Lecture Notes in Computer Science

Edited by G. Goos, J. Hartmanis, and J. van Leeuwen

Springer
Berlin
Heidelberg
New York
Barcelona
Hong Kong
London
Milan
Paris
Tokyo

Alberto H.F. Laender   Arlindo L. Oliveira (Eds.)

String Processing and Information Retrieval

9th International Symposium, SPIRE 2002
Lisbon, Portugal, September 11-13, 2002
Proceedings

 Springer

Series Editors

Gerhard Goos, Karlsruhe University, Germany
Juris Hartmanis, Cornell University, NY, USA
Jan van Leeuwen, Utrecht University, The Netherlands

Volume Editors

Alberto H.F. Laender
Universidade Federal de Minas Gerais
Departamento de Ciência da Computação
31270-901 Belo Horizonte, MG, Brazil
E-mail: laender@dcc.ufmg.br

Arlindo L. Oliveira
Instituto Superior Técnico, INESC-ID
R. Alves Redol 9, 1000-029 Lisboa, Portugal
E-mail: aml@inesc-id.pt

Cataloging-in-Publication Data applied for

Die Deutsche Bibliothek - CIP-Einheitsaufnahme

String processing and information retrieval : 9th international symposium ;
proceedings / SPIRE 2002, Lisbon, Portugal, September 11 - 13, 2002.
Alberto H. F. Laender ; Arlindo L. Oliveira (ed.). - Berlin ; Heidelberg ;
New York ; Hong Kong ; London ; Milan ; Paris ; Tokyo : Springer, 2002
    (Lecture notes in computer science ; Vol. 2476)
    ISBN 3-540-44158-1

CR Subject Classification (1998):H.3, H.2.8, I.2, E.1, E.5, F.2.2

ISSN 0302-9743
ISBN 3-540-44158-1 Springer-Verlag Berlin Heidelberg New York

Springer-Verlag Berlin Heidelberg New York
a member of BertelsmannSpringer Science+Business Media GmbH

http://www.springer.de

© Springer-Verlag Berlin Heidelberg 2002

Typesetting: Camera-ready by author, data conversion by DA-TeX Gerd Blumenstein
Printed on acid-free paper   SPIN 10871372   06/3142   5 4 3 2 1 0

Preface

This volume of the Lecture Notes in Computer Science series provides a comprehensive, state-of-the-art survey of recent advances in string processing and information retrieval. It includes invited and research papers presented at the 9th International Symposium on String Processing and Information Retrieval, SPIRE 2002, held in Lisbon, Portugal. SPIRE has its origins in the South American Workshop on String Processing which was first held in Belo Horizonte, Brazil, in 1993. Starting in 1998, the focus of the workshop was broadened to include the area of information retrieval due to its increasing relevance and its inter-relationship with the area of string processing.

The call for papers for SPIRE 2002 resulted in the submission of 54 papers from researchers around the world. Of these, 19 were selected for inclusion in the program (an acceptance rate of 35%). In addition, the Program Committee decided to accept six other papers, considered as describing interesting ongoing research, in the form of short papers. The authors of these 25 papers came from 18 different countries (Argentina, Australia, Brazil, Canada, Czech Republic, Chile, Colombia, Finland, France, Germany, Japan, Italy, Mexico, Saudi Arabia, Switzerland, Spain, United Kingdom, and USA). These papers cover a variety of research topics and were grouped in the following technical sessions:

- *String Matching*
- *String Processing*
- *Web Ranking and Link Analysis*
- *Pattern Matching*
- *Digital Libraries and Applications*
- *Approximate Searching*
- *Indexing Techniques*

Three internationally recognized scholars in the areas of string processing and information retrieval were also invited to submit papers and delivered the following keynote speeches at SPIRE 2002:

- Michael Ley (University of Trier, Germany), *The DBLP Computer Science Bibliography: Evolution, Research Issues, Perspectives*;
- Dan Suciu (University of Washington, USA), *From Searching Text to Querying XML Streams*; and
- Gaston H. Gonnet (ETH Informatik, Zurich, Switzerland), *String Matching Problems from Bioinformatics Which Still Need Better Solutions.*

Several people have contributed to making this symposium possible. First of all, we would like to thank Ricardo Baeza-Yates, who, on behalf of the Steering Committee, invited us to organize SPIRE 2002. We would also like to thank the other members of the Organizing Committee, Edgar Chavez (Publicity Chair),

Cuauhtémoc Rivera Loaiza (Webmaster), Ana Cardoso Cachopo (Local Arrangements), and Ana de Jesus (Administrative Assistant), for their constant support
and the great job done. We are particularly grateful to Stephen W. Liddle, from
Brigham Young University, for allowing us to use his Web-based conference management software that enabled the online submission of papers and reviews and
that made the virtual PC meeting possible. The PC members also deserve our
deep appreciation not only for providing timely and detailed reviews of the submitted papers but also for actively participating in the endless e-mail discussions
that took place before we could assemble our final technical program. Last, but
not least, we would also like to thank the authors who answered the call for
papers and made SPIRE 2002 the most successful meeting in this series, so far.

September 2002   Alberto H. F. Laender
                                                     Arlindo L. Oliveira

SPIRE 2002 Organization

General Chair
Arlindo L. Oliveira, Instituto Superior Técnico / INESC-ID, Portugal

Program Committee Chair
Alberto H. F. Laender, Universidade Federal de Minas Gerais, Brazil

Publicity Chair
Edgar Chavez, Universidad Michoacana, Mexico

Webmaster
Cuauhtémoc Rivera Loaiza, Universidad Michoacana, Mexico

Local Arrangements
Ana Cardoso Cachopo, Instituto Superior Técnico, Portugal

Steering Committee
Ricardo Baeza-Yates, Universidad de Chile, Chile
Gonzalo Navarro, Universidad de Chile, Chile
Arlindo L. Oliveira, Instituto Superior Técnico / INESC-ID, Portugal
Berthier Ribeiro-Neto, Universidade Federal de Minas Gerais, Brazil
Nivio Ziviani, Universidade Federal de Minas Gerais, Brazil

Program Committee

Alberto Apostolico (Purdue University, USA)
Ricardo Baeza-Yates (Universidad de Chile, Chile)
Michael Benedikt (Bell Labs, USA)
Elisa Bertino (University of Milan, Italy)
Nieves Brisaboa (Universidad de A. Coruña, Spain)
Edgar Chavez (Universidad Michoacana, Mexico)
Roger Chiang (University of Cincinnati, USA)
Fabio Crestani (University of Strathclyde, UK)
Maxime Crochemore (Université Marne-la-Vallee, France)
Bruce Croft (University of Massachusetts, USA)
David W. Embley (Brigham Young University, USA)
Daniela Florescu (XQRL Inc., USA)
Juliana Freire (Bell Labs, USA)

Edward Fox (Virginia Tech, USA)
Pablo de la Fuente (Universidad de Validolid, Spain)
Carlos Alberto Heuser (UFRGS, Brazil)
Costas S. Iliopoulos (King's College London, UK)
Vicente Lopez (Universitat Pompeu Fabra, Spain)
João Meidanis (UNICAMP, Brazil)
Ruy Milidiu (PUC-Rio, Brazil)
Alistair Moffat (University of Melbourne, Australia)
Mario Nascimento (University of Alberta, Canada)
Gonzalo Navarro (Universidad de Chile, Chile)
Arlindo L. Oliveira (Instituto Superior Técnico / INESC-ID, Portugal)
Ee-Peng Lim (Nanyang Technological University, Singapore)
Berthier Ribeiro-Neto (UFMG, Brazil)
Marie-France Sagot (INRIA Rhône-Alpes, France)
Fabrizio Sebastiani (CNR, Italy)
João Carlos Setúbal (UNICAMP, Brazil)
Ayumi Shinohara (Kyushu Univeristy, Japan)
Veda C. Storey (Georgia State University, USA)
Jorma Tarhio (Helsinki University of Technology, Finland)
Nivio Ziviani (UFMG, Brazil)
Justin Zobel (RMIT, Australia)

External Referees

Hiroki Arimura
Anne Bergeron
Pavel Calado
M. Christodoulakis
Cecil Chua
Zanoni Dias
Carina Dorneles
Ana Teresa Freitas
Luke A. D. Hutchison
M. Kurokawa
Monica Landoni
Wesley Dias Maciel

M. Mohamed
Edleno Silva de Moura
Hannu Peltola
Yoan Pinzón
Cinzia Pizzi
Ian Ruthven
Altigran Soares da Silva
Renato Stehling
Jesús Vegas
Maria Emilia M. T. Walter
Raymond Wan

Table of Contents

Pattern Matching

Digital Libraries and Applications

Approximate Searching

Indexing Techniques

The DBLP Computer Science Bibliography: Evolution, Research Issues, Perspectives

Michael Ley

University of Trier, FB 4 – Informatik
D-54286 Trier, Germany
ley@uni-trier.de

Abstract. Publications are essential for scientific communication. Access to publications is provided by conventional libraries, digital libraries operated by learned societies or commercial publishers, and a huge number of web sites maintained by the scientists themselves or their institutions. Comprehensive meta-indices for this increasing number of information sources are missing for most areas of science. The DBLP Computer Science Bibliography of the University of Trier has grown from a very specialized small collection of bibliographic information to a major part of the infrastructure used by thousands of computer scientists. This short paper first reports the history of DBLP and sketches the very simple software behind the service. The most time-consuming task for the maintainers of DBLP may be viewed as a special instance of the authority control problem: how to normalize different spellings of person names. The third section of the paper discusses some details of this problem which might be an interesting research issue for the information retrieval community.

1   History

1.1   The Beginning

DBLP was started at the end of 1993 as a simple test of Web technology which became popular with the Xmosaic browsers and the NCSA HTTP server in this year. A byproduct of the author's just finalized PhD thesis was a collection of photocopied tables of contents (TOCs) of important proceedings and journals from the fields of database systems and logic programming. These TOCs were typed in and formatted with some basic HTML markup, and a few entry pages were added. The server was called "Data Bases and Logic Programming" (DBLP) and announced in the dbworld mail list. Surprisingly this very primitive Web server seemed to be useful for others.

A.H.F. Laender and A.L. Oliveira (Eds.): SPIRE 2002, LNCS 2476, pp. 1-10, 2002.

1.2   Two Very Early Decisions

It is obvious that a simple hierarchy of text pages neither explores the expressibility of the medium hypertext nor constitutes an adequate interface for a bibliography. By adding a hyperlink from each author's name to a page which enumerates this person's publications a network orthogonal to the TOC hierarchy was introduced. The author pages contain links to coauthors and to the corresponding TOC pages. To make this "person-publication network" [L] browsable makes sense, because it is a result of the social network behind research. A click to a person page may answer questions like "Did the author publish other papers about this subject/project?", "In which journals/conferences did the author publish?", "When did the author start publishing?", etc. An important implication of the introduction of author pages is that the spelling of person names has to be normalized to get a 1:1 mapping between persons and person pages whenever possible. The person name normalization now is the hardest problem for the maintenance of DBLP. We will discuss it in the third section.

A second and perhaps unusual decision in an academic environment was that DBLP is a service and not a research project. The service is operated with very limited resources. There is always a trade-off between the development of new features or supporting software and entering or maintaining contents on a satisfactory level of quality. Most time we decided in favor of contents. This was supported by the experience that maintenance of complex software systems may cost more time than the gain in productivity justifies for our (almost) single user mode of operation. The authoritative version of DBLP has not used a database management system until today. In 1996 a student developed software to operate DBLP with the object-oriented DBMS SHORE from the University of Wisconsin. Two years later another student repeated the experiment with DB2 from IBM. Both diploma theses resulted in operational software, but it was too time consuming to keep them running on changing machines and operating system versions of the Unix/Linux family. For the production of DBLP a small set of programs and scripts written in C, Perl, Shell, and Java is still sufficient. The only non-standard software package we use is the MG information retrieval system described in the excellent "Managing Gigabytes" book [WMB].

1.3   Early Recognition

In 1997 we received the ACM SIGMOD Service Award and a VLDB Endowment Special Recognition Award. These awards by leading institutions of the database research field helped to give DBLP a more official status at the department of computer science and to get a small initial fund which enabled us to hire a student for entering data into DBLP for a year.

1.4   SIGMOD Anthology

In November 1997 we were contacted by Rick Snodgrass, chair of ACM SIGMOD. With its conferences SIGMOD had made some profit. Rick's idea was to use the money to scan in as much as possible of the "historical" publications of the database field and to combine the papers with an enhanced version of DBLP to a CDROM archive. Most money was spent to scan in the material and to convert it to PDF; this was done by Pinehurst Inc. In Trier we hired students from SIGMOD funds to improve the coverage of DBLP for the database field and for many boring editorial tasks during the project. To get a better idea of what is missing in DBLP and/or the SIGMOD Anthology we entered more than 100000 citation links for mainstream database publications. Many database publications are now annotated with a (partial) "referenced by" list of incoming citations.

The first 5 CDROMs of the Anthology were distributed in 1999 to the SIGMOD members. After this the project was joined by more and more conference organizers and journal editors which wanted to include their publications into the CDROM collection. Until the end of 2001 we produced 21 CDROMs with more than 150000 pages of material. Finally all material including a snapshot of DBLP from January 2002 was composed on two DVDs to get a very compact digital library containing most important research publications from the database field written before 2000. The realization of this huge collection was only possible with the help of more than 60 people which contributed material and permissions from copyright holders. The excellent management by Rick Snodgrass was essential to make it happen.

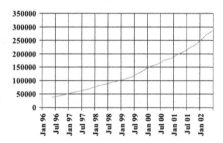

Fig. 1. Growth of DBLP

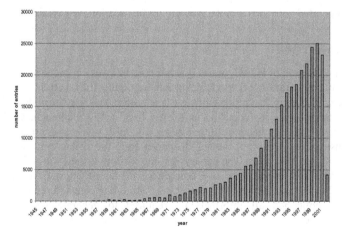

Fig. 2. DBLP entries by publication year

1.5   Sponsor Found

The Anthology project helped to make DBLP the most comprehensive bibliography of the database field. This field is a central part of computer science and has strong ties to other fields like operating systems, information retrieval, programming languages, algorithms, complexity theory etc. The goal is to extend the coverage of DBLP to all areas of computer science. With the generous support of the Microsoft Bay Area Research Center and Jim Gray we were able to hire students which work toward this direction. For the non-database fields DBLP is far from being "complete", but feedback from users indicates that it is becoming useful for researchers from a wide range of fields. As of now (June 2002), the bibliography lists more than 286000 publications. For more than 76000 of them it provides direct links to the abstracts and/or full texts stored on the publishers Web sites. Fig.1 shows the growth of DBLP and Fig. 2 shows the number of entries by publication year.

1.6   Undergraduate Software Labs

For CS students DBLP may be a convenient access path to primary scientific publications. But there is another important usage of the DBLP data set: At the University of Trier we teach Java as the first programming language. Students have to write programs which analyze the structure of DBLP, for example by applying classical graph algorithms to the coauthor relationship or by generating visualizations of simple statistics. The XML representation of DBLP is a medium size (>100MB) 'real' data set. To process it efficiently, careful selection of algorithms and clean design of programs is necessary. The number of temporary objects constructed often becomes the most time-critical parameter of student programs. DBLP data are used as a test set by several researchers, for example [LS], [PG].

2   Technical Background

DBLP is operated with very simple software. In this section we explain how it works.

2.1   HTML TOCs

The initial collection of HTML tables of contents had a very homogenous structure. A TOC is an enumeration of article level bibliographic information. Session titles, volume level bibliographic information, or cross-references may be added. The article level information was included in "unordered lists" (<ul> elements), anything else was outside of <ul>. To generate author pages we took a two step approach:

(1) A customized version of the HTML parser from the xmosaic browser was used to parse the TOC files. The parser was started from a shell script for each TOC. Volume level information like conference names or journal names was hard coded in the shell-script. The result was a large line oriented refer-style like file which contained all information   required to generate the author pages ("TOC_OUT").

(2) A second program ("mkauthors") reads this file into a main memory data structure and generates all author pages. We considered computing author pages on demand, but we decided that it is simpler and cheaper to provide the disk space for the materialized pages than to generate an index and to compose each page when required. mkauthors runs every evening if any DBLP data has been changed.

2.2   Mirrors

When DBLP was started, the University of Trier only had a slow connection to the Internet. The reliability of this connection and our computing environment was poor. To make DBLP a useful service, it should have a high availability. To achieve this, we decided to establish mirrors of the server. The first one was implemented on the SunSite Central Europe host operated by the group of Matthias Jarke at Aachen University of Technology. The technique of mirroring DBLP is primitive: The TOC_OUT file and all HTML pages except the author pages are packed into a compressed tar-file. The transfer of this archive is triggered manually or by a simple demon process on the mirror host. After unpacking mkauthor is run on the mirror.

2.3   Simple Search

Two very simple search programs were added to DBLP: The author search program is a sequential substring matching algorithm which runs through a file with all author names. This file is produced as a side effect by mkauthors. Author search is insensitive to umlauts and accents. The title search directly operates on the TOC_OUT file. Both search engines are C programs triggered by the HTTP demon via the CGI interface. The sequential search never was a serious performance problem, but substring matching author or title words without (Boolean) operators, stemming, ranking etc. is an insufficient level of service. The important advantage of this primitive technique is that it never was a problem to install it on mirror hosts.

2.4   XML Records

It soon became apparent that it is not a good design to use the HTML formatted tables of contents as the primary location to store all bibliographic information. Citation linking, annotated bibliographies, reading lists etc. make it necessary to assign a unique ID to each publication and to store the information in more classical bibliographic records. The standard format for bibliographic records in computer science is BibTeX. Because BibTeX is not easy to parse, we decided to use HTML-style markup but BibTeX publication types and field names. Again we customized the xmosaic parser. Later we noticed that our records perfectly fit into the new XML framework, we only had to adapt some minor syntactic details. Fig. 3 shows an example of a DBLP record. On the primary host each record is stored in a separate file; the key is interpreted as a file name.

```
<article key="journals/algorithmica/NavarroB01">
 <author>Gonzalo Navarro</author>
 <author>Ricardo A. Baeza-Yates</author>
 <title>Improving an Algorithm for Approximate
     Pattern Matching.</title>
 <pages>473-502</pages>
 <year>2001</year>
 <volume>30</volume>
 <journal>Algorithmica</journal>
 <number>4</number>
 <ee>http://link.springer.de/link/service/journals/00453/
     contents/01/0034/</ee>
 <url>db/journals/algorithmica/algorithmica30.html#NavarroB01</url>
</article>
```

Fig. 3. A DBLP XML Record

2.5   BHT (Bibliography HyperText)

Not all information from the tables of content was moved to the XML records. Session titles, cross-references between HTML pages and many unstructured comments and annotations can not be represented in BibTeX style records without lots of new but rarely used fields. We decided to leave this information in the tables of content. The XML records are imported into the tables of contents by a simple include mechanism which is implemented by a macro-processor: 'mkhtml' reads a 'bibliography hypertext' (BHT) file and replaces each <cite key="..." style="..."> by the XML record with the specified key using the format indicated by the style attribute. Additionally mkhtml knows tags to generate logos and page footers with navigation bars. Again all HTML pages are produced in advance. This requires more disk space than an 'on demand' strategy, but it requires less disk bandwidth.

2.6   MG

The XML records are loaded into the MG information retrieval system. A CGI based Web interface represents query results of this 'advanced search' engine in a style similar to the author pages. The MG backend treats each XML record as a small text document, only the front end is able to interpret the field structure of the records for filtering out 'false drops' caused by hits in fields different from the query specification.

During the ACM SIGMOD Anthology project students have been entering more than 100000 citation links into DBLP. Each reference from selected papers had to be located in the DBLP collection. The keys of hits are stored in <cite>-fields added to the XML-records of the starting nodes of the citation arcs. The plain text based MG system without the Web front end proved to be a superior tool for this highly repetitive task after a short time of familiarization.

2.7   Anthology Full Text Search

Another kind of information retrieval engine is employed on the CDROMs/DVDs of the SIGMOD Anthology: With Acrobat it is possible to build full text indices of collections of PDF documents. The Acrobat Reader version "with search" uses these indices for efficient full text search on complete CDROMs or DVDs. A prerequisite for indexing scanned material is to run all documents through an OCR algorithm, which is available as a part of the Acrobat software.

3   Research Issues

3.1   Person Names

Person names are ubiquitous in information systems. They are the only widely accepted method to identify persons. For humans the use of familiar person names is superior to all artificial identifiers. For information systems person names have many drawbacks compared to synthetically generated identifiers. Person names may not be unique; several persons with the same name may exist. A person may change his or her name; often several variations of a person name are used.

Variations of names may be caused by abbreviations (for example Jeffrey D. Ullman may become J. D. Ullman, J. Ullman or Jeff Ullman), nicknames (e.g. Michael may become Mike, William / Bill, Joseph / Joe etc.), permutations (e.g. Liu Bin may be the same person as Bin Liu), different transcriptions (e.g. Andrei / Andrey / Andrej may be identical), accents (Stephane vs. Stéphane), umlauts (Muller / Müller / Mueller), ligatures (Weiß / Weiss or Åström / Aastrom ...), case (Al-A'Ali vs. Al-A'ali), hyphens (Hans-Peter vs. Hans Peter), composition (MaoLin Qin vs. Mao Lin Qin), postfixes (Jr./Sr., a number, or a parents name), and by typos. Names may be changed at marriage or emigration to another cultural environment.

For DBLP the variations in person names have two consequences: (1) It is unclear how to search persons best, and (2) it may be hard to normalize different spellings of names to get correct author pages.

3.2   Person Search

The DBLP author search engine on the Web uses a simple substring matching algorithm which is insensitive to case, accents, and umlauts. If a known part of the name, usually the last name, is longer than 4 or 5 characters, the algorithm is practicable to locate the correct author page. For very common short names like Kim, Chen, Chan etc. the precision may be very poor.

The CDROM/DVD version of DBLP published as part of the ACM SIGMOD Anthology uses another search program: The Java Applet accepts queries which are sets of space separated strings. Names in the collection are tokenized into name parts. A name matches a query, if all query strings are prefixes of the parts of the name, i.e. the query "J Ullm" finds "J. D. Ullman", "Jeff Ullman", "Jeffrey D. Ullman", etc. The data structure behind the Applet is an ordered list of all permutations of the name parts (a KWIC). The list is stored in a simple file based tree. The longest query string is used to select a part of the tree; this sub list is filtered according to the other query strings. In most situations this algorithm is superior to the first one.

3.3   Normalization

We ourselves are often very heavy users of the person search programs. For each publication to be entered into DBLP we try to locate the authors (or editors) in the existing collection. If the spellings differ, but we are very confident that they are variations of the same person's name, we make them equal. It may be necessary to change the spelling in the new entry, in old entries, or both. We try to use a name variation preferred by the person which writes out most of the name parts. For persons who authored or edited many publications the name spelling usually converges very fast to a stable and correct state. For persons with a few known publications the likelihood for duplicate author pages, incorrect, or incomplete spellings is much higher.

The decision of when to unify two spellings may be very complex. To increase the productivity of maintaining DBLP (and many other information systems), this step should be supported by specialized tools. Many of the heuristics we use in the decision process are computable, but some of them require massive background knowledge which isn't available to a realistic system.

A very simple observation is that most publications have been written by groups of authors. These groups are part of working groups or collaborations embedded in theme-oriented communities. The coauthor relationship often gives very strong indications for the identity of persons. Conference series or specialized journals are condensation points for communities. These are larger and fuzzier than coauthor groups, but nevertheless it is often very helpful to look at the journal and conference names to get a rating. The focus of research of persons, groups, and communities changes with the time, an important precondition is that the new facts are consistent with the time frame of known facts.

3.4   Rating Functions

Throughout the last years the focus of information retrieval research has moved from large collections of isolated texts to hypermedia. For most search engines the link structure of documents has become a very important for rating functions. Terms inside Web pages are weighted in dependence of their position in the markup tree, e.g. words inside headings usually are considered more important than words inside long paragraphs. Bibliographic records are typical "semi-structured" documents. Information about authors and the coordinates of the publication (journal, volume, page, year, etc.) are database fields with well known semantics. Titles, abstracts, annotations, and reviews are examples of information inside of bibliographic records which may have a more irregular rich structure.

The idea is to develop specialized weight functions for the name normalization problem. The "query" is a set of names, a title, and the coordinates of the new publication. The task is to add the new bibliographic record to the collection in an "intelligent" manner. For DBLP name normalization has high priority, but a positive side effect of the decision process is that we may find other inconsistencies in the collection.

3.5   DBLP Browser

The ideas on how to support name normalization are at a very early stage. Any system support will require extensive experimentation and evaluation. A very fast interactive environment to explore the DBLP collection is needed. It should provide a convenient graphical user interface with specialized visualization facilities for the DBLP collection.

From an information retrieval viewpoint DBLP is a small collection. As of June 2002 it contains 286000 records, the XML representation of the data set has a size of approx. 115Mbytes. With known data compression techniques it is possible to build a representation which requires <30Mytes. This data structure contains all information from the XML records and is suitable for easy navigation and search within the data set. A Java prototype of the DBLP browser needs only a few seconds to load this compressed representation from a file into the main memory.

The compressed file is a text file, which only contains bytes in the range 0x20-0xff and line breaks. In the main section each bibliographic record is represented by one line. In the file header the total number of bytes and the number of records is specified. The first character of each line is a code for the publication type (article, book, inproceedings, ...); the remainder is a sequence of fields. The first byte of each field is a code for the field type (author, title, ...); the interpretation of the field value depends on the type.

For titles we use canonical Huffman codes on the word level. The lexicon is stored in a separate section of the text file using the "3-in-4 front-coding" strategy described in the MG book [WMB]. Contrary to MG, we do not use binary Huffman codes. We construct a Huffman tree of degree 213. The digits of the Huffman codes are represented as characters in the range 0x2a-0xff. Title fields are terminated by ')' (=0x29). The use of byte codes makes it very convenient to search on the compressed text [SNZB]. The degree 213 (and not 255) was chosen to make it easy to embed the Huffman coded titles into the byte coded bibliographic records.

Person names in author or editor fields are normalized. Normalization is favorable for a simple compression technique: All person names are stored in a separate section of the file, sorted by frequency of occurrence. For author or editor fields the values are person numbers. The numbers are represented as sequences of base 111 digits. The first digits are bytes in the range 0x21-0x8f the last digit of each number is marked by the transformation to the range 0x90-0xfe.

The same technique is used for other normalized domains: journal names, booktitles (conference names), series names and publisher names are stored in different sections of the file. On the field level only numbers are used.

DBLP records contain paths in several fields. They are keys or URLs. Because many paths share their prefixes, it makes sense to tokenize paths and to store the path elements in an extra section of the file. The path elements in this section are linked bottom-up: Each number stored in a record field points to the rightmost path element. The table entry contains its string representation and the index of the next path element on the left. Roots contain a circular link.

Other domain specific compression techniques proofed to be very efficient: Year values are represented as difference from the maximum year value. The maximum value is stored in the file header. This results in a considerable compression because most DBLP records describe "new" publications [Fig. 2]. Page fields many contain arbitrary strings, but most page values specify intervals of the type "start page – end page". This type of page field values is represented by two base 111 numbers (start page, number of pages). Only page values which are not of this type are represented by strings.

Our intention is to use the DBLP browser as a framework for experiments. It already provides an improved version of the person pages. The compressed version of the DBLP data and the source code of the browser prototype are available on **http://dblp.uni-trier.de/dblpbr/**, we encourage others to use and/or improve it.

4   Perspectives

With better tools it should be possible to improve productivity. But a really comprehensive portal to computer science literature requires more resources and staff. In a very recently approved project we will cooperate with the producer of CompuScience (FIZ Karlsruhe http://www.zblmath.fiz-karlsruhe.de/), the German Computer Society (GI, http://www.gi-ev.de/) and others. The project will be funded by the German Federal Ministry of Education and Research. The objective is to provide an open portal with improved coverage and additional services.

References

[L]   Michael Ley: Die Trierer Informatik-Bibliographie DBLP. GI-Jahrestagung 1997: 257-266.
[LS]   Hartmut Liefke, Dan Suciu: XMill: an Efficient Compressor for XML Data. SIGMOD Conf. 2000, 153-164.
[PG]   Neoklis Polyzotis, Minos N. Garofalakis: Statistical Synopses for Graph-Structured XML Databases. SIGMOD Conf. 2002.
[SNZB]   Edleno Silva de Moura, Gonzalo Navarro, Nivio Ziviani, Ricardo Baeza-Yates: Fast and Flexible Word Searching on Compressed Text. TOIS 18(2): 113-139 (2000).
[WMB]   Ian H. Witten, Alistair Moffat, Timothy C. Bell: Managing Gigabytes, Compressing and Indexing Documents and Images, 2nd Ed., Morgan Kaufmann, 1999.

Michael Ley was born in Düsseldorf, Germany, in 1959. He received his Diploma in computer science (with honors) from Aachen University of Technology in 1986 and the Ph.D. in computer science (with honors) from the University of Trier in 1993. He is a lecturer at the Department of Computer Science at the University of Trier.

From Searching Text to Querying XML Streams

Dan Suciu

University of Washington, USA
suciu@cs.washington.edu
http://www.cs.washington.edu/homes/suciu

Abstract. XML data is queried with XPath expressions, which are a limited form of regular expressions. New XML stream processing applications, such as content-based routing or selective dissemination of information, require thousands or millions of XPath expressions to be evaluated simultaneously on the incoming XML stream at a high, sustained rate. Conceptually, the XPath evaluation problem is analogous to the text search problem, in which one or several regular expressions need to be matched to a given text, but the number of regular expressions here is much larger, while the "text" is much shorter, since it corresponds to the depth of the XML stream. In this paper we examine techniques that have been proposed for XML stream processing, which are variations of either a non-deterministic or a deterministic finite automata (NFA and DFA). For the latter, we describe a series or theoretical results establishing lower and upper bounds on the number of DFA states for sets of XPath expressions.

1 Databases, Text, and XML

Data in relational databases is *structured*. It has a schema, which is usually stored in a part of the of the database called the catalog, while the data values are stored separately, in tables, following a layout that is completely described by the schema. User queries, expressed in SQL, refer both to the schema components, such as relation names and their attributes, and to the data values, in the form of equality predicates, inequality predicates, or string matches. Research on query processing has focused on join processing techniques, join ordering, and indexes.

Text documents are *unstructured*. There is no schema, only the text, and the data consists of some large collection of documents. A query consists of a regular expression, often as simple as a single word, and the answer consists of the set of text documents that match the given query. Indexes are used here too, and they are conceptually similar to, although technically different from those in relational databases (e.g. inverted files v.s. B$^+$-trees). Research on query processing has focused, among other things, on how to process efficiently regular expressions on a text document, and has produced celebrated results such as Knuth-Morris-Pratt's string search algorithm, suffix trees, and suffix arrays. These techniques have often been based on, and even expanded automata theory.

A new kind of data is *semistructured data*. Although considered in one form or another for a long time, semistructured has gained main-stream acceptance

A.H.F. Laender and A.L. Oliveira (Eds.): SPIRE 2002, LNCS 2476, pp. 11–26, 2002.

only recently, since the introduction of XML. Like in structured data here we have schema components (the tags and attributes in XML), and data values are organized along these components. But here the schema is embedded with the data, thus allowing each data item to describe its own local schema. This allows much more freedom in designing the structure, and often leads to structures that were explicitly disallowed in the relational data, such as nested collections, multiple or missing subelements, elements of the same type but with different structures, heterogeneous collections, etc. Hence the term *semistructured*. In the past, researchers have studied instances of data that we would call today semistructured, either in the form of SGML documents, or as *structured documents*, i.e. documents with a predefined grammar. Many interesting research results have been produced in this context, and they are definitely relevant today [9, 8, 5, 24, 20]. What is different today are the new applications in which XML is being used, which create new challenges for efficient query processing.

An Application of XML Stream Processing For illustration, consider XML Routing [25, 12, 13]. Here a network of *XML routers* forwards a continuous stream of XML packets from data producers to consumers. The "packet" is really an instance of a semistructured data, only expressed in XML. Each router in the network receives incoming XML packets, and forwards each packet to a subset of its output links (other routers or clients). In order to determine where to forward a given packet, the router needs to evaluate a large number of XPath filters on that packet, which usually correspond to clients' subscription queries, on the stream of XML packets. For example: "if the packet satisfies the expression:

```
/Envelope[Header/@dest="Lisabon"][@priority>100]/Body//*[@keyword="SPIRE"]
```

then forward the packet to servers S_{64} and S_{108}".

Data processing in XML packet routing is minimal: there is no need for the router to have an internal representation of the packet, or to buffer the packet after it has forwarded it. However the performance requirements are high, because routers often need to process packets at the rate of the network, for example one may want to process XML packets at a rate of, say, 10MB/s. In one experimental system [25] publicly available tools were used to parse the XML documents and evaluate the XPath expressions, and the resulting performance was quite poor: about 2.6KB/s for 10,000 XPath expressions[1].

The XPah expressions used here are very similar to queries considered before, in the context of structured text processing. For example all XPath expressions in this paper can be translated into the PAT algebra [23], for which efficient processing techniques are known. So, one may ask: what is new here ?

The answer lies in the different assumptions on the data and the queries. First we need to compute on a *stream* of incoming XML packets. Stream data processing is only now emerging as a mainstream research topic [3]. One issue in

---

[1] The authors in [25] report parsing a 262 bytes XML document in $64.2\mu s$, and evaluating one short XPath expression in 10 μs. This translates into a throughput of $262/100064.2 = 2.6$KB/s for 10,000 XPath expressions.

stream data is that we cannot use an index, at least not in the traditional sense, which makes some of the most efficient processing techniques for PAT algebra expressions useless. The second is the scale of the queries. Although each predicate is simple, like the one above, there may be lots of them, perhaps thousands or millions. How can we evaluate 10^6 XPath expressions on an incoming XML stream, and do this at, say, 10MB/s ? Finally, XML stream applications often have additional knowledge about the data or the queries that we did not have in processing structured text, and which we need to exploit to improve query processing. For example we may know the schema of the XML data, or we may know certain selectivities for some of the predicates used in the XPath expressions and we could use them to do cost-based optimizations like in relational database systems.

This paper defines the XML stream processing problem, and describes some of the techniques that have been considered in this context, with a strong bias toward the author's own work, in the context of the XML Toolkit project [11, 10, 14].

Outline The XML stream processing problem is described and discussed in Sec. 2. Two of the existing processing techniques, based on NFAs and DFAs respectively, are discussed in Sec. 3. An analysis of the number of states in the DFA in presented in Sec. 4. The lazy DFA is described, analyzed, and evaluated in Sec. 5. We conclude in Sec. 6.

2   XML Stream Processing

We start by describing the architecture of an XML stream processing system [10], to illustrate the context in which XPath expressions are processed. This defines a simple event-based XML processing model, extending the well-known SAX parsing model[2]. Several correlated XPath expressions are arranged in a tree, called the *query tree*. An input XML stream is first parsed by a SAX parser that generates a stream of *SAX events* (Fig. 1); this is input to the query processor that evaluates the XPath expressions and generates a stream of *application events*. The application is notified of these events, and usually takes some action such as forwarding the packet, notifying a client, or computing some values. In [10], an optional Stream Index (called SIX) may accompany the XML stream to speed up processing [10].

An application starts by defining a query tree, Q. This is a tree in which the nodes are labeled with variables and the edges with linear XPath expressions, P, given by the following grammar:

$$P ::= /N \mid //N \mid PP$$
$$N ::= E \mid A \mid text(S) \mid * \tag{1}$$

Here E, A, and S are an element constant, an attribute constant, and a string constant respectively, and $*$ is the wild card. The function text(S) matches

---

[2] Simple API for XML, http://www.megginson.com/SAX/.

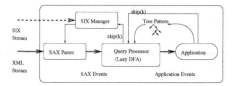

Fig. 1. System's Architecture

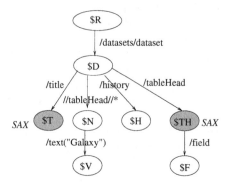

Fig. 2. A Query Tree

a text node whose value is the string S. In addition to the query tree, the application specifies the variables for which it requests SAX events. There is a distinguished variable, R, which is always bound to the root.

Example 1. The following is a query tree[3]:

```
$D  IN $R/datasets/dataset
$T  IN $D/title
$N  IN $D//tableHead//*
$V  IN $N/text("Galaxy")
$H  IN $D/history
$TH IN $D/tableHead
$F  IN $TH/field
```

Fig. 2 shows this query tree graphically, where the SAX events are requested for $T and $TH. Fig. 3 shows the result of evaluating this query tree on an XML input stream: the first column shows the XML stream, the second shows the SAX events generated by the parser, and the last two columns show the application events. Only some of the SAX events are forwarded to the application, namely exactly those that occur within a $T or $TH variable event.

Filters XPath expressions are rarely linear, but instead have branches called *filters*. It is possible to implement filters on top of query trees, using a simple

---

[3] The tags are from an XML astronomical database [19].

XML Stream	Parser SAX Events	Application Events	
		Variable Events	SAX Events
`<datasets>`	`start(datasets)`	`start($R)`	
`<dataset>`	`start(dataset)`	`start($D)`	
`<history>`	`start(history)`	`start($H)`	
`<date>`	`start(date)`		
`5/1/59`	`text("5/1/59")`		
`</date>`	`end(date)`		
`</history>`	`end(history)`	`end($H)`	
`<title>`	`start(title)`	`start($T)`	
			`start(title)`
`<subtitle>`	`start(subtitle)`		`start(subtitle)`
`Study`	`text(Study)`		`text(Study)`
`</subtitle>`	`end(subtitle)`		`end(subtitle)`
`</title>`	`end(title)`		`end(title)`
		`end($T)`	
`...`			
`</dataset>`	`end(dataset)`	`end($D)`	
`...`	`...`		
`</datasets>`	`end(datasets)`	`end($R)`	

Fig. 3. Events generated by a Query Tree

and direct method [11], whose throughput decreases with the number of filters in the query tree. In order to support filters efficiently one needs to combine the techniques for linear XPath expressions with event detection methods, e.g. like those described in [21]. We will not further discuss filters here, and assume instead that every XPath expressions is linear. Notice, however, that XPath expressions can already be arranged in a tree.

The XML Stream Processing Problem The problem that we address is: given a query tree Q, pre-process it, then evaluate it on an incoming XML stream. The goal is to maximize the throughput at which we can process the XML stream. A special case of a query tree, Q, is one in which every node is either the root or a leaf node, i.e. has the form: X_1 in R/e_1, X_2 in $R/e_2, \ldots, X_p$ in R/e_p (each e_i may start with // instead of /): we call Q a *query set*, or simply a *set*. Query sets are typical of many applications (e.g. XML routing), and are convenient for analyzing the problem as a function of their cardinality, p. It actually suffices to restrict the theoretical analysis to query sets only, since every query tree Q can be converted into an equivalent query set Q'. An implementation does not have to do that, but it suffices for us to restrict the theoretical analysis in Sec. 4 to query sets.

3 XML Stream Processing Techniques

Current approaches to processing sets of XPath expressions on an XML stream are based either on a nondeterministic finite automaton (NFA) or on a deterministic finite automaton (DFA). We review here both of them.

3.1   Processing with NFAs

Recall that the query tree may be a very large collection of XPath expressions. The first step is to translate the XPath expressions into one, single Nondeterministic Finite Automaton, denoted A_n. The automaton can then be executed directly on the input XML stream, using a stack of sets of NFA states. As usual we will denote $\delta(q, a)$ the transition function returning a set of states, i.e. $q' \in \delta(q, a)$ if there exists a transition labeled a from q to q'. We also extend δ to words, by defining $\delta(q, wa) = \delta(\delta(q, w), a)$. Notice that a here may be a tag, attribute label, string, or wild-card $(*)$.

To illustrate, consider the query tree P shown in Fig. 4(a). The NFA, denoted A_n, is shown in Fig. 4(b). Transitions labeled $*$ correspond to $*$ or $//$ in P; there is one initial state; there is one terminal state for each variable ($X, Y, \ldots$); and there are ε-transitions [4]. It is straightforward to generalize this to any query tree. Importantly, the number of states in A_n is proportional to the size of P.

To execute the NFA on the input XML stream we maintain a set of current states, S, and a stack of sets of states, ST. On a start(a) SAX event, with tag a, we push S on ST and replace S with the set of all successor states: $\{q' \mid q' \in \delta(q, a), q \in S\}$, where δ is the transition function. The transition function is implemented as a hash table at each state. On an end(a) SAX event we pop one set from the stack, and that becomes the current S.

Let us analyze the time and space complexity of the NFA evaluation method. The space of the NFA is proportional to the size of P. In addition we need a stack, whose depth is that of the XML input document, i.e. can be assumed to be bound by a constant, for all practical purposes. The elements on the stack are sets of states, whose cardinality is bounded by the size of P. Hence the space complexity is linear in the size of P. Consider now the time complexity. The time to process one SAX events can be as large as the number of states in A_n, hence is linear in the size of P. As a consequence, the more XPath expressions we have, the slower we can process the input XML stream.

Application: XFilter The XFilter system [2] is designed for efficient processing of XPath expressions on XML streams, with applications in Selective Dissemination of Information. We explain XFilter here putting emphasis on its relationship to NFAs, and refer the reader to [2] for details. More precisely, we will describe it as a sequence of optimization steps over the direct NFA evaluation method. The first step is to replace δ with a new transition function δ' defined by: $\delta'(q, a) = \{q' \mid \exists k.k \geq 0 \wedge q' \in \delta(q, *^k.a)\}$. That is, multiple $*$ transitions are collapsed, and, in the process, some states may be eliminated. Due to the special form of the linear XPath expressions, for every state q' there exists now a unique "predecessor" state q s.t. $q' \in \delta'(q, a)$ for some symbol a, and we denote $q = \delta^{-1}(q')$. Also define a "relative position" predicate for each state q', describing the number of symbols needed to reach q' from $\delta^{-1}(q')$ (the k in the

---

[4] These are needed to separate the loops from the previous state. For example if we merge states 2, 3, and 6 into a single state then the $*$ loop (corresponding to $//$) would incorrectly apply to the right branch.

definition of δ', plus one). The predicate can be either $= n$, or $\geq n$, for some $n \geq 1$. To illustrate δ', consider the the NFA in Fig. 4 (b). We transform into a new NFA having only the states $1, 2, 5, 7, 10$; the new transition function is $\delta'(1, a) = \{2\}$, $\delta'(2, b) = \{5, 7\}$, $\delta'(7, d) = \{10\}$, while the distance predicates for the states $2, 5, 7, 10$ are $= 1, \geq 2, = 1, = 2$ respectively (i.e. we can go from state 1 to state 2 by following exactly one symbol, we can go from state 2 to state 5 by following ≥ 2 symbols, etc). When applied to query sets rather than query trees, each state q has a unique transition, i.e. there is a unique a for which $\delta'(q, a) \neq \emptyset$, and, moreover, $\delta'(q, a)$ contains exactly one state, q'. Hence, we can drop the a argument from δ', and simply write $q' = \delta'(q)$.

The next optimization in XFilter is the way in which it represents at runtime the current set of states and the stack of sets of states, which we denoted S and ST respectively. The basic idea is to store in S and ST the values $\delta'(q)$ rather than q: this, as will see, speeds up execution at runtime. More precisely, XFilter maintains one hash table indexed by the symbols a (tags and attribute labels) occurring in all the XPath expressions. The hash table entry for a symbol a is a list, called *candidate list*, CL, which is updated at runtime as follows. The CL corresponding to a contains, at any given moment, all pairs $(\delta'(q, a), D)$, where q is any NFA state that has been visited by the current sequence of open XML tags, and D is a depth predicate of the form $= d$ or $\geq d$, representing the depth where a has to occur in order for the NFA to make the transition $q \rightarrow \delta'(q, a)$: the depth is computed by adding the depth at which q was reached to the relative position predicate for q'.

At runtime XFilter works as follows. On a start(a) SAX event, occurring at depth d, the CL for entry a is inspected, and for each pair (q', D), the predicate D is checked on d: if it is true, then we compute the successor of q', say $\delta'(q', b)$, and insert the pair (q'', D') in the CL at entry b. Thus, while processing an a event, we may need to update the CL's at several entries b. However, only the states at entry a need to be inspected, and this is an improvement over the direct NFA evaluation method. To see this, recall that in the direct NFA processing we have a set of states S and need to compute $\{q' \mid q' \in \delta'(q', a), q \in S\}$. When iterating q over S, many states may not have an a transition at all. For example, given the XPath expressions $/b/a$, $/b/c$, $/b/d$, $/b/e$, after seeing a start(b) event S has three states. If start(a) is the next event, then the direct NFA evaluation method needs to scan over all three states in S, and discover that only one has an a transition, while XFilter checks directly the CL at entry a, which has a single state. An end(a) event is processed similarly only in reverse, i.e. we need to find all matching elements in the CL for entry a, and remove the appropriate $\delta'(q', b)$ elements.

Another technique, XTrie [4], introduces additional optimization that further increase the throughput by a factor of four or so.

3.2 Processing with DFAs

Alternatively, we can evaluate the XPath expressions by constructing a DFA from the NFA. We review this construction here briefly and refer the reader to a standard textbook [15] for more details.

Let Σ denote the set of all tags, attributes, and text constants occurring in the query tree P, plus a special symbol ω representing any other symbol that could be matched by $*$ or $//$. For $w \in \Sigma^*$ let $A_n(w)$ denote the set of states in A_n reachable on input w, i.e. $\delta(q_0, w)$ where q_0 is the initial state in A_n. In our example (Fig. 4 (b)) we have $\Sigma = \{a, b, d, \omega\}$, and $A_n(\varepsilon) = \{1\}$, $A_n(a.b) = \{3, 4, 7\}$, $A_n(a.\omega) = \{3, 4\}$, $A_n(b) = \emptyset$.

The DFA for P, A_d, has the following set of states:

$$states(A_d) = \{A_n(w) \mid w \in \Sigma^*\} \tag{2}$$

For our running example A_d is illustrated[5] in Fig. 4 (c). Each state has unique transitions, and one optional [other] transition, denoting any symbol in Σ *except* the explicit transitions at that state: this is different from $*$ in A_n which denotes *any* symbol. For example [other] at state $\{3, 4, 8, 9\}$ denotes either a or ω, while [other] at state $\{2, 3, 6\}$ denotes a, d, or ω. Terminal states may be labeled now with more than one variable, e.g. $\{3, 4, 5, 8, 9\}$ is labeled $Y and $Z.

Processing an XML stream with a DFA is similar to that of an NFA, only simpler, since now we have a single current state, and the stack contains one single state per entry. Both a start(element) and a end(element) take now $O(1)$ time to process, and, assuming an upper bound on the depth of the XML document, we can preallocate the stack statically and there is no need to do any dynamic memory management. The space taken by the DFA, however, can be prohibitive since, in general, the number of states in a DFA can be exponentially larger that that in the NFA. The solution, as we will see, is to compute the DFA lazily.

Application: the XML Toolkit The XML Toolkit [10] is an application using a lazy DFA to process large collections of XPath expressions on an input XML stream. The toolkit, available from xmltk.sourceforge.net, implements an API to a processor for pattern trees, as described in Sec. 3. In addition it implements a number of XML Unix commands that scale to large XML files, like xsort (for sorting an XML document), xagg (for aggregation), xnest, xflatten.

4 Analyzing the Size of the DFA

While the size of a DFA for a general regular expression may be exponential [15], this general statement needs to be revisited in our context for two reasons. First the regular expressions we are considering are restricted to XPath expressions

---

[5] Technically, the state $\emptyset$ is also part of the DFA, and behaves like a "sink" state, collecting all missing transitions. We do not illustrate the sink state in our examples.

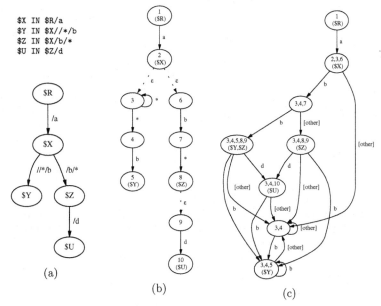

Fig. 4. (a) A query tree; (b) its NFA, A_n, and (c) its DFA, A_d

given by the grammar in Sec. 2. Second, in the XML applications that we target the regular expressions are over the structure of an XML stream, and, hence they are essentially evaluated on short sequences (whose length is bound by the depth of the XML tree). For example it can be in the range 20-30. By contrast, regular expressions in text processing need to inspect large documents, of at least a few thousands of characters.

Upper and lower bounds on the number of states in the DFA for XPath expressions were given in [11]. We review here those results.

Single XPath Expression We start with one linear XPath expression, which has the form $P = p_0//p_1//\ldots//p_k$ where each p_i is $N_1/N_2/\ldots/N_{n_i}$, $i = 0,\ldots,k$, and each N_j is given by (1). This case has already been considered in traditional text processing. For example, consider $P = //a/b/a/a/b$ the NFA and DFA are shown in Fig. 5 (a) and (b), and they have the same number of states. The DFA corresponds to Knuth-Morris-Pratt's string matching algorithm [6] applied to the word $abaab$. However, the construction in the KMP algorithm does not extend to all linear XPath expressions, and in general we may have some exponential blowup:

Theorem 1 ([11]). *Given a linear XPath expression P with the parameters in Fig. 5 (e), define:*

$$prefix(P) = n_0$$

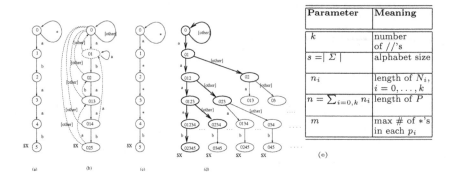

Parameter	Meaning
k	number of $//$'s
$s = \mid \Sigma \mid$	alphabet size
n_i	length of N_i, $i = 0, \ldots, k$
$n = \sum_{i=0,k} n_i$	length of P
m	max # of $*$'s in each p_i

(e)

Fig. 5. The NFA (a) and the DFA (b) for `//a/b/a/a/b`. The NFA (c) and the DFA (with back edges removed) (d) for `//a/*/*/*/b`: here the eager DFA has $2^5 = 32$ states, while the lazy DFA, assuming the DTD `<!ELEMENT a (a*|b)>`, has at most 9 states. Parameters for a linear XPath expression (e): $P = p_0//p_1// \ldots //p_k$, with $p_i = N_1/N_2/ \ldots /N_{n_i}$, $i = 0, \ldots, k$

$$suffix(P) = k + k(n - n_0)s^m$$

Then the eager DFA for P has at most prefix(P) + suffix(P) states. In particular, when $k = 0$ the DFA has at most n states, and when $k > 0$ the DFA has at most $k + k(n - n_0)s^m$ states.

When no wild-cards occur ($m = 0$), then the number of states in the DFA is at most $k + k(n - n_0)$. When wild cards are present ($m > 0$), then the nubmer of states in the DFA can be exponentially larger than that of the NFA's This is illustrated in Fig. 5 (c), (d) showing that the DFA for $p = //a/*/*/*/b$, has 2^5 states. It generalizes to the DFA for $//a/*/ \ldots /*/b$ having 2^{m+2} states, where m is the number of $*$'s.

Thus, for the case of only one linear XPath expression, the number of wild cards between two consecutive occurrences of $//$ is the only source of exponential size for the eager DFA of one linear XPath expression. One expects this number to be small in most practical applications; arguably users are more likely to write expressions like `/catalog//product//color` rather than expressions like `/catalog//product/*/*/*/*/*/*/*/*/color`. Indeed, some implementations of XQuery already translate a *single* linear XPath expression into DFAs [16].

Multiple XPath Expressions The case when P consists of several XPath expressions also has an analogy in text processing: it is related to Aho and Corasick's dictionary matching problem [1, 22]. We are given a dictionary consisting of p words, $\{w_1, \ldots, w_p\}$, and have to retrieve all their occurrences in a given text. This translates into constructing the DFA for the set of XPath expressions $Q = \{//w_1, \ldots, //w_p\}$. Hence, the dictionary matching problem corresponds to the special case where each XPath expression has a single, leading //, and has no *. The main result in the dictionary matching problem is that the number of DFA states is linear in the total size of Q. However, when we allow allow multiple occurrences of //, as we need in XML applications, the number of DFA states grows exponentially in the size of P, as illustrated in the following example.

Example 2. Consider four XPath expressions:

```
$X1 IN $R//book//figure
$X2 IN $R//table//figure
$X3 IN $R//chapter//figure
$X4 IN $R//note//figure
```

The DFA needs to remember what subset of tags of {book, table, chapter, note} it has seen, resulting in at least 2^4 states.

It is easy to generalize this exaple, and prove that p XPath expressions my have a DFA with 2^p states [11]. In terms of an upper bound, we have:

Theorem 2 ([11]). *Let Q be a set of XPath expressions. Then the number of states in the eager DFA for Q is at most:*

$$\sum_{P \in Q} (prefix(P)) + \prod_{P \in Q} (1 + suffix(P))$$

In particular, if A, B are constants s.t. $\forall P \in Q$, $prefix(P) \leq A$ and $suffix(P) \leq B$, then the number of states in the eager DFA is $\leq p \times A + B^{p'}$, where p' is the number of XPath expressions $P \in Q$ that contain //.

Recall that $suffix(P)$ already contains an exponent, which we argued is small in practice. The theorem shows that the extra exponent added by having multiple XPath expressions is precisely the number of expressions with //'s.

Sets of XPath expressions like the ones we saw in Example 2 are common in practice, and rule out the eager DFA, except in trivial cases. The solution is to construct the DFA lazily, which we discuss next.

5   Processing XML Streams with Lazy DFAs

An answer to the exponential blowup in the number of DFA states is to construct the DFA lazily. The *lazy DFA* is constructed at run-time, on demand. Initially it has a single state (the initial state), and whenever we attempt to make a transition into a missing state we compute it, and update the transition. The hope is that only a small set of the DFA states needs to be computed.

This idea has been used before in text processing, but it has never been applied to such large number of expressions as required in XML stream processing (say, 100,000): a careful analysis of the size of the lazy DFA is needed to justify its feasibility. Unlike our analysis of the eager DFA, in Sec. 4, when analyzing the lazy DFA we need to take into account both the set of XPath expressions, and the XML data instance. Two results have been shown in [11], which apply to two different classes of XML data.

Data-Centric XML Documents Call a DTD *simple* if any two distinct cycles in the DTD graph have disjoint sets of elements. For example non-recurisve DTDs are simple, because they have no cycles at all. Data-centric XML instances are either non-recursive, or have a limited form of recursion that usually corresponds to a hierarchy (part-subpart, or unit-subunit, etc). Thus, they have self-recursive elements, where an element a may contain a subelement a, but not mutual recursion, where a may contain b and b may contain a. These are also simple DTDs, since all cycles contain a single element and, hence, distinct ccyles are disjoint. Here we have:

Theorem 3 ([11]). *Let D be the number of simple paths in a simple DTD, and let d be the maximum number cycles on any simple path. Let Q be a set of XPath expressions of maximum depth n. Then the lazy DFA has at most $1 + D \times (1+n)^d$ states.*

Document-oriented XML instances encoding document-centric information, however, often have non-simple DTDs: for example a `table` may contain a `table` or a `footnote`, and a `footnote` may also contain a `table` or a `footnote`. In such cases one can give an upper bound on the size of the lazy DFA in terms of *Data Guides* [7]. For a given XML instance, the data guide G is defined to be the trie of all root-to-leaf element sequences. An empirical observation is that real XML data instances tends to have small data guides, regardless of its DTD. For example users occasionally place a `footnote` within a `table`, or vice versa, but don't nest all available element in all possible combinations. All XML data instances described in [17] have very small data guides, except for Treebank [18], where the data guide has $G = 340,000$ nodes. This is useful for the lazy DFA because of the following:

Corollary 1 ([11]). *Let G be the number of nodes in the data guide of an XML stream. Then, for any set Q of XPath expressions the lazy DFA for Q on that XML stream has at most $1 + G$ states.*

5.1   Validation of the Size of the Lazy DFA

An experimental evaluation of the size of the lazy DFA was conducted in [11]. We briefly review here those findings on six DTDs, of which four are simple (`protein.dtd` is even non-recursive), and two are not. Three sets of queries of depth $n = 20$ were generated, with 1,000, 10,000, and 100,000 XPath expressions[6], with 5% probabilities for both the $*$ and the $//$. Next, synthetic data was generated for all six DTDs[7], and the three query sets were executed on the data. The number of states in the lazy DFA is shown in Fig. 6 (a). For three DTDs

---

[6] With the generator described in [2].

[7] Using `http://www.alphaworks.ibm.com/tech/xmlgenerator`.

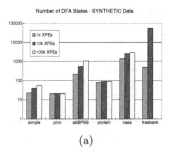

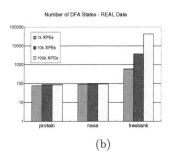

(a)   (b)

Fig. 6. Size of the lazy DFA for (a) synthetic data, and (b) real data. 1k means 1000 XPath expressions. For 100k XPath exrpession for the **treebank** DTD with synthetic data we ran out of memory

(**protein**, **nasa**, and **treebank**) real XML data was also availble: the number of states in the lazy DFA on the real data is shown in Fig. 6 (b).

The first four DTDs in Fig. 6 (a) are simple, and indeed the number of states in the lazy DFA is small. The last two DTDs are non-simple, and the number of states was significantly larger. In fact, we ran out of memory on **treebank** while processing the largest query set (100,000 XPath expressions).

By contrast Fig. 6 (b) shows that the number of states in the lazy DFA is significantly smaller when ran on *real* XML data, rather than synthetic one. The explanation is that real XML data tends to have a relatively small dataguide, hence Corollary 1 applies, while synthetic data has (by definition) a large data guide.

5.2   The Throughput of Lazy DFAs

As expected, at runtime the DFA outperforms any NFA-based approach. The graph in Figure 7, taken from [11], illustrates the point. It shows the measured throughput, as a function of the amount of data consumed, for the lazy DFA, for XFilter [2] (without list balancing), and for the parser only. The data is the NASA XML dataset [19], and is about 25MB. The four sets of XPath expressions were synthetically generated, and contain 1k (= 1000), 10k, 100k, and 1000k XPath expressions respetively. In all cases, the probability of both a * and a // is 10%. After a "warm-up" period, when most of the lazy DFA states are being constructed, the throughput of the lazy DFA stabilizes at about 5.4MB/s. This is about 1/2 the parser's througput. Importantly, the stable throughput is independent on the number of XPath expressions in the query set. By constrast, XFilter does not need a warm-up phase, however the throughput degrades as we increase the number of XPath expressions, until it is about 50,000 smaller than that of the lazy DFA.

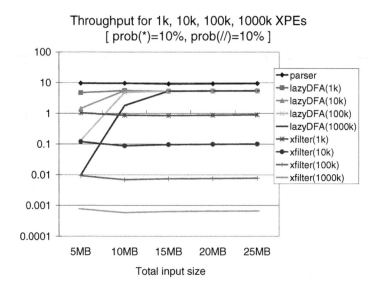

Fig. 7. Experiments illustrating the throughput of the DFA v.s. XFilter [2], as a function of the amount of XML data consumed. The number of XPath expressions varies from 1k (1000), to 1000k ($= 10^6$)

6   Conclusions

XML stream processing provides a new class of applications for automata-based processing techniques. Unlike traditional text processing applications, which have to search words or regular expressions in long text documents, here the match is on the XML's structure, and usually applies to a short sequence of elements, bounded by the detph of the XML document. However, the number of expressions that we need to evaluate on the input XML stream is much larger than what traditional text-based processing has previously attempted to process.

This paper has argued that lazy Deterministic Finite Automata are the most efficient technique for processing sets of *linear* XPath expressions, and that they work on *most* XML data streams. Both emphasis highlight limitations, and point to future work. First, the techniques described here apply only to linear XPath expression. In practice one encounters almost always expressions with filters. For example, consider /hr/person[name/text()="John"][age/text()="48"]. The lazy DFA can detect both branches /hr/person/name/text("John") and /hr/person/age/text("48"), but we need to identify persons that match *both* branches. While processing linear XPath expression is a neccessary first step, it is insufficient yet for practical purposes. The challenge is to extend the lazy DFA idea to branches, and obtain similarly high throughputs. Second, despite the positive results in Theorem 3 and Corollary 1, they fall short of offering a hard upper bound guarantee on the number of states in the lazy DFA in all cases. Production systems need hard guarantees, and they can only be obtained by offering a safety valve that adds an NFA-based proceesing component to the lazy DFAs. Designing, optimizing, and evaluating such mixed methods is part of future work.

Acknowledgment

Most of the results mentioned in this paper have been obtained in work done in collaboration with T.J. Green, A. Gupta, G. Miklau, and M. Onizuka. The author was partially supported by the NSF CAREER Grant 0092955, a gift from Microsoft, and an Alfred P. Sloan Research Fellowship.

References

[1] A. Aho and M. Corasick. Efficient string matching: an aid to bibliographic search. *Communications of the ACM*, 18:333–340, 1975. 20

[2] M. Altinel and M. Franklin. Efficient filtering of XML documents for selective dissemination. In *Proceedings of VLDB*, pages 53–64, Cairo, Egipt, September 2000. 16, 22, 23, 24

[3] B. Babcock, S. Babu, M. Datar, R. Motwani, and J. Widom. Models and issues in data stream systems. In *Proceedings of the ACM SIGART/SIGMOD Symposium on Principles of Database Systems*, pages 1–16, June 2002. 12

[4] C. Chan, P. Felber, M. Garofalakis, and R. Rastogi. Efficient filtering of XML documents with XPath expressions. In *Proceedings of the International Conference on Data Engineering*, 2002. 17

[5] V. Christophides, S. Abiteboul, S. Cluet, and M. Scholl. From structured documents to novel query facilities. In R. Snodgrass and M. Winslett, editors, *Proceedings of 1994 ACM SIGMOD International Conference on Management of Data*, pages 313–324, Minneapolis, Minnesota, May 1994. 12

[6] T. H. Cormen, C. E. Leiserson, and R. L. Rivest. *Introduction to Algorithms*. MIT Press, 1990. 19

[7] R. Goldman and J. Widom. DataGuides: enabling query formulation and optimization in semistructured databases. In *Proceedings of Very Large Data Bases*, pages 436–445, September 1997. 22

[8] G. Gonnet, R. Baeza-Yates, and T. Snider. Lexicographical indices for text: inverted files vs. PAT trees. In W. B. Frakes and R. A. Baeza-Yates, editors, *Information Retrieval: Data Structures & Algorithms*, pages 66–82. Prentice-Hall, 1992. 12

[9] G. Gonnet and F. Tompa. Mind your grammar: A new approach to modelling text. In *Proceedings of 13th International Conference on Very Large Databases*, pages 339–346, 1987. 12

[10] T. J. Green, A. Gupta, M. Onizuka, and D. Suciu. XMLTK: an XML toolkit for scalable XML stream processing, 2002. manuscript. 13, 18

[11] T. J. Green, G. Miklau, M. Onizuka, and D. Suciu. Processing xml streams with deterministic automata and stream indexes, 2002. manuscript. 13, 15, 19, 21, 22, 23

[12] M. Gudgin, M. Hadley, J. Moreau, and H. Nielsen. SOAP version 1.2 part 1: Messaging framework, 2001. available from the W3C, http://www.w3.org/2000/xp/Group/. 12

[13] M. Gudgin, M. Hadley, J. Moreau, and H. Nielsen. SOAP version 1.2 part 2: Adjuncts, 2001. available from the W3C, http://www.w3.org/2000/xp/Group/. 12

[14] A. Gupta, A. Halevy, and D. Suciu. View selection for XML stream processing. In *WebDB'2000*, 2002. 13

[15] J. Hopcroft and J. Ullman. *Introduction to automata theory, languages, and computation*. Addison-Wesley, 1979. 18

[16] Z. Ives, A. Halevy, and D. Weld. An XML query engine for network-bound data. Unpublished, 2001. 20

[17] H. Liefke and D. Suciu. XMill: an efficent compressor for XML data. In *Proceedings of SIGMOD*, pages 153–164, Dallas, TX, 2000. 22

[18] M. Marcus, B. Santorini, and M. A.Marcinkiewicz. Building a large annotated corpus of English: the Penn Treenbak. *Computational Linguistics*, 19, 1993. 22

[19] NASA's astronomical data center. ADC XML resource page. http://xml.gsfc.nasa.gov/. 14, 23

[20] G. Navarro and R. Baeza-Yates. Proximal nodes: a model to query document databases by content and structure. *ACM Transactions on Information Systems*, 15(4):400–435, October 1997. 12

[21] B. Nguyen, S. Abiteboul, G. Cobena, and M. Preda. Monitoring XML data on the web. In *Proceedings of the ACM SIGMOD Conference on Management of Data*, pages 437–448, Santa Barbara, 2001. 15

[22] G. Rozenberg and A. Salomaa. *Handbook of Formal Languages*. Springer Verlag, 1997. 20

[23] A. Salminen and F. W. Tompa. PAT expressions: An algebra for text search. In *Papers in Computational Lexicography: COMPLEX'92*, pages 309–332, 1992. 12

[24] A. Salminen and F. W. Tompa. PAT expressions: An algebra for text search. *Acta Linguistica Hungarica*, 41(1-4):277–306, 1994. 12

[25] A. Snoeren, K. Conley, and D. Gifford. Mesh-based content routing using XML. In *Proceedings of the 18th Symposium on Operating Systems Principles*, 2001. 12

String Matching Problems from Bioinformatics Which Still Need Better Solutions
Extended Abstract

Gaston H. Gonnet

ETH Informatik
Zurich, Switzerland

Abstract. Bioinformatics, the discipline which studies the computational problems arising from molecular biology, poses many interesting problems to the string searching community. We will describe two problems arising from Bioinformatics, their preliminary solutions, and the more general problem that they pose. We hope that this will encourage researchers to find better, general, algorithms to solve these problems.

1 Introduction

String searching problems in bioinformatics are normally posed in terms of returning a score as opposed to a binary answer. This is quite fundamental, most of the time these searching problems return the likelihood of a certain event. Consequently we will assume that all of our searches return a score, and we will be searching for the highest scoring strings.

Molecular information, for the purpose of this paper, consists of sequences of DNA/RNA (4 symbols) or sequences of amino acids (20 symbols) normally called proteins.

2 Identifying α-Helices

The first problem is related to the identification of α-helices in protein sequences. A similar, but simpler, problem arises with the identification of β-sheets (or β-strands). We will concentrate on the first problem.

An α-helix is a secondary structure of proteins, found in almost every protein. About 10% of the total amino acids in any genome are part of α-helices. Recognition of α-helices from the primary structure, that is the sequence of amino acids, is usually called "secondary structure prediction", and is a very important and active area of research. An α-helix is a helical structure which rotates exactly 100° with every amino acid. Its existence and stability is normally due to its surroundings, a helix cannot stand by itself. In particular, most helices find themselves in the interface between the inner and outer part of the protein. This information is very useful to find (or confirm) helices, as one side of the

A.H.F. Laender and A.L. Oliveira (Eds.): SPIRE 2002, LNCS 2476, pp. 27–30, 2002.

helix is hydrophobic (the inner side) and the other is hydrophilic (the outer side, typically exposed to water).

Each amino acid has an index of hydrophobicity. Hydrophobicity indices range from -1 to 1. A natural score for a sequence of L amino acids starting at position j is the the internal product:

$$R = \sum_{i=j}^{j+L-1} H_i \sin(\frac{2\pi i \times 100}{360} + \theta)$$

where θ is the phase angle of the helix with respect to the inner/outer limit and H_i is the hydrophobicity index of amino acid i. Expanding and collecting we obtain:

$$R = S_j \cos\theta + C_j \sin\theta$$

with

$$S_j = \sum_{i=j}^{j+L-1} H_i \sin 5/9\pi i \qquad C_j = \sum_{i=j}^{j+L-1} H_i \cos 5/9\pi i$$

The phase angle θ which gives the maximum score for each j is easily obtained by solving the derivative of R equated to 0. The maximum score is given by:

$$R = \sqrt{C_j^2 + S_j^2}$$

A linear time algorithm is easy to derive (for a fixed L). The values of C_j and S_j can be updated in constant time by adding the $(j + L)^{th}$ term and subtracting the jth term.

It is clear that such an algorithm will work for any score which is a function of sums (or other functions with an inverse) over individual values.

This optimal score has a surprisingly simple geometrical interpretation. If every H_i is viewed as a vector from $(0,0)$ to $(H_i \cos 5/9\pi i, H_i \sin 5/9\pi i)$, then we are looking for the longest path of L consecutive vectors.

Problem 1: Is there a more efficient algorithm to search an amino acid sequence for various values of L, e.g. L=5..30 ? (Even if it is more efficient in the constant term, not necessarily asymptotically.)

Problem 2: Are there any mathematical properties of the score R which make this search more efficient?

3 Matching Profiles or Probabilistic Sequences

A probabilistic pattern is a sequence which is defined by probability vectors in each position. It is interpreted as each position having several choices (all the values of the probability vector which are non zero). This is a natural generalization of matching a regular expression, where we additionally want to find the most likely match (highest probability) of all the possible ones.

There are three main uses of probabilistic sequences: Probabilistic ancestral sequences, Patterns and Motifs. The scores that we compute in this section can

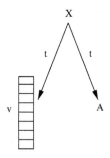

Fig. 1. Matching a probabilistic position against an amino acid

be used for direct string matching or can be used in the dynamic programming alignment of sequences with indels.

Scoring an amino acid against a probabilistic sequence is not completely trivial if it is to be done according to the standard model of evolution. The score is given by the quotient between the probability of being homologous, i.e. coming from a common ancestor divided the probability of being matched by chance (null hypothesis).

Let v be the probability vector to be scored against amino acid A and t the distance between x and A and between x and v as shown in figure 1. The quotient of probabilities is:

$$\frac{Pr\{\text{common ancestor}\}}{Pr\{\text{random occurrence}\}} = \frac{\sum_x f_x \left(\sum_i Pr\{x \to i\}v_i\right) Pr\{x \to A\}}{\left(\sum_i v_i f_i\right) f_A}$$

That is, the probability is simply summed over all possible values of the ancestor (x) and all possible values of the probabilistic position (i). Using Dayhoff's mutation matrices, doing some simplifications and taking logarithms to have an additive score, we simplify the score to:

$$R = 10 \log_{10} \frac{u_A}{fv}$$

where $f = (f_1, f_2, ...)$ is the vector of natural amino acid frequencies, $u = v^T M^{2t}$ and M is a 1-PAM mutation matrix. By precomputing the vectors u and fv for the pattern, we can compute the score for each position in time $O(1)$.

Scoring a probabilistic sequence against another is done following the same lines. Figure 2 describes the situation of scoring one particular position against another. This time we have a triple sum, over the ancestor and over each of the two probabilistic descendants, i.e.:

$$\frac{Pr\{\text{common ancestor}\}}{Pr\{\text{random occurrence}\}} = \frac{\sum_x \sum_i \sum_j f_x Pr\{x \to i\}v_i Pr\{x \to j\}w_j}{fv\, fw}$$

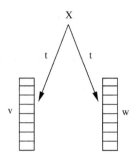

Fig. 2. Matching two probabilistic positions

We use the same technique as before to simplify the computation and obtain:

$$R = 10 \log_{10}(u^* w^*)$$

where $v^* = \frac{v}{f_v}$ can be precomputed for the first sequence, $w^* = \frac{w^T M^{2t} F}{f w}$ can be precomputed for the second sequence and F is a diagonal matrix containing the natural frequencies, i.e. $F_{ii} = f_i$. The computation of the score, besides precomputation, requires an internal product of two vectors of size 20 (number of symbols). This is quite efficient since the precomputation is dwarfed by the matching phase.

Problem 3: Is is possible to compute the scores more efficiently for this case?

Problem 4: All these string matching algorithms assume a brute force underlying string searching strategy. Is it possible to improve the efficiency by using the ideas of better string searching algorithms to these scores?

Optimal Exact String Matching
Based on Suffix Arrays

Mohamed Ibrahim Abouelhoda, Enno Ohlebusch, and Stefan Kurtz

Faculty of Technology, University of Bielefeld
P.O. Box 10 01 31, 33501 Bielefeld, Germany
{mibrahim,enno,kurtz}@TechFak.Uni-Bielefeld.DE

Abstract. Using the suffix tree of a string S, decision queries of the type "Is P a substring of S?" can be answered in $O(|P|)$ time and enumeration queries of the type "Where are all z occurrences of P in S?" can be answered in $O(|P|+z)$ time, totally independent of the size of S. However, in large scale applications as genome analysis, the space requirements of the suffix tree are a severe drawback. The suffix array is a more space economical index structure. Using it and an additional table, Manber and Myers (1993) showed that decision queries and enumeration queries can be answered in $O(|P|+\log|S|)$ and $O(|P|+\log|S|+z)$ time, respectively, but no optimal time algorithms are known. In this paper, we show how to achieve the optimal $O(|P|)$ and $O(|P|+z)$ time bounds for the suffix array. Our approach is not confined to exact pattern matching. In fact, it can be used to efficiently solve all problems that are usually solved by a top-down traversal of the suffix tree. Experiments show that our method is not only of theoretical interest but also of practical relevance.

1 Introduction

The suffix tree of a sequence S can be computed and stored in $O(n)$ time and space [13], where $n = |S|$. Once constructed, it allows one to answer queries of the type "Is P a substring of S?" in $O(m)$ time, where $m = |P|$. Furthermore, all z occurrences of a pattern P can be found in $O(m+z)$ time, totally independent of the size of S. Moreover, typical string processing problems like searching for all repeats in S can be efficiently solved by a bottom-up traversal of the suffix tree of S. These properties are most convenient in a "myriad" of situations [2], and Gusfield devotes about 70 pages of his book [8] to applications of suffix trees.

While suffix trees play a prominent role in algorithmics, they are not as widespread in actual implementations of software tools as one should expect. There are two major reasons for this: (i) Although being asymptotically linear, the space consumption of a suffix tree is quite large; even the recently improved implementations (see, e.g., [10]) of linear time constructions still require $20n$ bytes in the worst case. (ii) In most applications, the suffix tree suffers from a poor locality of memory reference, which causes a significant loss of efficiency on cached processor architectures. On the other hand, the suffix array (introduced in [12] and in [6] under the name PAT array) is a more space efficient data

A.H.F. Laender and A.L. Oliveira (Eds.): SPIRE 2002, LNCS 2476, pp. 31–43, 2002.
© Springer-Verlag Berlin Heidelberg 2002

structure than the suffix tree. It requires only $4n$ bytes in its basic form. However, at first glance, it seems that the suffix array has two disadvantages over the suffix tree:

(1) The direct construction of the suffix array takes $O(n \cdot \log n)$ time.
(2) It is not clear that (and how) every algorithm using a suffix tree can be replaced with an algorithm based on a suffix array solving the same problem in the same time complexity. For example, using only the basic suffix array, it takes $O(m \cdot \log n)$ time in the worst case to answer decision queries.

Let us briefly comment on the two seemingly drawbacks:

(1) The $O(n \cdot \log n)$ time bound for the direct construction of the suffix array is not a real drawback, neither from a theoretical nor from a practical point of view. The suffix array of S can be constructed in $O(n)$ time in the worst case by first constructing the suffix tree of S; see [8]. However, in practice the improved $O(n \cdot \log n)$ time algorithm of [11] to directly construct the suffix array is reported to be more efficient than building it indirectly in $O(n)$ time via the suffix tree.

(2) We strongly believe that every algorithm using a suffix tree can be replaced with an equivalent algorithm based on a suffix array and additional information. As an example, let us look at the exact pattern matching problem. Using an additional table, Manber and Myers [12] showed that decision queries can be answered in $O(m + \log n)$ time in the worst case. However, no $O(m)$ time algorithm based on the suffix array was known for this task. In this paper, we will show how decision queries can be answered in optimal $O(m)$ time and how to find all z occurrences of a pattern P in optimal $O(m+z)$ time. This new result is achieved by using the basic suffix array enhanced with two additional tables; each can be computed in linear time and requires only $4n$ bytes. In practice each of these tables can even be stored in n bytes without loss of performance. Our new approach is not confined to exact pattern matching. In general, we can simulate any top-down traversal of the suffix tree by means of the enhanced suffix array. Thus, our method can efficiently solve all problems that are usually solved by a top-down traversal of the suffix tree. By taking the approach of Kasai et al. [9] one step further, it is also possible to efficiently solve all problems with enhanced suffix arrays that are usually solved by a bottom-up traversal of the suffix tree; see Abouelhoda et al. [1] for details.

Clearly, it would be desirable to further reduce the space requirement of the suffix array. Recently, interesting results in this direction have been obtained. The most notable ones are the compressed suffix array introduced by Grossi and Vitter [7] and the so-called opportunistic data structure devised by Ferragina and Manzini [4]. These data structures reduce the space consumption considerably. However, due to the compression, these approaches do not allow to answer enumeration queries in $O(m+z)$ time; instead they require $O(m + z \log^{\varepsilon} n)$ time, where $\varepsilon > 0$ is a constant. Worse, experimental results [5] show that the gain in space reduction has to be paid by considerably slower pattern matching; this is true even for decision queries. According to [5], the opportunistic index is 8-13 times more space efficient than the suffix array, but string matching based on the opportunistic index is 16-35 times slower than their implementation based on the suffix array. So there is a trade-off between time and space consumption. In contrast to that, suffix arrays can be queried at speeds comparable to suffix trees, while being much more space efficient than these. Moreover, experimental results show that our method can compete with the method of [12]. In case of DNA sequences, it is even 1.5 times faster than the method of [12]. Therefore, it is not only of theoretical interest but also of practical relevance.

2   Basic Notions

In order to fix notation, we briefly recall some basic concepts. Let S be a string of length $|S| = n$ over an ordered alphabet Σ. To simplify analysis, we suppose that the size of the alphabet is a constant, and that $n < 2^{32}$. The latter implies that an integer in the range $[0, n]$ can be stored in 4 bytes. We assume that the special symbol $\$$ is an element of Σ (which is larger then all other elements) but does not occur in S. $S[i]$ denotes the character at position i in S, for $0 \leq i < n$. For $i \leq j$, $S[i..j]$ denotes the substring of S starting with the character at position i and ending with the character at position j.

The *suffix array* suftab is an array of integers in the range 0 to n, specifying the lexicographic ordering of the $n + 1$ suffixes of the string $S\$$. That is, $S_{\text{suftab}[0]}, S_{\text{suftab}[1]}, \ldots, S_{\text{suftab}[n]}$ is the sequence of suffixes of $S\$$ in ascending lexicographic order, where $S_i = S[i..n-1]\$$ denotes the ith nonempty suffix of the string $S\$$, $0 \leq i \leq n$. The suffix array requires $4n$ bytes. The direct construction of the suffix array takes $O(n \cdot \log n)$ time [12], but it can be build in $O(n)$ time via the construction of the suffix tree; see, e.g., [8].

The lcp-table lcptab is an array of integers in the range 0 to n. We define lcptab$[0] = 0$ and lcptab$[i]$ is the length of the longest common prefix of $S_{\text{suftab}[i-1]}$ and $S_{\text{suftab}[i]}$, for $1 \leq i \leq n$. Since $S_{\text{suftab}[n]} = \$$, we always have lcptab$[n] = 0$; see Fig. 1. The lcp-table can be computed as a by-product during the construction of the suffix array, or alternatively, in linear time from the suffix array [9]. The lcp-table requires $4n$ bytes. However, in practice it can be implemented in little more than n bytes; see section 8.

3   The lcp-Intervals of a Suffix Array

To achieve the goals outlined in the introduction, we need the following concepts.

Definition 1. *Interval* $[i..j]$, $0 \leq i < j \leq n$, *is an lcp-interval of lcp-value* ℓ *if*

1. lcptab$[i] < \ell$,
2. lcptab$[k] \geq \ell$ *for all* k *with* $i + 1 \leq k \leq j$,
3. lcptab$[k] = \ell$ *for at least one* k *with* $i + 1 \leq k \leq j$,
4. lcptab$[j + 1] < \ell$.

	suf-tab	lcp-tab	cldtab 1.	2.	3.	$S_{\text{suftab}[i]}$
0	2	0	②		6	aaacatat$
1	3	2				aacatat$
2	0	1	1 ③		4	acaaacatat$
3	4	3				acatat$
4	6	1	3 5			atat$
5	8	2				at$
6	1	0	2 ⑦		8	caaacatat$
7	5	2				catat$
8	7	0	7 ⑨		10	tat$
9	9	1				t$
10	10	0	9			$

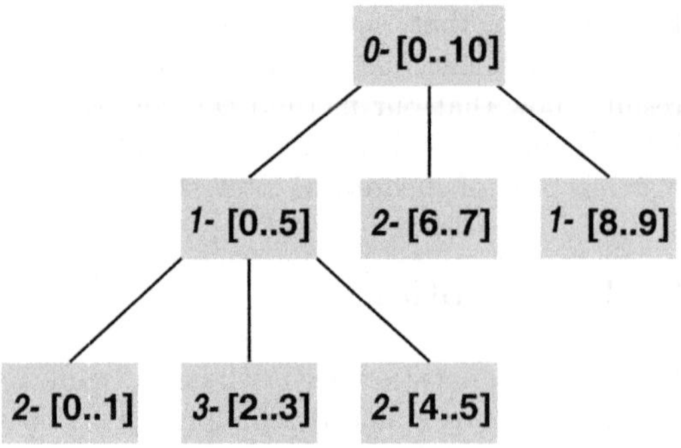

Tree:

0-[0..10]

1-[0..5]   2-[6..7]   1-[8..9]

2-[0..1]   3-[2..3]   2-[4..5]

Fig. 1. Enhanced suffix array of the string $S = $ acaaacatat$ and its lcp-interval tree. The fields 1, 2, and 3 of the cldtab denote the *up*, *down*, and *nextℓIndex* field, respectively; see Section 4. The encircled entries are redundant because they also occur in the *up* field

We will also use the shorthand ℓ-interval (or even ℓ-$[i..j]$) for an lcp-interval $[i..j]$ of lcp-value ℓ. Every index k, $i + 1 \leq k \leq j$, with lcptab$[k] = \ell$ is called ℓ-index. The set of all ℓ-indices of an ℓ-interval $[i..j]$ will be denoted by $\ell Indices(i, j)$. If $[i..j]$ is an ℓ-interval such that $\omega = S[\text{suftab}[i]..\text{suftab}[i]+\ell-1]$ is the longest common prefix of the suffixes $S_{\text{suftab}[i]}, S_{\text{suftab}[i+1]}, \ldots, S_{\text{suftab}[j]}$, then $[i..j]$ is also called ω-interval.

Definition 2. *An m-interval $[l..r]$ is said to be embedded in an ℓ-interval $[i..j]$ if it is a subinterval of $[i..j]$ (i.e., $i \leq l < r \leq j$) and $m > \ell$.[1] The ℓ-interval $[i..j]$ is then called the interval enclosing $[l..r]$. If $[i..j]$ encloses $[l..r]$ and there is no interval embedded in $[i..j]$ that also encloses $[l..r]$, then $[l..r]$ is called a child interval of $[i..j]$.*

This parent-child relationship constitutes a conceptual (or virtual) tree which we call the lcp-interval tree of the suffix array. The root of this tree is the 0-interval $[0..n]$; see Fig. 1. The lcp-interval tree is basically the suffix tree without leaves (note, however, that it is not our intention to build this tree). These leaves are left implicit in our framework, but every leaf in the suffix tree, which corresponds to the suffix $S_{\text{suftab}[l]}$, can be represented by a singleton interval $[l..l]$. The parent interval of such a singleton interval is the smallest lcp-interval $[i..j]$ with $l \in [i..j]$. The child intervals of an ℓ-interval can be computed according to the following lemma.

Lemma 3. *Let $[i..j]$ be an ℓ-interval. If $i_1 < i_2 < \ldots < i_k$ are the ℓ-indices in ascending order, then the child intervals of $[i..j]$ are $[i..i_1 - 1]$, $[i_1..i_2 - 1], \ldots, [i_k..j]$ (note that some of them may be singleton intervals).*

---

[1] Note that we cannot have both $i = l$ and $r = j$ because $m > \ell$.

Proof. Let $[l..r]$ be one of the intervals $[i..i_1 - 1], [i_1..i_2 - 1], \ldots, [i_k..j]$. If $[l..r]$ is a singleton interval, then it is a child interval of $[i..j]$. Suppose that $[l..r]$ is an m-interval. Since $[l..r]$ does not contain an ℓ-index, it follows that $[l..r]$ is embedded in $[i..j]$. Because $\mathsf{lcptab}[i_1] = \mathsf{lcptab}[i_2] = \ldots = \mathsf{lcptab}[i_k] = \ell$, there is no interval embedded in $[i..j]$ that encloses $[l..r]$. That is, $[l..r]$ is a child interval of $[i..j]$. Finally, it is not difficult to see that $[i..i_1 - 1], [i_1..i_2 - 1], \ldots, [i_k..j]$ are all the child intervals of $[i..j]$, i.e., there cannot be any other child interval.

Based on the analogy between the suffix array and the suffix tree, it is desirable to enhance the suffix array with additional information to determine, for any ℓ-interval $[i..j]$, all its child intervals in constant time. We achieve this goal by enhancing the suffix array with two tables. In order to distinguish our new data structure from the basic suffix array, we call it the *enhanced suffix array*.

4   The Enhanced Suffix Array

Our new data structure consists of the suffix array, the lcp-table, and an additional table: the child-table cldtab; see Fig. 1. The lcp-table was already presented in Section 2. The child-table is a table of size $n + 1$ indexed from 0 to n and each entry contains three values: *up*, *down*, and *nextℓIndex*. Each of these three values requires 4 bytes in the worst case. We shall see later that it is possible to store the same information in only one field. Formally, the values of each cldtab-entry are defined as follows (we assume that $\min \emptyset = \max \emptyset = \bot$):

$$\mathsf{cldtab}[i].up = \min\{q \in [0..i - 1] \mid \mathsf{lcptab}[q] > \mathsf{lcptab}[i]$$
$$\text{and } \forall k \in [q + 1..i - 1] : \mathsf{lcptab}[k] \geq \mathsf{lcptab}[q]\}$$
$$\mathsf{cldtab}[i].down = \max\{q \in [i + 1..n] \mid \mathsf{lcptab}[q] > \mathsf{lcptab}[i]$$
$$\text{and } \forall k \in [i + 1..q - 1] : \mathsf{lcptab}[k] > \mathsf{lcptab}[q]\}$$
$$\mathsf{cldtab}[i].nextℓIndex = \min\{q \in [i + 1..n] \mid \mathsf{lcptab}[q] = \mathsf{lcptab}[i]$$
$$\text{and } \forall k \in [i + 1..q - 1] : \mathsf{lcptab}[k] > \mathsf{lcptab}[i]\}$$

In essence, the child-table stores the parent-child relationship of lcp-intervals. Roughly speaking, for an ℓ-interval $[i..j]$ whose ℓ-indices are $i_1 < i_2 < \ldots < i_k$, the $\mathsf{cldtab}[i].down$ or $\mathsf{cldtab}[j + 1].up$ value is used to determine the first ℓ-index i_1. The other ℓ-indices $i_2, \ldots i_k$ can be obtained from $\mathsf{cldtab}[i_1].nextℓIndex$, $\ldots \mathsf{cldtab}[i_{k-1}].nextℓIndex$, respectively. Once these ℓ-indices are known, one can determine all the child intervals of $[i..j]$ according to Lemma 3. As an example, consider the enhanced suffix array in Fig. 1. The 1-[0..5] interval has the 1-indices 2 and 4. The first 1-index 2 is stored in $\mathsf{cldtab}[0].down$ and $\mathsf{cldtab}[6].up$. The second 1-index is stored in $\mathsf{cldtab}[2].nextℓIndex$. Thus, the child intervals of [0..5] are [0..1], [2..3], and [4..5]. In Section 6, it will be shown in detail how the child-table can be used to determine the child intervals of an lcp-interval in constant time.

5   Construction of the Child-Table

For clarity of presentation, we introduce *two* algorithms to construct the *up/down* values and the *nextℓIndex* value of the child-table separately. It is not difficult, however, to devise an algorithm that constructs the whole child-table in one scan of the lcptab. Both algorithms use a stack whose elements are indices of the lcptab. *push* (pushes an element onto the stack) and *pop* (pops an element from the stack and returns that element) are the usual stack operations, while *top* is the topmost element of the stack. Algorithm 4 scans the lcptab in linear order and pushes the current index on the stack if its lcp-value is greater than or equal to the lcp-value of *top*. Otherwise, elements of the stack are popped as long as their lcp-value is greater than that of the current index. Based on a comparison of the lcp-values of *top* and the current index, the *up* and *down* fields of the child-table are filled with elements that are popped during the scan.

Algorithm 4 *Construction of the up and down values.*

$lastIndex := -1$
$push(0)$
for $i := 1$ **to** n **do**
   while lcptab$[i]$ < lcptab$[top]$
      $lastIndex := pop$
      if (lcptab$[i]$ ≤ lcptab$[top]$) ∧ (lcptab$[top]$ ≠ lcptab$[lastIndex]$) **then**
           cldtab$[top].down := lastIndex$
   if lcptab$[i]$ ≥ lcptab$[top]$ **then**
      if $lastIndex \neq -1$ **then**
         cldtab$[i].up := lastIndex$
         $lastIndex := -1$
      $push(i)$

For a correctness proof, we need the following lemma.

Lemma 5. *The following invariants are maintained in the **while**-loop of Algorithm 4: If $i_1, \ldots, i_p$ are the indices on the stack (where i_p is the topmost element), then $i_1 < \cdots < i_p$ and lcptab$[i_1] \leq \cdots \leq$ lcptab$[i_p]$. Moreover, if lcptab$[i_j]$ < lcptab$[i_{j+1}]$, then for all k with $i_j < k < i_{j+1}$ we have lcptab$[k]$ > lcptab$[i_{j+1}]$.*

Theorem 6. *Algorithm 4 correctly fills the up and down fields of the child-table.*

Proof. If the cldtab$[top].down := lastIndex$ statement is executed, then we have lcptab$[i]$ ≤ lcptab$[top]$ < lcptab$[lastIndex]$ and $top < lastIndex < i$. Recall that cldtab$[top].down$ is the maximum of the set $M = \{q \in [top + 1..n] \mid$ lcptab$[q]$ > lcptab$[top]$ and $\forall k \in [top + 1..q - 1]$: lcptab$[k]$ > lcptab$[q]\}$. Clearly, $lastIndex \in [top + 1..n]$ and lcptab$[lastIndex]$ > lcptab$[top]$. Furthermore, according to Lemma 5, for all k with $top < k < lastIndex$ we have lcptab$[k]$ > lcptab$[lastIndex]$. In other words, $lastIndex$ is an element of M. Suppose that $lastIndex$ is not the maximum of M. Then there is an element q'

in M with $lastIndex < q' < i$. According to the definition of M, it follows that lcptab$[lastIndex] >$ lcptab$[q']$. This, however, implies that $lastIndex$ must have been popped from the stack when index q' was considered. This contradiction shows that $lastIndex$ is the maximum of M.

If the cldtab$[i].up := lastIndex$ statement is executed, then lcptab$[top] \leq$ lcptab$[i] <$ lcptab$[lastIndex]$ and $top < lastIndex < i$. Recall that cldtab$[i].up$ is the minimum of the set $M' = \{q \in [0..i-1] \mid$ lcptab$[q] >$ lcptab$[i]$ and $\forall k \in [q+1..i-1]$: lcptab$[k] \geq$ lcptab$[q]\}$. Clearly, we have $lastIndex \in [0..i-1]$ and lcptab$[lastIndex] >$ lcptab$[i]$. Moreover, for all k with $lastIndex < k < i$ we have lcptab$[k] \geq$ lcptab$[lastIndex]$ because otherwise $lastIndex$ would have been popped earlier from the stack. In other words, $lastIndex \in M'$. Suppose that $lastIndex$ is not the minimum of M'. Then there is a $q' \in M'$ with $top < q' < lastIndex$. According to the definition of M', it follows that lcptab$[lastIndex] \geq$ lcptab$[q'] >$ lcptab$[i] \geq$ lcptab$[top]$. Hence, index q' must be an element between top and $lastIndex$ on the stack. This contradiction shows that $lastIndex$ is the minimum of M'.

The construction of the $next\ell Index$ field is easier. One merely has to check whether lcptab$[i] =$ lcptab$[top]$ holds true. If so, then index i is assigned to the field cldtab$[top].next\ell Index$. It is not difficult to see that Algorithms 4 and 7 construct the child-table in linear time and space.

Algorithm 7 *Construction of the $next\ell Index$ value.*

```
push(0)
for i := 1 to n do
    while lcptab[i] < lcptab[top]
        pop
    if lcptab[i] = lcptab[top] then
        lastIndex := pop
    cldtab[lastIndex].nextℓIndex := i
    push(i)
```

To reduce the space requirement of the child-table, only one field is used in practice. The *down* field is needed only if it does not contain the same information as the *up* field. Fortunately, for an ℓ-interval, only one *down* field is required because an ℓ-interval $[i..j]$ with k ℓ-indices has at most $k+1$ child intervals. Suppose $[l_1..r_1], [l_2..r_2], \ldots, [l_k..r_k], [l_{k+1}..r_{k+1}]$ are the $k+1$ child intervals of $[i..j]$, where $[l_q..r_q]$ is an ℓ_q-interval and i_q denotes its first ℓ_q-index for any $1 \leq q \leq k+1$. In the *up* field of cldtab$[r_1+1]$, cldtab$[r_2+1], \ldots,$ cldtab$[r_k+1]$ we store the indices $i_1, i_2, \ldots, i_k$, respectively. Thus, only the remaining index i_{k+1} must be stored in the *down* field of cldtab$[r_k+1]$. This value can be stored in cldtab$[r_k+1].next\ell Index$ because r_k+1 is the last ℓ-index and hence cldtab$[r_k+1].next\ell Index$ is empty; see Fig. 1. However, if we do this, then for a given index i we must be able to decide whether cldtab$[i].next\ell Index$ contains the next ℓ-index or the cldtab$[i].down$ value. This can be accomplished as follows. cldtab$[i].next\ell Index$ contains the next ℓ-index if lcptab$[$cldtab$[i].next\ell Index] =$ lcptab$[i]$, whereas it stores the cldtab$[i].down$ value if $\mathsf{lcptab}[\mathsf{cldtab}[i].next\ell Index] > \mathsf{lcptab}[i]$. This follows directly from the definition of the $next\ell Index$ and $down$ field, respectively. Moreover, the memory cells of $\mathsf{cldtab}[i].next\ell Index$, which are still unused, can store the values of the up field. To see this, note that $\mathsf{cldtab}[i+1].up \neq \perp$ if and only if $\mathsf{lcptab}[i] > \mathsf{lcptab}[i+1]$. In this case, we have $\mathsf{cldtab}[i].next\ell Index = \perp$ and $\mathsf{cldtab}[i].down = \perp$. In other words, $\mathsf{cldtab}[i].next\ell Index$ is empty and can store the value $\mathsf{cldtab}[i+1].up$; see Fig. 1. Finally, for a given index i, one can decide whether $\mathsf{cldtab}[i].next\ell Index$ contains the value $\mathsf{cldtab}[i+1].up$ by testing whether $\mathsf{lcptab}[i] > \mathsf{lcptab}[i+1]$. To sum up, although the child-table theoretically uses three fields, only space for one field is actually required.

6   Determining Child Intervals in Constant Time

Given the child-table, the first step to locate the child intervals of an ℓ-interval $[i..j]$ in constant time is to find the first ℓ-index in $[i..j]$, i.e., $\min \ell Indices(i,j)$. This is possible with the help of the up and $down$ fields of the child-table:

Lemma 8. *For every ℓ-interval $[i..j]$ the following statements hold:*

1. *$i < \mathsf{cldtab}[j+1].up \leq j$ or $i < \mathsf{cldtab}[i].down \leq j$.*
2. *$\mathsf{cldtab}[j+1].up$ stores the first ℓ-index in $[i..j]$ if $i < \mathsf{cldtab}[j+1].up \leq j$.*
3. *$\mathsf{cldtab}[i].down$ stores the first ℓ-index in $[i..j]$ if $i < \mathsf{cldtab}[i].down \leq j$.*

Proof. (1) First, consider index $j+1$. Suppose $\mathsf{lcptab}[j+1] = \ell'$ and let I' be the corresponding ℓ'-interval. If $[i..j]$ is a child interval of I', then $\mathsf{lcptab}[i] = \ell'$ and there is no ℓ-index in $[i+1..j]$. Therefore, $\mathsf{cldtab}[j+1].up = \min \ell Indices(i,j)$, and consequently $i < \mathsf{cldtab}[j+1].up \leq j$. If $[i..j]$ is not a child interval of I', then we consider index i. Suppose $\mathsf{lcptab}[i] = \ell''$ and let I'' be the corresponding ℓ''-interval. Because $\mathsf{lcptab}[j+1] = \ell' < \ell'' < \ell$, it follows that $[i..j]$ is a child interval of I''. We conclude that $\mathsf{cldtab}[i].down = \min \ell Indices(i,j)$. Hence, $i < \mathsf{cldtab}[i].down \leq j$.
(2) If $i < \mathsf{cldtab}[j+1].up \leq j$, then the claim follows from $\mathsf{cldtab}[j+1].up = \min\{q \in [i+1..j] \mid \mathsf{lcptab}[q] > \mathsf{lcptab}[j+1], \mathsf{lcptab}[k] \geq \mathsf{lcptab}[q] \ \forall k \in [q+1..j]\} = \min\{q \in [i+1..j] \mid \mathsf{lcptab}[k] \geq \mathsf{lcptab}[q] \ \forall k \in [q+1..j]\} = \min \ell Indices(i,j)$.
(3) Let i_1 be the first ℓ-index of $[i..j]$. Then $\mathsf{lcptab}[i_1] = \ell > \mathsf{lcptab}[i]$ and for all $k \in [i+1..i_1 - 1]$ the inequality $\mathsf{lcptab}[k] > \ell = \mathsf{lcptab}[i_1]$ holds. Moreover, for any other index $q \in [i+1..j]$, we have $\mathsf{lcptab}[q] \geq \ell > \mathsf{lcptab}[i]$ but *not* $\mathsf{lcptab}[i_1] > \mathsf{lcptab}[q]$.

Once the first ℓ-index i_1 of an ℓ-interval $[i..j]$ is found, the remaining ℓ-indices $i_2 < i_3 < \ldots < i_k$ in $[i..j]$, where $1 \leq k \leq |\Sigma|$, are obtained successively from the $next\ell Index$ field of $\mathsf{cldtab}[i_1], \mathsf{cldtab}[i_2], \ldots, \mathsf{cldtab}[i_{k-1}]$. It follows that the child intervals of $[i..j]$ are the intervals $[i..i_1 - 1], [i_1..i_2 - 1], \ldots, [i_k..j]$; see Lemma 3. The pseudo-code implementation of the following function *getChildIntervals* takes a pair (i,j) representing an ℓ-interval $[i..j]$ as input and returns a list containing the pairs $(i, i_1 - 1), (i_1, i_2 - 1), \ldots, (i_k, j)$.

Algorithm 9 *getChildIntervals, applied to an lcp-interval $[i..j] \neq [0..n]$.*

intervalList = [ ]
if $i <$ cldtab$[j + 1].up \leq j$ **then**
    $i_1 :=$ cldtab$[j + 1].up$
else $i_1 :=$ cldtab$[i].down$
$add($intervalList$, (i, i_1 - 1))$
while cldtab$[i_1].next\ell Index \neq \bot$ **do**
    $i_2 :=$ cldtab$[i_1].next\ell Index$
    $add($intervalList$, (i_1, i_2 - 1))$
    $i_1 := i_2$
$add($intervalList$, (i_1, j))$

The function *getChildIntervals* runs in constant time, provided the alphabet size is constant. Using *getChildIntervals* one can simulate every top-down traversal of a suffix tree on an enhanced suffix array. To this end, one can easily modify the function *getChildIntervals* to a function *getInterval* which takes an ℓ-interval $[i..j]$ and a character $a \in \Sigma$ as input and returns the child interval $[l..r]$ of $[i..j]$ (which may be a singleton interval) whose suffixes have the character a at position ℓ. Note that all the suffixes in $[l..r]$ share the same ℓ-character prefix because $[l..r]$ is a subinterval of $[i..j]$. If such an interval $[l..r]$ does not exist, *getInterval* returns $\bot$.

With the help of Lemma 8, it is also easy to implement a function $getlcp(i, j)$ that determines the lcp-value of an lcp-interval $[i..j]$ in constant time as follows: If $i <$ cldtab$[j+1].up \leq j$, then $getlcp(i, j)$ returns the value lcptab[cldtab$[j+1].up$], otherwise it returns the value lcptab[cldtab$[i].down$].

7   Answering Queries in Optimal Time

As already mentioned in the introduction, given the basic suffix array, it takes $O(m \cdot \log n)$ time in the worst case to answer decision queries. By using an additional table (similar to the lcp-table), this time complexity can be improved to $O(m + \log n)$; see [12]. The logarithmic terms are due to binary searches, which locate P in the suffix array of S. In this section, we show how enhanced suffix arrays allow us to answer decision and enumeration queries for P in optimal $O(m)$ and $O(m + z)$ time, respectively, where z is the number of occurrences of P in S.

Algorithm 10 *Answering decision queries.*

$c := 0$
$queryFound := True$
$(i, j) := getInterval(0, n, P[c])$
while $(i, j) \neq \bot$ and $c < m$ and $queryFound = True$
    if $i \neq j$ **then**
        $\ell := getlcp(i, j)$
        $min := \min\{\ell, m\}$
        $queryFound := S[$suftab$[i] + c..$suftab$[i] + min - 1] = P[c..min - 1]$

$c := min$
$(i, j) := getInterval(i, j, P[c])$
else $queryFound := S[\mathsf{suftab}[i] + c..\mathsf{suftab}[i] + m - 1] = P[c..m - 1]$
if $queryFound$ **then**
$Report(i, j)$ /* the P-interval */
else print "pattern P not found"

The algorithm starts by determining with $getInterval(0, n, P[0])$ the lcp or singleton interval $[i..j]$ whose suffixes start with the character $P[0]$. If $[i..j]$ is a singleton interval, then pattern P occurs in S if and only if $S[\mathsf{suftab}[i]..\mathsf{suftab}[i] + m-1] = P$. Otherwise, if $[i..j]$ is an lcp-interval, then we determine its lcp-value ℓ by the function $getlcp$; see end of Section 6. Let $\omega = S[\mathsf{suftab}[i]..\mathsf{suftab}[i] + \ell - 1]$ be the longest common prefix of the suffixes $S_{\mathsf{suftab}[i]}, S_{\mathsf{suftab}[i+1]}, \ldots, S_{\mathsf{suftab}[j]}$. If $\ell \geq m$, then pattern P occurs in S if and only if $\omega[0..m - 1] = P$. Otherwise, if $\ell < m$, then we test whether $\omega = P[0..\ell - 1]$. If not, then P does not occur in S. If so, we search with $getInterval(i, j, P[\ell])$ for the ℓ'- or singleton interval $[i'..j']$ whose suffixes start with the prefix $P[0..\ell]$ (note that the suffixes of $[i'..j']$ have $P[0..\ell - 1]$ as a common prefix because $[i'..j']$ is a subinterval of $[i..j]$). If $[i'..j']$ is a singleton interval, then pattern P occurs in S if and only if $S[\mathsf{suftab}[i'] + \ell..\mathsf{suftab}[i'] + m - 1] = P[\ell..m - 1]$. Otherwise, if $[i'..j']$ is an ℓ'-interval, let $\omega' = S[\mathsf{suftab}[i']..\mathsf{suftab}[i'] + \ell' - 1]$ be the longest common prefix of the suffixes $S_{\mathsf{suftab}[i']}, S_{\mathsf{suftab}[i'+1]}, \ldots, S_{\mathsf{suftab}[j']}$. If $\ell' \geq m$, then pattern P occurs in S if and only if $\omega'[\ell..m - 1] = P[\ell..m - 1]$ (or equivalently, $\omega[0..m - 1] = P$). Otherwise, if $\ell' < m$, then we test whether $\omega[\ell..\ell' - 1] = P[\ell..\ell' - 1]$. If not, then P does not occur in S. If so, we search with $getInterval(i', j', P[\ell'])$ for the next interval, and so on.

Enumerative queries can be answered in optimal $O(m + z)$ time as follows. Given a pattern P of length m, we search for the P-interval $[l..r]$ using the preceding algorithm. This takes $O(m)$ time. Then we can report the start position of every occurrence of P in S by enumerating $\mathsf{suftab}[l], \ldots, \mathsf{suftab}[r]$. In other words, if P occurs z times in S, then reporting the start position of every occurrence requires $O(z)$ time in addition.

8   Implementation Details

We store most of the values of table lcptab in a table lcptab_1 using n bytes. That is, for any $i \in [1, n]$, $\mathsf{lcptab}_1[i] = \max\{255, \mathsf{lcptab}[i]\}$. There are usually only few entries in lcptab that are larger than or equal to ≥ 255; see Section 9. To access these efficiently, we store them in an extra table llvtab. This contains all pairs $(i, \mathsf{lcptab}[i])$ such that $\mathsf{lcptab}[i] \geq 255$, ordered by the first component. At index i of table lcptab_1 we store 255 whenever, $\mathsf{lcptab}[i] \geq 255$. This tells us that the correct value of lcptab is found in llvtab. If we scan the values in lcptab_1 in consecutive order and find a value 255, then we access the correct value in lcptab in the next entry of table llvtab. If we access the values in lcptab_1 in arbitrary order and find a value 255 at index i, then we perform a binary search in llvtab using i as the key. This delivers $\mathsf{lcptab}[i]$ in $O(\log_2 |\mathsf{llvtab}|)$ time.

In cldtab we store relative indices. For example, if $j =$ cldtab$[i].next\ell Index$, then we store $j-i$. The relative indices are almost always smaller than 255. Hence we use only one byte for storing a value of table cldtab. The values ≥ 255 are not stored. Instead, if we encounter the value 255 in cldtab, then we use a function that is equivalent to *getInterval*, except that it determines a child interval by a binary search, similar to the algorithm of [12, page 937]. Consequently, instead of 4 bytes per entry of the child-table, only 1 byte is needed. The overall space consumption for tables suftab, lcptab, and cldtab is thus only $6n$ bytes.

Additionally, we use an extra bucket table. For a given parameter q, we store for each string w of length q the smallest integer i, such that $S_{\mathsf{suftab}[i]}$ is a prefix of w. In this way, we can answer small queries of length $m \leq q$ in constant time. For larger queries, this bucket table allows us to locate the interval containing the q-character prefix $P[0..q-1]$ of the query P in constant time. Then our algorithm, which searches for the pattern P in S, starts with this interval instead of the interval $[0..n]$. The advantage of this hybrid method is that only a small part of the suffix array is actually accessed. In particular, we only rarely access a field with value 255 in cldtab.

9   Experimental Results

For our experiments, we collected a set of four files of different sizes and types:

1. *ecoli* is the complete genome of the bacterium *Escherichia coli*, i.e., a DNA sequence of length 4,639,221. The alphabet size is 4.
2. *yeast* is the complete genome of the baker's yeast *Saccharomyces cerevisiae*, i.e., a DNA sequence of length 12,156,300. The alphabet size is 4.
3. *swiss* is a collection of protein sequences from the Swissprot database. The total size of all protein sequences is 2,683,054. The alphabet size is 20.
4. *shaks* is a collection of the complete works of William Shakespeare. The total size is 5,582,655 bytes. The alphabet size is 92.

We use the algorithm of [3] to sort suffixes, i.e., to compute table suftab. Table lcptab is constructed as a by-product of the sorting. The construction of the enhanced suffix array (including storage on file) requires: 6.6 sec. and 21 MB RAM for *ecoli*, 27 sec. and 51 MB RAM for *yeast*, 7 sec. and 13 MB for *swiss*, 7 sec. and 32 MB for *shaks*. These and all other timings include system time and refer to a computer with a 933 MHz Pentium PIII Processor and 512 MB RAM, running Linux. We ran three different programs for answering enumeration queries:

1. *stree* is based on an improved linked list suffix tree representation as described in [10]. Searching for a pattern and enumerating the z occurrences takes $O(m + z)$ time. The space requirement is $12.6n$ bytes for *ecoli* and *yeast*, $11.6n$ bytes for *swiss*, and $9.6n$ bytes for *shaks*.
2. *mamy* is based on suffix arrays and uses the algorithm of [12, page 937]. We used the original program code developed by Gene Myers. Searching for

Table 1. Running times (in seconds) for one million enumeration queries searching for exact patterns in the input strings

	$minpl = 20, maxpl = 30$			$minpl = 30, maxpl = 40$			$minpl = 40, maxpl = 50$		
	stree	mamy	esamatch	stree	mamy	esamatch	stree	mamy	esamatch
file	time	time	time	time	time	time	time	time	time
ecoli	7.40	4.86	3.09	7.47	5.00	3.23	7.63	5.12	3.35
yeast	8.97	5.18	3.41	9.16	5.35	3.53	9.20	5.43	3.66
swiss	10.53	3.40	3.34	10.47	3.53	3.40	10.55	3.65	3.45
shaks	44.55	3.43	28.54	18.45	3.47	27.14	13.15	3.58	27.00

a pattern and enumerating its occurrences takes $O(m \log n + z)$ time. The space requirement is $4n$ bytes for all files.

3. *esamatch* is based on enhanced suffix arrays (tables suftab, lcptab, cldtab) and uses Algorithm 10. Searching a pattern takes $O(m + z)$ time. The space requirement is $6n$ bytes.

The programs *stree* and *mamy* first construct the index in main memory and then perform pattern searches. *esamatch* accesses the enhanced suffix array from file via memory mapping.

Table 1 shows the running times in seconds for the different programs when searching for one million patterns. This seems to be a large number of queries to be answered. However, at least in the field of genomics, it is relevant; see [8]. For example, when comparing two genomes it is necessary to match all substrings of one genome against all substrings of the other genome, and this requires to answer millions of enumeration queries in very short time.

The smallest running times in Table 1 are underlined. The time for index construction is not included. Patterns were generated according to the following strategy: For each input string S of length n we randomly sampled $p = 1,000,000$ substrings $s_1, s_2, \ldots, s_p$ of different lengths from S. The lengths were evenly distributed over different intervals $[minpl, maxpl]$, where $(minpl, maxpl) \in \{(20, 30), (30, 40), (40, 50)\}$. For $i \in [1, p]$, the programs were called to search for pattern p_i, where $p_i = s_i$, if i is even, and p_i is the reverse of s_i, if i is odd. Reversing a string s_i simulates the case that a pattern search is often unsuccessful.

The running time of all three programs is only slightly dependent on the size of the input strings and the length of the pattern. The only exception is *stree* applied to *shaks*, where the running time increases by a factor of about 2.5, when searching for smaller patterns. This is due to the fact that there are many patterns of length between 20 and 30 that occur very often in *shaks* (for example, lines that consist solely of white spaces). Enumerating their occurrences requires to traverse substantial parts of the suffix tree, which are often far apart in main memory. This slows down the enumeration. In contrast, in the suffix array the positions to be enumerated are stored in one consecutive memory area. As a consequence, for *esamatch* and *mamy* enumerating occurrences requires virtually no extra time. As expected, the running times of *stree* and *esamatch* depend on the alphabet size, while *mamy* shows basically the same speed for all files. For *shaks* it is much faster than the other programs, due to the large alphabet. For the other files, *esamatch* is always more than twice as fast as *stree* and slightly faster than *mamy* (1.5 times faster for DNA). This shows that *esamatch* is not only of theoretical interest.

Acknowledgments

We thank Dirk Strothmann, who observed that the values of the *up* field can also be stored in the *nextℓIndex* field of the child-table. Gene Myers provided his code for constructing and searching suffix arrays.

References

[1] M. I. Abouelhoda, S. Kurtz, and E. Ohlebusch. The Enhanced Suffix Array and its Applications to Genome Analysis. In *Proceedings of the Second Workshop on Algorithms in Bioinformatics*. Springer Verlag, Lecture Notes in Computer Science, accepted for publication, 2002. 32

[2] A. Apostolico. The Myriad Virtues of Subword Trees. In *Combinatorial Algorithms on Words, Springer Verlag*, pages 85–96, 1985. 31

[3] J. Bentley and R. Sedgewick. Fast Algorithms for Sorting and Searching Strings. In *Proceedings of the ACM-SIAM Symposium on Discrete Algorithms*, pages 360–369, 1997. 41

[4] P. Ferragina and G. Manzini. Opportunistic data structures with applications. In *IEEE Symposium on Foundations of Computer Science*, pages 390–398, 2000. 32

[5] P. Ferragina and G. Manzini. An experimental study of an opportunistic index. In *Symposium on Discrete Algorithms*, pages 269–278, 2001. 32

[6] G. Gonnet, R. Baeza-Yates, and T. Snider. New Indices for Text: PAT trees and PAT arrays. In W. Frakes and R. A. Baeza-Yates, editors, *Information Retrieval: Algorithms and Data Structures*, pages 66–82. Prentice-Hall, Englewood Cliffs, NJ, 1992. 31

[7] R. Grossi and J. S. Vitter. Compressed Suffix Arrays and Suffix Trees with Applications to Text Indexing and String Matching. In *ACM Symposium on the Theory of Computing (STOC 2000)*, pages 397–406. ACM Press, 2000. 32

[8] D. Gusfield. *Algorithms on Strings, Trees, and Sequences*. Cambridge University Press, 1997. 31, 32, 33, 42

[9] T. Kasai, G. Lee, H. Arimura, S. Arikawa, and K. Park. Linear-Time Longest-Common-Prefix Computation in Suffix Arrays and its Applications. In *Proceedings of the 12th Annual Symposium on Combinatorial Pattern Matching, July 2001, Lecture Notes in Computer Science 2089, Springer Verlag*, pages 181–192, 2001. 32, 33

[10] S. Kurtz. Reducing the Space Requirement of Suffix Trees. *Software—Practice and Experience*, **29**(13):1149–1171, 1999. 31, 41

[11] N. J. Larsson and K. Sadakane. Faster Suffix Sorting. Technical Report LU-CS-TR:99-214, Dept. of Computer Science, Lund University, 1999. 32

[12] U. Manber and E. W. Myers. Suffix Arrays: A New Method for On-Line String Searches. *SIAM Journal on Computing*, **22**(5):935–948, 1993. 31, 32, 33, 39, 41

[13] P. Weiner. Linear Pattern Matching Algorithms. In *Proceedings of the 14th IEEE Annual Symposium on Switching and Automata Theory*, pages 1–11, The University of Iowa, 1973. 31

Faster String Matching with Super–Alphabets

Kimmo Fredriksson

Department of Computer Science, University of Helsinki
Kimmo.Fredriksson@cs.Helsinki.FI

Abstract. Given a text $T[1 \ldots n]$ and a pattern $P[1 \ldots m]$ over some alphabet Σ of size σ, finding the exact occurrences of P in T requires at least $\Omega(n \log_\sigma m/m)$ character comparisons on average, as shown in [19]. Consequently, it is believed that this lower bound implies also an $\Omega(n \log_\sigma m/m)$ lower bound for the execution time of an optimal algorithm. However, in this paper we show how to obtain an $\mathcal{O}(n/m)$ average time algorithm. This is achieved by slightly changing the model of computation, and with a modification of an existing algorithm. Our technique uses a super–alphabet for simulating suffix automaton. The space usage of the algorithm is $\mathcal{O}(\sigma m)$. The technique can be applied to many other string matching algorithms, including dictionary matching, which is also solved in expected time $\mathcal{O}(n/m)$, and approximate matching allowing k edit operations (mismatches, insertions or deletions of characters). This is solved in expected time $\mathcal{O}(nk/m)$ for $k \leq \mathcal{O}(m/\log_\sigma m)$. The known lower bound for this problem is $\Omega(n(k + \log_\sigma m)/m)$, given in [6]. Finally we show how to adopt a similar technique to the shift–or algorithm, extending its bit–parallelism in another direction. This gives a speed–up by a factor s, where s is the number of characters processed simultaneously. Some of the algorithms are implemented, and we show that the methods work well in practice too. This is especially true for the shift–or algorithm, which in some cases works faster than predicted by the theory. The result is the fastest known algorithm for exact string matching for short patterns and small alphabets. All the methods and analyses assume the RAM model of computation, and that each symbol is coded in $b = \lceil \log_2 \sigma \rceil$ bits. They work for larger b too, but the speed–up is decreased.

1   Introduction

We address the well studied exact string matching problem. The problem is to search the occurrences of the pattern $P[1 \ldots m]$ from the text $T[1 \ldots n]$, where the symbols of P and T are taken from some finite alphabet Σ, of size σ. Numerous efficient algorithms solving the problem have been obtained. The first linear time algorithm was given in [11], and the first sublinear expected time algorithm in [5]. The sublinearity is obtained by skipping some characters of the input text by *shifting* the pattern over some text positions by using the information obtained by matching only a few characters of the pattern.

In [19] Yao showed that the string matching problem requires at least $\Omega(n \log_\sigma m/m)$ character comparisons on average. Later in [6] this result was

A.H.F. Laender and A.L. Oliveira (Eds.): SPIRE 2002, LNCS 2476, pp. 44–57, 2002.
© Springer-Verlag Berlin Heidelberg 2002

generalized to the k differences problem, where up to k edit operations (mismatches, insertions or deletions of characters) are allowed in the match. At least $\Omega(n(k + \log_\sigma m)/m)$ character comparisons are required on average to solve this problem. In both articles an algorithm achieving the given bound was given too.

In this article we show how to obtain faster algorithms. In particular, we achieve average time bounds $\mathcal{O}(n/m)$ for the exact matching, and $\mathcal{O}(nk/m)$ for the approximate matching. These results do not contradict with the above lower bounds; we use a super–alphabet to process $\mathcal{O}(\log_\sigma m)$ characters in $\mathcal{O}(1)$ time. It should be emphasized that in the RAM model of computation, this is always possible regardless of σ or m, if the input string T is packed such that each symbols takes just $\lceil \log_2 \sigma \rceil$ bits. Therefore, the method gives a true asymptotic, not a constant factor, speed–up.

Super–alphabet methods have appeared before, and the idea was mentioned already in [11, 5]. In [2] the BMH algorithm [9] was modified to use a super–alphabet. This effectively reduced the probability of match of two random characters, thus yielding longer shifts. Similar methods were presented in [17, 16]. These techniques differ from the one taken here; we apply our method to a suffix automaton [7] (often called BDM, for backward DAG matching), which is also able to skip characters of T, but we do not try to make the shifts larger, in fact the shifts are exactly the same as in the original method. Instead, we use the super–alphabet to process the characters faster, to obtain the shift faster. This leads to an asymptotic improvement. A similar idea was used in the "Four Russians" algorithm to compute the edit distance between two strings [12]. The edit distance is computed using precomputed and tabled blocks of the dynamic programming matrix. This technique achieves a speed–up by a factor of $\mathcal{O}(\log n)$.

We also apply the super–alphabet method to the well–known shift–or algorithm [4, 18]. Shift–or algorithm uses bit–parallelism to simulate a non–deterministic automaton efficiently. It is therefore natural to extend this parallelism to another dimension, to process several characters at a single step.

The algorithms are not only of theoretical interest. We have implemented some of the methods, and give some preliminary experimental results. The performance is clearly improved, and in some cases even more than the theory predicts.

2   Preliminaries

Let $T[1 \ldots n]$ and $P[1 \ldots m]$ be arrays of symbols taken from a finite alphabet $\Sigma = \{0, 1, \ldots, \sigma - 1\}$. The array T is called *text*, and the array P is called *pattern*. Usually $m \ll n$. We want to find all the exact occurrences of P in T. This is called an exact string matching problem.

String matching problem is easily solved using deterministic finite automaton in time $\mathcal{O}(n)$.

Definition 1. *Deterministic finite automaton* (DFA) *is a quintuple* $(\mathcal{Q}, q, \mathcal{F}, \Sigma, \delta)$, *where* $\mathcal{Q}$ *is a set of* states, $q \in \mathcal{Q}$ *is the* initial state, *and* $\mathcal{F} \subseteq \mathcal{Q}$ *is a set of*

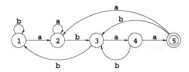

Fig. 1. DFA finding the occurrences of string abaa

final states, Σ *is the input alphabet, and δ is the state transition function, i.e. a mapping $\mathcal{Q} \times \Sigma \to \mathcal{Q}$.*

Fig. 1 shows an example of a DFA that finds the occurrences of $P =$ abaa. In our example $q = 1$, $\mathcal{F} = \{4\}$, and $\Sigma = \{a, b\}$. DFA can be simulated using the Alg. 1.

Alg. 1 Simulation of DFA.

Input: DFA recognizing the language $\mathcal{L}(P)$ and a text T
Output: (starting) positions where P occurs in T

1   **for** $i \leftarrow 1$ **to** n
2         $q \leftarrow \delta(q, T[i])$
3   **if** $q \in \mathcal{F}$ **then** output$(i - m + 1)$

The string v is a *prefix* and the string w is a *suffix* of the string u, if u can be written as vw. The set of all suffixes of P is denoted by $\mathcal{S}(P)$. The reverse of the pattern $P = p_1, p_2, \ldots, p_m$ is $P^r = p_m, p_{m-1}, \ldots, p_1$. A *suffix automaton* (SA) is a DFA that recognizes the language $\mathcal{L}(\mathcal{S}(P^r))$. SA lacks the backward transitions, for reasons that become apparent later. SA can be used to solve the exact pattern matching problem in $\mathcal{O}(n \log m / m)$ average time, which matches the lower bound. The worst case running time of this algorithm is $\mathcal{O}(nm)$, but it can be improved to $\mathcal{O}(n)$, see [7]. The automaton can be built in $\mathcal{O}(m)$ time, and the number of states and transitions is $\mathcal{O}(m)$. We do not give the construction algorithm of the automaton here. Fig. 2 shows a SA for our example pattern, and Alg. 2 gives the simulation algorithm.

Alg. 2 works as follows. The search algorithm uses a window of length m, that is slid from left to right along the text, 1 to m symbol positions at a time. The text window is searched from right to left using the automaton. The automaton remembers, in variable *shift*, the window position corresponding to the starting position of the longest suffix of P^r, that matches inside the window. The characters are matched until the first mismatch, or an occurrence of the pattern is found. After that, the window is slid *shift* symbol positions to the right. For the proof of correctness and further elaboration, see [7].

Alg. 2 Simulation of SA

Input: SA recognizing the language $\mathcal{L}(\mathcal{S}(P^r))$ and a text T
Output: (starting) positions where P occurs in T

```
1      i ← 1
2      while i ≤ n − m + 1
3          j ← m
4          shift ← m
5          while j ≥ 1 and δ(q, T[i + j − 1]) ∈ Q
6              q ← δ(q, T[i + j − 1])
7              j ← j − 1
8              if q ∈ F and j ≥ 1 then
9                  shift ← j
10         if j = 0 then
11             output( i )
12         i ← i + shift
```

3   Super–Alphabet Simulation of SA

Consider now processing several, say s, symbols of T at a time. That is, we use a super–alphabet of size σ^s, packing s symbols of T to a single super–symbol. Each symbol in T and P requires $b = \lceil \log_2 \sigma \rceil$ bits. Often eight bits are allocated for each symbol, even if $\lceil \log_2 \sigma \rceil < 8$ (8 bit bytes). This means that we can process $\lfloor w/b \rfloor$ symbols at the same time. Assume that we want to process s symbols at the same time. We map T to T', such that

$$T'[i] = T[is] + T[is + 1] \ll b + \ldots + T[is + s − 1] \ll ((s − 1)b). \qquad (1)$$

That is, we pack as many symbols of T as possible to one word with sb bits. Thus the input for our automaton is a "compressed" version of T, called T'. Note that the "packing" can be implicit. For example, if T is 8 bit ascii text, we may just address the string as if it was, say, an array of $\lfloor |T|/2 \rfloor$ 16bit integers. This is straight–forward for example in C/C++. For simplicity, and without loss of generality, we assume that the packing is implicit, and use the notation $T^s[i]$ to address the s consecutive symbols of T, starting from $T[i]$, that is, $T^s[i] = T[i], T[i + 1], \ldots, T[s − 1]$.

Fig. 2. Suffix automata for patterns $P_1 = \text{aba}$ and $P_2 = \text{abaa}$. The set of suffixes are $\mathcal{S}(P_1^r) = \{\text{aba}, \text{ba}, \text{a}, \epsilon\}$, and $\mathcal{S}(P_2^r) = \{\text{aaba}, \text{aba}, \text{ba}, \text{a}, \epsilon\}$

Alg. 3 converts the ordinary suffix automaton to use a super–alphabet. The states of the automaton remain the same, but the transition function δ is replaced by a new one, called Δ. This transition function is also augmented with some information. The conversion algorithm basically looks for each state and for each s–tuple of symbols what transitions the automaton takes, and then the transition Δ is just a short–cut to the state where the s–tuple leads.

Let $(q, aw) \vdash (q', w)$ denote the move the automaton makes for character a, where w is a string of characters, and $q' = \delta(q, a)$. The closure of $\vdash$ is denoted by $\vdash^*$. Let u be an s–tuple of characters. Now $\Delta(q, u) = q'$, iff $(q, u) \vdash^* (q', aw)$, where aw is a suffix of u, $a \in \Sigma \cup \epsilon$, $w \in (\Sigma \cup \epsilon)^*$, and $\delta(q', a) \notin Q$. There are a couple of problems with this. The sequence of transitions the automaton makes for string u may go through several accepting states, but the last state q' may not be an accepting state. Therefore, we associate the transitions Δ with information that tells if it is accepting transition (SetTerminalTrans) or not, instead of augmenting the states with the acceptance information. Also, the transition Δ is augmented with the path length (of single characters) to the last accepting state along the path (SetTransitionOffset). This is needed for implementing the shift. It may also happen that for some states there are not anymore any out–going transitions, because these are effectively skipped by the short–cut. These are labeled with SetTerminalState.

Note that for simplicity the algorithm in the pseudo–code is brute force in a sense that it generates all the possible s–tuples, while it would be sufficient to generate only those that are really present in the original automaton paths. This would be simple to implement with depth–first search.

Fig. 3 shows the resulting automaton for our example pattern. The offsets to the accepting states are denoted by o, and the accepting transitions are in dotted lines.

Alg. 4 gives the simulation algorithm for the super–alphabet suffix automaton. This is similar to Alg. 2, except that now we must keep track of the offsets to the final states among the transitions. Note that the packing of T^s may cause that the address of some $T^s[i]$ does not start within byte/word boundary, but $T^s[i]$ can still be trivially retrieved in constant time with simple bit–operations.

Theorem 1. *Alg. 4 solves the exact string matching problem in* $\mathcal{O}(n\lceil(\log_\sigma m)/s\rceil/m)$ *average time, using* $\mathcal{O}(m\sigma^s)$ *space.*

Fig. 3. Suffix automata with super–alphabet ($s = 2$) for patterns $P_1 = $ aba and $P_2 = $ abaa. Read the transition labels from right to left. The isolated state (2) in the automaton for P_2 can be removed

---

Alg. 3 Build a super–alphabet SA

Input: SA
Output: new transition function Δ

```
1       for each q ∈ Q
2           SetTerminalState(q, TRUE)
3       SetTerminalState(q₀, FALSE)
4       for each q ∈ Q
5           for each C = {cₛ, cₛ₋₁, ..., c₁} ∈ Σˢ
6               j ← 0
7               q₀ ← q
8               f ← fail
9               t ← FALSE
10              for i ← 1 to s
11                  qᵢ ← δ(qᵢ₋₁, cᵢ)
12                  if qᵢ ∉ Q then
13                      t ← TRUE
14                      break
15                  if qᵢ ∈ F then
16                      j ← i
17                      f ← qᵢ
18              if f ≠ fail then
19                  Δ(q, C) ← f
20                  SetTerminalTrans(Δ(q, C), t)
21                  if not t
22                      SetTerminalState(f, FALSE)
23                  SetTransitionOffset(Δ(q, C), j)
24      for each q ∈ Q
25          if TerminalState(q)
26              for each C ∈ Σˢ
27                  Δ(q, C) ← fail
28      return Δ
```


Input: SA
Output: new transition function Δ

1   **for each** $q \in \mathcal{Q}$
2   SetTerminalState$(q, TRUE)$
3   SetTerminalState$(q_0, FALSE)$
4   **for each** $q \in \mathcal{Q}$
5   **for each** $C = \{c_s, c_{s-1}, \ldots, c_1\} \in \Sigma^s$
6            $j \leftarrow 0$
7            $q_0 \leftarrow q$
8            $f \leftarrow fail$
9            $t \leftarrow FALSE$
10   **for** $i \leftarrow 1$ **to** s
11              $q_i \leftarrow \delta(q_{i-1}, c_i)$
12   **if** $q_i \notin \mathcal{Q}$ **then**
13                 $t \leftarrow TRUE$
14   break
15   **if** $q_i \in \mathcal{F}$ **then**
16                 $j \leftarrow i$
17                 $f \leftarrow q_i$
18   **if** $f \neq fail$ **then**
19              $\Delta(q, C) \leftarrow f$
20   SetTerminalTrans$(\Delta(q, C), t)$
21   **if not** t
22   SetTerminalState$(f, FALSE)$
23   SetTransitionOffset$(\Delta(q, C), j)$
24   **for each** $q \in \mathcal{Q}$
25   **if** TerminalState(q)
26   **for each** $C \in \Sigma^s$
27              $\Delta(q, C) \leftarrow fail$
28   **return** Δ

Proof. The ordinary suffix automaton solves the problem in $\mathcal{O}(n \log_\sigma m/m)$ expected time [7]. The automaton inspects $\mathcal{O}(\log_\sigma m)$ characters of T for each window position on average, as the automaton constitutes on m suffixes of length $\mathcal{O}(m)$. However, Alg. 4 processes T in blocks of s characters, and each block is processed in $\mathcal{O}(1)$ time, so the average time spent in each window is $\mathcal{O}(\lceil (\log_\sigma m)/s \rceil)$. Alg. 2 and Alg. 4 make exactly the same shifts. Hence the total average time is $\mathcal{O}(n \lceil (\log_\sigma m)/s \rceil /m)$. There are $\mathcal{O}(m)$ states in the automaton, and the transitions can be implemented using a lookup tables of size $\mathcal{O}(\sigma^s)$, for a total space usage of $\mathcal{O}(m\sigma^s)$. □

Corollary 1. *Alg. 4 can be used to solve the exact string matching problem in $\mathcal{O}(n/m)$ average time, using $\mathcal{O}(m^2\sigma)$ space.*

Proof. Follows from Theorem 1 by selecting $s = \lceil \log_\sigma m \rceil < 1 + \log_\sigma m$. □

Alg. 4 Simulation of a super–alphabet SA

Input: super–alphabet SA recognizing the language $\mathcal{L}(\mathcal{S}(P^r))$ and a text T
Output: (starting) positions where P occurs in T

```
1        i ← 1
2        while i ≤ n − m
3            j ← m − s + 1
4            shift ← m
5            t ← FALSE
6            while not t and j ≥ 1 and Δ(q, Tˢ[i + j − 1]) ∈ Q
7                o ← GetTransitionOffset(Δ(q, Tˢ[i + j − 1]))
8                t ← IsTerminal(Δ(q, Tˢ[i + j − 1]))
9                q ← Δ(q, Tˢ[i + j − 1])
10               j ← j − s
11               if o ≠ 0 and j ≥ 1 then
12                   shift ← j + s − o
13           if j ≤ 0 then
14               output( i )
15           i ← i + shift
```

Note that this does not contradict with Yao's lower bound; the number of characters of T inspected, is still $\mathcal{O}(n \log_\sigma m/m)$ on average. The only difference is that now $\mathcal{O}(\log_\sigma m)$ characters are inspected in time $\mathcal{O}(1)$.

Remark 1. We have used base σ logarithm for selecting the value for s. However, the $\mathcal{O}(n/m)$ time bound holds also for base c logarithm, where c is arbitrary (large) constant, because this would affect only to the constant factor of the time bound. Large c can be used to make the space usage of the algorithm smaller. Still, in practice the base $c = \sigma$ logarithm is optimal. This minimizes the constant factor work in each window position on average, while using $c < \sigma$ would not help on average case. In the worst case we would need $s = \mathcal{O}(m)$, which is not possible in most practical cases.

Remark 2. The worst case running time of Alg. 4 is $\mathcal{O}(nm/s)$, but it can be improved to $\mathcal{O}(n)$ by using exactly the same technique as in [3, 7], that is, by augmenting it with the famous KMP–algorithm [11]. Moreover, the KMP–algorithm can also be simulated using the super–alphabet technique, which improves the worst case running time of Alg. 4 to $\mathcal{O}(n/s + t) = \mathcal{O}(n/\log_\sigma m + t)$, where t is the number of occurrences of P in T. In the worst case, $t = \mathcal{O}(n)$. Note that the previous lower bound for the worst case running time is $\mathcal{O}(n)$, even if $t = 0$.

SA can be generalized for dictionary matching [8], that is, instead of one pattern we have a set of patterns that are simultaneously searched from T. The algorithm of [8] runs in $\mathcal{O}(n \log m/m)$ average time, where m is the length of the shortest pattern of the set, and the number of patterns and the length of the longest pattern are polynomial in m. This algorithm runs in $\mathcal{O}(n)$ worst case time when augmented with the AC–machine [1]. This algorithm is very similar to the Alg. 2, and the super–alphabet technique works the same for the dictionary matching also, leading again to $\mathcal{O}(n/m)$ average time algorithm.

3.1 Applicability

On average, SA inspects only $\mathcal{O}(\log_\sigma m)$ characters of T in each window position. Therefore, to achieve the bound of Theorem 1, it is enough to use the super–alphabet method with $s = \lceil \log_\sigma m \rceil$ only for the initial state. That is, we use the transition function Δ in the initial state, and δ in the other states. In other words, we use a bucket of s characters of T to go directly to the state of the automaton where the search is bound to finish for that window position. The size of this bucket array is $\mathcal{O}(\sigma^s)$. If we again select $s = \lceil \log_\sigma m \rceil < 1 + \log_\sigma m$, the space requirement is $\mathcal{O}(\sigma m)$.

Theorem 2. *The exact string matching problem can be solved in $\mathcal{O}(n/m)$ average time, using $\mathcal{O}(\sigma m)$ space.* $\qquad\square$

If the transition function δ is implemented using look–up tables of size $\mathcal{O}(\sigma)$, the ordinary suffix automaton and the super–alphabet method need asymptotically the same space.

Note that the super–alphabet gives asymptotic speed–up. At first glance, it may seem that the number of bits in the machine word limits the method to some constant factor speed–up, but in the RAM–model of computation, one always have enough bits to process $\mathcal{O}(\log_\sigma m)$ symbols at a time, if the input is packed.

4   Approximate Matching

Approximate matching can be reduced to exact matching by using a well–known *pattern partitioning technique* [18]. Assume that there can be up to k differences (mismatches, insertions or deletions of characters) in the match. In any such a match there must be an exact match of a subpattern of P. We divide P to $k + 1$ pieces. Now one of the pieces must have an exact match in any match of the whole P with at most k differences. We search the pieces simultaneously using the above dictionary matching method. This *filtering* takes average time $\mathcal{O}(n/(m/k)) = \mathcal{O}(nk/m)$, since the pieces are of length m/k. Every time when an exact match of a subpattern of P is found, we check if there is a complete match of the whole P. This can be done using e.g. dynamic programming, which requires $\mathcal{O}(m^2)$ time in the worst case for each verification. Assuming random text, where each character occurs independently from the others in probability $1/\sigma$, the total expected number of verifications is $\mathcal{O}(nk(1/\sigma)^{m/k})$. It follows that for $k < \Theta(m/\log_\sigma m)$ the filtering time dominates, and hence the total expected time is $\mathcal{O}(nk/m)$. The lower bound result of [6] states that any algorithm must make $\Omega(n(k + \log_\sigma m)/m)$ character comparisons on average. Our time bound $\mathcal{O}(nk/m)$ goes below that lower bound for $k \leq \Theta(m/\log_\sigma m)$, where the average time is $\mathcal{O}(n/\log_\sigma m)$.

Theorem 3. *The k differences approximate string matching problem can be solved in average time $\mathcal{O}(nk/m)$ for $k < \Theta(m/\log_\sigma m)$.* $\square$

5   Pattern Matching in Compressed Text

Huffman coding [10] is a compression method that uses short bit–patterns to represent frequently occurring symbols of the text. The more frequent the symbol is, the shorter the bit–pattern. The bit–pattern coded symbols are packed in a contiguous string of bits, which is stored, and thus a compression is achieved. Pattern matching in Huffman compressed texts is easy without decompression. The pattern can be compressed using the same set of character codes, and then a DFA with binary alphabet is built that recognizes the pattern. The super–alphabet method can be used also in DFA. The automaton can read s bits at a time, and thus an $\mathcal{O}(n'/s)$ time simulation algorithm is obtained, where n' is the number of bits in the compressed string. See also [13].

However, a straight–forward implementation of this method would mean that the matches should be verified, as the automaton may find incorrect occurrences, due to synchronization errors; the "match" may be incorrectly aligned, starting from the middle of a code word. This problem was solved in [14] by using *tagged byte–oriented codes* (instead of bits). They generate the code words for whole (natural language) words, instead of symbols, as in the bit–oriented technique. In their method one bit in each byte tells whether or not a text word starts in that position. This representation works also for the super–alphabet SA, but the downside is that only natural language can be compressed. The average time for this method is $\mathcal{O}(n'/m')$, where n' and m' are the lengths of the compressed text and pattern, respectively. Both strings should compress the same amount on average [14], so $n'/m' \approx n/m$.

6   Shift–Or

In this section we build a non–deterministic finite–state automaton (NFA). Each step of the automaton is simulated using bit–parallel techniques [4, 18]. Fig. 4 gives an example automaton. The automaton gets T for input, and whenever the accepting state becomes active, there is a match.

We use the following notation. A machine word has w bits, numbered from the least significant bit to the most significant bit. For bit–wise operations of words a C–like notation is used, & is **and**, | is **or**, and $\ll$ is shift to left, with zero padding. The notation 1^i denotes a bit–string of i consecutive 1–bits.

The automaton is constructed as follows. The automaton has states $1, 2, \ldots,$ $m + 1$. The state 1 is the initial state, state $m + 1$ is the final (accepting) state, and for $i = 1, \ldots, m$ there is a transition from the state i to the state $i + 1$ for character $P[i]$. In addition, there is a transition for every $c \in \Sigma$ from and to the initial state.

The preprocessing algorithm builds a table B. The table have one bit–mask entry for each character in the alphabet. For $1 \le i \le m$, the mask $B[c]$ has ith bit set to 0, iff $P[i] = c$, and to 1 otherwise. The bit–mask table correspond to the transitions of the implicit automaton. That is, if the bit i in $B[c]$ is 0, then there is a transition from the state i to the state $i + 1$ with character c.

We also need a bit–vector D for the states of the automaton. The ith bit of the state vector is set to 0, iff the state i is active. Initially each bit in the state vector is set to 1.

For each new text symbol $T[i]$, we update the vector as follows:

$$D \leftarrow (D \ll 1) \mid B[T[i]] \qquad (2)$$

Each state gets its value from the previous one ($D \ll 1$), which remains active only if the text character matches the corresponding transition ($\mid B[T[i]]$). The first state is set active automatically by the shift operation, which sets the least significant bit to 0. If after the simulation step (2), the mth bit of D is zero, then there is an occurrence of P.

Clearly each step of the automaton is simulated in time $\mathcal{O}(\lceil m/w \rceil)$, which leads to $\mathcal{O}(n\lceil m/w \rceil)$ total time. For small patterns, where $m = \mathcal{O}(w)$, this is a linear time algorithm.

It is possible to improve the NFA simulation by using bit–parallelism also in the indexing of the table B. In effect we use a super–alphabet of size σ^s. It must be emphasized that we do *not* modify the automaton, that is, the automaton does *not* use any super–alphabet, but the super–alphabet is only used to simulate the original automaton faster. Now our simulation algorithm is

$$D \leftarrow (D \ll s) \mid B'[T'[i]]. \qquad (3)$$

Note that here we use the notation T', instead of T^s, see Sec. 3. To compute the table B', we must simulate what happens for the information, in s steps, that we bit–wise or into the vector D in the basic algorithm. Let $C = c_s \ll (s-1)b + c_{s-1} \ll (s-2)b + \ldots + c_1$, where $c_1, \ldots, c_s$ form one super–symbol. Now

$$B'[C] \leftarrow ((B[c_1] \& 1^m) \ll (s-1)) \mid ((B[c_2] \& 1^m) \ll (s-2)) \mid \ldots \mid \qquad (4)$$
$$(B[c_s] \& 1^m).$$

$B'[C]$ therefore pre–shifts and bit–wise ors the state transition information for s consecutive original symbols, and the state vector D is then updated with this precomputation.

After the simulation step any of the bits numbered $m \ldots m + s - 1$ may be zero in D. This indicates an occurrence at location $T[is - d + m - 1]$, where $d = m \ldots m + s - 1$, corresponding to the offset of the zero bit in D.

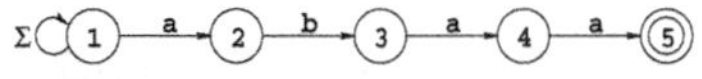

Fig. 4. Forward transitions of the non–deterministic finite automaton for $P =$ abaa

Theorem 4. *Equation (3) correctly evaluates the value of the state–vector D, using the table B' of Equation (5).*   □

The size of the new table B' is $\mathcal{O}(\sigma^s)$. This restricts the full potential of the method. Our implementation uses at most $w/2 = 16$ bits for the super–alphabet. The bit–vectors have length $m + s - 1$, due to the need of $s - 1$ extra bits to handle the super–alphabet. The simulation algorithm works in time $\mathcal{O}(n/s\lceil (m + s - 1)/w \rceil + t)$, where t is the number of matches reported. This is $\mathcal{O}(nm \log_2 \sigma / w^2 + t)$.

Theorem 5. *The super–alphabet shift–or algorithm runs in time $\mathcal{O}(nm \log_2 \sigma / w^2 + t)$, where t is the number of matches reported, using $\mathcal{O}(\sigma^s)$ space.*   □

7   Experimental Results

We have implemented the super–alphabet versions of suffix automaton and shift–or algorithm. The implementation is in C, compiled with gcc 2.96. The computer was 1333MHz ATHLON, 512MB RAM, running Linux 2.4 operating system.

The test data was a 64MB generated DNA file, in ASCII format. We experimented with the shift–or algorithm using super–alphabets $s = 1$ (the original algorithm) and $s = 2$. As the alphabet size for the DNA is 4, we also packed the same data, such that each byte contains four characters. For the packed DNA we run experiments with $s = 4$ and $s = 8$. The algorithm only counted the number of matches, without explicitly reporting each of them. We experimented with different pattern lengths, but as expected the length did not affect the timings (the automaton fitted in one machine word in each case).

Table 1 gives the timings for the shift–or algorithm. The experimental results show that the method gives a speed–up in practice too. The simplicity of the super–alphabet shift–or method makes it particularly fast in practice. In fact, for packed DNA the shift–or method can work faster than predicted by the theory. For example, with $s = 4$, the algorithm was over 5 times faster than with $s = 1$. This is probably due to the smaller input size, so the total number of cache misses is smaller than in the original method. However, using $s = 8$ did not improve the performance that much anymore. This may be partly attributed to the larger table B', and therefore more probable cache misses.

We also implemented the super–alphabet method for the *shift–add* algorithm [4]. The algorithm computes the number of mismatches (Hamming distance) between the pattern and each text location bit–parallelly. The algorithm

Table 1. Shift–or execution times in seconds for various super–alphabets. Pattern length $m = 16$

super–alphabet	$s = 1$ (ASCII)	$s = 2$ (ASCII)	$s = 4$ (packed)	$s = 8$ (packed)
time (s)	0.97	0.52	0.21	0.15

Table 2. Shift–add execution times in seconds for various super–alphabets. Pattern length $m = 12$

super–alphabet	$s = 1$ (ASCII)	$s = 2$ (ASCII)	$s = 4$ (packed)
$k = 0$, time (s)	1.82	0.99	0.54
$k = 1$, time (s)	1.82	1.00	0.68
$k = 2$, time (s)	1.83	1.00	0.71
$k = 4$, time (s)	1.83	1.15	0.72

is very similar to the shift–or algorithm. The results are presented in Table 2. The parameter k tells the maximum number of mismatches allowed. The times for the super–alphabet grow slightly as k increases. This is due to our implementation; the checking if some position has at most k mismatches is not done entirely parallelly. However, this could be easily fixed by table look–ups. Even so, the super–alphabet is quite effective.

The performance of the suffix automaton improved too, but not so dramatically, as the super–alphabet suffix automaton is more complex than the original automaton, and the implementation is not very optimized at the moment. Some timings for the DNA file are reported in Table 3. The current implementation uses only ASCII alphabet, and $s = 1$ or $s = 2$. For comparison, Table 3 shows timings also for the bit–parallel version [15] of the suffix automaton, without the super–alphabet. This is claimed to be the fastest known algorithm for short patterns. However, the super–alphabet shift–or clearly beats this algorithm in 32 bit computers and DNA alphabets (assuming that only one machine word is used for the state vector in the simulation of the non–deterministic automata). It is also possible to use super–alphabet in the bit–parallel version of the suffix automaton.

The problem with the bit–parallel algorithms is that the word length of the computer architecture (typically 32 or 64) restricts the maximum pattern length. Simulating longer words is easy, but it also causes performance penalty. The shift–or algorithm needs $m + s - 1$ bits for patterns of length m, and super–alphabets of size σ^s. The shift–add algorithm needs $(m+s-1)(\lceil \log_2(k + s) \rceil + 1)$ bits. Table 4 shows maximal m for various s and k for $w = 64$.

Table 3. SA execution times in seconds for various pattern lengths. The first row is for the bit–parallel version of the suffix automaton, and the second and the third rows are for the ordinary suffix automaton with super–alphabet

$|P|$	8	12	16	24	32
bit–parallel SA	0.41	0.34	0.30	0.25	0.23
SA, $s = 1$	1.23	0.87	0.74	0.58	0.48
SA, $s = 2$	1.05	0.73	0.58	0.42	0.36

Table 4. Maximal m for various s and k for the shift–add algorithm, when the word length is 64 bits

	$k = 1$	$k = 2$	$k = 4$	$k = 8$
$s = 1$	32	21	16	12
$s = 2$	20	20	15	11
$s = 3$	19	14	14	10
$s = 4$	13	13	13	9

Intel and AMD have added to their processors SIMD extensions that allow fast (i.e. constant time) operations for longer than 32 bit words, even when the processors are 32 bit. For example, Pentium 4 have instructions that work on 128 bit words in constant time. This extends the applicability of many bit–parallel algorithms. The problem is that most current compilers do not directly support these data types and operations. However, e.g. gcc 3.1 defines these vector data types, and gives built–in functions that directly translate to these fast vector instructions[1].

8   Conclusions

We have shown that using a simple trick of moving to a super–alphabet gives efficient algorithms for string matching. The new algorithms are faster than assumed by the comparison model lower bounds of [19, 6]. We have also applied the method to a shift–or algorithm, achieving a similar speed–up. Besides improved theoretical results, the method works well in practice too, and can be applied to many other string matching algorithms.

An open problem remains. What are the average case lower bounds for exact and approximate string matching, if super–alphabet and bit–parallelism are allowed?

References

[1] A. V. Aho and M. J. Corasick. Efficient string matching: an aid to bibliographic search. *Commun. ACM*, 18(6):333–340, 1975. 51
[2] R. A. Baeza-Yates. Improved string searching. *Softw. Pract. Exp.*, 19(3):257–271, 1989. 45
[3] R. A. Baeza-Yates. String searching algorithms revisited. In F. Dehne, J. R. Sack, and N. Santoro, editors, *Proceedings of the 1st Workshop on Algorithms and Data Structures*, number 382 in Lecture Notes in Computer Science, pages 75–96, Ottawa, Canada, 1989. Springer-Verlag, Berlin. 50
[4] R. A. Baeza-Yates and G. H. Gonnet. A new approach to text searching. *Commun. ACM*, 35(10):74–82, 1992. 45, 52, 54

---

[1] http://www.gnu.org/software/gcc/gcc.html

[5] R. S. Boyer and J. S. Moore. A fast string searching algorithm. *Commun. ACM*, 20(10):762–772, 1977. 44, 45

[6] W. I. Chang and T. Marr. Approximate string matching with local similarity. In M. Crochemore and D. Gusfield, editors, *Proceedings of the 5th Annual Symposium on Combinatorial Pattern Matching*, number 807 in Lecture Notes in Computer Science, pages 259–273, Asilomar, CA, 1994. Springer-Verlag, Berlin. 44, 51, 56

[7] M. Crochemore, A. Czumaj, L. Gąsieniec, S. Jarominek, T. Lecroq, W. Plandowski, and W. Rytter. Speeding up two string matching algorithms. *Algorithmica*, 12(4/5):247–267, 1994. 45, 46, 49, 50

[8] M. Crochemore, A. Czumaj, L. Gąsieniec, T. Lecroq, W. Plandowski, and W. Rytter. Fast practical multi-pattern matching. *Inf. Process. Lett.*, 71((3–4)):107–113, 1999. 50

[9] R. N. Horspool. Practical fast searching in strings. *Softw. Pract. Exp.*, 10(6):501–506, 1980. 45

[10] D. A. Huffman. A method for the construction of minimum redundancy codes. *Proc. I. R. E.*, 40:1098–1101, 1951. 52

[11] D. E. Knuth, J. H. Morris, Jr, and V. R. Pratt. Fast pattern matching in strings. *SIAM J. Comput.*, 6(1):323–350, 1977. 44, 45, 50

[12] W. J. Masek and M. S. Paterson. A faster algorithm for computing string edit distances. *J. Comput. Syst. Sci.*, 20(1):18–31, 1980. 45

[13] M. Miyazaki, S. Fukamachi, M. Takeda, and T. Shinohara. Speeding up the pattern matching machine for compressed texts. *Transactions of Information Processing Society of Japan*, 39(9):2638–2648, 1998. 52

[14] E. Moura, G. Navarro, N. Ziviani, and R. Baeza-Yates. Fast and flexible word searching on compressed text. *ACM Transactions on Information Systems (TOIS)*, 18(2):113–139, 2000. 52

[15] G. Navarro and M. Raffinot. A bit-parallel approach to suffix automata: Fast extended string matching. In M. Farach-Colton, editor, *Proceedings of the 9th Annual Symposium on Combinatorial Pattern Matching*, number 1448 in Lecture Notes in Computer Science, pages 14–33, Piscataway, NJ, 1998. Springer-Verlag, Berlin. 55

[16] G. Navarro and J. Tarhio. Boyer-Moore string matching over ziv-lempel compressed text. In R. Giancarlo and D. Sankoff, editors, *Proceedings of the 11th Annual Symposium on Combinatorial Pattern Matching*, number 1848 in Lecture Notes in Computer Science, pages 166–180, Montréal, Canada, 2000. Springer-Verlag, Berlin. 45

[17] J. Tarhio and H. Peltola. String matching in the DNA alphabet. *Softw. Pract. Exp.*, 27(7):851–861, 1997. 45

[18] S. Wu and U. Manber. Fast text searching allowing errors. *Commun. ACM*, 35(10):83–91, 1992. 45, 51, 52

[19] A. C. Yao. The complexity of pattern matching for a random string. *SIAM J. Comput.*, 8(3):368–387, 1979. 44, 56

On the Size of DASG for Multiple Texts

Maxime Crochemore* and Zdeněk Troníček[2] **

[1] Institute Gaspard-Monge, University Marne-la-Vallée
[2] Dept. of Comp. Science and Eng., FEE CTU Prague

Abstract. We present a left-to-right algorithm building the automaton accepting all subsequences of a given set of strings. We prove that the number of states of this automaton can be quadratic if built on at least two texts.

1 Introduction

A *subsequence* of a string T is any string that can be obtained by deleting zero or more symbols from T. Problems related to subsequences arise in molecular biology (sequence alignment, longest common subsequence), text processing (differences between two files), signal processing (episode matching), and in many other areas.

A basic task is the *subsequence matching problem*: given two strings S and T, we are to determine whether S is a subsequence of T. The string S is called *pattern* and the string T *text*. We consider the case of multiple texts, *i.e.* given a pattern S and texts $T_1, T_2, \ldots, T_k$, we are to determine whether S is a subsequence of T_i for any $i \in \langle 1, k \rangle$. We can preprocess the texts and build the automaton accepting all their subsequences. The automaton accepting all subsequences of the given text was mentioned for the first time probably by Jean-Jacques Hébrard and Maxime Crochemore in [2]. Ricardo A. Baeza-Yates [1] called this automaton Directed Acyclic Subsequence Graph (DASG). He also defined the DASG for a set of texts and gave a right-to-left algorithm of its building. In subsection 3.1 we give an example of a quadratic-size DASG associated with two texts. The derived lower bound corrects a flaw in [1]. Application of the DASG was found by Masahiro Hirao *et al.* in [3], where the DASG was used to find the best subsequence patterns. The best subsequence pattern is a string which distinguishes two input sets of strings in best way. The problem has application in machine learning.

The paper is organized as follows. In section 2 we recall the algorithm building the DASG for one text from Zdeněk Troníček and Bořivoj Melichar [5]. In section 3 we present a left-to-right algorithm building the DASG for a set of texts and put new bounds for the number of states and transitions. The presented algorithm seems slower than the algorithm described by Hiromasa Hoshino *et al.*

---

* http://www-igm.univ-mlv.fr/~mac/ ; partially supported by CNRS action AlBio, NATO Science Programme grant PST.CLG.977017

** http://cs.felk.cvut.cz/~tronicek/; supported by GAČR grant 201/01/1433

A.H.F. Laender and A.L. Oliveira (Eds.): SPIRE 2002, LNCS 2476, pp. 58–64, 2002.

in [4]. Despite that it is interesting for at least two reasons: 1) historically it was found earlier than the algorithm in [4], and 2) the algorithm is very understandable and this may help for solving the problem of the tight upper bound on the number of states.

Let Σ be a finite alphabet of size σ and let ε be the empty word. Given a word $\alpha \in \Sigma^*$, we denote by $Sub(\alpha)$ the set of all subsequences of α. A finite automaton is, in this paper, a 5-tuple $(Q, \Sigma, \delta, q_0, F)$, where Q is a finite set of states, Σ is an input alphabet, $\delta : Q \times \Sigma \to Q$ is a transition function, q_0 is the initial state, and $F \subseteq Q$ is the set of final states. Notation $\langle i, j \rangle$ means the interval of integers from i to j, including both i and j. Given $T = t_1 t_2 \ldots t_n$ and $i, j \in \langle 1, n \rangle, i \leq j$, notation $T[i \ldots j]$ means the string $t_i t_{i+1} \ldots t_j$. If we consider a string over an alphabet Σ, we assume that all symbols of Σ are contained in the string, *i.e.* that Σ has the minimum size.

2   DASG for One Text

We consider a string $T = t_1 t_2 \ldots t_n$ and describe $Sub(T)$ recurrently by the regular expression: $Sub_0(T) = \varepsilon$, $Sub_i(T) = Sub_{i-1}(T)(\varepsilon + t_i)$, and $Sub(T) = Sub_n(T)$. For $Sub_n(T)$ we get: $Sub_n(T) = Sub_{n-1}(T) + Sub_{n-1}(T)t_n = \ldots = \varepsilon + Sub_0(T)t_1 + Sub_1(T)t_2 + \ldots + Sub_{n-1}(T)t_n$. This expression will help to define and build the automaton accepting all subsequences of T. The automaton is called DASG for T.

Let $Q = \{q_0, q_1, \ldots, q_n\}$ and $F = Q$. For each $a \in \Sigma$ and each $i \in \langle 0, n \rangle$ we define the transition function δ as follows:
$\delta(q_i, a) = q_j$ if there exists $k > i$ such that $a = t_k$ and j is the minimal such k,
$\delta(q_i, a) = \emptyset$ otherwise.
Then the automaton $A = (Q, \Sigma, \delta, q_0, F)$ accepts a pattern S if and only if S is a subsequence of T. We note that the automaton can be partial, *i.e.* each state needs not have transitions for all $a \in \Sigma$. The DASG can be built by the algorithm BUILD_DASG that requires $O(n\sigma)$ time and $O(\sigma)$ extra space.

3   DASG for a Set of Texts

Let P denote a set of texts $T_1, T_2, \ldots, T_k$. Let n_i be the length of T_i and $T_i[j]$ be j-th symbol of T_i for all $j \in \langle 1, n_i \rangle$ and all $i \in \langle 1, k \rangle$. We say that S is a subsequence of P if and only if exists $i \in \langle 1, k \rangle$ such that S is a subsequence of T_i.

During the preprocessing of texts $T_1, T_2, \ldots, T_k$ we build the deterministic finite automaton that accepts all subsequences of T_i for all $i \in \langle 1, k \rangle$. Such automaton accepts the language $h(V)$, where $V = \sum_{i=1}^{k} (\prod_{j=1}^{n_i} (\varepsilon + T_i[j]))$.

Each state of the DASG corresponds to a position in texts. We start in front of the first symbol of each text. When a new symbol is read, the positions in texts can change. If we read a symbol a, we move the position in each text behind the first a after the actual position. If there is no a after the actual position in text T_i, we move behind the last symbol of T_i. Below we formalize this idea.

procedure BUILD_DASG $(t_1 t_2 \ldots t_n)$
input: text $T = t_1 t_2 \ldots t_n$
output: the DASG for text T
1: **for all** $a \in \Sigma$ **do**
2:    $f[a] \leftarrow 0$
3: **end for**
4: create state q_0 and mark it as final
5: **for** $i = 1$ to n **do**
6:    add state q_i and mark it as final
7:    **for** $j = f[t_i]$ to $(i - 1)$ **do**
8:       add a transition labeled t_i between states q_j and q_i
9:    **end for**
10:    $f[t_i] \leftarrow i$
11: **end for**

Algorithm 1: Building the DASG for one string

Definition 1. *We define a position point of the set P as an ordered k-tuple $[p_1, p_2, \ldots, p_k]$, where $p_i \in \langle 0, n_i \rangle$ is a position in string T_i. If $p_i \in \langle 0, n_i - 1 \rangle$ then it denotes the position in front of $(p_i + 1)$-th symbol of T_i, and if $p_i = n_i$ then it denotes the position behind the last symbol of T_i, for all $i \in \langle 1, k \rangle$.*

A position point $[p_1, p_2, \ldots, p_k]$ is called *initial position point* if $p_i = 0$ for all $i \in \langle 1, k \rangle$. We denote by ipp the initial position point and by $Pos(P)$ the set of all position points of P.

Definition 2. *For a position point $[p_1, p_2, \ldots, p_k]$ we define the subsequence position alphabet as the set of all symbols which are contained in text T_i at positions $p_i + 1, \ldots, n_i$ for all $i \in \langle 1, k \rangle$, i.e. $\Sigma_p([p_1, p_2, \ldots, p_k]) = \{a \in \Sigma;\ \exists i \in \langle 1, k \rangle\ \exists j \in \langle p_i + 1, n_i \rangle : T_i[j] = a\}$.*

Definition 3. *For $a \in \Sigma$ and a position point $[p_1, p_2, \ldots, p_k]$ we define the subsequence transition function:*
$sf([p_1, p_2, \ldots, p_k], a) = [r_1, r_2, \ldots, r_k]$, *where* $r_i = min\ (\{j : j > p_i$ *and* $T_i[j] = a\} \cup \{n_i\})$ *for all* $i \in \langle 1, k \rangle$ *if* $a \in \Sigma_p([p_1, p_2, \ldots, p_k])$, *and* $sf([p_1, p_2, \ldots, p_k], a) = \emptyset$ *otherwise.*

Let sf^* be reflexive-transitive closure of sf, *i.e.*
$sf^*([p_1, p_2, \ldots, p_k], \varepsilon) = [p_1, p_2, \ldots, p_k]$,
$sf^*([p_1, p_2, \ldots, p_k], a_1) = sf([p_1, p_2, \ldots, p_k], a_1)$,
$sf^*([p_1, p_2, \ldots, p_k], a_1 a_2 \ldots a_l) = sf^*(sf([p_1, p_2, \ldots, p_k], a_1), a_2 a_3 \ldots a_l)$,
where $a_j \in \Sigma_p(sf^*([p_1, p_2, \ldots, p_k], a_1 a_2 \ldots a_{j-1}))$ for all $j \in \langle 1, l - 1 \rangle$.

Lemma 1. *For each $pos \in Pos(P)$ automaton $A' = (Pos(P), \Sigma, sf, pos, Pos(P))$ accepts a string S iff exists $i \in \langle 1, k \rangle$ such that S is a subsequence of $T_i[pos[i] + 1 \ldots n_i]$.*

Proof. Let $S = s_1 s_2 \ldots s_m$. We prove two implications:

1. If A' accepts S then exists $i \in \langle 1, k \rangle$ such that S is a subsequence of $T_i[pos[i] + 1 \ldots n_i]$. A' accepts S, i.e. $sf^*(pos, s_1 s_2 \ldots s_m) \neq \emptyset$. From definition of sf^* directly follows that exists at least one $j \in \langle 1, k \rangle$ such that $T_j[pos[j] + 1 \ldots n_j]$ contains the symbols $s_1, s_2, \ldots, s_m$ in this order. In other words, S is a subsequence of $T_j[pos[j] + 1 \ldots n_j]$.

2. If S is a subsequence of $T_i[pos[i] + 1 \ldots n_i]$ then A' accepts S. Let $u_0 = pos[i]$ and $u_j = min\{v : v \in \langle u_{j-1} + 1, n_i \rangle$ and $T_i[v] = s_j\}$ for all $j \in \langle 1, m \rangle$. Clearly, $u_1, u_2, \ldots, u_m$ is an occurrence of S in $T_i[pos[i] + 1 \ldots n_i]$. Then, $sf^*(pos, s_1 s_2 \ldots s_m) = [r_1, r_2, \ldots, r_k]$ and $r_i = u_m$. Hence, A' accepts S. □

Lemma 2. *The automaton $A = (Pos(P), \Sigma, sf, ipp, Pos(P))$ accepts a string S iff S is a subsequence of P.*

Proof. Follows from lemma 1. □

Definition 4. *A position point $pos \in Pos(P)$ is called reachable iff there exists string $a_1 a_2 \ldots a_l$ such that $a_i \in \Sigma_p(sf^*(ipp, a_1 \ldots a_{i-1}))$ for all $i \in \langle 1, l \rangle$ and $sf^*(ipp, a_1 a_2 \ldots a_l) = pos$.*

Let $RP(P)$ be the set of all reachable position points of P. We note that $ipp \in RP(P)$ for arbitrary $P \neq \emptyset$.

Definition 5. *We say that position points $pos_1, pos_2 \in Pos(P)$ are equivalent iff the automata $(Pos(P), \Sigma, sf, pos_1, Pos(P))$ and $(Pos(P), \Sigma, sf, pos_2, Pos(P))$ accept the same language.*

Lemma 3. *If the set $RP(P)$ contains equivalent position points then exist $i, j \in \langle 1, k \rangle, i \neq j$ such that a suffix of T_i is a subsequence of T_j.*

Proof. Let pos_1, pos_2 be two distinct equivalent position points. Then exists $i \in \langle 1, k \rangle$ such that $pos_1[i] \neq pos_2[i]$. Without loss of generality, we suppose $pos_1[i] < pos_2[i]$ and denote $T' = T_i[pos_1[i] + 1 \ldots n_i]$. The points pos_1, pos_2 are equivalent and hence the automaton with the initial state pos_2 has to accept T'. From lemma 1 follows that exists $j \in \langle 1, k \rangle$ such that T' is a subsequence of $T_j[pos_2[j] + 1 \ldots n_j]$. Clearly, $i \neq j$. □

Lemma 4. *The set $RP(P)$ contains for all $i \in \langle 1, k \rangle$ and for all $j \in \langle 0, n_i \rangle$ at least one position point pos such that $pos[i] = j$.*

Proof. (by contradiction) We suppose $i \in \langle 1, k \rangle$ and $j \in \langle 0, n_i \rangle$ such that no such position point exists and denote $T' = T_i[1 \ldots j]$. Clearly, $sf^*(ipp, T') = pos$ and $pos[i] = j$. □

3.1   Lower Bound for the Number of States

We show a quadratic lower bound for the maximum number of states of the DASG for two strings of the same length.

Lemma 5. *We consider the texts* $T_1 = a(ba)^{2y}a^{3y+2}, T_2 = ba(bba)^{y}b^{4y+1}$, *where* $y \in Z, y \geq 1$ *and denote by* R *the set of all reachable position points of* T_1, T_2. *Then,* R *contains the position points* $[2(i + j) - 3, 3i - 1]$ *for all* $i \in \langle 1, y \rangle$ *and all* $j \in \langle 1, i + 1 \rangle$ *and no of these position points are equivalent.*

Proof. Since there are $2y$ b's in T_1, no suffix of T_2 of length greater than $2y$ is a subsequence of T_1, and since there are $y + 1$ a's in T_2, no suffix of T_1 of length greater than $y + 1$ is a subsequence of T_2. Hence, no two position points stated in the lemma are equivalent. Further we prove by induction that R contains points $[2(i + j) - 3, 3i - 1]$ for all $i \in \langle 1, y \rangle$ and all $j \in \langle 1, i + 1 \rangle$:
1. $i = 1$: Clearly, $[1, 2], [3, 2] \in R$.
2. We write the position points for i (from the lemma): $[2i - 1, 3i - 1], [2i + 1, 3i - 1], \ldots, [4i - 1, 3i - 1]$. Further, we find out the transitions for each of these position points and generate new points:

$$[2i - 1, 3i - 1] \xrightarrow{a} [2i + 1, 3i + 2]$$
$$[2i + 1, 3i - 1] \xrightarrow{a} [2i + 3, 3i + 2]$$
$$\vdots$$
$$[4i - 1, 3i - 1] \xrightarrow{a} [4i + 1, 3i + 2]$$
$$[4i - 1, 3i - 1] \xrightarrow{b} [4i, 3i] \xrightarrow{b} [4i + 2, 3i + 1] \xrightarrow{a} [4i + 3, 3i + 2]$$

The new generated points $[2i + i, 3i + 2], [2i + 3, 3i + 2], \ldots, [4i + 1, 3i + 2], [4i + 3, 3i + 2]$ are exactly the same as the points from the lemma for $i + 1$. □

Lemma 6. *We suppose the texts* T_1, T_2 *such that* $|T_1| = |T_2| = n$. *Then the maximum number of reachable position points of* T_1, T_2 *is* $\Omega(n^2)$.

Proof. The lemma is direct consequence of lemma 5. □

3.2   Building DASG

We use the DASGs for each text T_i to evaluate effectively the subsequence position alphabet and the subsequence transition function. Further we suppose that we have built the DASG $(Q_i, \Sigma, \delta_i, q_0^i, F_i)$ for each T_i and let $Q_i = \{q_0^i, q_1^i, \ldots, q_{n_i}^i\}$.

The algorithm building the DASG starts at the initial position point, that corresponds to the initial state of the DASG, and generates step by step all reachable position points (states),

We assume $n_1 = n_2 = \ldots = n_k = n$ and use k-dimensional array for mapping between position points and states. The complexity of the algorithm depends on the number of states. Unfortunately, we have found no tight upper bound for the number of reachable position points. The trivial upper bound is $1 + n^k$. Providing that the total number of states is $O(t)$, the algorithm requires $O(k\sigma t)$

procedure BUILD_DASG_FOR_SET_OF_TEXTS $(T_1, T_2, \ldots, T_k)$
input: texts $T_1, T_2, \ldots, T_k$
output: the DASG for texts $T_1, T_2, \ldots, T_k$
1: build the DASG for each text T_i
2: put the initial position point into *queue* and create the initial state
3: **while** *queue* is not empty **do**
4:     store to *pos* the next position point from *queue* and remove it from *queue*
5:     store to *orig* the state corresponding to *pos*
6:     **for all** $a \in \Sigma_p(pos)$ **do**
7:         $r \leftarrow$ SUBSEQUENCE_TRANSITION_FUNCTION (pos, a)
8:         **if** r is a new position point **then**
9:             add a new state corresponding to r
10:            insert r into *queue*
11:        **end if**
12:        store to *ns* the state corresponding to r
13:        add the transition from *orig* to *ns* labeled a
14:     **end for**
15: **end while**

Algorithm 2: Building the DASG for a set of texts

time and $O(k\sigma n + n^k)$ extra space. The required space can be reduced using *e.g.* a balanced tree. The time complexity is then multiplied by the factor giving the time complexity of one mapping, in the case of balanced tree by $k \log n$. In general case, the DASG built by the algorithm above can contain equivalent states. Therefore, it should be minimized using a standard algorithm if a minimal automaton is expected.

4   Conclusion

We have developed the algorithm building the DASG for a set of texts. We have also proved that the maximum number of states of the DASG for two texts is at least quadratic in the length of the input text, which could be considered as the main result of this paper. Despite our effort, the problem of a tight upper bound on the number of states remains open.

References

[1] R. A. Baeza-Yates. Searching subsequences. *Theor. Comput. Sci.*, 78(2):363–376, 1991. 58
[2] J.-J. Hébrard and M. Crochemore. Calcul de la distance par les sous-mots. *RAIRO Inform. Théor. Appl.*, 20(4):441–456, 1986. 58
[3] M. Hirao, H. Hoshino, A. Shinohara, M. Takeda, and S. Arikawa. A practical algorithm to find best subsequence patterns. In *Proceedings of the 3rd International Conference on Discovery Science*, volume 1967, pages 141–154. Springer-Verlag, Berlin, 2000. 58

[4] H. Hoshino, A. Shinohara, M. Takeda, and S. Arikawa. Online construction of subsequence automata for multiple texts. In *Proceedings of the Symposium on String Processing and Information Retrieval 2000*, La Coruña, Spain, 2000. IEEE Computer Society Press. 59

[5] Z. Troníček and B. Melichar. Directed acyclic subsequence graph. In J. Holub and M. Šimánek, editors, *Proceedings of the Prague Stringology Club Workshop '98*, pages 107–118, Czech Technical University, Prague, Czech Republic, 1998. Collaborative Report DC–98–06. 58

Sorting by Prefix Transpositions

Zanoni Dias [*] and João Meidanis [**]

University of Campinas, Institute of Computing
P.O.Box 6167, 13084-971, Campinas, Brazil
{zanoni,meidanis}@ic.unicamp.br

Abstract. A transposition is an operation that exchanges two consecutive, adjacent blocks in a permutation. A prefix transposition is a transposition that moves the first element in the permutation. In this work we present the first results on the problem of sorting permutations with the minimum number of prefix transpositions. This problem is a variation of the transposition distance problem, related to genome rearrangements. We present approximation algorithms with performance ratios of 2 and 3. We conjecture that the maximum prefix transposition distance is $D(n) = n - \lfloor \frac{n}{4} \rfloor$ and present the results of several computational tests that support this. Finally, we propose an algorithm that decides whether a given permutation can be sorted using just the number of transpositions indicated by the breakpoint lower-bound.

1 Introduction

Sequence comparison is one of the most studied problems in computer science. Usually we are interested in finding the minimum number of local operations, such as insertions, deletions, and substitutions that transform a given sequence into another given sequence. This is the edit distance problem, described in many Computational Biology textbooks [19]. Several studies, however, have shown that global operations such as reversals and transpositions (also called rearrangement events) are more appropriate when we wish to compare the genomes of two species [18].

A new research area called Genome Rearrangements appeared in the last years to deal with problems such as, for instance, to find the minimum number of rearrangement events needed to transform one genome into another. In the context of Genome Rearrangements, a genome is represented by an n-tuple of genes (or gene clusters). When there are no repeated genes, this n-tuple is a permutation. We proceed with a brief overview of the literature related to the present work.

The best studied rearrangement event is the reversal. A reversal inverts a block of any size in a genome. Caprara [5] proved that finding the minimum number of reversals needed to transform one genome into another is an NP-Hard problem. Bafna and Pevzner [3] have presented an algorithm with approximation

---

[*] Research supported by FAPESP

[**] Research supported in part by CNPq and FAPESP

factor 2 for this problem. Later Christie [6] presented the best known algorithm for the problem, with factor $\frac{3}{2}$.

Hannenhalli and Pevzner [10] have studied the reversal distance problem when the orientation of genes is known. In this case they proved that there is a polynomial algorithm for the problem. This algorithm has been refined successively until Kaplan, Shamir and Tarjan [14] presented a quadratic algorithm. When just the distance is needed, a faster, linear algorithm due to Bader, Moret, and Yan [2] can be used. Meidanis, Walter e Dias [17] have shown that all the reversal theory developed for linear genomes can be easily adapted to circular genomes.

Another interesting variation of this problem is the so-called prefix reversal problem or pancake problem as it was originally called [8]. In this variation only reversals involving the first consecutive elements of a genome are permitted. Heydari and Sudborough [11] have proved that this problem is NP-Hard. Gates and Papadimitriou [9] and Heydari and Sudborough [12] have studied the diameter of prefix reversals (see further details on diameter problems in Section 4).

The rearrangement event called transposition has the property of exchanging two adjacent blocks of any size in a genome. The transposition distance problem, that is, the problem of finding the minimum number of transpositions necessary to transform one genome into another, has been studied by Bafna and Pevzner [4], who presented the best approximation algorithm for the problem, with factor $\frac{3}{2}$. The transposition distance problem is still open: we do not know of any NP-Hardness proof, and there are no evidences that an exact polynomial algorithm exists. Christie [7] and Meidanis, Walter and Dias [16] have proved partial results on the transposition diameter.

In this work we present the first known results on the variation of the transposition distance problem that we call prefix transposition distance, that is, the rearrangement distance problem where only transpositions affecting two consecutive blocks of the genome, with one of these blocks formed by the first consecutive elements of the genome.

The paper is divided as follows. Initially, in Section 2, we define important concepts that will be used throughout. In Section 3 we present two approximation algorithms for the prefix transposition distance problem, with factors 3 and 2. In Section 4 we present several results on the prefix transposition diameter, leading to the conjecture that $D(n) = n - \lfloor \frac{n}{4} \rfloor$, and tests with programs that we implemented to help validate our conjectures. We show in Section 5 an algorithm that verifies whether a given genome can be sorted using the minimum number of prefix transpositions according to the breakpoint lower-bound (Lemma 5). Finally, in Section 6, we exhibit our conclusions and suggestions for future work.

2   Definitions

Here we introduce a number of basic concepts used in Genome Rearrangements. Notice that some definitions, for instance that of transposition, is different from the definition used in other areas.

Definition 1. *An arbitrary genome formed by n genes will be represented as a permutation $\pi = [\pi[1]\ \pi[2]\ \ldots\ \pi[n]]$ where each element of π represents a gene. The identity genome ι_n is defined as $\iota_n = [1\ 2\ \ldots\ n]$.*

Definition 2. *A transposition $\rho(x, y, z)$, where $1 \leq x < y < z \leq n + 1$, is an rearrangement event that transforms π into the genome $\rho\pi = [\pi[1]\ \ldots\ \pi[x - 1]\ \pi[y]\ \ldots\ \pi[z - 1]\ \pi[x]\ \ldots\ \pi[y - 1]\ \pi[z]\ \ldots\ \pi[n]]$.*

Definition 3. *A prefix transposition $\rho(1, x, y)$, where $1 < x < y \leq n + 1$, is an rearrangement event that transforms π into the genome $\rho\pi = [\pi[x]\ \ldots\ \pi[y - 1]\ \pi[1]\ \ldots\ \pi[x - 1]\ \pi[y]\ \ldots\ \pi[n]]$.*

Definition 4. *Given two genomes π and σ we define the transposition distance $d_\tau(\pi, \sigma)$ between these two genomes as being the least number of transpositions needed to transform π into σ, that is, the smallest r such that there are transpositions $\rho_1, \rho_2, \ldots \rho_r$ with $\rho_r \ldots \rho_2\rho_1\pi = \sigma$. We call sorting distance by transpositions, $d_\tau(\pi)$, the transposition distance between the genomes π and ι_n, that is, $d_\tau(\pi) = d_\tau(\pi, \iota_n)$.*

Definition 5. *Given two genomes π and σ we define the prefix transposition distance $d(\pi, \sigma)$ between these two genomes as being the least number of prefix transpositions needed to transform π into σ, that is, the smallest r such that there are prefix transpositions $\rho_1, \rho_2, \ldots \rho_r$ with $\rho_r \ldots \rho_2\rho_1\pi = \sigma$. We call sorting distance by prefix transpositions, $d(\pi)$, the prefix transposition distance between genomes π and ι_n, that is, $d(\pi) = d(\pi, \iota_n)$.*

3   Approximation Algorithms

The first important observation is the following.

Lemma 1. *For any permutation π, we have $d(\pi) \geq d_\tau(\pi)$.*

Proof: This follows from the observation that every prefix transposition is a transposition. The converse is not always true. $\square$

3.1   Approximation Algorithm with Factor 3

Lemma 2. *For every transposition $\rho(x, y, z)$ with $x \neq 1$, there are prefix transpositions $\rho_1(1, r, s)$ and $\rho_2(1, t, u)$ such that $\rho_2\rho_1\pi = \rho\pi$.*

Proof: Indeed, it suffices to take $r = y$, $s = z$, $t = z - y + 1$ and $u = z - y + x$, or, alternatively, $r = x$, $s = y$, $t = y - x + 1$ and $u = z$. Figure 1 shows how two prefix transpositions can simulate a transposition. $\square$

Lemma 3. *Any k-approximation algorithm for the transposition distance problem can be transformed into a $2k$-approximation algorithm for the prefix transposition distance problem.*

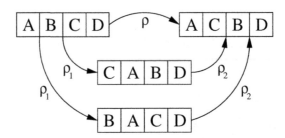

Fig. 1. Two examples of how it is possible to obtain prefix transpositions ρ_1 and ρ_2 such that $\rho\pi = \rho_2\rho_1\pi$, for a given transposition $\rho = \rho(x, y, z)$, with $x \neq 1$

Proof: Immediate from Lemma 2. $\square$

Therefore it is easy to obtain an approximation algorithm with factor 3 for the prefix transposition distance problem using the approximation algorithms with factor $\frac{3}{2}$ for the transposition distance problem given by Bafna and Pevzner [4] and by Christie [7].

3.2   Approximation Algorithm with Factor 2

We need to define a few important concepts before proceeding.

Definition 6. *A breakpoint for the prefix transposition problem is a position i of a permutation π such that $\pi[i] - \pi[i-1] \neq 1$, and $2 \leq i \leq n$. By definition, position 1 (beginning of the permutation) is always considered a breakpoint. Position $n+1$ (end of the permutation) is considered a breakpoint when $\pi[n] \neq n$. We denote by $b(\pi)$ the number of breakpoints of permutation π.*

By the former definition $b(\pi) \geq 1$ for any permutation π and the only permutations with exactly one breakpoint are the identity permutations ($\pi = \iota_n$, for all n).

Definition 7. *A strip is a subsequence $\pi[i..j]$ of π ($i \leq j$) such that i and $j+1$ are breakpoints and there are no breakpoints between these positions.*

Definition 8. *Given a permutation π and a prefix transposition ρ, we define $\Delta b(\pi, \rho)$ as the variation on the number of breakpoints due to operation ρ, that is, $\Delta b(\pi, \rho) = b(\rho\pi) - b(\pi)$.*

The first important observation about breakpoints is the following.

Lemma 4. *Given a permutation π and a prefix transposition ρ, we have that $\Delta b(\pi, \rho) \in \{-2, -1, 0, 1, 2\}$.*

Lemma 5. *For every permutation π, we have that $d(\pi) \geq \left\lceil \frac{b(\pi)-1}{2} \right\rceil$.*

Proof: Immediate from Lemma 4. $\square$

Lemma 6. *Given a permutation $\pi \neq \iota_n$, where $n = |\pi|$, it is always possible to obtain a prefix transposition ρ such that $\Delta b(\pi, \rho) \leq -1$.*

Proof: Let k be the last element of the first strip of π. If $k < n$, then there is a strip beginning with the element $k + 1$, such that $\pi^{-1}[k] < \pi^{-1}[k + 1]$ and $\rho = \rho(1, \pi^{-1}[k] + 1, \pi^{-1}[k + 1])$ suffices. If $k = n$, take $\rho = \rho(1, \pi^{-1}[k] + 1, n + 1)$. $\square$

Lemma 7. *Let π be a permutation and $\rho(1, x, y)$ a prefix transposition such that $\rho\pi = \iota_n$, where $n = |\pi|$. Then $\pi[x] = 1$ and $\Delta b(\pi, \rho) = -2$.*

Lemma 8. *For every permutation π, we have $d(\pi) \leq b(\pi) - 2$.*

Proof: Immediate by Lemmas 6 and 7. $\square$

Theorem 1. *For every permutation π, we have $\left\lceil \frac{b(\pi)-1}{2} \right\rceil \leq d(\pi) \leq b(\pi) - 2$.*

Theorem 2. *Any algorithm that produces the prefix transpositions according to Lemmas 6 and 7 is an approximation algorithm with factor 2 for the prefix transposition distance problem.*

Another important point regarding genome rearrangments is the possibility of sorting a permutation without ever increasing the number of breakpoints. Christie [7] has proved that this is true for transposition events. The following lemma establishes the analogous result for prefix transpositions. The proof is a bit lengthy and is omitted here, but appears in the full version of this paper.

Lemma 9. *Let π be an arbitrary permutation and $d(\pi) = k$ its prefix transposition distance. Then there exists an optimal sequence of prefix transpositions $\rho_1, \ldots, \rho_k$, such that $\rho_k \ldots \rho_1 \pi = \iota_n$, where $n = |\pi|$, and $\Delta b(\rho_{i-1} \ldots \rho_1 \pi, \rho_i) \leq 0$ for every $1 \leq i \leq k$.*

4   The Diameter of Prefix Transpositions

We call rearrangement diameter the largest rearrangement distance between two permutations of a certain size n. We Denote by $D(n)$ the diameter of prefix transpositions and by $D_\tau(n)$ the diameter of transpositions. Bafna and Pevzner [4] proved the following result.

Theorem 3. *The diameter of transpositions for permutations of size n is such that $\frac{n}{2} \leq D_\tau(n) \leq \frac{3n}{4}$.*

We can present a similar result for the prefix transposition distance problem.

Theorem 4. *The diameter of prefix transpositions for permutations of size n is such that $\frac{n}{2} \leq D(n) \leq n - 1$.*

Proof: To begin with note that $D(n) \geq D_\tau(n)$, since $d(\pi) \geq d_\tau(\pi)$ for any permutation π (Lemma 1). We can then use the result of Aigner and West [1] that says that the diameter for the rearrangement distance problem that considers only insertion of the first element, that is, transpositions of the form $\rho(1, 2, x)$, is $n - 1$. $\square$

Definition 9. *Let R_n be the family of permutations defined as follows: $R_n = [n \ n-1 \ \dots \ 2 \ 1]$. Permutation R_n is formed by odd cycles only: just one cycle when n is odd, and two cycles otherwise.*

The following result was proved independently by Christie [7] and Meidanis, Walter and Dias [16].

Theorem 5. *For $n \geq 3$, we have $d_\tau(R_n) = \lfloor \frac{n}{2} \rfloor + 1$.*

When dealing with prefix transpositions, we could state, based solely on Theorem 1, that $\lceil \frac{n}{2} \rceil \leq d(R_n) \leq n - 1$. However, a stronger statement holds.

Theorem 6. *For $n \geq 4$, we have $d(R_n) \leq n - \lfloor \frac{n}{4} \rfloor$.*

Proof: The algorithm of Figure 2 sorts R_n using exactly $n - \lfloor \frac{n}{4} \rfloor$ prefix transpositions. A step-by-step execution of this algorithm on permutation R_{13} can be seen in Figure 3. $\square$

ALGORITHM TO SORT $R_n()$
1   Input: $\pi = R_n$, with $n \geq 4$
2   $m \leftarrow 4 \lfloor \frac{n}{4} \rfloor$
3   {Phase 1: Shuffling}
4   **for** $i \leftarrow 1$ to $(\frac{m}{4}) - 1$
5   **do** $\pi \leftarrow \rho(1, 5, m - 2(i - 1))\pi$
6   $\pi \leftarrow \rho(1, 3, \frac{m}{2} + 2)\pi$
7   {Phase 2: Greedy Phase}
8   $x \leftarrow \pi^{-1}[n] + 1$
9   $y \leftarrow m + 1$
10 **for** $i \leftarrow 1$ to $(\frac{m}{2})$
11 **do** $z \leftarrow \pi[x]$
12      $\pi \leftarrow \rho(1, x, y)\pi$
13      $y \leftarrow \pi^{-1}[z - 1] + 1$
14      $w \leftarrow \pi[y] - 1$
15      $x \leftarrow \pi^{-1}[w] + 1$
16 {Phase 3: Positioning the Last Elements}
17 **for** $i \leftarrow (m + 1)$ to n
18 **do** $\pi \leftarrow \rho(1, i, i + 1)\pi$
19 Output: $n - \lfloor \frac{n}{4} \rfloor$

Fig. 2. Algorithm to sort R_n

```
•13 •12 •11 •10 • 9 • 8 • 7 • 6 • 5 • 4 • 3 • 2 • 1 •

• 9 • 8 • 7 • 6 • 5 • 4 • 3 •13 •12 •11 •10 • 2 • 1 •

• 5 • 4 • 3 •13 •12 • 9 • 8 • 7 • 6 •11 •10 • 2 • 1 •

• 3 •13 •12 • 9 • 8 • 5 • 4 • 7 • 6 •11 •10 • 2 • 1 •

•12 • 9 • 8 • 5 • 4 • 7 • 6 •11 •10 • 2    3 •13 • 1 •

• 8 • 5 • 4 • 7 • 6 •11   12 • 9   10 • 2    3 •13 • 1 •

• 4 • 7   8 • 5   6 •11   12 • 9   10 • 2    3 •13 • 1 •

• 9   10 • 2    3   4 • 7   8 • 5   6 •11   12   13 • 1 •

• 7    8    9   10 • 2    3   4    5   6 •11   12   13 • 1 •

• 2    3    4    5    6    7    8    9   10   11   12   13 • 1 •

• 1    2    3    4    5    6    7    8    9   10   11   12   13
```

Fig. 3. Steps to sort R_{13}

Lemma 10. *For $n \geq 1$, we have $d(R_{n+1}) \geq d(R_n)$.*

Proof: It is easy to see that any series of prefix transpositions that sorts R_{n+1} will also sort R_n, provided we adapt the movements that include the element $n+1$. □

Christie [7] and Meidanis, Walter and Dias [16] have proposed the following conjecture, still open today.

Conjecture 1. The transposition diameter $D_\tau(n)$, for $n \geq 3$, is given by $D_\tau(n) = d_\tau(R_n) = \lfloor \frac{n}{2} \rfloor + 1$.

Likewise, we believe that the following statement is true.

Conjecture 2. The diameter of prefix transpositions $D(n)$, for $n \geq 4$, is given by $D(n) = d(R_n) = n - \lfloor \frac{n}{4} \rfloor$.

4.1 Tests

The tests that will be presented in this section were performed in a Digital Alpha Server GS140 computer, with 10 Alpha 21264 EV6 processors of 524MHz and 64-bit word length, with 8 GB of physical memory and running the OSF1 version 4.0 operating system. All programs were written in C++ and compiled with g++ using compilation directive "-O3". Our programs use just one processor and during the tests the machine was always executing other processes as well. The measured times are the times effectively spent by the programs (user + system time) and not the total time of execution (real time).

We implemented two "branch and bound" algorithms to compute the exact distance of prefix transpositions. The first version considers all possible prefix

Table 1. distance of prefix transposition for reverse permutations with 16 or less elements. The times in column "without optimization" refer to the "branch and bound" algorithm that considers all prefix transpositions possible, while the column "with optimization" presents the results of the implementation that considers only prefix transpositions that do not create new breakpoints, according to Lemma 9. We could not compute $d(R_{16})$ directly using any of the two implementations; instead we present an estimate of the time necessary for each algorithm to compute correctly the distance. Note also that it is possible to infer the distance $d(R_{16})$ from Theorem 6 and Lemma 10

n	$d(R_n)$	Time without optimization (seconds)	Time with optimization (seconds)
02	01	0	0
03	02	0	0
04	03	0	0
05	04	0	0
06	05	0	0
07	06	0	0
08	06	4	2
09	07	9	3
10	08	59	22
11	09	1011	373
12	09	8872	2607
13	10	16294	4305
14	11	118463	45168
15	12	2771374	1081631
16	12*	750 days *	300 days *

transpositions, while the second version considers only prefix transpositions that do not create new breakpoints, according to Lemma 9. Using these programs it was possible to obtain directly the prefix transposition distance for all reverse permutations R_n with $n \leq 15$. Table 1 and Figure 4 show result summaries.

To further support the correctness of Theorem 6, we implemented the algorithm that sorts reverse permutations R_n in polynomial time (Figure 2). We tested our implementation using all reverse permutations R_n for $n \leq 50000$. The algorithm correctly sorted all tested instances. Note that these instances are several times bigger than the biggest instances used in practice in genome rearrangement problems. Execution times for this algorithm are plotted in Figure 5.

Lastly we implemented two programs to verify the conjectures proposed in Section 4. The two programs are based in the same strategy. We built a graph as follows: we created a vertex for each of the $n!$ permutations with n elements and an edge for each pair of permutations that differ by a rearrangement event. In this graph we search for the permutations that posses the largest distance from the identity permutation. This strategy can be implemented in linear time on

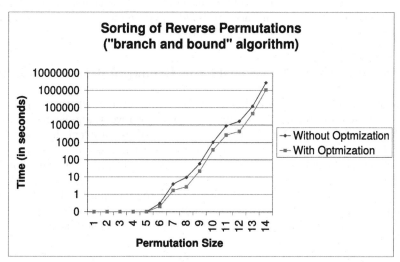

Fig. 4. Results for the "branch and bound" algorithm. Total approximate time of 47 days nonstop processing, with about 34 days for the version not optimized and 13 days for the optimized version

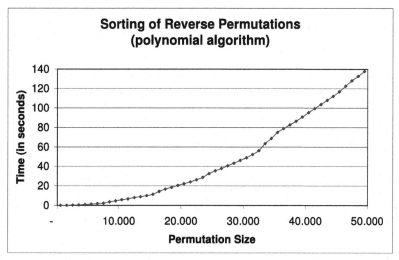

Fig. 5. Results for the polynomial algorithm. Total approximate time of 27 days nonstop processing

the graph size. With this method we could certify in slightly over 20 hours that both conjectures are true for permutations with $n \leq 11$ elements. Unfortunately 30 GB of physical memory are need to build the graph for $n = 12$, what made the test of our conjectures for $n \geq 12$ impossible.

5   Permutations that Satisfy the Breakpoint Lower-Bound

Kececioglu and Sankoff [15] conjectured that to determine whether a permutation can be sorted using the minimum number of reversals indicated by the breakpoint lower-bound for reversals was an NP-Hard problem, just like the general problem of sorting by reversals. Irving and Christie [13] and Tran [20] independently proved that this conjecture is false, exhibiting a polynomial algorithm for the problem.

In the case of prefix transpositions we know from Lemma 5 that for every permutation π we have $d(\pi) \geq \lceil (b(\pi) - 1)/2 \rceil$. However, given a permutation π, is it possible to determine whether $d(\pi) = (b(\pi) - 1)/2$? The following results prove that the answer is yes.

Lemma 11. *Let π be an arbitrary permutation. Then there exists at most one prefix transposition ρ such that $\Delta b(\pi, \rho) = -2$.*

Proof: Suppose that π and $\rho(1, x, y)$ are such that $\Delta b(\pi, \rho) = -2$. In this case we have $\pi = [\pi[1] \ldots \pi[x-1]\pi[x] \ldots \pi[y-1]\pi[y] \ldots]$ and $\rho\pi = [\pi[x] \ldots \pi[y-1]$ $\pi[1] \ldots \pi[x-1]\pi[y] \ldots]$, where $\pi[x-1] \neq \pi[x] - 1$, $\pi[y-1] \neq \pi[y] - 1$, $\pi[y-1] = \pi[1] - 1$ and $\pi[x-1] = \pi[y] - 1$. Finally, note that $\pi[1]$ determines uniquely the index y, and y determines uniquely the index x. $\square$

Theorem 7. *Let π be an arbitrary permutation. Then it is possible to determine in polynomial time whether $d(\pi) = \frac{b(\pi)-1}{2}$.*

Proof: Immediate by the algorithm of Figure 6, that has complexity $O(n^2)$. $\square$

Given an integer k, is it always possible to find a permutation π such that there is a series of k prefix transpositions $\rho_1, \ldots, \rho_k$ with $\Delta b(\rho_{i-1}\rho_{i-2} \ldots \rho_1 \pi, \rho_i)$ $= -2$, for $1 \leq i \leq k$? Once again the answer is affirmative.

Definition 10. *Let B_k be the family of permutations defined as follows: $B_k = [k+1 \ k \ k+2 \ k-1 \ k+3 \ k-2 \ \ldots \ 2k-1 \ 2 \ 2k \ 1]$. Permutation B_k possesses $2k+1$ breakpoints.*

Lemma 12. *For every integer k it is possible to obtain a series of k prefix transpositions $\rho_1, \rho_2, \ldots, \rho_k$ that sort B_k such that $\Delta b(\rho_{i-1}\rho_{i-2} \ldots \rho_1 \pi, \rho_i) = -2$, for $1 \leq i \leq k$.*

Proof: Immediate from the algorithm of Figure 7, that can be implemented in linear time. $\square$

VERIFYING WHETHER π SATISFIES THE BREAKPOINTS LOWER-BOUND()
1   Input: π
2   $n \leftarrow |\pi|$
3   OK $\leftarrow$ TRUE
4   **While** $\pi \neq \iota_n$ and OK
5   **do** $y \leftarrow \pi^{-1}[\pi[1] - 1] + 1$
6       $x \leftarrow \pi^{-1}[\pi[y] - 1] + 1$
7   {Verifies whether there exists a movement that removes two breakpoints}
8   **if** $x < y$
9   **then** $\pi \leftarrow \rho(1, x, y)\pi$
10   **else** OK $\leftarrow$ FALSE
11 Output: OK

Fig. 6. The algorithm that verifies whether π has distance $d(\pi) = \frac{b(\pi) - 1}{2}$

ALGORITHM TO SORT B_k()
1   Input: $\pi = B_k$, with $k \geq 1$
2   **for** $i \leftarrow 1$ to k
3   **do** $\pi \leftarrow \rho(1, 2i, 2i + 1)\pi$
4   Output: k

Fig. 7. The algorithm that sorts B_k

6   Conclusions

We introduced in this work a new problem of Genome Rearrangement that we called distance of prefix transpositions. We showed a number of results for this problem, including two approximation algorithms (the best of them with factor 2), a proof that any permutation can be sorted without "cutting strips," a conjecture on the prefix transposition diameter stating that $D(n) = n - \left\lfloor \frac{n}{4} \right\rfloor$, and an algorithm for determining whether a permutation can be sorted using a series of prefix transpositions removing two breakpoints per step. The problem of sorting an arbitrary permutation with prefix transpositions remains open.

Acknowledgments

We gratefully acknowledge the financial support of Brazilian agencies CNPq (National Council of Scientific and Technological Development) and FAPESP (The State of São Paulo Research Foundation).

References

[1] M. Aigner and D. B. West. Sorting by insertion of leading element. *Journal of Combinatorial Theory*, 45:306–309, 1987.   70

[2] D. A. Bader, B. M. E. Moret, and M. Yan. A linear-time algorithm for computing inversion distance between signed permutations with an experimental study. *Journal of Computational Biology*, 8(5):483–491, 2001. 66

[3] V. Bafna and P. A. Pevzner. Genome rearrangements and sorting by reversals. *SIAM Journal on Computing*, 25(2):272–289, 1996. 65

[4] V. Bafna and P. A. Pevzner. Sorting by transpositions. *SIAM Journal on Discrete Mathematics*, 11(2):224–240, May 1998. 66, 68, 69

[5] A. Caprara. Sorting by reversals is difficult. In *Proceedings of the First International Conference on Computational Molecular Biology - (RECOMB'97)*, pages 75–83, New York, USA, January 1997. ACM Press. 65

[6] D. A. Christie. A 3/2-approximation algorithm for sorting by reversals. In *Proceedings of the Ninth Annual ACM-SIAM Symposium on Discrete Algorithms*, pages 244–252, San Francisco, USA, January 1998. 66

[7] D. A. Christie. *Genome Rearrangement Problems*. PhD thesis, Glasgow University, 1998. 66, 68, 69, 70, 71

[8] H. Dweighter. *American Mathematical Monthly*, volume 82, page 1010. The Mathematical Association of America, 1975. 66

[9] W. H. Gates and C. H. Papadimitriou. Bounds for sorting by prefix reversals. *Discrete Mathematics*, 27:47–57, 1979. 66

[10] S. Hannenhalli and P. A. Pevzner. Transforming cabbage into turnip: Polynomial algorithm for sorting signed permutations by reversals. *Journal of the ACM*, 46(1):1–27, January 1999. 66

[11] M. H. Heydari and I. H. Sudborough. Sorting by prefix reversals is np-complete. To be submitted. 66

[12] M. H. Heydari and I. H. Sudborough. On the diameter of the pancake network. *Journal of Algorithms*, 25:67–94, 1997. 66

[13] R. W. Irving and D. A. Christie. Sorting by reversals: on a conjecture of kececioglu and sankoff. Technical Report TR-95-12, Department of Computing Science, University of Glasgow, May 1995. 74

[14] H. Kaplan, R. Shamir, and R. E. Tarjan. Faster and simpler algorithm for sorting signed permutations by reversals. *SIAM Journal on Computing*, 29(3):880–892, January 2000. 66

[15] J. D. Kececioglu and D. Sankoff. Exact and approximation algorithms for sorting by reversals, with application to genome rearrangement. *Algorithmica*, 13:180–210, January 1995. 74

[16] J. Meidanis, M. E. Walter, and Z. Dias. Transposition distance between a permutation and its reverse. In R. Baeza-Yates, editor, *Proceedings of the 4th South American Workshop on String Processing (WSP'97)*, pages 70–79, Valparaiso, Chile, 1997. Carleton University Press. 66, 70, 71

[17] J. Meidanis, M. E. M. T. Walter, and Z. Dias. Reversal distance of signed circular chromosomes. Technical Report IC-00-23, Institute of Computing - University of Campinas, December 2000. 66

[18] J. D. Palmer and L. A. Herbon. Plant mitochondrial dna evolves rapidly in structure, but slowly in sequence. *Journal of Molecular Evolution*, 27:87–97, 1988. 65

[19] J. C. Setubal and J. Meidanis. *Introduction to Computional Molecular Biology*. PWS Publishing Company, 1997. 65

[20] N. Q. Tran. An easy case of sorting by reversals. In A. Apostolico and J. Hein, editors, *Proceedings of the 8th Annual Symposium of the Combinatorial Pattern Matching (CPM'97)*, volume 1264 of *Lecture Notes in Computer Science*, pages 83–89, Aarhus, Denmark, June 1997. Springer. 74

Efficient Computation
of Long Similar Subsequences

Abdullah N. Arslan and Ömer Eğecioğlu⋆

Department of Computer Science, University of California, Santa Barbara
Santa Barbara, CA 93106 USA
{arslan,omer}@cs.ucsb.edu

Abstract. Given sequences X of length n and Y of length m with $n \geq m$, let LAt^* and $NLAt^*$ denote the maximum ordinary, and maximum *length normalized* scores of local alignments with length at least a given threshold value t. The alignment length is defined as the sum of the lengths of the involved subsequences, and length normalized score of an alignment is the quotient of the ordinary score by the alignment length. We develop an algorithm which finds an alignment with ordinary score $\geq LAt^*$, and length $\geq (1 - \frac{1}{r})t$ for a given r, in time $O(rnm)$ and space $O(rm)$. The algorithm can be used to find an alignment with length normalized score $> \lambda$ for a given positive λ with the same time and space complexity and within the same approximation bounds. Thus this algorithm provides a length-approximate answer to a query such as "Do X and Y share a (sufficiently long) fragment with more than 70% of similarity?" We also show that our approach gives improved approximation algorithms for the *normalized local alignment* problem. In this case we can efficiently find an alignment with length $\geq (1 - \frac{1}{r})t$ which has a length normalized score $\geq NLAt^*$.

Keywords: Local alignment, normalized local alignment, approximation algorithm, dynamic programming, ratio maximization.

1 Introduction

Local sequence alignment aims to reveal similar regions in a given pair of sequences X and Y. The common notion of local similarity suffers from some well-known anomalies resulting from not taking into account the lengths of the subsequences involved in the alignments. The so-called *mosaic effect* in an alignment is observed when a very poor region is sandwiched between two regions with high similarity scores. *Shadow effect* is observed when a biologically important short alignment is not detected because it overlaps with a significantly longer yet biologically inadequate alignment with higher overall score. Several studies in the literature have aimed to describe methods to reduce these anomalies (Arslan and Eğecioğlu, 2002 [6], Arslan et al., 2001 [5], Zhang et al., 1999 [11], Zhang et al., 1998 [10], Altschul et al., 1997 [4]).

⋆ Supported in part by NSF Grants No. CCR–9821038 and No. EIA–9818320.

A.H.F. Laender and A.L. Oliveira (Eds.): SPIRE 2002, LNCS 2476, pp. 77–90, 2002.

It is well-known that the statistical significance of local alignment depends on both its score and length (Altschul and Ericson, 1986 [2], 1988 [3]). Alexandrov and Solovyev, 1998 [1] proposed to normalize the alignment score by its length and demonstrated that this new approach leads to better protein classification. Arslan et al., 2001 [5] defined the *normalized local alignment problem* in which the goal is to find subsequences I and J that maximize $s(I, J)/(|I| + |J|)$ among all subsequences I and J with $|I| + |J| \geq t$, where $s(I, J)$ is the score, and t is a threshold for the overall length of I and J. The standard dynamic programming solution to this problem requires cubic time. By dropping the length constraint and changing the objective to the maximization of $s(I, J)/(|I| + |J| + L)$ for real parameter L, it is possible to have some control over the desired alignment lengths while keeping the computational complexity small [5].

In this paper we concentrate on the length constrained version of normalized local alignment. The problem is *feasible* if there is an alignment with positive normalized score and length at least t, where the *length* of an alignment is defined as the sum of the lengths of the subsequences involved in the alignment. We develop an algorithm which provides an approximate control over the total length of the resulting alignment while guaranteeing that the normalized score is maximum achievable by any alignment of length $\geq t$. The approximation ratio is controlled by a parameter r. For a feasible problem, the algorithm returns subsequences with total length $\geq (1 - \frac{1}{r})t$. The computations take $O(rnm)$ time and $O(rm)$ space (Theorem 1, section 3). We subsequently revisit the two normalized local alignment algorithms proposed in [5]. In these algorithms we change the subproblems involving ordinary local alignments to those which have a length constraint, and we use the approximation algorithm we present in this paper to solve them. We show that this way we can obtain an alignment which has a normalized score no smaller than the optimum score of the original normalized local alignment problem with total length at least $(1 - \frac{1}{r})t$ provided that the original problem is feasible (Theorem 2, section 4). In both resulting algorithms the space complexity is $O(rm)$. The number of subproblems that need to be solved is the same as in [5] : While one algorithm establishes that $O(\log n)$ invocations of our approximation algorithm is sufficient, experiments suggest that the other algorithm requires only $3 - 5$ iterations, resulting in observed $O(rnm)$ time complexity.

2 Background

Given two sequences $X = x_1 x_2 \ldots x_n$ and $Y = y_1 y_2 \ldots y_m$ with $n \geq m$, *alignment graph* $G_{X,Y}$ is used to represent all possible *alignments* between all subsequences of X and Y. It is a directed acyclic graph having $(n + 1)(m + 1)$ lattice points (u, v) as vertices for $0 \leq u \leq n$, and $0 \leq v \leq m$ (See for example, [9, 6]). An *alignment path* for subsequences $x_i \cdots x_k$, and $y_j \cdots y_l$ is a directed path from vertex $(i - 1, j - 1)$ to (k, l) in $G_{X,Y}$ where $i \leq k$ and $j \leq l$. We will use the terms alignment and alignment path interchangeably.

The objective of sequence alignment is to quantify the similarity between two sequences. There are various scoring schemes for this purpose. In the *basic scoring scheme*, the arcs of $G_{X,Y}$ are assigned weights determined by non-negative reals δ (*mismatch penalty*) and μ (*indel* or *gap penalty*). We assume that $s(x_i, y_j)$ is the similarity score between the symbols x_i, and y_j which is 1 for a match $(x_i = y_j)$ and $-\delta$ for a mismatch $(x_i \neq y_j)$. The following is the classical dynamic programming formulation ([9]) to compute the maximum local alignment score $\mathcal{S}_{i,j}$ ending at each vertex (i, j):

$$\mathcal{S}_{i,j} = \max\{0,\ \mathcal{S}_{i-1,j} - \mu,\ \mathcal{S}_{i-1,j-1} + s(x_i, y_j),\ \mathcal{S}_{i,j-1} - \mu\} \qquad (1)$$

for $1 \leq i \leq n$, $1 \leq j \leq m$, with the boundary conditions $\mathcal{S}_{i,j} = 0$ whenever $i = 0$ or $j = 0$.

Let $\subseteq$ indicate the subsequence relation. The *local alignment* (*LA*) problem seeks subsequences $I \subseteq X$ and $J \subseteq Y$ with the highest similarity score. The optimum local alignment score $LA^*(X, Y)$ is defined as $LA^*(X, Y) = \max\{s(I, J) \mid I \subseteq X, J \subseteq Y\} = \max_{i,j} \mathcal{S}_{i,j}$, where $s(I, J) > 0$, hereinafter, is the best local alignment score between I and J. LA^* can be computed using the Smith-Waterman algorithm [8] in time $O(nm)$ and space $O(m)$.

In what follows, for any optimization problem $\mathcal{P}$, we denote by $\mathcal{P}^*$ its optimum value, and sometimes drop the parameters from the notation when they are obvious from the context. We call $\mathcal{P}$ *feasible* if it has a solution with the given parameters.

As in [5] the objective of the *normalized local alignment* problem (*NLAt*) can be written as

$$NLAt^*(X, Y) = \max\{s(I, J)/(|I| + |J|) \mid I \subseteq X, J \subseteq Y, |I| + |J| \geq t\} \qquad (2)$$

In general optimal alignments for *LA* and *NLAt* are different (see [5] for a detailed example).

3 Finding Long Alignments with High Ordinary Score

For a given t, we define the *local alignment with length threshold* score between X and Y as

$$LAt^*(X, Y) = \max\{s(I, J) \mid I \subseteq X, J \subseteq Y, \text{ and } |I| + |J| \geq t\} \qquad (3)$$

To solve *LAt* we can extend the dynamic programming formulation in (1) by adding another dimension. At each entry of the dynamic programming matrix we store optimum scores for all possible lengths up to $m+n$, increasing the time and space complexity to $O(n^2m)$ and $O(nm)$, respectively, which are unacceptably high in practice.

We give an approximation algorithm *APX-LAt* which computes a local alignment whose score is at least LAt^*, and whose length is at least $(1 - \frac{1}{r})t$ provided that the *LAt* problem is feasible, i.e. $s(\widehat{I}, \widehat{J}) \geq LAt^*$ and $|\widehat{I}| + |\widehat{J}| \geq (1 - \frac{1}{r})t$.

For simplicity, we assume a basic scoring scheme. Our approximation idea is similar to that in Arslan and Eğecioğlu, 2002 [6]. Instead of a single score, we maintain at each node (i, j) of $G_{X,Y}$, a list of alignments with the property that for positive s where s is the optimum score achievable over the set of alignments with length $\geq t$ and ending at (i, j), at least one element of the list actives score s and length $t - \Delta$ where Δ is a positive integral parameter. We show that the dynamic programming formulation can be extended to preserve this property through the nodes. In particular, an alignment with score $\geq LAt^*$, and length $\geq t - \Delta$ will be observed in one of the nodes (i, j) during the computations.

We imagine the vertices of $G_{X,Y}$ as grouped into $\lfloor (n+m)/\Delta \rfloor$ diagonal slabs at distance Δ from each other as shown in Figure 1. The length of a diagonal arc is 2 while the length of each horizontal, or vertical arc is 1 . Each slab consists of $\lfloor \Delta/2 \rfloor + 1$ diagonals. Two consecutive slabs share a diagonal which we call a *boundary* . The *left* and the *right boundaries* of slab b are respectively the boundaries shared by the left and right neighboring slabs of b. As a subgraph, a slab contains all the edges in $G_{X,Y}$ incident to the vertices in the slab except for the horizontal and vertical edges incident to the vertices on the left boundary (which belong to the preceding slab), and the diagonal edges incident to the vertices on the first diagonal following the left boundary.

Now to a given diagonal d in $G_{X,Y}$, we associate a number of slabs as follows. Let *slab 0 with respect to diagonal d* be the slab that contains the diagonal d itself. The slabs to the left of *slab 0* are then ordered consecutively as *slab 1, slab 2, ...* with respect to d. In other words, *slab k* with respect to diagonal d is the subgraph of $G_{X,Y}$ composed of vertices placed inclusively between diagonals $\lfloor d/\Delta \rfloor$ and d if $k = 0$, and between diagonal $(\lfloor d/\Delta \rfloor - k)\Delta$ and $(\lfloor d/\Delta \rfloor - k + 1)\Delta$, otherwise. Figure 1 includes sample slabs with respect to diagonal d, and alignments ending at some node (i, j) on this diagonal.

Let $\mathcal{S}_{i,j,k}$ represent the optimum score achievable at (i, j) by any alignment starting at slab k with respect to diagonal $i + j$ for $0 \leq k < \lceil t/\Delta \rceil$. For $k = \lceil t/\Delta \rceil$, $\mathcal{S}_{i,j,k}$ is slightly different: It is the maximum of all achievable scores by an alignment starting in or before slab k . Also let $\mathcal{L}_{i,j,k}$ be the length of an optimal alignment starting at slab k, and achieving score $\mathcal{S}_{i,j,k}$. A single slab can contribute at most Δ to the length of any alignment. We store at each node (i, j) $\lceil t/\Delta \rceil + 1$ score-length pairs $(\mathcal{S}_{i,j,k}, \mathcal{L}_{i,j,k})$ for $0 \leq k \leq \lceil t/\Delta \rceil$ corresponding to $\lceil t/\Delta \rceil + 1$ optimal alignments that end (i, j) . Figure 2 shows the steps of our approximation algorithm   *APX-LAt*. The processing is done row-by-row starting with the top row $(i = 0)$ of $G_{X,Y}$.

Step 1 of the algorithm performs the initialization of the lists of the nodes in the top row $(i = 0)$. Step 2 implements computation of scores as dictated by the dynamic programming formulation in (1). Let maxp of a list of score-length pairs be a pair with the maximum score in the list. We obtain an optimal alignment with score $\mathcal{S}_{i,j,k}$ by extending an optimal alignment from one of the nodes $(i-1, j)$, $(i-1, j-1)$, or $(i, j-1)$. We note that extending an alignment at (i, j) from node $(i-1, j-1)$ increases the length by 2 and the score by $s(x_i, y_j)$,

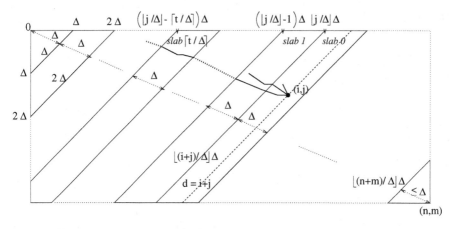

Fig. 1. Slabs with respect to diagonal d, and alignments ending at node (i, j) starting at different slabs

whereas from nodes $(i - 1, j)$ or $(i, j - 1)$ adds 1 to the length and $-\mu$ to the score of the resulting alignment. There are two cases:

(1) If the current node (i, j) is not on the first diagonal after a boundary then nodes $(i - 1, j)$, $(i - 1, j - 1)$ and $(i, j - 1)$ share the same slabs with node (i, j). In this case $(\mathcal{S}_{i,j,k}, \mathcal{L}_{i,j,k})$ is calculated by using $(\mathcal{S}_{i-1,j,k}, \mathcal{L}_{i-1,j,k})$, $(\mathcal{S}_{i-1,j-1,k}, \mathcal{L}_{i-1,j-1,k})$, and $(\mathcal{S}_{i,j-1,k}, \mathcal{L}_{i,j-1,k})$ as shown in Step 2.*b* where $(\mathcal{S}_{i-1,j-1,k}, \mathcal{L}_{i-1,j-1,k}) \oplus (s(x_i, y_j), 2) = (\mathcal{S}_{i-1,j-1,k} + s(x_i, y_j), \mathcal{L}_{i-1,j-1,k} + 2)$ if $\mathcal{S}_{i-1,j-1,k} > 0$ or $k = 0$; and $(0, 0)$ otherwise. This is because, by definition, every local alignment has a positive score, and it is either a single match, or it is an extension of an alignment whose score is positive. Therefore we do not let an alignment with no score be extended unless the resulting alignment is a single match in the current slab.

(2) If the current node is on the first diagonal following a boundary (i.e. $i + j$ mod $\Delta = 1$) then the slabs for the nodes involved in the computations for node (i, j) differ as shown in Figure 3. In this case slab k for node (i, j) is slab $k - 1$ for nodes $(i - 1, j)$, $(i - 1, j - 1)$ and $(i, j - 1)$. Moreover any alignment ending at (i, j) starting at slab 0 for (i, j) can only include one of the edges $((i - 1, j), (i, j))$ or $((i - 1, j - 1), (i, j))$ both of which have negative weight $-\mu$. Therefore, $(\mathcal{S}_{i,j,0}, \mathcal{L}_{i,j,0})$ is set to $(0, 0)$. Steps 2.*a*.1 and 2.*a*.2 show the calculation of $(\mathcal{S}_{i,j,k}, \mathcal{L}_{i,j,k})$ respectively for $0 < k < \lceil t/\Delta \rceil$ and for $k = \lceil t/\Delta \rceil$.

The running maximum score $\widehat{LAt}$ is updated whenever a newly computed score for an alignment with length $\geq t - \Delta$ is larger than the current maximum which can only happen with alignments starting in or before slab $\lceil t/\Delta \rceil - 1$. The final value $\widehat{LAt}$ is returned in Step 3. The alignment position achieving this score may also be desired. This can be done by maintaining for each optimal alignment a start and end position information besides its score and length. In

Algorithm $APX\text{-}LAt(\delta, \mu)$
1. Initialization:
   set $\widehat{LAt} = 0$
   set $(\mathcal{S}_{0,j,k}, \mathcal{L}_{0,j,k}) = (0,0)$ for all j, k, $0 \leq j \leq m$, and $0 \leq k \leq \lceil t/\Delta \rceil$
2. Main computations:
   for $i = 1$ to n do
   {
     set $(\mathcal{S}_{i,0,k}, \mathcal{L}_{i,0,k}) = (0,0)$ for all k, $0 \leq k \leq \lceil t/\Delta \rceil$
     for $j = 1$ to m do
     {
       if $(i + j \bmod \Delta = 1)$ then
       {
         set $(\mathcal{S}_{i,j,0}, \mathcal{L}_{i,j,0}) = (0,0)$
         for $k = 1$ to $\lceil t/\Delta \rceil - 1$ do

2.a.1   set $(\mathcal{S}_{i,j,k}, \mathcal{L}_{i,j,k}) = \mathrm{maxp}\{\ (0,0),\ (\mathcal{S}_{i-1,j,k-1}, \mathcal{L}_{i-1,j,k-1}) + (-\mu, 1),$
$(\mathcal{S}_{i-1,j-1,k-1}, \mathcal{L}_{i-1,j-1,k-1}) \oplus (s(x_i, y_j), 2),$
$(\mathcal{S}_{i,j-1,k-1}, \mathcal{L}_{i,j-1,k-1}) + (-\mu, 1)\ \}$

         for $k = \lceil t/\Delta \rceil$

2.a.2   set $(\mathcal{S}_{i,j,k}, \mathcal{L}_{i,j,k}) = \mathrm{maxp}\{\ (0,0),\ (\mathcal{S}_{i-1,j,k-1}, \mathcal{L}_{i-1,j,k-1}) + (-\mu, 1),$
$(\mathcal{S}_{i-1,j-1,k-1}, \mathcal{L}_{i-1,j-1,k-1}) \oplus (s(x_i, y_j), 2),$
$(\mathcal{S}_{i,j-1,k-1}, \mathcal{L}_{i,j-1,k-1}) + (-\mu, 1),$
$(\mathcal{S}_{i-1,j,k}, \mathcal{L}_{i-1,j,k}) + (-\mu, 1),$
$(\mathcal{S}_{i-1,j-1,k}, \mathcal{L}_{i-1,j-1,k}) \oplus (s(x_i, y_j), 2),$
$(\mathcal{S}_{i,j-1,k}, \mathcal{L}_{i,j-1,k}) + (-\mu, 1)\ \}$

       } else
       {
         for $k = 0$ to $\lceil t/\Delta \rceil$ do

2.b   set $(\mathcal{S}_{i,j,k}, \mathcal{L}_{i,j,k}) = \mathrm{maxp}\{\ (0,0),\ (\mathcal{S}_{i-1,j,k}, \mathcal{L}_{i-1,j,k}) + (-\mu, 1),$
$(\mathcal{S}_{i-1,j-1,k}, \mathcal{L}_{i-1,j-1,k}) \oplus (s(x_i, y_j), 2),$
$(\mathcal{S}_{i,j-1,k}, \mathcal{L}_{i,j-1,k}) + (-\mu, 1)\ \}$
       }
       for $k = \lceil t/\Delta \rceil - 1$ if $\mathcal{L}_{i,j,k} \geq t - \Delta$ then set $\widehat{LAt} = \max\{\widehat{LAt}, \mathcal{S}_{i,j,k}\}$
       for $k = \lceil t/\Delta \rceil$ set $\widehat{LAt} = \max\{\widehat{LAt}, \mathcal{S}_{i,j,k}\}$
     }
   }
3. Return $\widehat{LAt}$

Fig. 2. Algorithm $APX\text{-}LAt$

this case in addition to the running maximum score, the start and end positions of a maximal alignment should be stored and updated.

We first show that $\mathcal{S}_{i,j,k}$ calculated by the algorithm is the optimum score achievable and $\mathcal{L}_{i,j,k}$ is the length of an alignment achieving this score over the set of all alignments ending at node (i, j) and starting with respect to diagonal $i + j$: 1) at slab k for $0 \leq k < \lceil t/\Delta \rceil$, 2) in or before slab k for $k = \lceil t/\Delta \rceil$. This claim can be proved by induction. If we assume that the claim is true for nodes $(i - 1, j)$, $(i - 1, j - 1)$ and $(i, j - 1)$, and for their slabs, then we can easily see

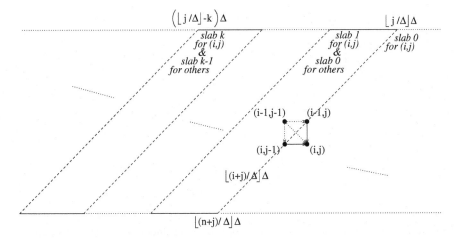

Fig. 3. Relative numbering of the slabs with respect to (i,j), $(i-1,j)$, $(i-1,j-1)$ and $(i,j-1)$ when node (i,j) is on the first diagonal following boundary $\lfloor (i+j)/\Delta \rfloor$

by following Step 2 of the algorithm that the claim holds for node (i,j) and its slabs.

Let optimum score LAt^* for the alignments of length $\geq t$ be achieved at node (i,j). Consider the calculations of the algorithm at (i,j) at which an optimal alignment ends. There are two possible orientations of an optimal alignment as shown in Figure 4: 1) It starts at some node (i',j') of slab $k = \lceil t/\Delta \rceil - 1$. By our previous claim an alignment starting at slab k with score $\mathcal{S}_{i,j,k} \geq LAt^*$ is captured in Step 2. The length of this alignment $\mathcal{L}_{i,j,k}$ is at least $t - \Delta$ since the length of the optimal alignment is $\geq t$, and both start at the same slab and end at (i,j). 2) It starts at some node (i'',j'') in or before slab $k = \lceil t/\Delta \rceil$. Again by the previous claim an alignment starting in or before slab k with score $\mathcal{S}_{i,j,k} \geq LAt^*$ is captured in Step 2. The length of this alignment $\mathcal{L}_{i,j,k}$ is at least $t - \Delta$ since slab k is at distance $\geq t - \Delta$ from (i,j). Therefore the final value $\widehat{LAt}$ returned in Step 3 is $\geq LAt^*$ and it is achieved by an alignment whose length is $\geq t - \Delta$. We summarize these results in the following theorem.

Theorem 1. *For a feasible LAt problem, Algorithm APX-LAt returns an alignment* $(\widehat{I}, \widehat{J})$ *such that* $s(\widehat{I}, \widehat{J}) \geq LAt^*$ *and* $|\widehat{I}| + |\widehat{J}| \geq (1 - \frac{1}{r})t$ *for any* $r > 1$. *The algorithm's complexity is* $O(rnm)$ *time and* $O(rm)$ *space.*

Proof. Algorithm *APX-LAt* is similar to the Smith-Waterman algorithm except that at each node instead of a single score, $\lceil t/\Delta \rceil + 1$ entries for score-length pairs are stored and manipulated. Therefore the resulting complexity exceeds that of the Smith-Waterman algorithm by a factor of $\lceil t/\Delta \rceil + 1$. That is, the time complexity of *APX-LAt* is $O(nmt/\Delta)$. The algorithm requires $O(mt/\Delta)$ space

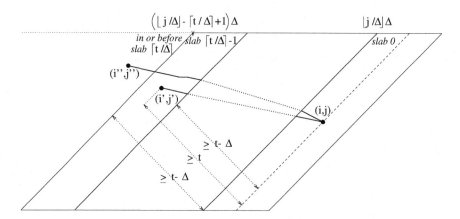

Fig. 4. Two possible orientations of an optimal alignment of length $\geq t$ ending at (i,j): it starts either at some (i',j') at slab $\lceil t/\Delta \rceil - 1$, or (i'',j'') in or before slab $\lceil t/\Delta \rceil$

since we need the entries in the previous and the current row to calculate the entries in the current row. When the LAt problem is feasible, it is guaranteed that Algorithm $APX\text{-}LAt$ returns an alignment $(\widehat{I}, \widehat{J})$ such that $s(\widehat{I}, \widehat{J}) \geq LAt^* > 0$ and $|\widehat{I}| + |\widehat{J}| \geq t - \Delta$ for any positive Δ. Therefore setting $\Delta = \lfloor t/r \rfloor$ for a choice of r, $1 < r \leq t$, and using Algorithm $APX\text{-}LAt$ we can achieve the approximation and complexity results expressed in the theorem. We also note that for $\Delta = 1$ the algorithm becomes a dynamic programming algorithm extending the dimension by storing all possible alignment lengths.

4 Finding Long Alignments with High Normalized Score

We consider the problem Qt of finding two subsequences with normalized score higher than λ, and total length at least t. More formally

$$Qt: \text{ find } (I,J) \text{ such that } I \subseteq X, J \subseteq Y, \ \frac{s(I,J)}{|I| + |J|} > \lambda \text{ and } |I| + |J| \geq t \quad (4)$$

We note that Qt is feasible iff $NLAt^* > \lambda$. We present an approximation algorithm which provided that Qt is feasible finds two subsequences $\widehat{I} \subseteq X$, and $\widehat{J} \subseteq Y$ with normalized score higher than λ, and $|\widehat{I}| + |\widehat{J}| \geq (1 - \frac{1}{r})t$.

Let AVt denote the *set of alignment vectors* between X and Y where (x, y, z) is an *alignment vector* if there is an alignment between subsequences $I \subseteq X$ and $J \subseteq Y$ with x matches, y mismatches, and z indels such that $|I| + |J| \geq t$. Then $s(I, J)$ and length $|I| + |J|$ are linear functions over AVt. Problems LAt and $NLAt$ can be rewritten as follows :

$$LAt_{\delta,\mu} \quad : maximize \; x - \delta y - \mu z \;\; s.t. \; (x, y, z) \in AVt$$
$$NLAt_{\delta,\mu} : maximize \; \tfrac{x-\delta y-\mu z}{2x+2y+z} \qquad s.t. \; (x, y, z) \in AVt$$

Also for a given λ, we have *the parametric local alignment with length threshold problem $LAt(\lambda)$*

$$LAt_{\delta,\mu}(\lambda) : maximize \; x - \delta y - \mu z \; - \; \lambda(2x + 2y + z) \;\; s.t. \; (x, y, z) \in AVt$$

A parametric local alignment with length threshold problem can be described in terms of a local alignment with length threshold problem.

Proposition 1. *For $\lambda \neq \frac{1}{2}$, the optimum value $LAt^*(\lambda)$ of the parametric LAt problem can be formulated in terms of the optimum value LAt^* of an LAt problem.*

Proof. The optimum value of the parametric problem, when $\lambda \neq \frac{1}{2}$, is

$$LAt^*(\lambda) = (1 - 2\lambda)LAt^*_{\delta',\mu'} \text{ where } \delta' = \frac{\delta + 2\lambda}{1 - 2\lambda}, \; \mu' = \frac{\mu + \lambda}{1 - 2\lambda} \, . \qquad (5)$$

Thus, computing $LAt^*(\lambda)$ involves solving the local alignment problem $LAt_{\delta',\mu'}$, and performing some simple arithmetic afterward.

We assume without loss of generality that for any alignment the score does not exceed the number of matches. Therefore for any alignment vector, its normalized score $\lambda \leq \frac{1}{2}$. We consider $\lambda = \frac{1}{2}$ as a special case since it can only happen when the alignment is composed of matches only.

An optimal solution to a ratio optimization problem $NLAt$ can be achieved via a series of optimal solutions of the parametric problem with different parameters $LAt(\lambda)$. In fact $\lambda = NLAt^*$ iff $LAt^*(\lambda) = 0$. Details for a very similar result can be found in [5].

Proposition 2. *When solving $LAt(\lambda)$, Algorithm APX-LAt returns an alignment $(\widehat{I}, \widehat{J})$ with normalized score higher than λ, and $|\widehat{I}| + |\widehat{J}| \geq (1 - \frac{1}{r})t$ if Problem Qt is feasible.*

Proof. Assume that Problem Qt is feasible. Then $NLAt^* > \lambda$, and therefore $LAt^*(\lambda) > 0$ which implies that Algorithm APX-LAt with parameters δ' and μ' (of Proposition 1) returns an alignment $(\widehat{I}, \widehat{J})$ such that its score is positive (i.e. $s(\widehat{I}, \widehat{J}) - \lambda(|\widehat{I}| + |\widehat{J}|) > 0$, or equivalently its normalized score is higher than λ) and $|\widehat{I}| + |\widehat{J}| \geq (1 - \frac{1}{r})t$ by the approximation results of Algorithm APX-LAt .

Theorem 2. *If $NLAt^* > 0$ then an alignment with normalized score at least $NLAt^*$, and total length at least $(1 - \frac{1}{r})t$ can be computed for any $r > 1$ in time $O(rnm \log n)$, and using $O(rm)$ space.*

```
Algorithm APX-RationalNLAt
If there is an exact match of size (1 − 1/r)t then return(1/2) and exit
σ ← 1/(qs(m+n)²) where δ = p/q, and μ = r/s
[e, f] ← [0, 1/2 σ⁻¹]
λ* ← 0
While (e + 1 < f) do
   k ← ⌈(e + f)/2⌉
     If APX-LAt(kσ) > 0 then {e ← k, and λ* ← (x−δy−μz)/(2x+2y+z) for (x, y, z) optimal
   }
     else f ← k
End {while}
Return(λ*)
```

Fig. 5. Algorithm *APX-RationalNLAt* for rational scores

```
Algorithm Dinkelbach
If APX-LAt(0) ≤ 0 then return(0) and exit
λ* ← (x−δy−μz)/(2x+2y+z) where (x, y, z) is optimal for APX-LAt(0)
Repeat
     λ ← λ*
     if APX-LAt(λ) > 0 then λ* ← (x−δy−μz)/(2x+2y+z) for (x, y, z) optimal
Until λ* ≤ λ
Return(λ*)
```

Fig. 6. Dinkelbach algorithm for *NLAt*

Proof. Algorithm *RationalNLAt* given in Figure 5 accomplishes this. The algorithm is based on a binary search for optimum normalized score over an interval of integers. This takes $O(\log n)$ parametric problems to solve. The algorithm is similar to the *RationalNLA* algorithm in [5], and the results are derived similarly.

If $NLAt^* > 0$ then we can also achieve the same approximation guarantee by using a Dinkelbach algorithm given in [5] as the template. The details of the resulting algorithm are presented in Figure 6. Solutions of the parametric problems through the iterations yield improved (higher) values to λ except for the last iteration. The resulting algorithm performs no more than $3 - 5$ iterations on the average as experiments suggest.

Our approximation and complexity results hold for two particularly important cases of scoring schemes: *affine gap penalties*, and *arbitrary scoring matrices*. We can develop variants of Algorithm *APX-LAt* for these scoring schemes with simple modifications. In the case of arbitrary scoring matrices, penalties depend on individual symbols involved in the operations. Varying penalties can easily be incorporated in the dynamic programming formulation. In the case of affine gap penalties, the total penalty of a *gap* (a block of insertions, or a block of deletions) of size k is $\alpha + k\beta$ where α, and β are the *gap open penalty*, and the *gap extension penalty*, respectively. Affine gap penalties require a slightly different dynamic programming formulation than the one given for basic scoring scheme (1). It can be described as follows ([9]) : Let $\mathcal{E}_{i,j} = \mathcal{F}_{i,j} = \mathcal{S}_{i,j} = 0$ when i or j is 0 then define

$$\mathcal{E}_{i,j} = \max\{\mathcal{S}_{i,j-1} - \alpha, \ \mathcal{E}_{i,j-1} - \beta\},$$
$$\mathcal{F}_{i,j} = \max\{\mathcal{S}_{i-1,j} - \alpha, \ \mathcal{F}_{i-1,j} - \beta\},$$
$$\mathcal{S}_{i,j} = \max\{0, \ \mathcal{S}_{i-1,j-1} + s(x_i, y_j), \ \mathcal{E}_{i,j}, \ \mathcal{F}_{i,j}\} \tag{6}$$

Affine gap penalties do not increase the complexity of the local alignment problem, i.e. the problem can be solved in time $O(nm)$ and using $O(m)$ space. Figure 7 shows the variant of Algorithm *APX-LAt* for affine gap penalties. The approximation and complexity results expressed in Theorem 1 can be obtained by Algorithm *APX-LAt-AFFINE* for affine gap penalties.

We can verify that in both cases of these scoring schemes a parametric *LAt* problem can easily be formulated in terms of an *LAt* problem. We can develop variants of *NLAt* algorithms for them such that the same approximation and complexity results hold.

5   Implementation and Test Results

We have implemented versions of Algorithm *APX-LAt* and *Dinkelbach* for affine gap penalties and tested our *Dinkelbach* program on *bli-4* locus in *C. elegans* and *C.briggsae* for various values of parameters t and r. We have observed that the program performs $3 - 5$ invocations of *APX-LAt* implementation on the average. Therefore for reasonable choice of r its time requirement is $3r$ to $5r$ times that of a Smith-Waterman implementation on the average. In Figure 9, we include results for optimal alignments obtained as t runs from $1,000$ to $22,000$ in increments of $1,000$, and from $30,000$ to $90,000$ in increments of $10,000$, and for fixed $r = 5$. On a Beowulf class super-computer which is composed of a cluster of 42 linux-based 400-500 Mhz workstations it took about 8 days to complete the tests. We note that we could use a fast heuristic algorithm to solve the parametric local alignment problems and improve the running time by orders of magnitude, but then the approximation guarantee of the results no longer holds.

We have used a score of 1 for a match, -1 for a mismatch, and $-6 - 0.2k$ for a gap of length k. In Figure 9, we have multiplied the normalized scores by $10,000$ to be able to display them on the same scale as the ordinary scores. As expected in general, normalized scores steadily decrease with the increasing alignment lengths. The alignments whose lengths exceed $32,100$ include regions with very poor scores.

Test runs like this can generate important statistical information. For instance in this case we can infer from our approximation results and from the normalized score 0.33 of the alignment with length $16,048$ that 0.33 cannot be obtained by any alignment whose length exceeds $16,048/(1 - 1/5) \approx 20,000$.

Algorithm $APX\text{-}LAt\text{-}AFFINE(\delta, \alpha, \beta)$

1. **Initialization:**
   set $\widehat{LAt} = 0$
   set $(\mathcal{E}_{0,j,k}, \mathcal{L}^{\mathcal{E}}_{0,j,k}) = (\mathcal{F}_{0,j,k}, \mathcal{L}^{\mathcal{F}}_{0,j,k}) = (\mathcal{S}_{0,j,k}, \mathcal{L}^{\mathcal{S}}_{0,j,k}) = (0,0)$
       for all j, k, $0 \le j \le m$, $0 \le k \le \lceil t/\Delta \rceil$

2. **Main computations :**
   for $i = 1$ to n do {
     set $(\mathcal{E}_{i,0,k}, \mathcal{L}^{\mathcal{E}}_{i,0,k}) = (\mathcal{F}_{i,0,k}, \mathcal{L}^{\mathcal{F}}_{i,0,k}) = (\mathcal{S}_{i,0,k}, \mathcal{L}^{\mathcal{S}}_{i,0,k}) = (0,0)$
         for all k, $0 \le k \le \lceil t/\Delta \rceil$
     for $j = 1$ to m do {
       if $(i + j \bmod \Delta = 1)$ then {
         set $(\mathcal{E}_{i,j,0}, \mathcal{L}^{\mathcal{E}}_{i,j,0}) = (\mathcal{F}_{i,j,0}, \mathcal{L}^{\mathcal{F}}_{i,j,0}) = (\mathcal{S}_{i,j,0}, \mathcal{L}^{\mathcal{S}}_{i,j,0}) = (0,0)$
         for $k = 1$ to $\lceil t/\Delta \rceil - 1$ do {
           set $(\mathcal{E}_{i,j,k}, \mathcal{L}^{\mathcal{E}}_{i,j,k}) = \max\{\ (\mathcal{S}_{i,j-1,k-1}, \mathcal{L}^{\mathcal{S}}_{i,j-1,k-1}) + (-\alpha, 1),$
                                    $(\mathcal{E}_{i,j-1,k-1}, \mathcal{L}^{\mathcal{E}}_{i,j-1,k-1}) + (-\beta, 1)\ \}$
           set $(\mathcal{F}_{i,j,k}, \mathcal{L}^{\mathcal{F}}_{i,j,k}) = \max\{\ (\mathcal{S}_{i-1,j,k-1}, \mathcal{L}^{\mathcal{S}}_{i-1,j,k-1}) + (-\alpha, 1),$
                                    $(\mathcal{F}_{i-1,j,k-1}, \mathcal{L}^{\mathcal{F}}_{i-1,j,k-1}) + (-\beta, 1)\ \}$
           set $(\mathcal{S}_{i,j,k}, \mathcal{L}^{\mathcal{S}}_{i,j,k}) = \max\{\ (0,0),$
                                    $(\mathcal{S}_{i-1,j-1,k-1}, \mathcal{L}^{\mathcal{S}}_{i-1,j-1,k-1}) \oplus (s(x_i, y_j), 2),$
                                    $(\mathcal{E}_{i,j,k}, \mathcal{L}^{\mathcal{E}}_{i,j,k}),\ (\mathcal{F}_{i,j,k}, \mathcal{L}^{\mathcal{F}}_{i,j,k})\ \}$
         }
         for $k = \lceil t/\Delta \rceil$ do {
           set $(\mathcal{E}_{i,j,k}, \mathcal{L}^{\mathcal{E}}_{i,j,k}) = \max\{\ (\mathcal{S}_{i,j-1,k-1}, \mathcal{L}^{\mathcal{S}}_{i,j-1,k-1}) + (-\alpha, 1),$
                                    $(\mathcal{E}_{i,j-1,k-1}, \mathcal{L}^{\mathcal{E}}_{i,j-1,k-1}) + (-\beta, 1),$
                                    $(\mathcal{S}_{i,j-1,k}, \mathcal{L}^{\mathcal{S}}_{i-1,j,k}) + (-\alpha, 1),$
                                    $(\mathcal{E}_{i,j-1,k}, \mathcal{L}^{\mathcal{E}}_{i,j-1,k}) + (-\beta, 1)\ \}$
           set $(\mathcal{F}_{i,j,k}, \mathcal{L}^{\mathcal{F}}_{i,j,k}) = \max\{\ (\mathcal{S}_{i-1,j,k-1}, \mathcal{L}^{\mathcal{S}}_{i-1,j,k-1}) + (-\alpha, 1),$
                                    $(\mathcal{F}_{i-1,j,k-1}, \mathcal{L}^{\mathcal{F}}_{i-1,j,k-1}) + (-\beta, 1),$
                                    $(\mathcal{S}_{i-1,j,k}, \mathcal{L}^{\mathcal{S}}_{i-1,j,k}) + (-\alpha, 1),$
                                    $(\mathcal{F}_{i-1,j,k}, \mathcal{L}^{\mathcal{F}}_{i-1,j,k}) + (-\beta, 1)\ \}$
           set $(\mathcal{S}_{i,j,k}, \mathcal{L}^{\mathcal{S}}_{i,j,k}) = \max\{\ (0,0),$
                                    $(\mathcal{S}_{i-1,j-1,k-1}, \mathcal{L}^{\mathcal{S}}_{i-1,j-1,k-1}) \oplus (s(x_i, y_j), 2),$
                                    $(\mathcal{S}_{i-1,j-1,k}, \mathcal{L}^{\mathcal{S}}_{i-1,j-1,k}) \oplus (s(x_i, y_j), 2),$
                                    $(\mathcal{E}_{i,j,k}, \mathcal{L}^{\mathcal{E}}_{i,j,k}),\ (\mathcal{F}_{i,j,k}, \mathcal{L}^{\mathcal{F}}_{i,j,k})\ \}$
         }
       }
     }
   ...

Fig. 7. Algorithm $APX\text{-}LAt\text{-}AFFINE$. The algorithm continues in Figure 8

6 Conclusion

We have developed an algorithm for finding sufficiently long similar subsequences in two sequences of lengths n and m respectively, with $n \ge m$. Given thresholds λ and t the proposed algorithm finds an alignment with a normalized score higher than λ and with total length no smaller than $(1 - \frac{1}{r})t$, provided that the corresponding normalized local alignment problem is feasible. The length of the

$$\begin{aligned}
&\text{else } \{ \\
&\quad \text{for } k = 0 \text{ to } \lceil t/\Delta \rceil \text{ do } \{ \\
&\qquad \text{set } (\mathcal{E}_{i,j,k}, \mathcal{L}^{\mathcal{E}}_{i,j,k}) = \max\{ \ (\mathcal{S}_{i,j-1,k}, \mathcal{L}^{\mathcal{S}}_{i,j-1,k}) + (-\alpha, 1), \\
&\qquad\qquad\qquad\qquad\qquad\qquad (\mathcal{E}_{i,j-1,k}, \mathcal{L}^{\mathcal{E}}_{i,j-1,k}) + (-\beta, 1) \ \} \\
&\qquad \text{set } (\mathcal{F}_{i,j,k}, \mathcal{L}^{\mathcal{F}}_{i,j,k}) = \max\{ \ (\mathcal{S}_{i-1,j,k}, \mathcal{L}^{\mathcal{S}}_{i-1,j,k}) + (-\alpha, 1), \\
&\qquad\qquad\qquad\qquad\qquad\qquad (\mathcal{F}_{i-1,j,k}, \mathcal{L}^{\mathcal{F}}_{i-1,j,k}) + (-\beta, 1) \ \} \\
&\qquad \text{set } \ (\mathcal{S}_{i,j,k}, \mathcal{L}^{\mathcal{S}}_{i,j,k}) \ = \ \max\{ \ (0,0), \ (\mathcal{S}_{i-1,j-1,k}, \mathcal{L}^{\mathcal{S}}_{i-1,j-1,k}) \ \oplus \\
&(s(x_i, y_j), 2), \\
&\qquad\qquad\qquad\qquad\qquad (\mathcal{E}_{i,j,k}, \mathcal{L}^{\mathcal{E}}_{i,j,k}), \ (\mathcal{F}_{i,j,k}, \mathcal{L}^{\mathcal{F}}_{i,j,k}) \ \} \\
&\quad \} \\
&\} \\
&\quad \text{for } k = \lceil t/\Delta \rceil - 1 \text{ if } \mathcal{L}^{\mathcal{E}}_{i,j,k} \geq t - \Delta \text{ then set } \widehat{LAt} = \max\{\widehat{LAt}, \mathcal{S}_{i,j,k}\} \\
&\quad \text{for } k = \lceil t/\Delta \rceil \text{ set } \widehat{LAt} = \max\{\widehat{LAt}, \mathcal{S}_{i,j,k}\} \\
&\} \\
&\} \\
&\text{3. Return } LAt^*
\end{aligned}$$

Fig. 8. Continuation of Algorithm $APX\text{-}LAt\text{-}AFFINE$ from Figure 7

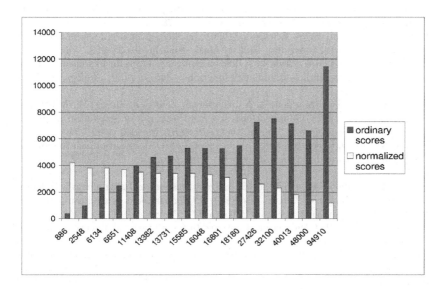

Fig. 9. Ordinary versus normalized scores on $bli\text{-}4$ locus in *C. elegans* and *C.briggsae* when score of a match is 1, mismatch score is -1, and score for a gap of length k is $-6 - 0.2k$

result can be made arbitrarily close to t by increasing r. This is done at the expense of allocating more resources as the time and space complexities depend on the parameter r as $O(rnm)$ and $O(rm)$ respectively.

Based on the techniques previously proposed in [5], and using the approximation algorithm we present in this paper, we have further developed ways to find an alignment with normalized score no smaller than the maximum normalized score achievable by alignments with length at least t. The alignment returned by the algorithm is guaranteed to have total length $\geq (1 - \frac{1}{r})t$. In our experiments we have observed that the time requirement of the Dinkelbach implementation is $O(rnm)$ on the average. This is better compared to the worst-case time complexity $O(n^2m)$ of the naive algorithm.

We believe that our approximation algorithms have made normalized scores a viable similarity measure in pairwise local alignment as they provide approximate control over the desired alignment lengths. Since the computed normalized score for a particular value of t is an upper bound for the actual normalized scores achievable by sequences of length at least t, these algorithms can also be used to collect statistics about scores of alignments versus length for a particular pair of input sequences.

References

[1] N. N. Alexandrov and V. V. Solovyev. (1998) Statistical significance of ungapped alignments. *Pacific Symposium on Biocomputing (PSB-98), (eds. R. Altman, A. Dunker, L. Hunter, T. Klein)*, pp. 463–472. 78

[2] S. F. Altschul and B. W. Erickson. (1986) Locally optimal subalignments using nonlinear similarity functions. *Bull. of Math. Biology*, 48:633–660. 78

[3] S. F. Altschul and B. W. Erickson. (1988) Significance levels for biological sequence comparison using nonlinear similarity functions. *Bull. of Math. Biology*, 50:77–92. 78

[4] S. F. Altschul, T. L. Madden, A. A. Schaffer, J. Zhang, Z. Zhang, W. Miller, and D. J. Lipman. (1997) Gapped Blast and Psi-Blast: a new generation of protein database search programs. *Nucleic Acids Research*, 25:3389–3402. 77

[5] A. N. Arslan, Ö. Eğecioğlu, and P. A. Pevzner. (2001) A new approach to sequence comparison: Normalized local alignment. *Bioinformatics*, 17(4):327–337. 77, 78, 79, 85, 86, 90

[6] A. N. Arslan and Ö. Eğecioğlu. (2001) Algorithms for local alignments with length constraints. *Technical Report TRCS2001-17*, Department of Computer Science, University of California at Santa Barbara. 77, 78, 80

[7] N. Megiddo. (1979) Combinatorial optimization with rational objective functions. *Mathematics of Operations Research*, 4:414–424.

[8] T. F. Smith and M. S. Waterman. (1981) The identification of common molecular subsequences. *J. Mol. Biol.*, 147, 195–197. 79

[9] M. S. Waterman. (1995) *Introduction to computational biology*. Chapman & Hall. 78, 79, 87

[10] Z. Zhang, P. Berman, and W. Miller. (1998) Alignments without low-scoring regions. *J. Comput. Biol.*, 5:197–200. 77

[11] Z. Zhang, P. Berman, T. Wiehe, and W. Miller. (1999) Post-processing long pairwise alignments. *Bioinformatics*, 15:1012–1019. 77

Stemming Galician Texts[*]

Nieves R. Brisaboa[1], Carlos Callón[2], Juan-Ramón López[1],
Ángeles S. Places[1], and Goretti Sanmartín[2]

[1] Laboratorio de Bases de Datos. Departamento de Computación.
brisaboa@udc.es
asplaces@mail2.udc.es
mon@dc.fi.udc.es
[2] Departamento de Galego-Portugués, Francés e Lingüística
Universidade da Coruña
cmct@megamail.pt
goretti@udc.es

Abstract. In this paper we describe a stemming algorithm for Galician language, which supports, at the same time, the four current orthographic regulations for Galician. The algorithm has already been implemented, and we have started to use it for its improvement. But this stemming algorithm cannot be applied over documents previous to the appearance of the first Galician orthographic regulation in 1977; therefore we have adopted an *exhaustive approach*, consisting in defining a huge collection of *wordsets* for allowing systematic word comparisons, to stem documents written before that date. We also describe here a tool to build the wordsets needed in this approach.

Keywords. Stemming, Digital Libraries, Text Retrieval

1   Introduction

Galician is the language spoken in Galicia, a region in the northwest of Spain. It is a language very close to Portuguese. They present a common syntactic, morphological and lexical base, but also many differences, especially in phonetics.

Galician and Portuguese used to be the same until the 14th century, when Portugal and Spain became different states and Galicia remained within the Spanish territory. Then, Galician entered a decline period suffering a sharp demotion for three centuries (16th-18th). Nevertheless, it continued being used, but its exclusively oral use caused a strong dialectalization. During the 19th century took place the literary, cultural, political and historical recovery of Galician. Writers of this age had to "invent" their own orthographic regulations, all of them strongly influenced by the Spanish ones. Unfortunately, the Civil War and the start of Franco's regime led to the disappearance

---

[*]   This work was partially granted by CICYT (TEL99-0335-C04-02) and the Vicerrectorado de Innovación Tecnolóxica (University of A Coruña).

A.H.F. Laender and A.L. Oliveira (Eds.): SPIRE 2002, LNCS 2476, pp. 91-97, 2002.
© Springer-Verlag Berlin Heidelberg 2002

of Galician from the public area, from education and from socio-economic activities. In the last years of the 20th century, with the new legal framework, it became alive again, being protected by law. Since 1977, an official orthographic regulation exists but having a lot of political implications, it has not been accepted by a lot of Galician writers and philologists, who have proposed and support two other different alternative regulations [[8]]. Therefore, four[1] orthographic regulations exist nowadays [[7]].

All of these conditions have produced the inclusion of Galician into the European Committee entitled *European Lesser Used Languages* [[4], [5]], and the UNESCO's list of 3,000 world endangered languages [[18]]. Besides, the absence nowadays of a language in the new technologies domain, in general, and in the Internet, in particular, increases its probability of disappearing. This two asserts lead us into an immediate conclusion: the presence of the Galician language in Internet is absolutely necessary.

In this direction, the *Galician Virtual Library* (BVG) project [[1]] has been started with the aim of promoting the use of the Galician language and spreading our literature and culture all over Internet. The first result of this effort has been a Web Portal with the same name [[1]], including a Virtual Library (containing not only a catalogue of Galician authors and works – as any literature encyclopaedia - but also hundreds of text, sound and video documents[2]). The Portal is fully described in [[2]].

The availability of a wide collection of Galician literature from all periods, which is in continuous growth, makes our Virtual Library an ideal source of information and resources for researchers and teachers of Galician language and literature. Taking this into account, it makes sense the consideration of a new research line in the BVG project, in order to provide our Library with text retrieval capabilities.

In this paper, a stemming algorithm is presented which supports, at the same time, the four current Galician orthographic regulations (to the best of our knowledge, an interesting and innovative approach). Sadly, our stemmer cannot be applied over documents previous to the appearance of the first Galician orthographic regulation in 1977. For texts produced before that date, an *exhaustive approach* is the only possible solution, defining a wide collection of *wordsets* for allowing systematic word comparisons.

The rest of this paper is organized as follows. Section 2 describes the two strategies we have chosen to provide BVG with text retrieval capabilities, including our stemming algorithm. Last section gives the conclusions and the directions for future work.

2   Stemming Strategies

Summarizing, the first orthographical regulation for the Galician language was defined during the 70's decade. Until then, no unified regulation (neither official nor *de facto*) had been adopted, and Galician authors had been forced to use their own rules (if any), frequently plenty of local or even personal particularities, in their

---

[1]   This includes the Portuguese one, which is the favourite for some of them.
[2]   Our catalogue includes 157 authors and 1975 works. 325 of these works are available for reading, accompanied by 30 audio and 17 video files.

writings. Since then, Galician writers have been using one of the four current orthographic regulations.

Our aim is to provide our Virtual Library with text retrieval capabilities, supporting documents from any historical period. This has leaded us to follow two different strategies: one suitable for documents previous to 1977 and another one for texts after that date. Both strategies are introduced in the following sections.

2.1   Stemming for Documents Previous to 1977

Dealing with documents written without using clear and stable linguistic rules, the use of conventional stemming techniques not practical. The *exhaustive* approach is maybe the only applicable one. It consists in defining a complete collection of *wordsets*, grouping each of them all the different orthographic shapes of a particular word (the wordset *root*) and all its derived forms. So the process of stemming each word of a document is reduced to its comparison against the content of each wordset, determining its correct classification, and thus its corresponding root.

All wordsets must be defined manually, usually from the analysis of a (wide enough) *corpus* of documents. Ambiguity must be taken into account, as a word can correspond, depending on its syntactical class, to more than one wordset: e.g., the Galician word *baixo* should be included into the wordsets *baixo-preposition* (*under* in English), *baixo-adjective* (*low*) and *baixar-verb* (*to walk down*).

In the BVG project, we plan to adapt and reuse a tool previously developed by our *Database Lab.* [[11], [12]] for the study of ancient Spanish documents, and which implements the exhaustive approach. It is organized into two different modules: a **document analysis module**, which processes new documents generating *multi-list indexes* [[15]] to support later text retrieval operations, and allows the semi-automatic refinement of the wordset collection; and a **document study module**, which allows different kinds of searches (*words*, *wordsets*, *sentences*) along the tool's corpus of documents. It is important to remark that ambiguity is not present in the search process, as all document words must have been classified into a particular wordset during the analysis stage.

Considering the adaptation of this tool to the Galician language and its integration into the BVG project, a new full wordset collection is needed. Some Galician philologists are going to start using this tool with the corpus of documents included until now in our virtual library. To ease their task, we plan to improve the analysis module with fully automatic lexical and syntactical analysis functionality. Well-known approaches and techniques from the natural language processing area could be very useful here.

2.2   Galician Stemming Algorithm

The Galician stemming algorithm is closely based on a stemming algorithm for Portuguese language, which has been designed by Viviane Moreira[3] and Christian Huyck. According to their authors this algorithm improves the word stemming with

---

[3]   We are very grateful to Viviane Moreira for her help in the implementation of the Galician stemmer.

regard to the Porter Stemming Algorithm for Portuguese. This comparison and a full description of the algorithm can be found in [[13]].

As stated, most of the words in Galician Language have a wide variety of forms [[8],[14]]. Besides, the Galician language standardization process is not finished yet, and nowadays there are four orthographical and morphological regulations with internal variants (for example, the official normative allows the endings –*bel* and –*ble* for the same word; this is the case of *amabel* and *amábel*) [[7]]. Due to this, the number of rules of the stemming algorithm for the Galician Language is significantly larger than for the Portuguese language.

The Galician stemmer, like the two other stemming algorithms, is based on rules. The syntax of the rules is the following:

Sintax: `"Suffix to replace", "Minimum size of the stem",`
            `"Replacement", "List of exceptions"`
Example: `"axe", 3, "", {coraxe, chantaxe, vantaxe}`

where

- `"Suffix to replace"` is the suffix to be removed. The rule in our example will be applied to words ending in –*axe*.
- `"Minimum size of the stem"`. The rule will be applied only if the length of the resulting stem is greater or equal than this measure. The rule in our example would never be applied to word *"traxe"* (*suit* in English) because the resulting stem would have only two characteres (*"tr-"*). This measure varies for each suffix. The inclusion of this measure in the rules helps to avoid overstemming.
- `"Replacement"`: A replacement suffix to be appended to the stem. This component can be an empty string.
- `"List of exceptions"`: The third condition that a word must fullfil for the rule to be applied. The rule in our example will not be applied to the list of words: *"coraxe"*, *"chantaxe"* and *"vantaxe"* (*courage*, *blackmail* and *advantage*).

So the rule in our example will be applied to words like *"contaxe"* (*recount* in English) because this word ends in –*axe*, its stem is over 3 chars and it is not included in the list of exceptions of the rule.

These rules are organized in eight steps according to the kind of suffixes that they treat. The rules in the steps are examined in sequence and only one rule in a step can be applied. The order of the rules within steps makes the longest suffix is always removed first. For example the plural suffix –*ais* should be tested before the suffix –*s*. The list of rules in each step and the lists of exceptions are not included in this paper due to space limitations. The complete list can be found online in [[9]]. This URL will be up to date with any future refinement of our list.

The sequence in which each step is applied is described below and the set of rules of each step can be found in the appendix of this paper:

Step 1. Plural Suffix Reduction. Only words ending in –*s* are tested in this step. Although the common end of plural forms in Galician language is –*s*, there are another suffixes denoting plural that have been consider. That is the case of the suffix *"is"*, that is replaced with *"il"* like in *fusis* → *fusil* (rifle in English).

Step 2. Adverb Suffix Reduction. There is just one rule in this step, just the one to remove the adverb suffix *–mente*. For example, *eternamente* (eternally) will be reduced to *eterna*.

Step 3. Feminine Suffix Reduction. Galician nouns and adjectives, just like in any other romance language, have a gender. The stemming consists in replacing the feminine suffixes by their corresponding masculine. Only words ended in *-a* are candidates to be stemmed by the rules in this step.

Step 4. Augmentative/Diminutive Suffix Reduction. Galician nouns and adjectives have augmentative, diminutive and superlative forms. Those cases are treated by this step. Due to the number orthographical regulations in Galician Language, the number of rules in this step is very large.

Step 5. Noun Suffix Reduction. This step tests words against noun and adjective endings. If a suffix is removed here, step 6 is not executed.

Step 6. Verb Suffix Reduction. Galician regular verbs have over 50 different forms. Each one has its specific suffix. The verbs can vary according to tense, person, number and mode. Verbal forms are reduced to their root.

Step 7: Accents Removal. Stems of Galician words are accented or not depending on their suffixes. In the cases of *prática* (*practice*) and *pratica* (*he/she practices*), previous steps will produce *prát-* and *prat-*, respectively. After this step both forms would be conflated to *prat*.

2.3   The Exploitation of the Galician Stemming Algorithm

We have already done a first test applying this algorithm to a series of corpus of Galician texts. The corpora are made up of literary texts (from BVG), economic texts, judicial texts, newspaper texts and technologic texts. So we have a representative collection of Galician texts in several fields. For each corpus we have counted the number of different words. Table 1 shows the obteined results.

It has been notice that the number of different words (vocabulary) in the Galician language is larger than it would be hoped for texts of that size (The vocabulary for the same size corpora in Spanish language is considerably smaller). Evidently it is due to dialectalization and the coexistence of four different orthographic normatives since that date.

Using our Galician stemming, the vocabulary was significantly reduced as shown in Table 1. However, due to the inexistence of other stemming algorithms for Galician language, we cannot estimate the eficiency and the quality of our algorithm by compared to others. So we are obliged to manually evaluate the eficiency of the algorithm. Specialists in Galician language will do this test. We hope this evaluation leads in an increase and a refinement of the rules of the algorithm in order to improve its overall working.

Table 1. Vocabulary in Galician texts before and after stemming

Files	Text Size (MB)	#Entries pre-stemming	#Entries post-stemming
ECO	4.0	42,839	18,489
JUS	3.3	32,822	15,319
LIT	13.0	110,722	42,862
NEW	10.0	88,029	38,901
TEC	3.6	45,340	20,438

3   Conclusions and Future Work

We have developed of a Galician stemming algorithm for any Galician text written after 1977 but there is still a long way to go until natural proccessing tools can be built. There are a lot of tools of Linguistic Engeneering that need to be developed (thesaurus of synonyms and antonyms, for example).

On the other hand, we need to build, using the tool described in section 2.1, the whole collection of wordsets needed in the *exhaustive approach*. Only then, we will be able to stem Galician texts previous to 1977.

Once both algorithms are satisfactory enough, we will be able to use them to provide BVG with Text Retrieval capabilities. It is still too early to know which text retrieval technique we are going to use, but whatever our decision is, it is sure it will benefit from these two stemming approaches.

References

[1]   Biblioteca Virtual Galega. http://bvg.udc.es.
[2]   Brisaboa, N. R., Ocaña, E., Penabad, M. R., Places, A. S., Rodríguez, F. J. Biblioteca 7Virtual de Literatura Gallega. In *Proc. of IDEAS'2002*, pp. 68-77. Cuba, 2002.
[3]   Database Lab. http://emilia.dc.fi.udc.es/labBD.
[4]   Euromosaic: The production and reproduction of the minority language groups in the European Union, ISBN 92-827-5512-6, Luxembourg 1996.
[5]   European Bureau for the Lesser Used Languages. http://www.eblul.org.
[6]   Honrado, A., Leon, R., O'Donnell, R. and Sinclair, D. A Word Stemming Algorithm for the Spanish Language. In *Proc. of the SPIRE'2000 – IEEE Computer Society*, pp.139-145, A Coruña, 2000.
[7]   Freixeiro Mato, X. R., *Gramática da lingua galega*, Laiovento, Santiago de Compostela, 1998-2000 (3 vols.).
[8]   Freixeiro Mato, X. R., *Lingua galega: normalidade e conflito*, Laiovento, Santiago de Compostela, 2000.
[9]   Galician Stemmer Rules. http://bvg.udc.es/recursos_lingua/stemming.html.

[10] Kraaij, W., Pohlmann, R. Porter's stemming algorithm for Dutch. In L.G.M. Noordman and W.A.M. de Vroomen, editors, *Informatiewetenschap 1994: Wetenschappelijke bijdragen aan de derde STINFON Conferentie*, pp. 167-180, Tilburg, 1994.

[11] López, J.R., Iglesias, E.L., Brisaboa, N.R., Paramá, J.R., Penabad, M.R. BBDD documental para el estudio del español del S. de Oro. In Proc. of *CIICC'97*, pp. 3-14. México, 1997.

[12] López, J.R., Iglesias, E.L., Brisaboa, N.R., Paramá, J.R., Penabad, M.R. BBDD documental para el estudio del español antiguo. In Proc. of *INFONOR'97*, pp. 2-8., Chile, 1997.

[13] Moreira, V., Huyck, C. A Stemming Algorithm for the Portuguese Language. In *Proc. of SPIRE'2001 – IEEE Computer Society*, pp.186-193, Chile, 2001.

[14] Portas, M., *Língua e sociedade na Galiza*, Bahía, A Coruña.

[15] Smith, P.D. and Barnes, G.M. Files and Databases: An introduction. Addison-Wesley, 1987.

[16] Snowball Project. http://snowball.sourceforge.net.

[17] Wechsler, M., Sheridan, P., Schäuble, P. Multi-Language Text Indexing for Internet Retrieval. In the *Proc. of the 5th RIAO Conference*. Montreal, Canada, 1997.

[18] Wurm, Stephen A. *Atlas of the World's Languages in Danger of Disappearing*. UNESCO Publishing, ISBN 92-3-103798-6.

Firing Policies for an Arabic Rule-Based Stemmer

Imad A. Al Sughaiyer and Ibrahim A. Al Kharashi

Computer and Electronics Research Institute
King Abdulaziz City for Science and Technology
P. O. Box 6086, Riyadh 11442, Saudi Arabia
Tel: 481-3273, Fax: 481-3764
{kharashi,imad}@kacst.edu.sa

Abstract. Processing morphology of Semitic languages requires more complicated systems. Arabic language, for example, exhibits very complex but very regular morphological structure that greatly affect its automation. Many approaches were proposed to analyze Arabic language at the morphological level. This paper studies the rule firing policies for Arabic rule-based stemmer. Proposed firing policies include the single, pair, triple and quadruple approaches. Generalization of these approaches was also investigated.

1   Introduction

Stemming techniques are processes that gather all words sharing the same stem with some semantic relation. Stemming is achieved by removing all possible affixes and thus reduces the word to its stem [1,2]. The major difference between Arabic and most of other languages resides mainly on its complicated, very regular and rich morphological structure. Arabic language is derivational while most of other languages are concatenate. Most of Arabic words are generated based on root-pattern structure. The generation process is highly affected by word morphological characteristics [3,4,5].

Computational Arabic morphology drew the attention during the last two decades. This, consequently, has led to the emerging of some morphological analysis techniques. Some researchers suggested analyzing Arabic words to reach their roots [3] while others suggested analyzing them to their stems only [4], [5]. Analyzing words to their roots is preferred in linguistic-based applications while analyzing words to their stems is more useful in some other applications such as information retrieval systems.

2   Rule-Based Arabic Stemmer

The rule-based stemmers [6,7] utilize the apparent symmetry of generated natural Arabic words to suggest the stem of a given Arabic word. In this approach, a unique regular expression-based rule is generated for group of similar Arabic words. Rules are used to describe the internal morphological structure of Arabic words and guide

A.H.F. Laender and A.L. Oliveira (Eds.): SPIRE 2002, LNCS 2476, pp. 98-103, 2002.
© Springer-Verlag Berlin Heidelberg 2002

the rule parser during the decomposition process of a given word into its main parts [8]. Rule complexity varies from very simple ones to very complicated rules that deal with complex morphological behaviors. Syntax of rules was generated after deep analysis of a data set of about 23000 Arabic words [9]. Of that data set, more than 1200 rules were generated [7] then merged into less than 600 [10]. Table 1 shows a small set of the total generated rules.

Table 1. Small set of sample rules

Rule Id	Applied Rule	Word	Resultant		
			Prefix	Stem	Suffix
1	7.	الـبكـترك		الـبكـترك	
2	<حية>3.<ال>	النارية	ال	نار	ية
3	<ال><أ>2.<أ^ا>.<ة><>	الأتربة	ال	تراب	
4	6.<ة>	متكاملة		متكامل	ة

To process rules and extract word morphological components, a very simple rule parser was developed [8]. The parser tries to match set of rules and a given Arabic word. The matching process is achieved when the parser successively analyzes the word and decomposes it to its valid components according to the parsed rule. A rule is said to be fired if it has the same length as the length of the processed word. A match is achieved if and only if a fired rule produces the correct morphological components. A given word should fire at least one rule and match only one rule.

Order of rule firing plays an important role in the correctness and the efficiency of the analyzer. For a given word, it is desirable to fire less number of rules and to maintain firing order in such a way that first fired rule is the matched one. Fig. 1 shows the firing behavior of the stemmer for the set of rules arranged according to their generation order [7]. Despite the uncontrolled list of rules in terms of its order, the experiment reveals promising behavior. For a given word that fires a set of rules, it is most likely that the first fired rule will achieve a match.

In order to optimize the stemmer performance, the curve in Fig. 1 should show a sharp drop. Although it is impractical to achieve such optimum state, it is possible to have certain rule ordering that produces the best performance for such a given rule set.

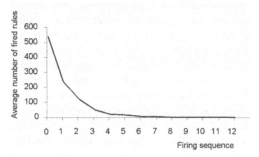

Fig. 1. Average number of fired rules per 1000 words

3   Firing Policies

In the rule-based stemmer, a given word may fire zero or more rules. If more than one rule is fired, it is desirable to achieve a correct firing at the first firing. A certain policy should be developed to achieve an optimum stemmer performance. A straightforward policy is to test all permutations of ordering rules of a given length then select the rule order that achieve the highest correctness score. Obtaining permutations for all lengths is impractical since it requires time complexity of $O(n!)$. Adapting heuristic to sort rules starting by very specific and ending with the most generic one would generate a good-sorted set of rules. This approach cannot guarantee neither optimum nor close to optimum solution.

In this work the correctness score cs is defined as follows:

$$cs = c / f \tag{1}$$

Where c denotes the number of correctly analyzed words and f is the number of fired words. The target is to achieve maximum correctness score. For that, scores of correctness for different permutations will be calculated and then highest score will be considered as optimum. Equation (2) measures how close the approach to the optimal state using the closeness factor cf

$$cf = (a - c) / (a - b) \tag{2}$$

Where a and b denote the highest and the lowest permutation scores respectively and c denotes the score of single, pair, triple or quadruple approaches. In this approach, achieving lower closeness factor will produce better ordered rule set. Ratio of correctly fired rules to the total firings per single rule showed that it can be used to enhanced the performance of a rule set generated for random text [7].

To enhance the correctness score, combination of two or more rules out of n where order is important are used to calculate the score of a set of a given rule length. Resultant scores of all combinations will be sorted in an ascending order. To obtain the best rule order of a given length, the first unique rule is selected and added to the best-ordered rule set. This approach reduces the time complexity of the problem to $O(n(n-1))$ as compared to $O(n!)$ for the case of generating all possible permutations for a set size of n. Applying this approach with combination of two rules out of n for rule sizes of 2 and 12 and comparing that against the results of permutation approach shows a very close to optimal results. For the case of length two the highest correctness score of permutations was one while the pair correctness score was 0.999659. For the case of length twelve, the highest correctness score is one while pair correctness score is one. This approach is also applied by selecting a random subset of six or seven rules with lengths 4,5,7,8 and 10. Comparing the pair correctness scores against corresponding permutations shows that seven out of nine sets achieve the optimum scores.

In the above-mentioned approach it is not clear how good the non-optimum cases are. To check the closeness of the pair approach to the optimum, the results of 500 runs were investigated. For each run, six rules were randomly selected. Sets are distributed evenly over rule lengths from 3 to 11. A comparison factor is defined to indicate the closeness of score of pair approach ps to the highest value obtained by permutations hs.

For each run, the score of rule order developed by pair approach *ps* and all scores of different permutations *hs* were calculate. The closeness factor equals one if pair score achieves as the highest score of permutations. The results of the 500 runs are shown in Fig. 2. This score, accumulated over the five hundred runs, shows 0.989021546% closeness. This approach shows that it can achieve a very close to optimum and hence it can be used as a simpler and cheaper policy for ordering rules.

A similar experiment using combination of three rules was conducted. Calculating the closeness factor for hundred runs shows 0.9769% closeness. This result shows that triple approach is also achieving close to optimum score. The problem of using triple approach is that it costs $O(n(n-1)(n-2))$ as compared to $O(n(n-1))$ for the pair approach.

Another judgment for the triple approach is performed by comparing it against the pair approach over hundred runs. Fig. 3 shows the results of this experiment that indicated that out of 300 runs, there are 273 ties and only 25 cases the triple approach outperform the pair approach. This experiment shows that the enhancement gained using the triple approach is not major given the complexity of it.

In another experiment the triple and quadruple approaches were studied by randomly selecting six rules hundred times. Results show that there are 91 ties and only 7 cases of enhancement.

To generalize this approach over larger number of rules a three stages experiment can be performed. Starting with three rules for every set then moving to four rules in the second stage and finally using five rules for every set. In the first stage the best order of rules using single and pair approaches were developed. In the second stage the triple approach was added. Finally, the quadruple approach was integrated. The results are shown in Fig. 4 which clearly indicates that the triple approach is applicable to higher number of rules without high loss in correctness compared to the single and pair approaches.

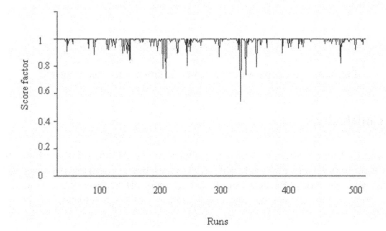

Fig. 2. Score factors of 500 runs

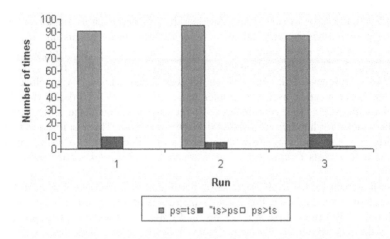

Fig. 3. Comparisons between pair and triple scores

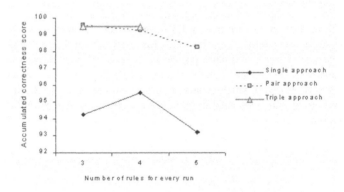

Fig. 4. Accumulated correctness scores for different number of rules

4   Conclusions

This paper thoroughly studied the firing policies of the Arabic rule-based stemmer. Results show that single, pair and triple approaches have promising performance in ordering rules. Selecting the best approach is a trade off between performance and cost. Taking generalization issue into consideration yields the selection of the triple approach.

References

[1]   Lovins, J.: Development of a stemming algorithm. Mechanical Translation and Computational Linguistics, 11(1968) 22-31

[2]   Dawson J.: Suffix removal and word conflation. ALLC Bulletin, 2(1974) vol 3. 33-46

[3]   Ali. N.: Arabic Language and Computer. Ta'reeb, 1988. (In Arabic)

[4]   Alsuwaynea. A.: Information Retrieval in Arabic language. King Fahad National Library, 1995 (In Arabic)

[5]   Al-Atram M.: Effectiveness of Natural Language in Indexing and Retrieving Arabic Documents. KACST, AR-8-47. 1990. (In Arabic)

[6]   Al Sughaiyer, I., Al Kharashi, I.: An Efficient Arabic Morphological Analysis Technique for Information Retrieval Systems. ACIDCA 2000. Tunis (2000)

[7]   Al Kharashi, I., Al Sughaiyer, I.: Pattern-Based Arabic Stemmer. Second Saudi Technical Conference and Exhibition. STCEX2002. Riyadh (2002)

[8]   Al Sughaiyer, I., Al Kharashi, I.: Rule Parser for Arabic Stemmer. Fifth International Conference on Text, Speech and Dialogue. TSD2002. Czech Republic (2002)

[9]   Al Kharashi I., Al Sughaiyer, I.: Data Set for Designing and Testing an Arabic Stemmer. Proceedings of Arabic Language Resources and Evaluation: Status and Prospects. Spain (2002)

[10]   Al Kharashi, I., Al Sughaiyer, I.: Rule Merging in a Rule-Based Arabic Stemmer. The 19th international conference on computational Linguistics. Coling 2002. Taipei (2002)

Enhancing the Set-Based Model
Using Proximity Information

Bruno Pôssas, Nivio Ziviani, and Wagner Meira, Jr.

Departamento de Ciência da Computação, Universidade Federal de Minas Gerais
30161-970 Belo Horizonte-MG, Brazil
{bavep,nivio,meira}@dcc.ufmg.br

Abstract. (SBM), which is an effective technique for computing term weights based on co-occurrence patterns, employing the information about the proximity among query terms in documents. The intuition that semantically related term occurrences often occur closer to each other is taken into consideration, leading to a new information retrieval model called proximity set-based model (PSBM). The novelty is that the proximity information is used as a pruning strategy to determine only related co-occurrence term patterns. This technique is time efficient and yet yields nice improvements in retrieval effectiveness. Experimental results show that PSBM improves the average precision of the answer set for all four collections evaluated. For the CFC collection, PSBM leads to a gain relative to the standard vector space model (VSM), of 23% in average precision values and 55% in average precision for the top 10 documents. PSBM is also competitive in terms of computational performance, reducing the execution time of the SBM in 21% for the CISI collection.

1 Introduction

In the area of information retrieval one of the most successful models in terms of the ability to locate answers that humans judge to be relevant is the vector space model (VSM). The main advantages of VSM are its term-weighting scheme that improves retrieval performance and its partial matching strategy that allows retrieval of documents that approximate the query conditions. In spite of its success, VSM has the disadvantage that index terms are assumed to be mutually independent, an assumption often made as a matter of mathematical convenience and simplicity of implementation. However, it is generally agreed that exploitation of the correlation among index terms in each document might be used to improve retrieval effectiveness for general collections.

Different approaches to take into account co-occurrence among terms during the information retrieval process have been proposed [23, 22, 15, 6, 14]. The set-based model [13] is the first information retrieval model that exploits term correlations effectively and provides significant gains in terms of precision, regardless of the size of the collection and of the size of the vocabulary, with processing costs close to the costs of VSM. Although the co-occurrence term

A.H.F. Laender and A.L. Oliveira (Eds.): SPIRE 2002, LNCS 2476, pp. 104–116, 2002.

patterns has been used, the intuition that semantically related term occurrences often occur closer to each other is not taken into consideration.

Recent experimentation [7, 4] indicates, however, that measurements involving the distance between term occurrences may provide good relevance assessments, and that these relevance calculations exhibit other properties for document retrieval that are not found with other document retrieval techniques. In particular, a very desirable property of distance-based relevance scores is their independence from collection statistics. Furthermore, consistent document rankings may be obtained across independent collections, even when those collections are distributed across the net.

An indirect way to considerer term proximity is the idea of passage level retrieval [16]. Underlying this idea is the fact that large documents may often contain considerably smaller passages of text that are relevant to a given query, but documents containing these passages are ranked low by many frequency-based relevance ranking algorithms. A passage is defined as a contiguous group of paragraphs or sections of a document [3, 26, 16], or as a block of words of fixed length [3], as a window over the document which may move in fixed-length jumps [26, 8, 9], as a non-contiguous but semantically linked thread of paragraphs through the document [11, 10].

In this work we present an extension to the set-based model (SBM), called proximity set-based model (PSBM), to employ the information about the proximity among query terms in documents. The proximity information does not modify the algebraic representation of the SBM. As a consequence, the changes to the original model are minimal, and is related only with the closed termsets enumeration phase.

We evaluated and validated PSBM through experimentation using four test collections. Our experimental results show that accounting for proximity between terms yields higher retrieval performance. For the CFC collection [19], containing 1,240 documents, PSBM yields average precision values that are 23.04% better than VSM and 4.20% better than the SBM. When only the first 10 answers are considered, this margin goes up to 55.06% and 6.22%, respectively.

PSBM is also competitive in terms of computational performance. The use of proximity information drops the execution time of PSBM even closer to the execution time of VSM. For the CISI [20] collection, where the average number of terms per query is 9.44, the reduction of the execution time for PSBM over the SBM is just 21%, and the increase over VSM is just 12%. These are relevant facts from both theoretical and practical points of view, considering that we incorporate term correlations and term proximity to a well known information retrieval model reducing its response time.

The paper is organized as follows. Section 2 describes SBM. In Section 3 we formalize the method for computing co-occurrences among query terms based in an association rules approach using the proximity information. In Section 4 we present the reference collection characteristics and the experimental results obtained through a comparison between VSM, SBM and PSBM. Finally we present some conclusions and future work in Section 5.

2   Set-Based Model Revisited

In the set-based model, a document is described by a set of closed termsets, where termset is simply an ordered set of terms extracted from the document itself [13]. With each closed termset we associate a pair of weights representing (a) its importance in each document and (b) its importance in the whole document collection. In a similar way, a query is described by a set of closed termsets with and each closed termset has a weight that represents its importance in the query.

2.1   Termset Weights

The best known term weighting schemes [18, 24, 17] use weights that are function of (i) $tf_{i,j}$, the number of times that an index term i occurs in a document j, and (ii) df_i, the number of documents that an index term i occurs in the whole document collection. Such term-weighting strategy is called $tf \times idf$ scheme. The expression for idf_i represents the importance of term i in the collection, assigning a high weight to terms that are found in a small number of documents in the collection, supposing that rare terms have high discriminating value.

In SBM, the association rules approach naturally quantifies representative patterns of term co-occurrences, a feature that is not part of the $tf \times idf$ scheme. To determine the weights associated with the closed termsets in a document or in a query, we also use the number of occurrences of a closed termset in a document, in a query, and in the whole collection. Formally, the weight of a closed termset i in a document j is defined as:

$$w_{i,j}^* = sf_{i,j} \times ids_i = sf_{i,j} \times \log \frac{N}{ds_i} \qquad (1)$$

where N is the number of documents in the collection, $sf_{i,j}$ is the number of occurrences of the closed termset i in document j (obtained from the index), and ids_i is the inverted frequency of occurrence of the closed termset in the collection. $sf_{i,j}$ generalizes $tf_{i,j}$ in the sense that it counts the number of times that the closed termset s_i appears in document j. The component ids_i also carries the same semantics of idf_i, but accounting for the cardinality of the closed termsets as follows. High-order closed termsets usually have low frequency, resulting in large inverted frequencies. Thus, this strategy assigns large weights to closed termsets that appear in a small number of documents, that is, rare closed termsets result in greater weights.

2.2   Similarity Calculation

Since documents and queries are represented as vectors, we assign a similarity measure to every document containing any of the query closed termsets, defined as the normalized scalar product between the set of document vectors d_j, $1 \leq j \leq N$, and the query vector q. The similarity between a document d_j and a query q is defined as:

$$sim(q, d_j) = \frac{\boldsymbol{d_j} \bullet \boldsymbol{q}}{|\boldsymbol{d_j}| \times |\boldsymbol{q}|} = \frac{\sum_{s \in C_q} w_{s,j}^* \times w_{s,q}^*}{\sqrt{\sum_{i=1}^{t} (w_{i,j})^2} \times \sqrt{\sum_{i=1}^{t} (w_{i,q})^2}}, \tag{2}$$

where $w_{s,j}^*$ is the weight associated with the closed termset s in document d_j, $w_{s,q}^*$ is the weight associated with the closed termset s in query q, these respective weights are calculated according to the Equation 1. C_q is the set of all closed termsets such that all $s \subseteq q$, $w_{i,j}$ is the weight of term i in document d_j, and $w_{i,q}$ is the weight of term i in query q. We observe that the normalization (i.e., the factors in the denominator) is performed using the terms (instead of closed termsets) that compose the query and document vectors. This simplification is important to reduce computational costs because computing the norm of a document d using closed termsets might be prohibitively costly. Experimental results for SBM [13] corroborate the validity of adopting this alternative form of normalization.

2.3 Query Mechanisms

In this section we describe a simple algorithm for implementing a search mechanism based on the set-based model and the indexing information.

The steps performed by the set-based model to the calculation of the similarity metrics are equivalent to the standard vector space model. First we create the data structures that are used for calculating the document similarities among all closed termsets s_i of a document d. Then, for each query term, we retrieve its inverted list, and determine the first frequent termsets, i.e., the frequent termsets of size equal to 1, applying the minimal frequency threshold. The next step is the enumeration of all closed termsets based on the 1-termsets. After enumerating all closed termsets, we employ the pruning scheme presented by Persin [12] to the evaluation of its inverted lists, allowing to discard closed termsets that will not influence the final ranking very early. After evaluating the closed termsets, we normalize the document similarities by dividing each document similarity by the respective document's norm. The final step is to select the k largest similarities and return the corresponding documents.

3   Accounting for Proximity Information in Closed Termsets

In this section we review the concept of closed termsets as a basis for computing term weights, extending its definition to account for the proximity information associated with each term occurrence in a document. Further, we analyze how closed termsets can be generated from a document inverted list. A detailed analysis of its computational costs is described in [13].

3.1   Closed Termsets

Let $T = \{k_1, k_2, ..., k_t\}$ be the vocabulary of a collection of documents D, that is, the set of t unique terms that may appear in a document from D. There is a total ordering among the vocabulary terms, which is based on the lexicographical order of terms, so that $k_i < k_{i+1}$, for $1 \leq i \leq t - 1$. We define an n-termset s as an ordered set of n unique terms, such that $s \subseteq T$ and the order among terms follows the aforementioned total ordering. Let $S = \{s_1, s_2, ..., s_{2^t}\}$ be the vocabulary-set of a collection of documents D, that is, the set of 2^t unique termsets that may appear in a document from D. Each document j from D is characterized by a vector in the space of the termsets.

With each termset s_i, $1 \leq i \leq 2^t$, we associate an inverted list ls_i composed of identifiers of the documents that contains the termset and the intra-document frequency. We also define the frequency ds_i of a termset s_i as the number of occurrences of s_i in D, that is, the number of documents where $s_i \subseteq d_j$ and $d_j \in D$, $1 \leq j \leq N$. The frequency ds_i of a termset s_i is the length of its associated inverted list ($| ls_i |$). Finally, we define s_i as a frequent termset if its frequency ds_i is greater than or equal to a given threshold, which is known as *support* in the scope of association rules [1].

A closed termset c is a frequent termset that is the largest termset among the termsets that are subsets of c and occur in the same set of documents. That is, given a set $\mathcal{D} \subseteq D$ of documents and the set $\mathcal{S}_\mathcal{D} \subseteq S$ of termsets that occur in all documents from $\mathcal{D}$ and only in these, a closed termset c satisfies the property that $\nexists s \in \mathcal{S}_\mathcal{D} | c \subset s$. For sake of information retrieval, closed termsets are interesting because they represent a reduction on the computational complexity and on the amount of data that has to be analyzed, without loosing information, since all termsets in a closure are represented by the respective closed termset.

3.2   Proximity Information

To employ the information about the proximity among query terms in documents, we extend the inverted list of the closed termset and the inverted list of the term in the inverted file representation.

In the implementation of PSBM the document collection has an inverted file [21]. An inverted file is typically composed of a *vocabulary* and a set of *inverted lists*. For each term in the vocabulary, there is an inverted list consisting of the identifiers of all documents containing the term and, with each identifier d_j, the intra-document frequency $tf_{i,j}$ of the term i in d_j and, the list of occurrence locations of term i in the document d_j, represented by $rp_{i,j}$. An occurrence location for a term i is equivalent to the number of term occurrences preceding that term in a document. Thus the inverted lists consists of triples of $< d_j, tf_{i,j}, rp_{i,j} >$ values.

We extend the original proposition of the closed termsets adding a new constraint to the elements of its inverted lists. The list elements must be composed only for term occurrences with locations bounded by a proximity threshold, called minimum proximity. This technique is equivalent to the intra-document passages defined by a window that moves in fixed-length jumps [26, 8, 9].

3.3   Algorithm Description

Determining closed termsets is a problem very similar to mining association rules and the algorithms employed for the latter is our starting point [1]. Our approach is based on an efficient algorithm for association rule mining, called CHARM [25], which has been adapted to handle terms and documents instead of items and transactions, respectively.

The algorithm for generating termsets is basically an incremental enumeration algorithm that employs a very powerful pruning strategy. More specifically, we start by verifying whether the frequency of 1-termsets is above a given threshold, since if a term is not frequent, none of the higher-order termsets that include it will be. These frequent 1-termsets will also be defined as closed. We then start grouping frequent termsets and verifying two criteria that are used to determine whether these new termsets are closed or not.

The first criterion verifies whether the termset is frequent and was introduced by the original Apriori algorithm [2]: an n-termset may be frequent only if all of its $n-1$-termsets are also frequent.

The second criterion checks whether a frequent termset f being verified is closed. A termset f is defined as closed if there is no closed termset that is also a closure of f. In this case, all current closed termsets are tested for having f as its closure, being discarded if such condition holds. Otherwise, f is discarded, since its closure is already determined.

The proximity information is used as a pruning strategy to find only the closed termsets occurrences bounded by an specified proximity threshold, conforming with the assumption that semantically related term occurrences often occur closer to each other. This pruning strategy, as discussed in Section 4.2, is very effective. This pruning strategy is incorporated in the closed termsets enumeration algorithm as a third criterion, which is verified before the first criterion. Verifying this new constraint is quite straightforward and consists of rejecting the closed termsets occurrences whose the difference of pairwise terms locations are greater than the given threshold.

To illustrate this new criterion, consider two 1-termsets s_1 and s_2 and a minimum proximity threshold of 10. Let $rp_{1,1} = \{2, 10, 35\}$ be the term locations of s_1 in a document d_1, and $rp_{2,1} = \{4, 11, 50\}$ be the term locations of s_2 in the same document d_1. A new termset is determined by the union of these sets $(s_1 \cup s_2)$, creating a 2-termset $s_{1,2}$. The list of documents where $s_{1,2}$ appears can be determined by intersecting the lists of the two concatenated sets $(l_{1,2} = l_1 \cap l_2)$. The pruning strategy is employed during the lists intersection and verifies if two pairwise term locations are bounded by the minimum proximity threshold. Thus, the term location $\{35, 50\}$ of $s_{1,2}$ is discarded because its difference $(|35 - 50| > 10)$ is greater than the minimum proximity threshold employed. We may expect that the number of termsets occurrences, and as a consequence, the number of closed termsets evaluated decrease with the application of this new criterion, dropping the execution time of the queries.

Table 1. Characteristics of the reference collections

Characteristics	Collection			
	CFC	CACM	CISI	MEDL
Number of Documents	1,240	3,204	1,460	1,033
Number of Distinct Terms	2,105	11,536	10,869	13,020
Number of Queries	100	64	50	30
Average Terms per Query	3.82	12.51	9.44	10.30
Average Terms per Document	146.43	58.86	126.60	150.99
Average Relevants per Query	29.04	15.61	49.84	23.20

4   Experimental Results

In this section we describe the experimental results for the evaluation of the proximity set-based model (PSBM) in terms of both effectiveness and computational efficiency. Our evaluation is based on a comparison to the standard vector space model (VSM) and to the set-based model (SBM). We first present the experimental framework and the reference collections employed, and then discuss the retrieval performance and the computational efficiency of each model.

In our evaluation we use four reference collections, CFC [19], CACM [5], CISI [20] and MEDL, respectively. Table 1 presents the main features of these collections, which comprise not only the documents, but also a set of example queries and the relevant responses for each query, as selected by experts. We quantify the retrieval effectiveness of the various approaches through standard measures of average recall and precision. The computational efficiency is evaluated through the query response time, that is, the processing time to select and rank the documents for each query.

We employed two aggregate metrics for measuring retrieval effectiveness: average precision over retrieved documents, that is, the percentage of relevant documents among the documents retrieved; and precision at 10, which is the percentage of relevant documents among the first 10 documents retrieved. The first metric is widely used for evaluating information retrieval systems, but assumes that the recall is high, i.e., the number of retrieved and inspected documents is large. On the other hand, the second metric is more suitable for a Web-like application environment, where precision in a small set of documents is more desirable.

The experiments were performed on a Linux-based PC with an AMD K6-II 500 MHz processor and 320 MBytes RAM. Next we present the results obtained for the four collections, which are characterized in Table 1.

4.1   Retrieval Performance

We start our evaluation by verifying the precision-recall values for each model when applied to the four collections. The results presented for SBM and PSBM use as minimal frequency 1 document. PSBM yields better average precision than both VSM and SBM, regardless the collection, as shown in Tables 2, 3, 4 and 5. These tables also present the overall average precision achieved for each

Table 2. Recall x Precision for CFC

Recall (%)	Precision(%)		
	VSM	SBM	PSBM
10	76.19	86.94	91.93
20	60.77	67.84	70.12
30	52.46	59.86	61.59
40	40.22	45.68	48.43
50	31.10	36.71	38.26
60	20.11	25.38	26.18
70	13.07	19.66	19.98
80	6.18	10.83	11.06
90	2.32	5.96	6.35
100	1.38	2.67	2.84
Average	30.38	36.15	37.67
Improvement		18.99	23.04

Table 3. Recall x Precision for CACM

Recall (%)	Precision(%)		
	VSM	SBM	PSBM
10	69.86	76.78	79.78
20	60.12	65.28	68.75
30	49.90	52.62	55.62
40	42.45	43.91	46.04
50	36.44	36.21	37.91
60	31.61	31.99	33.29
70	26.38	25.82	26.82
80	20.44	19.45	19.53
90	15.38	14.07	14.37
100	11.28	10.13	10.23
Average	36.39	37.63	39.23
Improvement		3.40	7.80

Table 4. Recall x Precision for CISI

Recall (%)	Precision(%)		
	VSM	SBM	PSBM
10	63.72	65.97	75.63
20	34.79	38.99	39.54
30	21.71	24.71	24.89
40	18.08	19.96	19.93
50	14.56	16.53	16.45
60	12.28	15.89	15.80
70	10.33	12.58	12.69
80	7.12	10.84	10.66
90	4.05	8.89	8.98
100	1.97	4.45	4.97
Average	18.86	21.88	22.95
Improvement		16.01	21.68

Table 5. Recall x Precision for MEDL

Recall (%)	Precision(%)		
	VSM	SBM	PSBM
10	91.59	92.99	94.59
20	80.23	85.29	88.29
30	72.90	78.65	80.15
40	66.37	74.26	76.65
50	60.39	64.96	66.06
60	50.46	52.87	54.97
70	44.36	45.98	47.98
80	40.16	40.85	41.15
90	30.23	28.88	31.28
100	18.18	15.97	23.27
Average	52.67	58.07	60.44
Improvement		10.25	14.75

model, and the overall improvement provided by the PSBM over the other two models.

We observe that, although the precision gains are not significant for the employed collections when compared to the SBM, there is always some gain. Furthermore, accounting for correlations among terms with its respective proximity information never degrades the quality of the response sets. In fact, we expect even better results if we consider just queries containing correlated terms. The PSBM outperforms SBM because it takes into account just the co-occurrence patterns that are closer to each other. The gains provided by PSBM over VSM ranged from 7.80% to 23.04%, being consistent for all queries.

PSBM provides even greater gains when we verify the average precision for the top 10 documents. This metric estimates the user "satisfaction" while using Web services such as search engines. We can see from Table 6 that the gains range from 14.80 to 55.06% when compared to VSM, and ranges from 5.09 to 7.18% when compared to SBM.

Table 6. Average precision values for top 10 documents and gains provided by the PSBM

Collection	Average Precision at 10 (%)			PSBM Gain(%)	
	VSM	SBM	PSBM	VSM	SBM
CFC	17.16	25.05	26.61	55.06	6.22
CACM	24.99	27.30	28.69	14.80	5.09
CISI	7.27	9.24	9.88	35.90	6.92
MEDL	28.57	33.41	35.81	25.34	7.18

One of the features of the set-based model is the possibility of controlling the minimal frequency threshold of a termset [13]. The variation of the minimal frequency allows us to exploit the trade-off between precision and the number of closed termsets taken into consideration. As presented next, variations in the minimal proximity threshold also affects the precision and the number of closed termsets evaluated.

We verified how variations in the minimal proximity threshold employed affect the precision achieved for all collections. We performed a set of PSBM executions where the minimal proximity threshold is fixed for all queries and varies from 1 to 250. The results for the CFC collection are illustrated in Figure 1 and we realize that the PSBM precision is significantly affected by the minimal proximity parameter employed. Initially, an increase in the minimal proximity results in better precision, achieving a maximum precision for minimal proximity between 50 and 80 words. When we increase the minimal proximity beyond 80, we observe that the precision decreases until it reaches almost the mean average precision obtained by the set-based model. We observed similar results for the other document collections. This behavior can be explained as follows. First, an increase in the minimal proximity implies in an increase in the number of closed termsets evaluated resulting in a better precision, since a greater number of correlations was used. When the minimal proximity gets above 80, the number of closed termsets representing weak correlations increase, leading to a reduction in terms of precision. For instance, occurrences of different words in the begin and in the end of a document means to a weak correlation.

In summary, PSBM is the first information retrieval model that exploits term correlations and term proximity effectively and provides significant gains in terms of precision. In the next section we discuss the computational costs associated with PSBM.

4.2   Computational Efficiency

In this section we compare PSBM to VSM and to SBM regarding the query response time, in order to evaluate its feasibility in terms of computational costs. This comparison is important because the closed termsets enumeration phase is the most costly computation part, being the major limitation of SBM.

We start our evaluation by verifying the average number of closed termsets and its average list sizes while using PSBM and SBM. The results show that

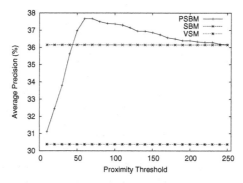

Fig. 1. Impact of varying minimal proximity threshold on average precision for CFC

Table 7. Average number of closed termsets and inverted list size

Collection	Closed Termsets		Inverted List Size	
	SBM	PSBM	SBM	PSBM
CFC	5.22	3.81	4.43	3.31
CACM	19.35	13.14	5.72	4.23
CISI	8.80	6.20	5.59	4.48
MEDL	13.23	10.12	3.16	2.05

the average case scenario is much better than the worst case theoretical bound presented in [13], as we can see in Table 7. We may expect that the response time for the PSBM is better than the SBM because the number of the closed termsets generated and its respective inverted list sizes is smaller.

To validate our analysis, we compared the response time for the models employed for the collections considered. The comparison is summarized in Table 8. We also calculated the response time increase of SBM and PSBM when compared to VSM. We observe that SBM results in a response time increase from 41.00 to 77.27% for the reference collections evaluated when compared to VSM, while the increase for the PSBM ranges from 12.23 to 50.00%. The results confirm the complexity analysis performed, showing that the PSBM outperforms the SBM due to the smaller number of closed termsets and its respective inverted lists sizes.

Table 8. Average response time

Collection	Average Response Time (s)			Increase(%)	
	VSM	*SBM*	*PSBM*	*SBM*	*PSBM*
CFC	0.0147	0.0229	0.0173	55.78	17.68
CACM	0.0134	0.0228	0.0164	70.14	22.38
CISI	0.0139	0.0196	0.0156	41.00	12.23
MEDL	0.0066	0.0117	0.0099	77.27	50.00

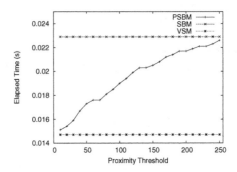

Fig. 2. Impact of minimal proximity on response time for CFC

As mentioned, we may control the number of closed termsets, and thus the query processing time, by varying the minimal frequency and the minimal proximity threshold. We varied the minimal proximity used in PSBM and measured the response time for all collections. Figure 2 shows the response time as a function of the minimal proximity employed for the CFC collection, where we see that the increase in the minimal proximity causes significant reductions on the response time, at a possible penalty in average precision values as presented in Section 4.1. For the other collections, we observe similar trade-offs.

5   Final Remarks

We present an extension to the set-based model (SBM), the proximity set-based model (PSBM), that accounts for the information about the proximity among query terms in documents. The proximity information does not modify the algebraic representation of SBM. As a consequence, the changes to the original model are minimal, and are related only with the closed termsets enumeration phase. We showed that it is possible to improve retrieval effectiveness, while reducing the computational costs.

We evaluated and validated PSBM using four test collections. We showed through values of recall-precision that the new model provides results that are superior for all the collections considered. The results show that the average case scenario for PSBM is much better than the worst theoretical bound found for the SBM, which is translated to a smaller number of closed termsets and its respective inverted lists sizes. In fact, the computational costs measured allow the use of PSBM with larger general document collections. Preliminary results indicates that the retrieval effectiveness for PSBM may increase, reducing even more the computational costs when applied to larger collections.

In addition to assessing document relevance, the proximity information have application in identifying phrases with a greater degree of precision. We will investigate the behavior of PSBM for phrases identification and ranking in future works. We will also propose an extension to PSBM to consider the logic distribution of the terms in documents, i.e., the model should identify parts, sections and paragraphs of the documents, using this information to increase the retrieval effectiveness of the model.

References

[1] R. Agrawal, T. Imielinski, and A. Swami. Mining association rules between sets of items in large databases. In *Proceedings of the ACM SIGMOD International Conference Management of Data*, pages 207-216, Washington, D.C., May 1993. 108, 109

[2] R. Agrawal and R. Srikant. Fast algorithms for mining association rules. In *The 20th International Conference on Very Large Data Bases*, pages 487-499, Santiago, Chile, September 1994. 109

[3] J.P. Callan. Passage-level evidence in document retrieval. In *Proceedings of the 17th ACM SIGIR Conference on Research and Development in Information Retrieval*, pages 302–310, Dublin, Ireland, 1994. 105

[4] C.L.A. Clarke, G.V. Cormack, and F.J. Burkowski. Shortest substring ranking. In *In Fourth Text REtrieval Conference (TREC-4)*, pages 295–304, Gaithersburg, Maryland, USA, November 1995. 105

[5] E. Fox. Characterization of two new experimental collections in computer and information science containing textual and bibliographical concepts. Technical report, 1983. http://www.ncstrl.org. 110

[6] D.J. Harper and C.J. Van Rijsbergen. An evaluation of feedback in document retrieval using co-occurrence data. In *Journal of Documentation*, volume 34, pages 189–216, 1978. 104

[7] D. Hawking and P. Thistlewaite. Proximity operators - so near and yet so far. In *In Fourth Text REtrieval Conference (TREC-4)*, pages 131–144, Gaithersburg, Maryland, USA, November 1995. 105

[8] M. Kaszkeil and J. Zobel. Passage retrieval revisited. In *Proceedings of the 20th ACM SIGIR Conference on Research and Development in Information Retrieval*, pages 178–185, Philadelphia, Philadelphia, USA, 1997. 105, 108

[9] M. Kaszkeil, J. Zobel, and R. Sacks-Davis. Efficient passage ranking for document databases. In *ACM Transactions on Information Systems (TOIS)*, volume 17(4), pages 406–439, 1999. 105, 108

[10] D. Knaus, E. Mittendorf, P. Schauble, and P. Sheridan. Highlighting relevant passages for users of the interactive spider retrieval system. In *Proceedings of the Fourth Text REtrieval Conference (TREC-4)*, pages 233–244, Gaithersburg, Maryland, USA, 1996. 105

[11] E. Mittendorf and P. Schauble. Document and passage retrieval based on hidden markov models. In *Proceedings of the 17th ACM SIGIR Conference on Research and Development in Information Retrieval*, pages 318–327, Dublin, Ireland, 1994. 105

[12] M. Persin, J. Zobel, and R. Sacks-Davis. Filtered document retrieval with frequency-sorted indexes. In *Journal of the American Society of Information Science*, pages 749–764, 1996. 107

[13] B. Pôssas, N. Ziviani, W. Meira, and B. Ribeiro-Neto. Set-based model: A new approach for information retrieval. In *The 25th ACM-SIGIR Conference on Research and Development in Information Retrieval*, Tampere, Finland, August 2002. 104, 106, 107, 112, 113

[14] V. V. Raghavan and C. T. Yu. Experiments on the determination of the relationships between terms. In *ACM Transactions on Databases Systems*, volume 4, pages 240–260, 1979. 104

[15] C. J. Van Rijsbergen. A theoretical basis for the use of co-occurrence data in information retrieval. In *Journal of Documentation*, volume 33, pages 106–119, 1977. 104

[16] G. Salton, J. Allan, and C. Buckley. Approaches to passage retrieval in full text information systems. In *Proceedings of the 16th ACM SIGIR Conference on Research and Development in Information Retrieval*, pages 49–58, Pittsburgh, Philadelphia, USA, 1993. 105

[17] G. Salton and C. Buckley. Term-weighting approaches in automatic retrieval. In *Information Processing and Management*, volume 24(5), pages 513–523, 1988. 106

[18] G. Salton and C. S. Yang. On the specification of term values in automatic indexing. In *Journal of Documentation*, volume 29, pages 351-372, 1973. 106

[19] W. M. Shaw, J. B. Wood, R. E. Wood, and H. R. Tibbo. The cystic fibrosis database: Content and research opportunities. In *Library and Information Science Research*, volume 13), pages 347–366, 1991. 105, 110

[20] H. Small. The relationship of information science to the social sciences: A co-citation analysis. In *Information Processing and Management*, volume 17(1), pages 39–50, 1981. 105, 110

[21] I. Witten, A. Moffat, and T. Bell. *Managing Gigabytes. Compressing and Indexing Documents and Images*. Morgan Kaufmann Publishers, 1999. 108

[22] S. K. M. Wong, W. Ziarko, V. V. Raghavan, and P. C. N. Wong. On modeling of information retrieval concepts in vector spaces. In *The ACM Transactions on Databases Systems*, volume 12(2), pages 299–321, June 1987. 104

[23] S. K. M. Wong, W. Ziarko, and P. C. N. Wong. Generalized vector space model in information retrieval. In *The 8th ACM-SIGIR Conference on Research and Development in Information Retrieval*, pages 18–25, New York, USA, 1985. 104

[24] C. T. Yu and G. Salton. Precision weighting – an effective automatic indexing method. In *Journal of the ACM*, volume 23(1), pages 76–88, January 1976. 106

[25] M. J. Zaki. Generating non-redundant association rules. In *6th ACM SIGKDD International Conference on Knowledge Discovery and Data Mining*, pages 34-43, Boston, MA, USA, August 2000. 109

[26] J. Zobel, A. Moffat, R. Wilkinson, and R. Sacks-Davis. Efficient retrieval of partial documents. In *Information Processing and Management*, volume 31(3), pages 361–377, 1995. 105, 108

Web Structure, Dynamics and Page Quality*

Ricardo Baeza-Yates, Felipe Saint-Jean, and Carlos Castillo

Computer Science Department, University of Chile
Blanco Encalada 2120, Santiago, Chile
{rbaeza,fsaint,ccastill}@dcc.uchile.cl

Abstract. This paper is aimed at the study of quantitative measures of the relation between Web structure, page recency, and quality of Web pages. Quality is studied using different link-based metrics considering their relationship with the structure of the Web and the last modification time of a page. We show that, as expected, Pagerank is biased against new pages. As a subproduct we propose a Pagerank variant that includes page recency into account and we obtain information on how recency is related with Web structure.

1   Introduction

The purpose of a Web search engine is to provide an infrastructure that supports relationships between publishers of content and readers. In this context, as the numbers involved are very big (550 million users [11] and more than 3 billion pages[1] in 39 million sites [10] at this time) it is critical to provide good measures of quality that allow the user to choose "good" pages. We think that this is the main element that explain Google's [7] success. However, the notion of what is a "good page" and how is related to different Web characteristics is not well known.

Therefore, in this paper we address the study of the relationships between the quality of a page, Web structure, and age of a page or a site. Age is defined as the time since the page was last updated (recency). For Web servers, we use the oldest page in the site as a lower bound on the age of the site.

The specific questions we explore are the following:

- How does the position of a website in the structure of the Web depends on the website age? Depends the quality of a webpage on where is located in the Web structure? We give some experimental data that sheds some light on these issues.
- Are link-based ranking schemes providing a fair score to newer pages? We find that the answer is no for Pagerank [12], which is the base technique of the ranking technique used by Google [7], and we propose alternative ranking schemes that take in account the recency of the pages, an important problem according to [9].

---

* Supported by Millenium Nucleus "Center for Web Research" (P01-029-F), Mideplan, Chile.

[1] This is a lower bound that comes from the coverage of search engines.

A.H.F. Laender and A.L. Oliveira (Eds.): SPIRE 2002, LNCS 2476, pp. 117–130, 2002.

Our study is focused in the Chilean Web, mainly the .cl domain on two different time instants: first half of 2000, when we collected 670 thousand pages in approximately 7,500 websites (Set1), and the last half of year 2001, when we collected 795 thousand pages, corresponding to approximately 21.200 websites (Set2). This data comes from the TodoCL search engine [13] which specializes on the Chilean Web and is part of a family of vertical search engines built using the Akwan search engine [1].

Most statistical studies about the Web are based either on a "random" subset of the complete Web, or on the contents of some websites. In our case, the results are based on a Web collection that represents a large % of the Chilean Web, so we believe that our sample is more homogeneous and coherent, because it represents a well defined cultural and linguistic context.

The remaining of this paper is organized as follows. Section 2 presents previous work and that main concepts used in the sequel of the paper. Section 3 presents several relations among Web structure, age, and quality of webpages. Section 4 presents the relation of quality of webpages and age (recency), followed by a modified Pagerank that is introduced in Section 5. We end with some conclusions and future work.

2 Previous Work

The most complete study of the Web structure [4] focus on page connectivity. One problem with this is that a page is not a logical unit (for example, a page can describe several documents and one document can be stored in several pages.) Hence, we decided to study the structure of how websites were connected, as websites are closer to be real logical units. Not surprisingly, we found in [2] that the structure in the domain at the website level was similar to the global Web[2] and hence we use the same notation of [4]. The components are:

a) MAIN, sites that are in the strong connected component of the connectivity graph of sites (that is, we can navigate from any site to any other site in the same component);
b) IN, sites that can reach MAIN but cannot be reached from MAIN;
c) OUT, sites that can be reached from MAIN, but there is no path to go back to MAIN; and
d) other sites that can be reached from IN (T.IN, where T is an abbreviation of tentacle), sites in paths between IN and OUT (TUNNEL), sites that only reach OUT (T.OUT), and unconnected sites (ISLANDS).

In [2] we analyzed Set1 and we extended this notation by dividing the MAIN component into four parts:

a) MAIN-MAIN, which are sites that can be reached directly from the IN component and can reach directly the OUT component;

---

[2] Another example of the autosimilarity of the Web, which gives a scale invariant.

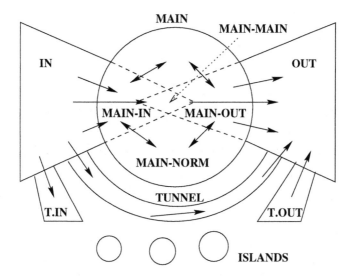

Fig. 1. Structure of the Web

b) MAIN-IN, which are sites that can be reached directly from the IN component but are not in MAIN-MAIN;
c) MAIN-OUT, which are sites that can reach directly the OUT component, but are not in MAIN-MAIN;
d) MAIN-NORM, which are sites not belonging to the previously defined subcomponents.

Figure 1 shows all these components.

We also gathered time information (last-modified date) for each page as informed by the webservers. How webpages change is studied in [6, 3, 5], but here we focus on webpage age, that is, the time elapsed after the last modification (recency). As the Web is young, we use months as time unit, and our study considers only the three last years as most websites are that young. The distribution of pages and sites for Set1 with respect to age is given in Figure 2.

The two main link based ranking algorithms known in the literature are Pagerank [12] and the hub and authority measures [8].

Pagerank is based on the probability of a random surfer to be on a page. This probability is modeled with two actions: the chance of the surfer to get bored and jump randomly to any page in the Web (with uniform probability), or choosing randomly one of the links in the page. This defines a Markov chain, that converges to a permanent state, where the probabilities are defined as follows:

$$PR_i = \frac{q}{T} + (1 - q) \sum_{j=1,\ j\neq i}^{k} \frac{PR_{m_j}}{L_{m_j}}$$

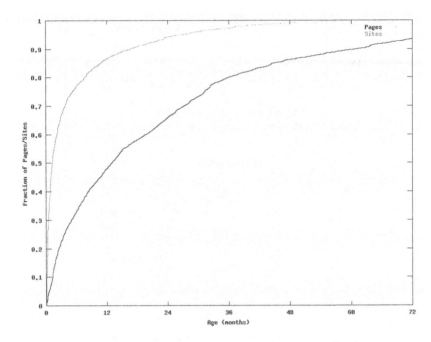

Fig. 2. Cumulative distribution of pages (bottom) and sites (top) in function of age for Set1

where T is the total number of webpages, q is the probability of getting bored (typically 0.15), m_j with $j \in (1..k)$ are the pages that point to page i, and L_j is the number of outgoing links in page j.

The hub and authority are complementary functions. A page will have a high hub rank if it points to good content pages. In the similar way a page will have a high authority rank if it is referred by pages with good links. In this way the authority of a page is defined as the sum of the hub ranks of the pages that point to it, and the hub rank of a page is the sum of the authority of the pages it points to.

When considering the rank of a website, we use the sum of all the ranks of the pages in the site, which is equivalent to the probability of being in any page of the site in the case of Pagerank [2].

3   Relations to the Web Structure

One of the initial motivations of our study was to find if the IN and OUT components were related to Web dynamics or just due to bad website design. In fact, websites in IN could be considered as new sites which are not linked because of causality reasons. Similarly, OUT sites could be old sites which have

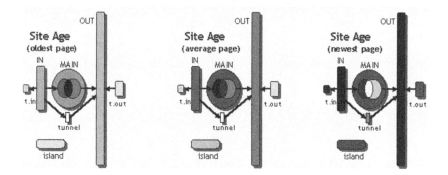

Fig. 3. Visualization of Web structure and website age

not been updated. Figure 3 shows the relation between the macro-structure of
the Web using the number of websites in each component to represent the area
of each part of the diagram for Set1. The colors represent website age, such that
a darker color represents older websites. We consider three ages: the oldest page
that is a lower bound to the website age, the average age that can be considered
as the freshness of a site, and the newest page which is a measure of update
frequency on a site. Figure 4 plots the cumulative distribution of the oldest page
in each site for Set 1 in each component of the Web structure versus date in a
logarithmic scale (these curves have the same shape as the ones in [4] for pages).
The central part is a line and represents the typical power laws that appear in
many Web measures.

These diagrams show that the oldest sites are in MAIN-MAIN, while the sites
that are fresher on average are in MAIN-IN and MAIN-MAIN. Finally, the last
diagram at the right shows that the update frequency is high in MAIN-MAIN
and MAIN-OUT, while sites in IN and OUT are updated less frequently.

We also obtain some confirmation to what can be expected. Newer sites are in
the ISLANDS component (and that is why they are not linked, yet). The oldest
sites are in MAIN, in particular MAIN-MAIN, so the kernel of the Web comes
mostly from the past. What is not obvious, is that on average, sites in OUT are
also newer than the sites in other components. Finally, IN shows two different
parts: there is a group of new sites, but the majority are old sites. Hence, a large
fraction of IN are sites that never became popular.

In Table 1 we give the numerical data for the average of website age (using
the oldest page) as well as the overall Web quality (sum for all the sites) in each
component of the macro-structure of the Web, as well as the percentage change
among both data sets in more than a year. Although Set1 did not include all
the ISLANDS at that time (we estimate that Set1 was 70% of the sites), we
can compare the core. The core has the smaller percentage but it is larger as
Set2 triples the number of sites of Set1. OUT also has increased, which may
imply a degradation of some part of the Web. Inside the core, MAIN-MAIN

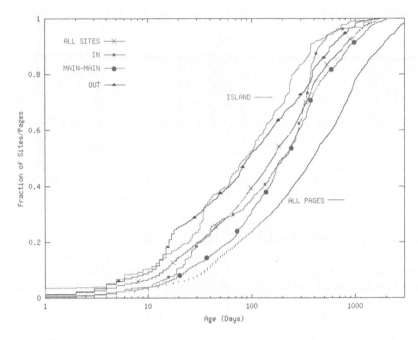

Fig. 4. Website age in the different components and webpage age (rightmost curve)

has increased in expense of MAIN-NORM. Overall, Set2 represents a Web much more connected than Set1.

Several observations can be made from Table 1. First, sites in MAIN have the higher Pagerank, and inside it, MAIN-MAIN is the subcomponent with highest Pagerank. In a similar way MAIN-MAIN has the largest authority. This makes MAIN-MAIN a very important segment of the Web. Notice that IN has the higher hub which is natural because sites in MAIN have the higher authority. ISLANDS have a low score in all cases.

Studying age, sites in MAIN are the oldest, and inside it, sites in MAIN-MAIN are the oldest. As MAIN-MAIN also has good quality, seems that older sites have the best content. This may be true when evaluating the quality of the content, but the value of the content, we believe in many cases, could be higher for newer pages, as we need to add novelty to the content.

Table 2 indicates the percentage of sites coming from Set1 in each part of the structure for Set2. Note that some are new sites (NEW) and that other sites from Set1 have disappeared (GONE). The main flows are from MAIN, IN and OUT to ISLANDS or from MAIN to OUT (probably sites that become outdated), and sites that disappear in OUT and ISLANDS (probably new sites that were not successful). On the other hand, it is interesting to notice the stability of the

Table 1. Age and page quality for Set2 in the different components of the macro-structure of the Chilean Web

Component	size(%,Set1)	size(%,Set2)	age (days)	Pagerank	hub	authority
MAIN	23%	9.25%	429	0.0002	0.0053	0.0009
IN	15%	5.84%	295	8.02e-05	0.0542	9.24e-08
OUT	45%	20.21%	288	6.12e-05	5.71e-08	1.00e-05
TUNNEL	1%	0.22%	329	2.21e-05	7.77e-08	3.78e-08
T.IN	3%	3.04%	256	3.45e-05	1.83e-12	1.53e-06
T.OUT	9%	1.68%	293	3.5e-05	4.12e-07	5.41e-09
ISLANDS	4%	59.73%	273	1.41e-05	1.10e-12	3.08e-11
MAIN-MAIN	2%	3.43%	488	0.0003	0.01444	0.0025
MAIN-OUT	6%	2.49%	381	0.0001	7.71e-05	4.19e-07
MAIN-IN	3%	1.16%	420	0.0001	1.14e-06	9.82e-06
MAIN-NORM	12%	2.15%	395	8.30e-05	3.31e-06	1.92e-07

Table 2. Relative percentage of sites coming from differents part of the structure, including new sites and sites that have disappeared among Set1 and Set2

2000 - 2001	MAIN	IN	OUT	ISLANDS	GONE
MAIN	36.36	5.31	27.46	11.57	19.30
IN	5.19	15.71	11.85	37.15	30.09
OUT	8.12	1.62	31.21	31.21	27.83
ISLANDS	3.31	2.58	22.84	39.23	32.04
NEW	5.20	6.30	14.40	74.10	
Rest	3.79	11.76	29.41	1.26	53.78

MAIN component. At the same time, all these changes show that the Web is very unstable as a whole.

Therefore there is a strong relation between the macro-structure of the Web and age/quality characteristics. This implies that the macro-structure is a valid partition of websites regarding these characteristics.

4   Link-Based Ranking and Age

In [2] we gave qualitative data that showed that link-based ranking algorithms had bad correlation and that Pagerank was biased against new pages. Here we present quantitative data supporting those observations.

Webpages sorted by recency were divided in 100 group segments of the same weight (that is, each segment has the same number of pages), obtaining a time division that is not uniform. Then we calculated the standard correlation[3] of each pair of average rank values. Three graphs were obtained: Figure 5 which

---

[3] This is defined as $\hat{\rho}(x,y) \equiv \frac{\hat{cov}(x,y)}{\hat{\sigma}_x \hat{\sigma}_y}$ where x and y are two random variables, $\hat{cov}$ is the covariance, and σ is the standard deviation.

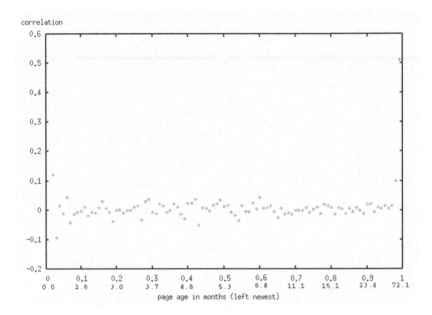

Fig. 5. Correlation among Pagerank and authority with age

shows the correlation between Pagerank and authority, Figure 6 the correlation among Pagerank and hub, and Figure 7 shows the correlation of authorities and hubs. Notice that the horizontal axis has two scales: at the top the fraction of groups and at the bottom the recency in months.

The low correlation between Pagerank and authority is surprising because both ranks are based on incoming links. This means that Pagerank and authority are different for almost every age percentile except the one corresponding to the older and newer pages which have Pagerank and authority rank very close to the minimum.

Notice the correlation between hub/authority, which is relatively low but with higher value for pages about 8 months old. New pages and old pages have a lower correlation. Also notice that hub and authority are not biased with time.

It is intuitive that new sites will have low Pagerank due to the fact that webmasters of other sites take time to know the site and refer to it in their sites. We show that this intuition is correct in Figure 8, where Pagerank is plotted against percentiles of page age. As can be seen, the newest pages have a very low Pagerank, similar to very old pages. The peak of Pagerank is in three months old pages.

In a dynamic environment as the Web, new pages have a high value so a ranking algorithm should take an updated or new page as a valuable one. Pages with high Pagerank are usually good pages, but the opposite is not necessarily

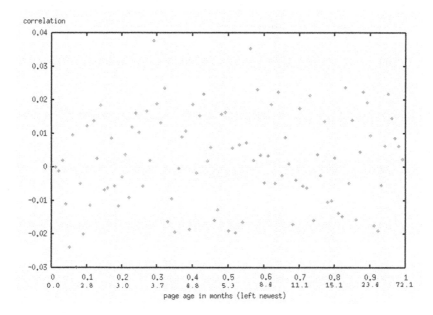

Fig. 6. Correlation among Pagerank and hub with age

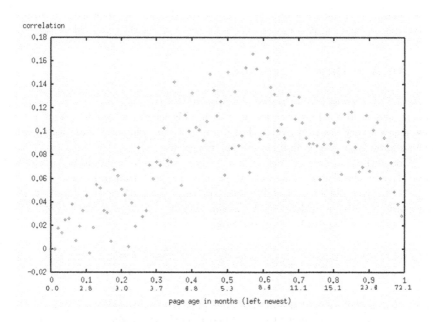

Fig. 7. Correlation among hubs and authorities with age

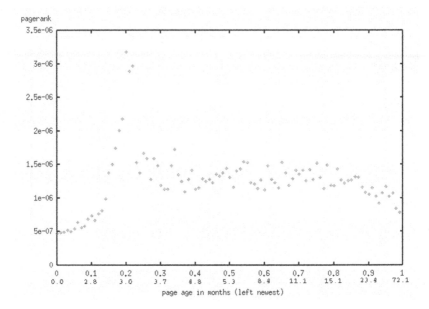

Fig. 8. Pagerank as a function of page age

true (good precision does not imply good recall). So the answer is incomplete and a missing part of it is in new pages. In the next section we explore this idea.

5   An Age Based Pagerank

Pagerank is a good way of ranking pages, and Google is a demonstration of it. But as seen before it has a tendency of giving higher ranks to older pages, giving new pages a very low rank. With that in mind we present some ideas for variants of Pagerank that give a higher value to new pages.

A page that is relatively new and already has links to it should be considered good. Hence, the Pagerank model can be modified such that links to newer pages are chosen with higher probability. So, let $f(age)$ be a decreasing function with age (present is 0), and define $f(x)$ as the weight of a page of age x. Hence, we can rewrite the Pagerank computation as:

$$PR_i = \frac{q}{T} + (1-q)\ f(age_i) \sum_{j=1,\ j\neq i}^{k} \frac{PR_{m_j}}{L_{m_j}}$$

where L_{m_j} as before is the number of links in page m_j. At each step, we normalize PR. Figures 9 and 10 shows the modified Pagerank by using $f(age) = (1 + A * e^{-B*age})$, $q = 0.15$, and different values of A and B.

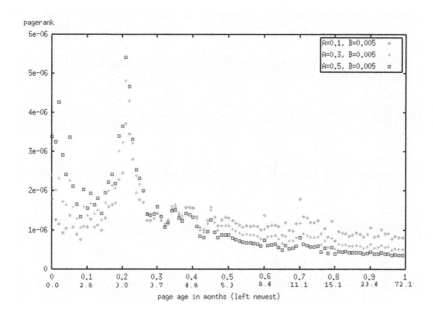

Fig. 9. Modified PageRank taking in account the page age (constant B)

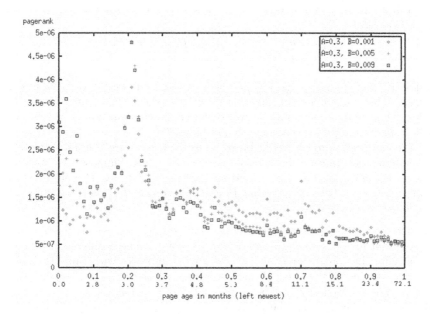

Fig. 10. Modified PageRank taking in account the page age (constant A)

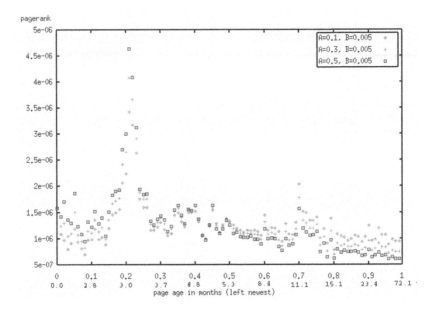

Fig. 11. Modified PageRank taking in account the page age (constant B)

Another possibility would be to take in account the age of the page pointing to i. That is,

$$PR_i = \frac{q}{T} + (1-q) \sum_{j=1,\ j \neq i}^{k} \frac{f(age_{m_j})\, PR_{m_j}}{F_{m_j}}$$

where $F(j) = \sum_{pages\ k\ linked\ by\ j} f(age_k)$ is the total weight of the links in a page. The result does not change to much, as shown in Figures 11 and 12 using the same parameters as before. However the computation is in this case slower, hence the previous scheme should be used.

Yet another approach would be to study how good are the links based in the modification times of both pages involved in a link. Suppose that page P_1 has an actualization date of t_1, and similarly t_2 and t_3 for P_2 and P_3, such that $t_1 < t_2 < t_3$. Let's assume that P_1 and P_3 reference P_2. Then, we can make the following two observations:

1. The link (P_3, P_2) has a higher value than (P_1, P_2) because at time t_1 when the first link was made the content of P_2 may have been different, although usually the content and the links of a page improves with time. It is true that the link (P_3, P_2) could have been created before t_3, but the fact that was not changed at t_3 validates the quality of that link.
2. For a smaller $t_2 - t_1$, the reference (P_1, P_2) is fresher, so the link should increase its value. On the other hand, the value of the link (P_3, P_2) should not depend on $t_3 - t_2$ unless the content of P_2 changes.

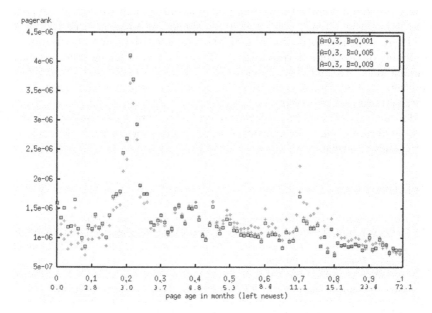

Fig. 12. Modified PageRank taking in account the page age (constant A)

A problem with the assumptions above is that we do not really know when a link was changed and that they use information from the servers hosting the pages, which is not always reliable. These assumptions could be strengthened by using the estimated rate of change of each page.

Let $w(t, s)$ be the weight of a link from a page with modification time t to a page with modification time s, such that $w(t, s) = 1$ if $t \geq s$ or $w(t, s) = f(s-t)$ otherwise, with f a fast decreasing function. Let W_j be the weight of all the outlinks of page j, then we can modify Pagerank using:

$$PR_i = \frac{q}{T} + (1 - q) \sum_{j=1,\ j \neq i}^{k} \frac{w(t_j, t_i)\ PR_{m_j}}{W_{m_j}}$$

where t_j is the modification time of page j. One drawback of this idea is that changing a page may decrease its Pagerank.

6   Conclusions

In this paper we have shown several relations between the macro structure of the Web, page and site age, and quality of pages and sites. Based on these results we have presented a modified Pagerank that takes in account the age of the pages. Google might be already doing something similar according to a BBC article[4].

There is plenty to do for mining the presented data and this is just the beginning of this kind of Web mining. We are currently trying other age-based ranking functions, and also applying the same ideas to hubs and authorities. In addition, ranking can also be based in where the page is with respect to the macro-structure of the Web.

Further related work includes how to evaluate the real goodness of a webpage link based ranking and the analysis of search engines logs to study user behavior with respect to time.

References

[1] Akwan search engine: Main page. http://www.akwan.com, 1999. 118

[2] BAEZA-YATES, R., AND CASTILLO, C. Relating web characteristics with link analysis. In *String Processing and Information Retrieval* (2001), IEEE Computer Science Press. 118, 120, 123

[3] BREWINGTON, B., CYBENKO, G., STATA, R., BHARAT, K., AND MAGHOUL, F. How dynamic is the web? In *9th World Wide Web Conference* (2000). 119

[4] BRODER, A., KUMAR, R., MAGHOUL, F., RAGHAVAN, P., RAJAGOPALAN, S., STATA, R., AND TOMKINS, A. Graph structure in the Web: Experiments and models. In *9th World Wide Web Conference* (2000). 118, 121

[5] CHO, J., AND GARCIA-MOLINA, H. The evolution of the Web and implications for an incremental crawler. In *The VLDB Journal* (2000). 119

[6] DOUGLAS, F., FELDMANN, A., KRISHNAMURTHY, B., AND MOGUL, J. Rate of change and other metrics: a live study of the World Wide Web. In *USENIX Symposium on Internet Technologies and Systems* (1997). 119

[7] Google search engine: Main page. http://www.google.com/, 1998. 117

[8] KLEINBERG, J. Authoritative sources in a hyperlinked environment. In *9th Symposium on discrete algorithms* (1998). 119

[9] LEVENE, M., AND POULOVASSILIS, A. Report on International Workshop on Web Dynamics, London, January 2001. 117

[10] Netcraft web server survey. http://www.netcraft.com/survey/, June 2002. 117

[11] Nua internet - how many online. http://www.nua.ie/surveys/how_many_online/, February 2002. 117

[12] PAGE, L., BRIN, S., MOTWANI, R., AND WINOGRAD, T. The Pagerank citation algorithm: bringing order to the Web. Tech. rep., Dept. of Computer Science, Stanford University, 1999. 117, 119

[13] TodoCL search engine: Main page. http://www.todocl.cl/, 2000. 118

---

[4] http://news.bbc.co.uk/hi/english/sci/tech/newsid_1868000/1868395.stm (in private communication with Google staff they said that the journalist had a lot of imagination.)

A Theoretical Analysis of Google's PageRank

Luca Pretto

Department of Information Engineering, University of Padua
Via Gradenigo 6/a, 35131 Padua, Italy
pretto@dei.unipd.it

Abstract. Our work starts from the definition of an intuitive formula that can be used to order the Web pages according to their importance, showing the need of a modification of this formula on a mathematical basis. Following the thread of this argument we get to a well-founded general formula, that covers many interesting different cases, and among them that of PageRank, the algorithm used by the Google search engine, as it is currently proposed in recent works [4, 7]. Then we prove the substantial equivalence between this PageRank formula and the classic formula proposed in [3]. As an example of the versatility of our general formula we derive from it a version of PageRank based on a user personalization. Finally, we discuss the problem of the "objectivity" of classic PageRank, demonstrating that a certain degree of subjectivity persists, since the order of Web pages given by this algorithm depends on the value of a parameter.

Keywords: Information retrieval (IR); IR and Web; Link-based analysis; Ranking; PageRank; Markov chains.

1 Introduction

PageRank is considered one of the earliest techniques of link-based analysis to increase the performance of Information Retrieval on the Web; this technique is used by Google, a Web search engine developed at Stanford University [3]. Google effects a retrieval of documents based on a boolean model, with no stemming, a brief stop words list, use of word proximity analysis and anchor text, and paying careful attention to capitalization and font dimension. A document is retrieved with regard to a particular query either if it contains all the words that are in the query or if these words are in the text of a link which is pointing to the document itself. Each document retrieved has a query-dependent score, called "traditional information retrieval score": for single-word queries, this score is computed giving a different weight to the occurrences of the word in the title, in the link text, and in the text with a different font dimension and then counting these occurrences; for multi-word queries this score is particularly sensitive to word proximity [3]. After retrieving the documents related to a particular query, Google orders them by merging information given by the traditional information retrieval score over the full-text with a query-independent score, called PageRank. PageRank is the result of the ambitious project of associating every existing Web page with just

A.H.F. Laender and A.L. Oliveira (Eds.): SPIRE 2002, LNCS 2476, pp. 131–144, 2002.

one number, its PageRank, which expresses the "importance", or rank, of that Web page in the whole Web. The information given by PageRank and by the traditional information retrieval score is used to express the ranking of Web pages, trying to solve the difficult and important problem of listing the results to a user's query in order of importance.

In this work we focus our attention on PageRank: we try to throw light on the classic PageRank definition, i.e. the definition given in [3] which is suggested with a slight change in recent works, for instance [4] and [7], explaining the intuitive and mathematical reasons that lead to this definition; we justify the convergence of PageRank algorithms in their various formulations; we analyze the dependence of PageRank on parameters. Since we are interested not only in classic PageRank formulation, but also in different modifications suggested in literature [10], we will get a well-founded general formula for PageRank, from which all particular cases (and, among them, the classic PageRank formula) can be obtained. This allows us to deal with all particular cases using a single theory, offering a unified view of all the different formulations.

This paper is organized in a progressive structure: we start from some known facts from the theory of PageRank and Markov chains, moving towards a general formula for PageRank; from this general formula we are able to examine some important particular cases; finally, we analyze the dependence of PageRank on parameters.

2   Related Works

The original definition of PageRank is given in [3], and PageRank is explained in [10]. Here we use a formulation that can be found in [7] for classic PageRank; it contains a minor correction from that in [3]; in Sect. 8 we will discuss the difference between the formulation in [3] and that in [7], and we will justify our choice. A mathematical formalization of classic PageRank can be found in [9]; it differs from our formalization because it only deals with classic PageRank, while our one is much more general, allowing us to deal with all the different formulations of PageRank suggested by developing a single theory. [6] is a recent work on the actual computation of PageRank. The case treated in [6] is that of pages with no out-links, giving a practical solution corresponding to the one we will consider in Subsect. 6.1: this present paper gives a theoretical justification of the convergence of the algorithm also in this case.

Many other works exist on the use of links to rank Web pages; generally the algorithms described in these works give a query-dependent ranking, i.e. the rank of Web pages depends on the particular query sent to the search engine, and so they are different from the one we are considering here. Among these, Kleinberg's algorithm [7] is considered one of the earliest and most famous. In [2] the authors consider the Kleinberg algorithm, a modification of the SALSA algorithm [8], and some new link-analysis query-dependent ranking algorithms; they compare their performance and develop a theoretical analysis of these algorithms.

3   The Intuitive Definition

The basic idea underlying the definition of PageRank is that of trying to infer the importance of a Web page from just the topological structure of a directed graph associated with the World Wide Web (WWW). We can in fact associate a directed graph with the WWW, where each node represents a Web page and each arc from node i to j represents a link from page i to j. Keeping this fact in mind, from now on we will use "page" or "node", and "link" or "arc" interchangeably and we will typically blend Web with graph terminology.

We will call "in-links" for a Web page the links that point to that page, "out-links" the links that start from that page. Using well-known graph terminology, we will call "in-degree" for a node the number of arcs pointing to that node, "out-degree" the number of arcs starting from that node. If a page i points to a page j, we will also say that "i links to j".

We could now think of the rank of a page as depending on the ranks of all the pages pointing to it, where each rank is divided by the number of out-links those pages have. So we could give an initial, intuitive definition of PageRank, saying that the PageRank of a page k, $P_r(k)$, is a non-negative real number given by the system of equations:

$$P_r(k) = \sum_{h \to k} \frac{P_r(h)}{o(h)} , \qquad k = 1, 2, \ldots, n \qquad (1)$$

where $P_r(h)$ is the PageRank of page h, $o(h)$ is the number of out-links of page h and the sum is extended to all Web pages h pointing to page k; n is the number of pages in the Web. If a page h has many out-links to the same page k, all these out-links count as one. According to this definition the rank of a page depends not only on the number of pages pointing to it but also on their importance. This definition raises some problems, however, substantially related to the fact that something like a *rank sink* can occur; a rank sink is a group of pages pointing to each other, with some links going to the group but with no links going out. In such a situation (see Fig. 1), once we calculate PageRank using the system of equations (1), the pages in the group abnormally increase their PageRank as we will show later. Some other considerations, suggesting a need to change (1), will be given in the following section.

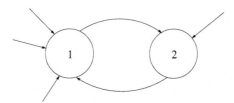

Fig. 1. An example of rank sink

4 Mathematical Aspects

To better understand the problems related to the intuitive definition (1) of PageRank, and why it must be changed, let us focus our attention on a possible way of interpreting (1). If we look at the graph representing the Web as the graphical representation of a discrete time Markov chain [5], the system of equations (1) can be considered as the system of equilibrium equations of this Markov chain. This Markov chain will have transition probabilities given by:

$$P_{ij} = \begin{cases} 1/o(i) & \text{if a link from page } i \text{ to } j \text{ exists,} \\ 0 & \text{otherwise,} \end{cases}$$

where, as in (1), $o(i)$ is the number of out-links of page i. Since we are only interested in relative values of PageRank, PageRank $P_r(h)$, $h = 1, 2, \ldots, n$ can be seen as the limit and stationary probability of being on state h, i.e. each PageRank can only take a value between 0 and 1, and $\sum_{h=1}^{n} P_r(h) = 1$, where, as usual, n is the number of all Web pages. If this limit and stationary probability exists it can be computed with an iterative procedure according to the equations:

$$P_r(k; t+1) = \sum_{h \to k} \frac{P_r(h; t)}{o(h)} , \qquad k = 1, 2, \ldots, n \qquad t = 0, 1, 2, \ldots \qquad (2)$$

where $P_r(h; t)$ is the PageRank of page h on step t, and the remaining notation is the same as in (1). The vector $\mathbf{P_r}(0) = [P_r(1; 0), P_r(2; 0), \ldots, P_r(n; 0)]$ gives the PageRank values of all pages at step 0, and can be chosen arbitrarily among all the possible values for PageRank. Let us consider two examples, to better justify the need for a mathematical theory underlying the computation (2).

Let us consider Fig. 2, where we can see that a rank sink exists, made by the two pages 3 and 4. Starting from the following values of PageRank:

$$P_r(1; 0) = P_r(2; 0) = P_r(3; 0) = P_r(4; 0) = \frac{1}{4}$$

it is easy to get, at a certain step t:

$$P_r(1; t) = P_r(2; t) = \frac{1}{4} \frac{1}{2^t} , \qquad P_r(3; t) = P_r(4; t) = \frac{1}{4}(1 + \frac{1}{2} + \cdots + \frac{1}{2^t})$$

and so:

$$\lim_{t \to +\infty} P_r(1; t) = \lim_{t \to +\infty} P_r(2; t) = 0 , \qquad \lim_{t \to +\infty} P_r(3; t) = \lim_{t \to +\infty} P_r(4; t) = \frac{1}{2} .$$

From these formulas we can see that the PageRank has been totally swallowed up by the rank sink. This situation happens every time we have a finite state Markov chain that is not irreducible, like the one depicted on Fig. 2, and it is particularly regrettable since all states that are outside the closed communicating class will have a PageRank equal to zero and so will be indistinguishable from each other. Another problem with Markov chains that are not irreducible is that

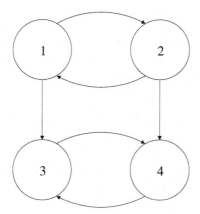

Fig. 2. Markov chain with a rank sink

if we do have two or more closed communicating classes, the PageRank values of the various pages computed through (2) are different, depending on the choice of $\mathbf{P_r}(0)$. In this case even the order of PageRank values of the various pages can change, depending on the choice of $\mathbf{P_r}(0)$.

Even if we have an irreducible Markov chain, however, problems can occur, as can be seen by examining Fig. 3. The very simple Markov chain depicted on Fig. 3 has only two states, 1 and 2, and behaves very strangely: if we have $P_r(1;0) = 1$, $P_r(2;0) = 0$, after one step it is $P_r(1;1) = 0$, $P_r(2;1) = 1$, and then $P_r(1;2) = 1$, $P_r(2;2) = 0$ and so on, in a kind of *rank ping pong* with no convergence. It is worthwhile noting that if we have $P_r(1;0) = 1/2$, $P_r(2;0) = 1/2$ we have a clear convergence:

$$\lim_{t \to +\infty} P_r(1;t) = \lim_{t \to +\infty} P_r(2;t) = \frac{1}{2} \ .$$

From these simple examples we can argue that to have a well-founded definition of PageRank we must have a Markov chain with properties ensuring the Markov chain has a unique strictly positive limit and stationary distribution, i.e. the Markov chain must be irreducible and aperiodic. The limit and stationary distribution is also called equilibrium distribution. It is easy to see that the

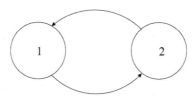

Fig. 3. Markov chain with rank ping pong

Markov chain depicted on Fig. 2 is not irreducible, and that the one depicted on Fig. 3 is periodic with period 2.

The Markov chain described by means of the graph representing the Web is typically not irreducible. The solution to this problem adopted for PageRank is simple and neat: we artificially change the topology of the graph by adding new arcs. In general this addition of new arcs can be done freely, and a new arc can be added between node h and node k even if an arc between these two nodes already exists, so that we can obtain a multigraph, rather than just a simple graph. In practice, as we will see later, in each particular case the addition of new arcs must be done keeping in mind two aims:

1. to disturb the influence of the existing graph as little as possible;
2. to pursue the aims of each particular case.

5   A General Formula for PageRank

Let us suppose to change the structure of the graph as said before, so that in general from a node h to a node k we can have an existing arc and a new arc; let us build a new Markov chain in which, when we are on state h, with a probability $d(h)$ we follow a new link and with a probability $1 - d(h)$ we follow an existing link. The probability $d(h)$ is called the *damping factor*. If we follow one of the existing links, the probability of moving from h to k is given by $\mathrm{elw}(h, k)$ (elw: existing link weight); if we follow one of the new links, the probability of moving from h to k is given by $\mathrm{nlw}(h, k)$ (nlw: new link weight.) So we can say that the transition probability from h to k of this Markov chain, P_{hk}, is given by:

$$
\begin{aligned}
P_{hk} = \mathrm{P}[h \rightarrow k] &= \text{(total probability theorem)} = \\
&= \mathrm{P}[h \rightarrow k | \text{an existing link is followed}]\mathrm{P}[\text{an existing link is followed}] + \\
&\quad + \mathrm{P}[h \rightarrow k | \text{a new link is followed}]\mathrm{P}[\text{a new link is followed}] = \\
&= \mathrm{elw}(h, k)(1 - d(h)) + \mathrm{nlw}(h, k)d(h) \,,
\end{aligned}
$$

where $\mathrm{P}[A]$ is the probability of the event A. If the Markov chain is irreducible and aperiodic (and it can be built in this way, since we are free in choosing the values of $\mathrm{nlw}(\cdot, \cdot)$), the values of PageRank are given by the system of equations:

$$
P_r(k) = \sum_{h=1}^{n} \{P_r(h)[\mathrm{elw}(h, k)(1 - d(h)) + \mathrm{nlw}(h, k)d(h)]\}, \quad k = 1, 2, \ldots, n \quad (3)
$$

where, as usual, n is the number of all the Web pages we consider. Of course, we will have to meet some constraints:

$$
\sum_{k=1}^{n} \mathrm{elw}(h, k) = 1, \qquad \sum_{k=1}^{n} \mathrm{nlw}(h, k) = 1, \qquad h = 1, 2, \ldots, n \,,
$$

and for PageRank we must have:

$$
P_r(k) \geq 0, \qquad k = 1, 2, \ldots, n \qquad \text{and} \qquad \sum_{k=1}^{n} P_r(k) = 1 \,,
$$

since it is a probability.

If the Markov chain is irreducible and aperiodic, from (3) we get a unique strictly positive distribution, i.e. the values of PageRank are univocally determined by (3), and they are all strictly positive. If we require the equilibrium distribution just to be unique, i.e. not necessarily strictly positive, the Markov chain need only have one closed communicating class, which must be aperiodic; even in this case we can use (3) to get the values of PageRank.

6   Deducing Classic PageRank

Starting from the general formula (3), we can easily get back the classic formula for PageRank; we must set:

$$
\mathrm{elw}(h, k) = \begin{cases} 1/o(h) & k = 1, 2, \ldots, n, \text{ if a link actually exists,} \\ 0 & \text{otherwise,} \end{cases} \tag{4}
$$

where $o(h)$ is the number of out-links from page h. Note that even if a page h has many existing out-links to the same page k, all these out-links count as one. Then we set:

$$
\mathrm{nlw}(\cdot, k) = 1/n, \qquad k = 1, 2, \ldots, n; \qquad d(h) = d, \qquad h = 1, 2, \ldots, n
$$

where n is the total number of Web pages considered. In this way we clearly have an irreducible and aperiodic Markov chain, and from (3) we obtain:

$$
P_r(k) = \frac{d}{n} + (1 - d) \sum_{h \to k} \frac{P_r(h)}{o(h)} \,, \qquad k = 1, 2, \ldots, n \tag{5}
$$

where we have used:

$$
\sum_{k=1}^{n} P_r(k) = 1 \ .
$$

The system of equations (5) gives the classic formula for PageRank, as it is suggested, for example, in [7, pages 619–620]; the sum is extended to all Web pages pointing to k.

6.1   Resolving Minor Problems

We can now test the usefulness of the general formula (3) by using it to give a formulation of PageRank which takes into account the possibility of having a page with no out-links. We could also be interested in counting the actual number of links from a page, say h, to another page k.

We might have a page h with no (existing) out-links. In this case we would set $d(h) = 1 \Rightarrow 1 - d(h) = 0$, since we would be forced to follow a new link when wanting to leave page h; for every other page k with at least one out-link we will generally have $d(k) = d$, $0 < d < 1$.

When we want to take into account the actual number of links from h to k we must change the definition (4) of elw(h, k) into:

$$\mathrm{elw}(h, k) = \frac{n_o(h \to k)}{o'(h)}$$

where $n_o(h \to k)$ (≥ 0) gives the actual number of out-links from h to k and $o'(h)$ is the actual number of out-links from page h (i.e. if there are $c > 1$ out-links from h to k, each of them contribute to $o'(h)$). With these changes we still have an irreducible and aperiodic Markov chain, and the formula (3) becomes:

$$P_r(k) = \frac{d}{n} + \frac{1-d}{n} \sum_{h \in S_1} P_r(h) + (1-d) \sum_{h \in S_2} P_r(h) \frac{n_o(h \to k)}{o'(h)} \qquad (6)$$

where $k = 1, 2, \ldots, n$ and, if $S = \{1, 2, \ldots, n\}$ is the set of all the n Web pages we are considering, $S_1 \subset S$ is the set of pages with no out-links, $S_2 \subseteq S$ is the set of pages with at least one out-link, where S_1 and S_2 form a partition of S, and all the other symbols have the usual meaning.

7   Building a Personalized PageRank

Another possible application of the formula (3) concerns a personalization of PageRank; the personalization proposed here gives a rigorous mathematical explanation of a kind of personalization proposed in [10]. In [10] the results of some experiments made considering this kind of personalization can also be found. Let us suppose that only a small number m of pages are considered really important by the user. We can personalize PageRank taking this fact into account, for example considering:

$$\mathrm{nlw}(\cdot, k) = \begin{cases} 1/m & k \in I \\ 0 & \text{otherwise} \end{cases} \qquad (7)$$

where I is the set of pages considered important by the user ($|I| = m$). From (7) we find that a new link is added from each node of the graph to each node in the set I. It is easy to see that in this case the Markov chain might not be irreducible. However, we can prove the following theorem:

Theorem 1. *Using the definition (7) for* nlw$(\cdot, \cdot)$ *we get a Markov chain with only one closed communicating class, the one which includes the states in I.*

Proof. Let us consider the set $\mathcal{C}$ of states that can be reached from at least one state of I; from (7) we get $I \subseteq \mathcal{C}$. The set $\mathcal{C}$ is clearly a closed communicating class: "closed" because no other state $j \notin \mathcal{C}$ can be reached from a state of $\mathcal{C}$, or it would be a state of $\mathcal{C}$; "communicating" because from (7) we learn that from every state j of $\mathcal{C}$ we can reach each state of I, and, according to the definition of $\mathcal{C}$, each state $i \in \mathcal{C}$ can be reached from a correct state of I.

Now we have to prove that this closed communicating class is the only one in this Markov chain. Let us suppose that the Markov chain has another closed communicating class C'; since these classes are equivalence classes, it must be $C' \cap C = \emptyset$. Let us consider a state $h \in C'$; from (7) we have that each state $i \in I$ is accessible from h, i.e. C' is not closed, which clashes with the hypothesis. □

Since the states in C are clearly aperiodic, it is well known from the theory of Markov chains that we can use the general formula to calculate PageRank; of course PageRank will be positive for the pages in the class C, and zero for all the other pages. So we have:

$$P_r(k) = \begin{cases} \sum_{h=1}^n [P_r(h)\mathrm{elw}(h,k)(1-d(h))] & \text{if } k \notin I \\ \sum_{h=1}^n [P_r(h)\mathrm{elw}(h,k)(1-d(h))] + \frac{1}{m}\sum_{h=1}^n (P_r(h)d(h)) & \text{if } k \in I. \end{cases}$$

Then this formula can be particularized choosing the desired values for $\mathrm{elw}(\cdot,\cdot)$ and $d(\cdot)$.

8   A Comparison between Two Different Formulations of Classic PageRank

Let us consider a case in which there are no Web pages without out-links, and the links between the same couple of pages count as one. The formula we use in this case for classic PageRank is

$$P_r(k) = \frac{d}{n} + (1-d)\sum_{h \to k} \frac{P_r(h)}{o(h)} , \qquad k = 1, 2, \ldots, n \qquad (8)$$

that is in [7, pages 619–620]; this formula is slightly different from

$$P_r'(k) = (1-c) + c\sum_{h \to k} \frac{P_r'(h)}{o(h)} , \qquad k = 1, 2, \ldots, n \qquad (9)$$

where c is a constant number, $0 < c < 1$; the formula (9) can be found in [3]. We choose (8) instead of (9) because (9) must be corrected, since in [3] it is written that it should be:

$$\sum_{k=1}^n P_r'(k) = 1$$

while from (9) we get:

$$\sum_{k=1}^n P_r'(k) = (1-c)n + c\sum_{k=1}^n \sum_{h \to k} \frac{P_r'(h)}{o(h)} = (1-c)n + c\sum_{k=1}^n P_r'(k)$$

that is

$$\sum_{k=1}^n P_r'(k) = n .$$

Anyway, the correction proposed in (8) does not change the order of PageRank values, nor adds or removes solutions, as can easily be seen. In fact, using matrix notation, if we write

$$\mathbf{P_r} = \begin{bmatrix} P_r(1) \\ P_r(2) \\ \vdots \\ P_r(n) \end{bmatrix} \qquad \mathbf{u} = \left.\begin{bmatrix} 1 \\ 1 \\ \vdots \\ 1 \end{bmatrix}\right\} n$$

and $\mathbf{\Pi} = [\pi_{hk}]$ $h, k = 1, 2, \ldots, n$, is a matrix with

$$\pi_{hk} = \begin{cases} 1/o(h) & \text{if an arc from } h \text{ to } k \text{ exists,} \\ 0 & \text{otherwise} \end{cases}$$

we find that (8) can be written:

$$\mathbf{P_r} = \frac{d}{n}\mathbf{u} + (1 - d)\mathbf{\Pi}^T\mathbf{P_r}$$

where $\mathbf{\Pi}^T$ is the transposed matrix of $\mathbf{\Pi}$, that is:

$$[\mathbf{I} - (1 - d)\mathbf{\Pi}^T]\mathbf{P_r} = \frac{d}{n}\mathbf{u}$$

where $\mathbf{I}$ is the identity matrix, or

$$\mathbf{P_r} = \frac{d}{n}[\mathbf{I} - (1 - d)\mathbf{\Pi}^T]^{-1}\mathbf{u} \tag{10}$$

since we know that in this case (8) has only one solution. Using the same notation and setting $d = 1 - c$, from (9) we get:

$$\mathbf{P_r}' = d\mathbf{u} + (1 - d)\mathbf{\Pi}^T\mathbf{P_r}'$$

that is

$$\mathbf{P_r}' = d[\mathbf{I} - (1 - d)\mathbf{\Pi}^T]^{-1}\mathbf{u} \ . \tag{11}$$

By a comparison between (10) and (11) we can see that they both have only one solution, since from the theory previously developed we know that $[\mathbf{I}-(1-d)\mathbf{\Pi}^T]$ is an invertible matrix, and the solution of (11) can be obtained from that of (10) by simply multiplying it by n:

$$\mathbf{P_r}' = n\mathbf{P_r} \ .$$

In particular, the order of PageRank values is kept.

9   On the Dependence of Classic PageRank on the Damping Factor

As we have seen before, the idea underlying the formulation of classic PageRank is to try to modify the graph representing the Web to solve the mathematical

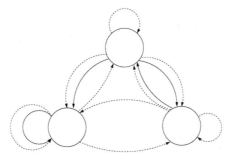

Fig. 4. The changes we must make to the graph to get the classic PageRank; after these changes we have a multigraph

problems related to (1). This must be done while trying not to favour one node over another. To change the structure of the graph in such a balanced way, new links are added to it, so that a new link is added between every couple of existing nodes in both directions, and a new link is also added from each node to itself. All these links have the same weight, and they are all followed with the same probability d, excepting the case in which a node h doesn't have an out-link; in that case we *must* set $d(h) = 1$. The general formula we get is:

$$P_r(k) = \frac{d}{n} + \frac{1-d}{n} \sum_{h \in S_1} P_r(h) + (1-d) \sum_{h \to k} \frac{P_r(h)}{o(h)} , \qquad k = 1, 2, \ldots, n \quad (12)$$

where, as in (6), S_1 is the set of pages with no out-links, d is the probability of following a new link when we leave a node with at least one out-link, and all the other symbols have the usual meaning. In Fig. 4 we depict the changes made in the graph, where the unbroken arcs represent existing arcs, and the dotted arcs represent the new arcs.

A question may now arise (personal communication [1]):

Does the order of PageRank values change if we consider different values for d?

In other words, let us suppose that with $d = d_0$, $0 < d_0 < 1$, the order of PageRank values is:

$$P_r(k_1) \leq P_r(k_2) \leq \ldots \leq P_r(k_n) \quad (13)$$

where $k_1, k_2, \ldots, k_n$ are the n Web pages we are considering. Are we sure that (13) gives the order of PageRank values even if $d \neq d_0$, $0 < d < 1$? Unfortunately, the answer is: "The order of PageRank values generally depends on the value of d", and so there is a certain degree of subjectivity in the order we get. Note that we are focusing our attention on the order of PageRank values, because it is important for ranking Web pages. The simple counter example that follows shows a situation in which the order of PageRank values depends on the value of d

(personal communication [11]). Let us suppose we have $n = 2N+1$ nodes, linked in the way shown in Fig. 5. We have nodes $1, 2, \ldots, N$ pointing to node 0, which has no out-links, and nodes $N+1, N+2, \ldots, 2N$ forming a separate complete directed graph, i.e. there is always an arc between every couple of nodes in both directions, and from a node to itself. In the second graph all PageRank values are the same, i.e. $r = P_r(j)$, $j = N+1, N+2, \ldots, 2N$, because of symmetry, so that by (12) we get:

$$P_r(0) = \frac{d[1 + N(1 - d)]}{n - (1 - d) - (1 - d)^2 N} ,$$

$$P_r(k) = \frac{d}{n} + \frac{1 - d}{n} \frac{d[1 + N(1 - d)]}{n - (1 - d) - (1 - d)^2 N} , \qquad k = 1, 2, \ldots, N$$

$$P_r(k) = \frac{1}{n} + \frac{1 - d}{d} \frac{1}{n} \frac{d[1 + N(1 - d)]}{n - (1 - d) - (1 - d)^2 N} = r , \ k = N+1, N+2, \ldots, 2N.$$

Let us consider the function

$$f(d) \triangleq r - P_r(0) = \frac{(1 - d)(1 - dN)}{n - (1 - d) - (1 - d)^2 N} .$$

It is easy to see that $f(d) > 0$ when $0 < d < 1/N$, $f(d) < 0$ when $1/N < d < 1$, and $f(d) = 0$ when $d = 1/N$, so that:

$$r > P_r(0) \quad \text{when } 0 < d < 1/N$$

$$r < P_r(0) \quad \text{when } 1/N < d < 1$$

$$r = P_r(0) \quad \text{when } d = 1/N .$$

For example, let us suppose $N = 10 \Rightarrow n = 21$. We have:

1. if $d = 0.01$

$$r \cong 0.098 \qquad P_r(0) \cong 0.011$$

that is $r > P_r(0)$;
2. if $d = 0.99$

$$r \cong 0.048 \qquad P_r(0) \cong 0.052$$

that is $r < P_r(0)$.

This example indicates the dependence of the order of PageRank values on d.

10   Conclusion

In this work we discussed the mathematical characteristics of the PageRank algorithm. Starting from an intuitive definition of the algorithm, we showed the need of a new definition with a strong mathematical basis. So we got a well-founded general formula, from which we could directly derive many different

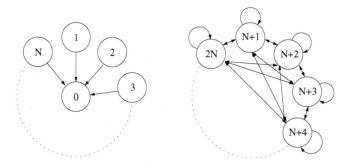

Fig. 5. A counter example to prove that the order of PageRank values depends on the value of d. Since the number of arcs is so large, we have replaced a couple of arcs between two nodes with an arc with one arrow at each end

cases, and among them the case of classic PageRank, in the formulation used in recent works. This formulation is slightly different from the first one given for classic PageRank: we showed that these two formulations are substantially equivalent, i.e. they both have a unique strictly positive solution, and these solutions are bound by a scale factor. Then, as another particularization of the general formula, we derived a personalized PageRank. Finally, we showed the dependence on parameters of the order of classic PageRank values.

This work can be seen as a starting point for new research in many different directions. We will restrict ourselves to three such directions.

1. We could think of a more sophisticated definition of personalized PageRank, for instance one that can dynamically change on the basis of users' feedback.
2. We could also use this work to give us a mathematical basis with a view to an efficient computation of PageRank, and possibly towards an incremental update of its computation as the Web crawler gives new information on the changing topology of the graph.
3. Finally we could think of a new algorithm, giving us the "importance" of a Web page on the basis of a completely "objective" formula, i.e. a formula with no parameters.

Acknowledgements

During the preparation of this work I greatly benefited from stimulating discussions with Maristella Agosti, Gianfranco Bilardi, Massimo Melucci, Nicola Orio and Enoch Peserico. I would also like to thank the anonymous reviewers of this paper for the numerous suggestions they gave me to improve its quality.

References

[1] G. Bilardi, Mar. 2002. Personal communication. 141

[2] A. Borodin, G. O. Roberts, J. S. Rosenthal, and P. Tsaparas. Finding authorities and hubs from link structures on the World Wide Web. In *Proceedings of the World Wide Web Conference*, May 2001. http://www.www10.org/cdrom/papers/314/index.html. 132

[3] S. Brin and L. Page. The anatomy of a large scale hypertextual Web search engine. In *Proceedings of the World Wide Web Conference*, 1998. http://www7.scu.edu.au/programme/fullpapers/1921/com1921.htm. 131, 132, 139

[4] M. R. Henzinger. Hyperlink analysis for the Web. *IEEE Internet Computing*, 5(1), Jan.-Feb. 2001. 131, 132

[5] S. Karlin. *A First Course in Stochastic Processes*. Academic Press, New York, 1966. 134

[6] S. J. Kim and S. H. Lee. An improved computation of the PageRank algorithm. In F. Crestani, M. Girolami, and C. J. van Rijsbergen, editors, *Advances in Information Retrieval*, number 2291 in LNCS, pages 73–85, 2002. 132

[7] J. M. Kleinberg. Authoritative sources in a hyperlinked environment. *Journal of the ACM*, 46(5):604–632, Sept. 1999. 131, 132, 137, 139

[8] R. Lempel and S. Moran. SALSA: The stochastic approach for link-structure analysis. *ACM Transactions on Information Systems*, 19(2):131–160, Apr. 2001. 132

[9] M. Mitzenmacher. Notes on Kleinberg's algorithm and PageRank. Unpublished manuscript. http://www.eecs.harvard.edu/ +michaelm/CS222/NOTES/Klein.ps (downloaded: January 2002). 132

[10] L. Page, S. Brin, R. Motwani, and T. Winograd. The PageRank citation ranking: bringing order to the Web. Unpublished manuscript. http://google.stanford.edu/ +backrub/pageranksub.ps (downloaded: January 2002), 1998. 132, 138

[11] E. Peserico, Mar. 2002. Personal communication. 142

Machine Learning Approach
for Homepage Finding Task

Wensi Xi, Edward A. Fox, Roy P. Tan, and Jiang Shu

Computer Science Department, Virginia Polytechnic Institute and State University
VA, 24060, U.S.A.
{xwensi,fox,rtan,jshu}@vt.edu

Abstract This paper describes new machine learning approaches to predict the correct homepage in response to a user's homepage finding query. This involves two phases. In the first phase, a decision tree is generated to predict whether a URL is a homepage URL or not. The decision tree then is used to filter out non-homepages from the web pages returned by a standard vector space information retrieval system. In the second phase, a logistic regression analysis is used to combine multiple sources of evidence based on the homepages remaining from the first step to predict which homepage is most relevant to a user's query. 100 queries are used to train the logistic regression model and another 145 testing queries are used to evaluate the model derived. Our results show that about 84% of the testing queries had the correct homepage returned within the top 10 pages. This shows that our machine learning approaches are effective since without any machine learning approaches, only 59% of the testing queries had their correct answers returned within the top 10 hits.

1   Introduction

With the rapid development of the internet and World Wide Web, information from the Web has become one of the primary sources of knowledge for human beings. Although traditional information retrieval (IR) techniques have provided many methods to seek relevant information from the internet in response to a user's need, they are still far from sufficient in some cases, such as when a user is seeking information that is too broadly or vaguely specified for a traditional IR system to give a precise result. On the other hand the linking structure and various tagged fields of a web page can be rich sources of information about the content of that page. Making use of this information can be very helpful in solving those information seeking problems that can not be satisfactorily solved by traditional IR techniques. Among this kind of user's information need are special information seeking tasks like "homepage finding" which involves trying to find the entry page to a website. This paper describes new methods of using machine learning approaches to consider extensive linking information, tagged fields, URLs, and other information sources to

A.H.F. Laender and A.L. Oliveira (Eds.): SPIRE 2002, LNCS 2476, pp. 145–159, 2002.
© Springer-Verlag Berlin Heidelberg 2002

best predict the relevant homepage in response to a user's homepage finding query. The rest of the paper is organized as follows: related work is introduced in Section 2; our approach is described in Section 3; the baseline IR system is explained in Section 4; machine learning models and results are reported in Sections 5 and 6; and results are summarized and discussed in Section 7.

2   Related Work

2.1   Link Analysis

In our research work, we analyze various types of linking information to find whether they can help to predict a homepage. Consequently, we herein briefly summarize previous studies of linking information. There have been two major methods to make use of link information to identify the correct web page in response to a user's query: the page rank algorithm and the HITS algorithm.

The page rank algorithm was first introduced by Brin and Page [2]. This algorithm was developed because in-degree is a weak predictor of quality. First, not all back pages are of the same importance. Second, in-degree is spammable. In their page rank algorithm each page was first evaluated as to quality. Then each page allows all the page links to it to distribute their "value" of quality to it. The quality value of each page was divided by the out-degree before they could distribute their "authority" to other pages. The algorithm can be summarized as:

$$PageRank(P) = \beta/N + (1 - \beta)\Sigma PageRank(B)/outdegree(B)$$

where β is the probability of a random jump to P and N is the total number of pages in the Web. B identifies a web page that contains a hyperlink to page P.

The HITS algorithm was first introduced by Kleinberg [9]. He assumes that a topic can be roughly divided into pages with good coverage of the topic, called authorities, and directory-like pages with many hyperlinks to pages on the topic, called hubs. The algorithm aims to find good authorities and hubs. For a topic, the HITS algorithm first creates a neighborhood graph. The neighborhood contains the top 200 matched web pages retrieved from a content based web search engine; it also contains all the pages these 200 web pages link to and pages that link to these 200 top pages. Then, an iterative calculation is performed on the value of authority and value of hub. Iteration proceeds on the neighborhood graph until the values converge. Kleinberg claimed that the small number of pages with the highest converged value should be the pages that are the best authorities for the topic. And the experimental results support the concept. Kleinberg also pointed out that there might be topic diffusion problems (with the answer shifting to a broader topic related to the query). There also might be multi-communities for a query, where each community is focused on one meaning of the topic. Sometimes the first/principal community is too broad for the topic and the 2nd and 3rd communities might contain the right answer to the user's query.

2.2   Combining Different Sources of Evidence

In our research work, we also use machine learning to combine different sources of evidence to help improve the retrieval results. Combining multiple sources of evidence (or data fusion) is not a new research approach in the information retrieval area. A number have investigated how document scores generated by different systems and methods can be combined to improve retrieval results. Some early work was done by Fuhr [5] and Gey [7]. Lee [10] combined pairs of weighting schemes used in the SMART system. He summed the normalized document scores produced by the various weighting schemes, and found that significant improvements could be obtained by combining two schemes in which one performed cosine normalization and the other did not, if the two schemes provided a similar level of retrieval effectiveness. Lee [11] also combined retrieval results from six different systems that participated in the TREC-3 conference. He took every pair of these systems and combined the retrieval scores for the documents. He found that combining two systems together generally gave better results than the individual systems. Taking the sum of individual scores gave the best results when the document scores were un-normalized. However, taking the sum of scores multiplied by the number of nonzero scores gave slightly better results when the scores were normalized. This method also gave the best results for the 3-way, 4-way, and 5-way combinations of the six systems and the combination of all the systems. Lee suggested that combining the scores from multiple systems increases retrieval effectiveness because the different systems retrieve similar sets of relevant documents but different sets of non-relevant documents. In the same study, Lee also investigated the combination of document ranks rather than scores, and found that combining document ranks gave better results than combining scores when the two systems generated very different rank-similarity curves.

Vogt and Cottrell [16] combined the retrieval scores from two systems by taking a weighted sum. They tried a series of relative weights ranging from 20 to 1/20. Their experiments were carried out in a "routing queries" context. The document collection was divided into two subsets. The first subset was used to determine the best relative weights to use for each query (i.e., a different relative weight was used for each query for combining the scores). The formulas for the individual queries were evaluated using the second subset of the document collection. The effectiveness of the combined system was compared with that of the two individual systems, as well as with the best possible performance determined by optimizing the relative weight using the second subset of documents. The result was disappointing because the combined system performed virtually identically to the better of the two systems for each query, and didn't achieve the best possible linear performance.

Chen [3] explored a range of methods for combining four factors for information retrieval. The first factor reflected the frequency of the matching terms in the query, the second factor reflected the frequency of the matching terms in the document, the third reflected the prevalence of the matching terms in the document collection, and the fourth factor was the number of matching terms. He combined the factors using various methods, and found that logistic regression, linear regression, neural networks, and the linear discriminant method gave equally good results when used to develop models for combining the 4 factors. However, he recommended using logistic regression because of its performance, efficiency, ease of interpretation of the output (the output can be interpreted as probability of relevance), and scalability. We build upon these results in the study described below.

2.3   Homepage Finding Task

The homepage finding task was defined in Craswell and Hawking's research work [4]. A related problem to homepage finding is identification of best entry points to structured documents as was done by Kazai et al. [8]. An early effort for homepage finding was carried out at HP Inc. (http://hpsearch.uni-trier.de/hp/), called "Search for Personal Home Pages of Computer Scientists".

In Craswell and Hawking's work, they used anchor text to retrieve documents in response to a homepage finding task, and compared their results with full-text retrieval. They found anchor text retrieval is far more effective than full-text retrieval. They also developed a method of taking the average of the reciprocal of the rank of the first correct homepage retrieved to evaluate retrieval performance. This method is called mean reciprocal rank or MRR.

This type of research work was presented in the TREC-10 Web track, where 16 research groups from all over the world explored various ways to find the relevant homepage based on the same web page collection and sample queries.

Westerveld and Hiemstra's approach [19] had among the best results for the TREC homepage finding task. They developed a prior probability for a page being a homepage. Their prior is simply based on the length of the URL length. The prior is computed by assigning URLs that only had one slash "/" (or are followed by index.html) a score of 4, URLs with 2 "/" score 3, and URLs with 3 "/" score 2; all other URLs have score 1.   Then, they linearly combine the scores from content retrieval, anchor text retrieval, as well as the URL prior. They achieved a Mean Reciprocal Rank of 0.82 on the training queries and MRR of 0.77 on testing queries.

In another work, Fijita [6] first searched the queries against an index file of server names. His single search on this had achieved a MRR of 0.64 on training queries. He also collected the anchor text of each page as well as the title description of each page, and linearly combined them with various linking information (number of in links of a page, number of out links of a page). He achieved a mean MRR of 0.76 on the test queries.

Savoy and Rasologo [12] proposed two search strategies in their homepage finding work. The first was to simply search the URL address. The second strategy was to first search the content of the web page and then to re-rank the returned list using URL length. In their final run, they combined the content search result with the URL search result as well as an adaptation of the Okapi model, and achieved an MRR of 0.63.

In this paper, based on work with the same TREC collection used by the three above mentioned groups, we report an MRR of approximately 0.8. We consider this of interest to explain further since our results are good and since our approach differs from the others.

3   Problem Context

Our research makes use of the WT10g web collection provided by the TREC staff. The WT10g collection is about 10GByte in size and contains 1,692,096 web pages crawled in 1997. The average size of a web page in the collection is 6.3 KBytes.

The TREC staff provided 100 sample homepage finding queries and their corresponding correct answers or homepages. (Note that some queries have multiple correct answers; thus, there are a total of 107 homepage provided by the TREC staff.) These sample queries can be used to train the homepage finding system developed. TREC also provided another 145 testing queries without the corresponding answers. These queries can be used to evaluate the system developed.

The 100 sample homepage finding queries are very short queries. Most of them only contain 2 to 3 words. They include the name of an institute (e.g., UVA English department), organization (e.g., Chicago Computer Society), or a person's name (e.g., Jim Edwards). Some of the queries also contain descriptive information (e.g., Unofficial Memphis Home Page). After a close analysis of the 100 training queries and URLs of their corresponding homepages, we developed the following heuristics:

- A homepage usually ends with a "/".
- Most homepages contain at most 2 other "/", beyond the 2 in http://.
- The last word in the homepage URL (if the URL is not ending with a "/") is usually: index.html, index1.html, homepage.html, home.html, main.html, etc.

Most of the 100 sample homepages confirm these rules. Yet there are exceptions, e.g.:

- McSportlight Media This Week ->
    http://www.mcspotlight.org:80/media/thisweek/
- LAB MOVIE REVIEW SITE ->
    http://www.ucls.uchicago.edu:80/projects/MovieMetropolis/
- The Boats and Planes Store -> http://www.psrc.usm.edu:80/macrog/boats.html

The basic rationale for our URL analysis is to filter out non-homepages that rank at the top of the list returned by the content based information retrieval system, so that real homepages can be ranked higher.

TREC also provided two files:

- in_links: which maps each page to a list of pages that contain incoming links to this page.
- out_links: which maps each page to a list of pages that are the destination of outgoing links from this page.

4   Baseline IR System, Collection Analysis, and Initial Results

At the beginning of this research, a vector space model IR system was developed to retrieve relevant web pages for each of the 100 training homepage finding queries. The vector space model IR system uses a stop word list to filter out high frequency words. Each word left is stemmed using Porter's algorithm [13]. The IR system uses the ntf*idf weighting scheme with cosine normalization to construct the query vectors and the tf*idf weighting scheme with cosine normalization to construct the document vectors [15]. ntf refers to normalized term frequency and is given by the formula:

$$ntf = 0.5 + 0.5 * tf / max\_tf$$

where max_tf is the highest term frequency obtained by terms in the vector. The retrieval score for the document is calculated by taking the inner product of the document and query vectors.

The WT10g Web collection contains 3,353,427 unique keywords (after filtering out stopwords, and stemming). The inverted file developed from this collection is about 3 GBytes in size.

Tagged fields: In order to investigate the importance of tagged fields in HTML files during the retrieval, several tagged fields were extracted from the WT10g collection. The tagged fields extracted were <title>, <meta>, and <h1>.

Anchor texts: Anchor texts are the text description of a hyperlink in a web page. Previous research found that anchor text retrieval could help improve retrieval performance [14]. In this research work, we extracted and combined the anchor texts with the destination web page it links to and built a separate anchor text collection, in which each page only contains all the anchor text of other pages describing it. Relevant related work was done by Attardi et al. [1].

Abstract: Some researchers had found that text summary and abstract retrieval could yield comparable or even better retrieval results than full text retrieval [14]. And abstract retrieval also can save substantial time and space. In this research work, we extracted an pseudo-abstract for each web page. The abstract contains the URL of the web page, <title> tagged field of that page, and the first 40 words following. The rationale for the abstract collection is that we believe a homepage is very likely to repeat its name in its URL title or at the beginning of the page, so this collection is more likely to achieve better results than full text retrieval. On the other hand, an abstract contains more information than that used for single tagged field retrieval and so is not likely to omit the correct answers to queries.

The statistical facts of the full-text, tagged field, anchor, and abstract collections are listed in Table 1.

Table 1. Statistical facts of the various collections

Collection	Collection Size	Number of Documents	Average Document Length	Inverted File Size	Number of Keywords
Full Text	10000MBytes	1692096	6.3KBytes	3000MBytes	3353427
Title Tag	100MBytes	1602137	62.5Bytes	59MBytes	158254
Meta Tag	50MBytes	306930	167Bytes	28MBytes	59122
H1 Tag	29MBytes	517132	56Bytes	15MBytes	82597
Anchor	180MBytes	1296548	138Bytes	53MBytes	219213
Abstract	710MBytes	1692096	420Bytes	400MBytes	646371

Retrieval Results

Table 2 and Figure 1 report the retrieval results for the 100 testing queries on different tagged fields. From the table we find that the <meta> tag and <h1> tag each performs poorly. This shows that the text in these fields is not a good indicator of the main topic of the web page. Full text retrieval doesn't work very well either. Abstract retrieval works much better than the full-text retrieval, as we expected. Anchor text retrieval performs slightly better than abstract retrieval in terms of MRR (Mean Reciprocal Rank). Title tag retrieval performs best of all.

Table 2. Baseline system retrieval results for training queries

Relevant Found in	Full-Text	Title Tag	Meta Tag	H1 Tag	Anchor Text	Abstract
Top1	5	34	4	7	22	23
Top5	18	62	8	11	47	40
Top10	25	68	11	14	54	49
Top20	34	73	14	14	57	59
Top100	48	85	18	15	65	73
Lost	0	5	73	84	18	2
MRR	0.115	0.456	0.058	0.09	0.336	0.313

MRR stands for Mean Reciprocal Rank
$MRR = \Sigma(1/rank)/N$ N: Number of queries

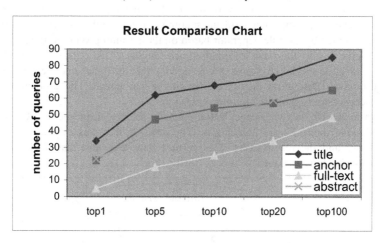

Fig. 1. Baseline retrieval results comparison chart for training queries

5   Decision Tree Model

In the second phase of our research work, a decision tree was generated to predict whether a URL is a homepage URL or not. The detailed steps are:

1. 91 non-homepages are manually selected from the WT10g collection. These pages are identified not only by the content but also by the in-links and out-links of the pages and by the structure of the URL.
2. Attribute vectors are developed for the 198 cases (107 positive cases provided from TREC and 91 negative cases derived manually); the attribute vectors contain these factors:

- URL length: the number of slashes in the URL;
- In link: the total number of in links;
- In link normalized by homepage: total number of in links divided by the length of the web page;
- In link from outer domain: the number of in links from outer domains;
- In link from same domain: the number of in links from the same domain;
- Out link: total number of out links of a web page;
- Out link normalized by homepage: the total number of out links divided by the length of the web page;
- Out link to outer domain: the number of out links pointing to other domains;
- Out link to same domain: the number of out links pointing to the same domain;
- Keyword: whether the URL ends with a keyword; these keywords are "home", "homepage", "index", "default", "main";
- Slash: whether the URL ends with "/";
- Result: whether it is a homepage or not.

3. The 198 training vectors were provided to the data mining tool C5 or See5 (available at http://www.rulequest.com/see5-info.html). A decision tree was developed by the rule generator based on these training vectors. It can be seen in Figure 2; only the slash information, the length of URL, and whether URL ends with some special keywords, are retained. Other attributes may be helpful but are not the determining factors in deciding a homepage. The correctness of the decision tree against the training cases is 97%.

4. Another 102 test web pages were manually selected from the TREC collection. Among them, 27 are homepages. The decision tree was evaluated on the test cases and the results were 92% correct. This indicates that the decision tree model is fairly reliable.

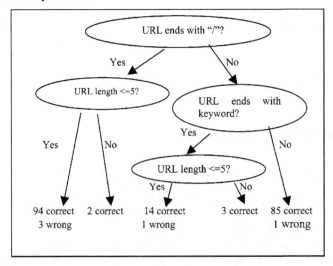

Fig. 2. Decision tree model

The decision tree was then applied to the results returned by the baseline IR system, in anticipation that we can filter out most of the non-web pages in these returned web page lists. The decision tree model was only applied to anchor, title field, and abstract retrieval. Results of the decision tree applied on the title and anchor text retrieval can be found in Table 3.

6   Logistic Regression Model

In the third stage of this research work, a logistic regression analysis model was developed to combine link information with the various scores returned by the standard IR system, in order to improve the rank of the correct homepages in response to the query. The logistic regression analysis was only made on the web pages that were retained by the decision tree model. Similar logistic regression was employed by Fuhr [5]. The detailed steps are:

1. Two training queries (No. 5 and No. 51) were taken out of consideration because their correct answer was already filtered out as non-homepages by the decision tree model. The top 1000 pages for each rank-list file of the remaining 98 training queries are fed into the logistic regression analysis. Thus, there are 67855 pages in the training set (not all the return lists contain more than 1000 pages; for those short lists, we just take all the pages returned); among them 104 pages are relevant to a specific query.
2. A logistic regression analysis was made using SAS, version 8.02. The evidence used in the logistic regression analysis includes IR scores from title, anchor, and abstract retrieval. (All scores are pre-normalized by the maximum score for each query, thus, the score ranges from 0 to 1.) Linking information (e.g., no. of in links, out links) and the URL length information are also used. The logs of all these factors are also thrown into the logistic regression analysis. The predicted factor is whether a page is relevant to a query (1) or not (0). The analysis result shows that the log of title retrieval score (l_title); title retrieval score (title); anchor retrieval score (anchor); abstract retrieval score (abstract); and the reciprocal of the URL length (r_url) can be used to predict the relevance of a web page to a query. The formula is shown below:

relevancy = 0.99*l_title+11.57*title+2.42* anchor+4.12*abstract+13.9*r_url – 22.21

The percent correlation of the system is 98%.
3. The formula derived from the logistic regression analysis was then applied to the 98 training queries; 70 queries found the correct answer on the top of the list; 96 queries found the correct answer within the top10 of the list. The MRR is 0.802 and is 13% better than the title retrieval after non-homepage removal using the decision tree model (the best of all the runs in the previous stage). Detailed results of the logistic regression analysis model can be found in Table 3.

Table 3. Machine learning model retrieval results for training queries

Relevant Found in	Anchor + Tree	Title + Tree	Abstract + Tree	Logistic Regression
Top1	43	62	50	70
Top5	61	83	67	94
Top10	63	84	75	96
Top20	65	86	79	96
Top100	72	92	92	97
Lost	19	7	4	3
MRR	0.504	0.710	0.597	0.802
Percentage Improvement	50% over Anchor	55.7% over Title	90.7% over Abstract	13% over Title + Tree

7   Testing Query Results and Discussion

Finally, 145 testing queries provided by the TREC conference were used to evaluate our system. The table below reports the retrieval result for the testing queries on different collections. From the table we find that testing queries perform substantially worse than the training queries on title collection; however, they perform much better than the training queries on the anchor retrieval.

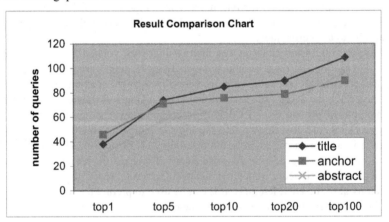

Fig. 3. Machine learning model retrieval results comparison chart for training queries

Table 4. Baseline system retrieval results for testing queries

Relevant Found in	Title Tag	Anchor Text	Abstract
Top1	38	46	30
Top5	74	71	58
Top10	85	76	66
Top20	92	79	70
Top100	109	90	97
Lost	17	33	2
MRR	0.378	0.401	0.295

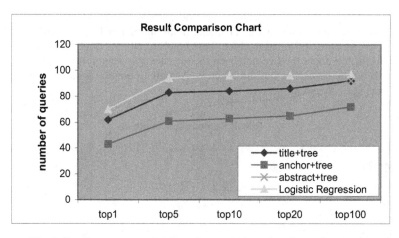

Fig. 4. Baseline system retrieval results comparison chart for testing queries

Then the decision tree model was applied to the returning rank lists of the 145 testing queries. The logistic regression model was applied to the result of the decision tree model. Results are shown in Table 5.

Table 5. Machine learning model retrieval results for testing queries

Relevant Found in	Anchor + Tree	Title + Tree	Abstract + Tree	Logistic Regression
Top1	68	77	61	96
Top5	81	97	84	118
Top10	84	102	96	121
Top20	88	108	105	128
Top100	98	114	124	130
Lost	38	27	13	15
MRR	0.511	0.595	0.501	0.727
Percentage Improvement	27.4% over Anchor	57.4% over Title	69.8% over Abstract	22.2% over Title + Tree

From Figure 4 and Figure 5 we can find that the overall performance of the testing queries is much worse than for the training queries. This is mainly because 11 testing queries corresponding to correct homepages do not confirm the decision tree model. Thus the correct homepage was filtered out of the rank list by the decision tree step. This greatly affects the final performance.

After a close examination of these 11 queries, we find that in 3 cases, an argument could be made regarding what should be classified as homepages. For example, for query No. 14 "Wah Yew Hotel", the correct answer provided by TREC is

http://www.fastnet.com.au:80/hotels/zone4/my/my00198.htm

Another example: query No.16 "Hotel Grand, Thailand", has correct answer:

http://www.fastnet.com.au:80/hotels/zone4/th/th00635.htm

When we go to the above locations we find each is only an introductory page to Wah Yew Hotel and Hotel Grand, Thailand, in an online hotel index website. It had no links to any other information about these hotels at all. Although this might be the only information about the two hotels on the Internet, this may not guarantee in itself that we have the homepages of these hotels. Actually, common sense would suggest these two pages are not homepages at all.

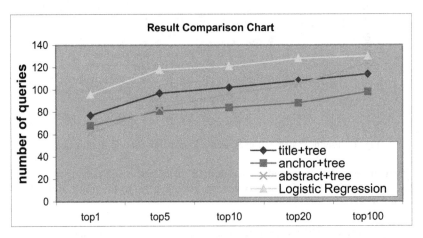

Fig. 5. Machine learning model retrieval results comparison chart for testing queries

One more example: query No. 134 "Kaye Bassman International" has the correct answer provided by TREC:

http://www.kbic.com:80/toc.htm

However, when you look at the actual page, you will find this is only a table of contents. The homepage of Kaye Bassman International is clearly

http://www.kbic.com:80/index.htm,

pointed to by the hyperlink at the table of contents page. These queries lead us to 2 basic questions: What is the definition of a homepage? Can a table of contents also be regarded as a homepage? These questions are not easily answered without further research on user behavior on the Internet.

8   Conclusion and Future Research Work

Our main conclusions from this research work are:
1. <Title> tagged field retrieval, Anchor text retrieval, and Abstract retrieval perform substantially better than the full text retrieval in the context of homepage finding task.

2. The decision tree model is an effective machine learning method to filter out non-homepages. This method can improve the retrieval performance by an average of 50%.

3. Logistic regression analysis is another effective machine learning approach to combine multiple sources of evidences to improve the retrieval result. Our research results show this method can improve the retrieval performance by 13% on training queries and 22% on testing queries.

4. By applying machine learning technologies to our system, our final testing results show 66% of the queries find the correct homepage on top of the return list and 84% of the queries find the correct homepage within the top 10 hits of the return list.

Future research may include:

1. Further looking into the homepages, finding more attributes that might indicate a homepage. For example, some homepages contain words such as: "welcome", "homepage", "website", "home", or "page" in the initial few lines of the text. Incorporating these new factors might help indicate whether a page is a homepage or not.

2. Making use of relevance feedback. The relevance feedback technique is found to be very successful at improving precision for very short queries. Since they are short, homepage finding queries might benefit from this approach.

3. Using a probabilistic rather than a binary decision tree, so the likelihood of being a homepage becomes a factor in the logistic regression.

4. Experimenting with large collections to give more thorough and realistic testing of the methods, such as with the 1 terabyte crawling of text we recently completed in collaboration with the University of Waterloo.

Acknowledgements

This research work was funded in part by America OnLine, Inc. Thanks go to Dr. A. Chowdhury from AOL for his kind help. Thanks also go to Fernando Das Neves, Hussein Suleman, and other colleagues in the Digital Library Research Laboratory at Virginia Tech for their very useful and important suggestions.

References

[1] G. Attardi, A. Gull, and F. Sebastiani. Automatic Web page categorization by link and context analysis. In *Proceedings of the First European Symposium on Telematics, Hypermedia and Artificial Intelligence*, pp. 105-119. Varese, Italy, 1999.

[2] S. Brin and L. Page. The anatomy of a large-scale hypertextual web search engine. *Proceedings of the 7th International WWW Conference*, pp. 107-117. 1998. http://www7.scu.edu.au/programme/fullpapers/1921/com1921.htm

[3]   Chen. "A comparison of regression, neural net, and pattern recognition approaches to IR," in *Proceedings of the 1998 ACM 7th International Conference on Information and Knowledge Management* (CIKM '98), pp. 140-147. New York: ACM, 1998.

[4]   N. Craswell, D. Hawking and S. Robertson. Effective Site Finding using Link Anchor Information. Proceedings of the 24th Annual International ACM SIGIR Conference on Research and Development in Information Retrieval, pp. 250-257. 2001.

[5]   N. Fuhr. Integration of Probabilistic fact and text retrieval. In Proceedings of the 15th Annual International ACM SIGIR Conference on Research and Development in Information Retrieval, pp. 211-222, 1992.

[6]   S. Fujita. More Reflections on "Aboutness". TREC-2001 Evaluation Experiments at Justsystem. In *Proceedings of the Tenth Text Retrieval Conference (TREC 2001)*. NIST Special Publication 500-250. 2002.

[7]   F.C. Gey, A. Chen, J. He, and J. Meggs. Logistic regression at TREC4: Probabilistic retrieval from full text document collections. In *Proceedings of the Fourth Text Retrieval Conference (TREC 4)*. NIST Special Publication 500-236. 1996.

[8]   G Kazai, M Lalmas and T Roelleke. A Model for the Representation and Focused Retrieval of Structured Documents based on Fuzzy Aggregation, In *Proceedings of the 8th International Symposium on String Processing and Information Retrieval*, pp. 123-135, Laguna de San Rafael, Chile, 2001.

[9]   J. Kleinberg. Authoritative sources in a hyperlinked environment. In *Proceedings of the 9th Annual ACM-SIAM Symposium on Discrete Algorithms*, pp. 668-677. 1998. http://www.cs.cornell.edu/home/kleinber/auth.ps

[10]   J.H. Lee. Combining multiple evidence from different properties of weighting schemes. In *Proceedings of the 18th Annual International ACM SIGIR Conference on Research and Development in Information Retrieval*, pp. 180-188. New York: ACM, 1995.

[11]   J.H. Lee. Analyses of Multiple Evidence Combination. In Proceedings of the 20th Annual International ACM SIGIR Conference on Research and Development in Information Retrieval, pp. 267-276. New York: ACM, 1997.

[12]   J. Savoy and Y. Rasolofo. Report on the TREC-10 Experiment: Distributed Collections and Entrypage Searching. In *Proceedings of the Tenth Text Retrieval Conference (TREC 2001)*. NIST Special Publication 500-250. 2002.

[13]   M. F. Porter. An algorithm for suffix stripping. Program 14, pp. 130-137. 1980.

[14]   T. Sakai and K. Sparck-Jones. Generic Summaries for Indexing in Information Retrieval. In Proceedings of the 24th Annual International ACM SIGIR Conference on Research and Development in Information Retrieval, pp. 190-198. 2001.

[15]   G. Salton and M. J. McGill. Introduction to Modern Information Retrieval. New York: McGraw Hill, 1983.

[16]   C.C. Vogt and G.W. Cottrell. "Fusion via linear combination for the routing problem". In *Proceedings of the Sixth Text Retrieval Conference (TREC 2001)*. NIST Special Publication 500-250. 1998.

[17] C.C. Vogt and G.W. Cottrell. "Predicting the performance of linearly combined IR systems". In *Proceedings of the 21st Annual International ACM SIGIR Conference on Research and Development in Information Retrieval,* pp. 190 – 196. New York: ACM, 1998.

[18] E. Voorhees and D.K. Harman. Overview of the Ninth Text Retrieval Conference (TREC-9). In *Proceedings of the Ninth Text Retrieval Conference (TREC-9),* pp. 1-28. NIST Special Publication 500-249. 2001.

[19] T. Westerveld and D. Hiemstra. More Retrieving Web Pages Using Content, Links, URLs and Anchors. In *Proceedings of the Tenth Text Retrieval Conference (TREC 2001).* NIST Special Publication 500-250. 2002.

Tree Pattern Matching for Linear Static Terms

Cedric Chauve

LaCIM and Département d'Informatique, Université du Québec à Montréal
Case Postale 8888, Succursale Centre-Ville, H3C 3P8, Montréal (QC), Canada
chauve@lacim.uqam.ca

Abstract. In this paper, we present a simple algorithm for pattern matching within a family of trees called linear terms, that have many applications in the design of programming languages, theorem proving and symbolic computation for example. Our algorithm relies on the representation of a tree by words. It has a quadratic worst-case time complexity, which is worse than the best known algorithm, but experimental results on uniformly distributed random binary terms suggest a linear expected time and interesting practical behavior.

The tree pattern matching (TPM) problem consists of finding all the occurrences of a pattern tree P as subtree of a target tree T. Aside from its theoretical interest (it is a natural generalization of the classical pattern matching in words (WPM) problem), it has applications in several areas of computer science from design of programming languages [1, 9] to computational molecular biology [15, 19]. In this paper, we consider a particular family of trees, called linear terms, which is very common in the field of compiler design and theorem proving for instance. We describe a very simple algorithm to search a set of pattern trees in a fixed (*static*) target tree. Our algorithm relies on encoding trees by words and on a classical data structure in the field of word algorithms, the *suffix tree*, and seems to have a good behavior in practice. In Section 1, we present a quick survey of linear terms and of the TPM problem for this family of trees. We continue by a precise description of our algorithm, followed by an experimental study. We conclude with some problems.

1   Tree Pattern Matching and Linear Terms

Linear terms. Let Σ be a finite alphabet and V a symbol not belonging to Σ. We associate to every symbol of Σ an integer value called its arity. We call a *target term* an ordered tree such that every vertex is labeled by a symbol of Σ and has a degree (its number of children) equal to the arity of its label. The definition of a *linear pattern tree* is similar to the one of a target term, except that the leaves (vertices of degree 0) of a linear pattern term can be labeled either by the symbols of Σ of arity 0 or by the symbol V. Terms are used, for instance, to represent boolean expressions (see Figure 1) in the field of automatic theorem proving, or derivation trees related to a grammar in the analysis of programs or in compiler design.

A.H.F. Laender and A.L. Oliveira (Eds.): SPIRE 2002, LNCS 2476, pp. 160–169, 2002.

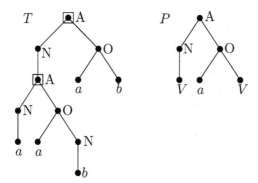

Fig. 1. A target term T, representing a parameterized boolean expression (A stands for And, O for Or and N for Not), and a linear pattern term P. There are two occurrences of P in T, at the vertices marked with a square

Tree pattern matching for linear terms. Let T be a target term and P a linear pattern term, of respective size (number of vertices) n and m. For a vertex v of T, there is an occurrence of the pattern P at v if there exists a one-to-one map from the vertices of P to the vertices of T such that:

- the root of P maps to v,
- if an internal vertex x maps to y then x has the same label as y (the two vertices have the same degree) and the ith child of x maps to the ith child of y,
- if a leaf x maps to y then either x is labeled with V or x and y have the same label.

The TPM problem for linear terms consists of computing the set of vertices of T where there is an occurrence of P.

Previous results. There is an immediate algorithm for solving the TPM problem, usually called the *naïve algorithm*, consisting of a traversal of T, calling at every visited vertex v a recursive procedure testing if there is an occurrence of P at v (see [17] for example). This algorithm is very simple to implement and achieves a quadratic $O(n\,m)$ time complexity[1], but Flajolet and Steyaert proved that the expected time is in $\Theta(n + m)$ [17].

The first non trivial algorithms were proposed by Hoffmann and O'Donnell [9], but their algorithms still have a quadratic time complexity (later, their bottom-up algorithm has been improved by Cai, Paige and Tarjan [3], and Thorup [18]). The first algorithm with a subquadratic time complexity is due to Kosaraju [11], who proposed an algorithm running in $O(n\,m^{3/4}\,\text{polylog}(m))$ time. This result has been improved successively by Dubiner, Galil and Magen [8], Cole and Hariharan [5], and Cole, Hariharan and Indyk [6], who achieved an almost linear $O(n\,\log^3 n)$ time complexity.

---

[1] Unless specified, in this paper we consider the worst-case time complexity.

The static case of the pattern matching problem. In a pattern matching problem, one usually distinguishes two cases. In the *dynamic* case, the target structure is not fixed (it can be modified between the search of different patterns) and the algorithm is based on a preprocessing of the pattern structure (for words we can cite the Knuth-Morris-Pratt and Boyer-Moore algorithms [10, 2]). In the *static* case, we assume that the target is fixed (if it is inserted in a data base for example) and that many patterns could be searched through this target tree. Thus we can preprocess the target in order to speed-up the pattern matching phase. For the WPM problem, the preprocessing of the target consists of computing an auxiliary data structure indexing the suffixes of the target, like the suffix tree, the suffix automaton or the suffix array (see [7, chapters 5 and 6]). For words, this preprocessing is linear (in space and time) in the size of the target and allows to compute the positions of the occurrences of P in T in time almost linear in the size of P ($O(|P| \log |\Sigma|)$ with a suffix tree or a suffix automaton, and $O(|P| + \log |T|)$ with a suffix array). This property makes this method very useful in the case of numerous pattern searches in the same target.

Motivation and results. In the context of the TPM problem for terms, we can notice that there are only two algorithms dealing with the static case, but that these two algorithms suffer from some limitations. The bottom-up algorithm of Hoffmann and O'Donnell [9] has an exponential time preprocessing in the general case and is very complicated to implement. The algorithm of Shibuya [16], based on a new suffix tree for a tree data-structure, allows only to treat particular instances of this problem: the target term must be a k-ary tree (every vertex other than a leaf has degree exactly k, for a given integer k) and the pattern term must be a balanced k-ary tree. Moreover, we should add that all the known algorithms for the TPM problem are quite sophisticated and difficult to implement efficiently, which often leads people to use the naive algorithm, which is very simple and very efficient in practice.

Our aim in this paper is to present a simple algorithm for the TPM problem for linear terms dedicated to the static case. The algorithm we propose relies on a classical representation of terms as words proposed by Luccio and Pagli for some tree matching problems [12, 13, 14] and on the classical suffix tree data structure. They have the following properties: the preprocessing phase has a $O(n \log |\Sigma|)$ time complexity and $O(n)$ space complexity, and the pattern matching phase has a quadratic $O(n\,m)$ time complexity. This time complexity is the same as the naive algorithm, but it appears from experiments that our simple algorithm seems to have a linear expected time and a better behavior than the naive algorithm.

2   The Algorithm

Terms and words. Our algorithm is based on the representation of a term T of size n by two words of size n, W_T and L_T, already used by Luccio and Pagli [12]. For a term T, if x is the ith vertex of T visited during a preorder traversal of T,

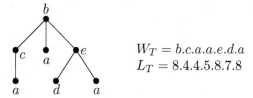

$$W_T = b.c.a.a.e.d.a$$
$$L_T = 8.4.4.5.8.7.8$$

Fig. 2. A term T and the associated words W_T and L_T

then $W_T[i]$ is the label of x and $L_T[i] = i + |T_x|$, where $|T_x|$ is the number of vertices in the subtree of T rooted at x.

Notation 1. In the rest of this section we consider two terms T and P, respectively on the alphabets Σ and $\Sigma \cup \{V\}$. T has size n and P has size m.

Definition 1. We say that the kth prefix of W_P ($W_P[1 \cdots k]$, $1 \le k \le m$) matches the factor $W_T[i \cdots j]$ of W_T ($1 \le i \le j \le m$) if there are k integers $i_1 = i < i_2 < \cdots < i_k = j$ such that

- for every $\ell \in [k]$, $W_P[\ell] \ne V \Rightarrow W_T[i_\ell] = W_P[\ell]$,
- for every $\ell \in [k]$, $W_P[\ell] \ne V \Rightarrow i_{\ell+1} = i_\ell + 1$, and $W_P[\ell] = V \Rightarrow i_{\ell+1} = L_T[i_\ell]$.

Let v be a vertex of T and i be the position of the corresponding symbol in W_T. It is clear that there is an occurrence of P in T at v if and only if there is a factor $W_T[i \cdots j]$ of W_T such that the mth prefix of W_P matches $W_T[i \cdots j]$. The following algorithm for the TPM problem is a simple iterative translation of the naive recursive algorithm in terms of words following from the above remark.

Algorithm 1: Naive algorithm for terms

---

for *every* $1 \le i \le n$ *such that* $W_T[i] = W_P[1]$ **do**

    $j := 2$ and $k := i + 1$;

    while $j \le m$ **do**

1

        if $W_T[k] = W_P[j]$ **then** $j := j + 1$ and $k := k + 1$;

        else if $W_P[j] = V$ **then** $j := j + 1$ and $k := L_T[k]$;

        else exit the **while** loop;

    if $j = m + 1$ **then** there is an occurrence of P at the ith vertex of T;

Notation 2. We denote by comp_1 the number of comparisons between a symbol of W_T and a symbol of W_P (that is the number of times the step 1 of the above algorithm is performed). It is clear that this parameter gives also the asymptotic time complexity of the algorithm.

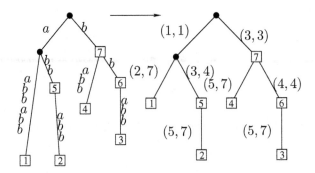

Fig. 3. The suffix tree of the word *aabbabb*

Suffix trees and pattern matching in terms. In the rest of this section, we propose an improvement of this algorithm, using the suffix tree of the word W_T.

We recall that the suffix tree of a word W, denoted by $ST(W)$, is a compressed digital search tree indexing the suffixes of W (see [7, chapter 5] for a survey on the suffix tree of a word and its applications). Every edge of $ST(W)$ is labeled by a factor of W, that can be represented by the position in W of its first and last symbols ((i,j) for a factor $W[i \cdots j]$). For a vertex u of $ST(W)$, we denote by $w(u)$ the word obtained by the concatenation of the labels of the edges on the path from the root of $ST(W)$ to u. For a word W and a vertex u of a suffix tree, we say that u accepts W if and only if $w(u) = W$ (see Figure 3).

The correctness of the algorithm we propose below relies on the notion of valid pair in the suffix tree of the word encoding a target term. Valid pairs will be used to represent the occurrences of a pattern tree in the target tree in such a suffix tree.

Definition 2. A *valid pair of* $ST(W_T)$ is a pair (e, ℓ) where:

- e is an edge of $ST(W_T)$ (say labeled by (b, f)),
- ℓ an integer satisfying $0 \leq \ell \leq (f - b)$.

We denote by $w(e, \ell)$ the word $W_T[(b - |w(u)|) \cdots (b + \ell)]$.

Notation 3. From now, for a valid pair (e, ℓ) (resp. (e', ℓ'), (e'', ℓ'')) we denote by u and v (resp. u' and v', u'' and v'') the vertices incident by the edge e (resp. e', e''), where u (resp. u', u'') is the parent of v (resp. v', v''), and by (b, f) (resp. (b', f'), (b'', f'')) the label of this edge.

Definition 3. We say that a word W *matches a valid pair* (e, ℓ) of a suffix tree $ST(W_T)$ if W is equal to $w(e, \ell)$.

Example 1. In the suffix tree of Figure 3, if we denote by e the edge incident to the vertices labeled by 6 and 3, then the word *bbab* matches the valid pair $(e, 2)$.

The following property is the central to our pattern matching algorithm.

Property 1. Let $W_P[1 \cdots k]$ $(k < m)$ be a prefix of W_P (e, ℓ) and (e', ℓ') be two valid pairs of $ST(W_T)$ such that

  - $W_P[k+1] = V$,
  - the kth prefix of W_P $(W_P[1 \cdots k])$ matches (e, ℓ),
  - v' is a descendant of v,
  - $w(e, \ell)$ is a proper prefix of $w(e', \ell')$.

If we denote by h the integer $|w(u')| - |w(u)| - (\ell + 1)$ (hence $W_P[1 \cdots k]$ matches $W_T[b' - h - 1 \cdots b']$), then $W_P[1 \cdots k + 1]$ matches (e', ℓ') if and only if $L_T[b' - h] = b' + \ell' + 1$.

The algorithm. The principle of our algorithm is to read the word W_P in $ST(W_T)$, as usual when searching a suffix tree for the occurrences of a word, the variable V being handled in a special way defined following Property 1. Hence we need two procedures to traverse $ST(W_T)$: the first, called **Reading**, is the classical procedure which reads a word in a suffix tree, but when the current symbol of W_P equals the variable V, it calls the **Jump** procedure, which performs a recursive traversal of the subtree of $ST(W_T)$ rooted at the current vertex of this suffix tree, computing valid pairs accepting the prefix of W_P ending on this symbol V. The fact that the following algorithm computes all the occurrences of the pattern term P in the target term T is a direct consequence of Property 1.

Algorithm 2: Pattern matching in terms

Input: W_T, L_T, W_P and $ST(W_T)$
let r be the root of $ST(W_T)$;
if *an edge e such that $W_T[b] = W_P[1]$ leaves r* **then Reading**$(1, (e, 0))$;

Analysis of the algorithm. The preprocessing of the target (computing W_T, L_T and $ST(W_T)$) can be done in $O(n)$ space and $O(n \ \log |\Sigma|)$ time, using classical results on encoding of trees and suffix trees.

The time complexity of the pattern matching phase depends on three parameters:

  - the number $comp_2$ of comparisons between symbols of the words W_T and W_P (which is the number of executions of the test $W_T[b+\ell] = W_P[k]$ in the loop marked 1 in **Reading**),
  - the number of calls to **Jump**,
  - the number of vertices of $ST(W_T)$ visited during the step 2 of **Reading**.

First, we notice that the number of vertices of $ST(W_T)$ visited during step 2 of **Reading** is at most two times the number of occurrences of P in T, which is less than or equal to n

---

Procedure Reading$(j, (e, \ell))$
$k := j$;
1 **while** $k \le m$, $\ell \le (f - b)$ *and* $W_T[b + \ell] = W_P[k]$ **do**
$\quad \lfloor \ k := k + 1$ *and* $\ell := \ell + 1$;

if $k > m$ **then**

2 $\quad \mid$ (* *the word* W_P *has been completely read* *) traverse the subtree of $ST(W_T)$
$\quad \mid$ rooted at v: visiting a vertex accepting the suffix $W_T[i \cdots n]$ indicates that
$\quad \mid$ there is an occurrence of P in T rooted at the vertex corresponding to the
$\quad \mid$ symbol $W_T[i]$;

else if $\ell > (f - b)$ **then**
$\quad \mid$ (* *the current edge* e *has been completely read* *) **if** *an edge* e' *such*
$\quad \mid$ *that* $W_T[b'] = W_P[k]$ *leaves* v **then Reading**$(k, (e', 0))$;
$\quad \mid$ **if** $W_P[k] = V$ **then for** *every edge* e'' *other than* e' *leaving* v **do**
$\quad \mid \quad \lfloor$ **Jump** $(k, e'', 0)$;

else (* *we exit the loop because* $W_T[b + \ell] \ne W_P[k]$ *) **if** $W_P[k] = V$ **then**
Jump$(k, e, -\ell)$;

Procedure Jump(k, e, h)
$j := L_T[b - h]$ (* j: *position of the next symbol of* W_T *to read (Property 1)**);
if $j \le (f + 1)$ **then** (* *this jump stops in the current edge* e *) **Reading**$(k + 1,$
$(e, j - b))$;
else (* *we must continue the jump in the suffix tree* *) **for** *every edge* e' *leaving* v
do Jump$(k, \ e', \ h + (f - b + 1))$;

Next, if we notice that between two consecutive calls to **Jump** on the same
edge of $ST(W_T)$ there has been at least one comparison between symbols of W_T
and W_P, we can state that the number of such calls is at most comp_2 plus the
number of edges of $ST(W_T)$ visited during the pattern matching phase (which
is at most $2n$).

Finally, the number comp_2 of comparisons between a symbol of W_T and
a symbol of W_P is at most comp_1. This last observation allows us to say that
the time complexity of our algorithm is $O(n + \text{comp}_1)$, i.e. $O(n\,m)$.

In fact, we can express this time complexity in a more precise way. Let us
denote, for any symbol $x \in \Sigma$, by $ST_x(W_T)$ the set of leaves u of $ST(W_T)$ such
that the first letter of $w(u)$ is the symbol x. If the root of P is labeled with x, it
is easy to see that

- $\text{comp}_2 <= m\,|ST_x(W_T)|$,
- the number of calls to **Jump** is at most $\text{comp}_2 + |ST_x(W_T)|$,
- the number of vertices of the suffix tree visited by the step 1 of **Reading** is
  at most $2\,|ST_x(W_T)|$.

Hence, if x is the label of the root of P, the time complexity of the pattern
matching phase is $O(m\,|ST_x(W_T)|)$.

Finally, it follows from the fact that the complexity of the pattern matching phase is $O(n + \text{comp}_1)$ and from the result of Flajolet and Steyaert [17] about the naive algorithm that, with uniformly distributed random terms, the expected time is at most $\Theta(n + m)$. Our experimental results (Section 3) suggest that the expected time of our algorithm is linear, with a better behavior than the naive algorithm.

Remark 1. We can slightly improve Algorithm 2, in time and space, by noticing that in the suffix tree $ST(W_T)$, we don't need, for a suffix $W_T[i \cdots n]$ of W_T, to store the entire suffix, but only the part $W_T[i \cdots L_T[i] - 1]$, which represents the subtree of T rooted at the vertex corresponding to $W_T[i]$. Hence, we can remove some states in $ST(W_T)$, with the consequence that a vertex of this modified suffix tree can accept many identical words (corresponding to identical subtrees of T). This operation can clearly be done in linear time after the construction of the classical version of $ST(W_T)$ and allows to save some space (the suffix tree has less vertices) and some time during the execution of the step 2 of the **Reading** procedure.

3   Experimental Results

In this section, we present the experimental results obtained with the two algorithms presented above (the naive algorithm, which is known to be fast in practice, and our improved suffix tree algorithm).

Our implementation was done on a Pentium 400 MHz running LINUX, with the C language (using GCC 2.91.66). The time spent in every procedure was recorded using the GPROF 2.9.1 program. We focused on the pattern matching phase and not on the preprocessing phase (i.e. converting the trees in words and computing the suffix tree).

Like Flajolet and Steyaert [17], we considered binary terms (every internal vertex has degree 2 or 0) and three cases, according to the probability p for the leaves of a random pattern to be labeled with the variable V: if $p = 1/(|\Sigma_0| + 1)$ where Σ_0 is the set of symbols of Σ having arity 0, if $p = 1/2$ or if $p = 1$ (this last case maximises the number of calls to **Jump**). Finally, our methodology was to generate at random thousands of targets of size 1000 or 10000 and search twenty small random patterns (of size from 4 to 40 vertices) in every target.

For the naive algorithm, we recorded the following statistics: the number comp_1 of comparisons between symbols of W_T and W_P (line 1 of the naive algorithm) and the time t_1 spent in this algorithm. For the improved algorithm, we recorded the following statistics: the number comp_2 of comparisons between symbols of W_T and W_P (line 1 of the improved algorithms), the number jumps of calls to the **Jump** procedure and the time t_2 spent during the pattern matching phase.

Finally, we may add that we used an implementation of suffix trees as binary trees, which is equivalent to consider that the branching structure (the structure used to store and retrieve the edges leaving a node) is an unsorted list.

Table 1. Experimental results for binary terms. First column: number of symbols comparisons with Algorithm 1. Second column: number of symbols comparisons with Algorithm 2. Third column: number of calls to **Jump** in Algorithm 2. Fourth column: time spent by Algorithm 1 / time spent by Algorithm 2

n	$\|\Sigma\|$	$comp_1$	$comp_2$	jumps	t_1/t_2
1000	2	3561/3318/3318	1294/536/536	817/297/297	$1, 18/2, 81/2, 81$
1000	3	1237/1115/1075	459/178/123	1091/381/257	$1, 19/2, 82/4, 16$
1000	4	647/577/545	242/91/50	1255/437/231	$1, 21/2, 83/4, 79$
1000	5	404/359/334	151/57/26	1362/475/209	$1, 25/2, 86/5, 83$
1000	6	334/297/274	124/47/18	1444/509/182	$1, 3/2, 9/6, 52$
10000	2	35604/33166/33166	11153/4446/4446	7238/2575/2575	$1, 01/2, 28/2, 28$
10000	3	12380/11137/10731	3985/1467/987	9730/3272/2206	$1, 04/2, 46/3, 38$
10000	4	6458/5759/5434	2080/757/391	11103/3745/1949	$1, 09/2, 51/4, 32$
10000	5	4035/3583/3335	1301/471/200	12156/4113/1743	$1, 11/2, 56/5, 08$
10000	6	3339/2960/2727	1077/391/138	12922/4414/1583	$1, 12/2, 58/5, 99$

In the following table, we give the average value of $comp_1$, $comp_2$, jumps and the value t_1/t_2 (we display from right to left, in each cell of the table, the values of these statistics for $p = 1/(|\Sigma_0| + 1)$, $p = 1/2$ and $p = 1$).

These experimental data suggest that our algorithm is more efficient, in practice, than the naive algorithm, even if, when $p = 1$, the two algorithms have a similar behavior.

4   Conclusion

In this paper, we propose a simple algorithm for matching linear patterns in static terms. They are, as far as we know, the first devoted to this precise problem and seem to be very efficient in practice. We believe that these simple algorithms are good candidates for the case where many pattern matching requests are dealing with the same target term. Among the works remaining to do on this problem of pattern matching in static trees, we can highlight some problems.

It would be interesting to study the practical behavior of our algorithm on real data and not only random binary terms.

Among other extensions, we can think to apply the principle of our algorithm in the design of algorithms for other TPM problems dealing with other kind of trees (like the non-linear pattern matching in terms, or the TPM problem, for general ordered trees, introduced in [4]).

Can we improve the theoretical analysis of our algorithm in order to understand its good practical behavior? For instance, it should be possible to study the average behavior of the parameter $comp_2$ using the method of Flajolet and Steyaert [17].

From an implementation point of view, it would be efficient to give a non recursive version of our algorithms, which implies using a $O(n)$ extra-space but would surely greatly improve their performances.

References

[1] A. V. Aho and M. Ganapathi. Efficient tree pattern matching : an aid to code generation. In *ACM Symposium on Principles of Programming Languages, POPL'85*, pages 334–340. Assoc. Comput. Mach. Press, 1985. 160

[2] M. S. Boyer and J. S. Moore. A fast string-searching algorithm. *Comm. ACM*, 20:762–772, 1977. 162

[3] J. Cai, R. Paige, and R. E. Tarjan. More efficient bottom-up multi-pattern matching in trees. *Theoret. Comput. Sci.*, 106(1):21–60, 1992. 161

[4] C. Chauve. Tree pattern matching with a more general notion of occurrence of the pattern. *Inform. Process. Letters*, 82(4):197–201, 2002. 168

[5] R. Cole and R. Hariharan. Tree pattern matching and subset matching in randomized $O(n \log^3 m)$ time. In *ACM Symposium on Theory of Computing, STOC'97*, pages 66–75. Assoc. Comput. Mach. Press, 1997. 161

[6] R. Cole, R. Hariharan, and P. Indyk. Tree pattern matching and subset matching in deterministic $O(n \log^3 n)$-time. In *ACM-SIAM Symposium on Discrete Algorithms, SODA'99*, pages 245–254. Assoc. Comput. Mach. Press, 1999. 161

[7] M. Crochemore and W. Rytter. *Text algorithms*. Oxford University Press, New York, 1994. 162, 164

[8] M. Dubiner, Z. Galil, and E. Magen. Faster tree pattern matching. *J. Assoc. Comput. Mach.*, 41(2):205–213, 1994. 161

[9] C. M. Hoffmann and M. J. O'Donnell. Pattern matching in trees. *J. Assoc. Comput. Mach.*, 29(1):68–95, 1982. 160, 161, 162

[10] D. E. Knuth, J. H. Jr. Morris, and V. R. Pratt. Fast pattern matching in strings. *SIAM J. Comput.*, 6(2):323–350, 1977. 162

[11] S. R. Kosaraju. Efficient tree pattern matching. In *IEEE Symposium on Foundations of Computer Science, FOCS'89*, pages 178–183. IEEE Comput. Soc. Press, 1989. 161

[12] F. Luccio and L. Pagli. An efficient algorithm for some tree matching problems. *Inform. Process. Lett.*, 39(1):51–57, 1991. 162

[13] F. Luccio and L. Pagli. Simple solutions for approximate tree matching problems. In *Theory and Practice of Software, TAPSOFT '91*, volume 493 of *Lecture Notes in Comput. Sci.*, pages 193–201. Springer, 1991. 162

[14] F. Luccio and L. Pagli. Approximate matching for two families of trees. *Inform. and Comput.*, 123(1):111–120, 1995. 162

[15] B. A. Shapiro and K. Zhang. Comparing multiple RNA secondary structures using tree comparisons. *Comput. Appl. Biosci.*, 6:309–318, 1990. 160

[16] T. Shibuya. Constructing the suffix tree of a tree with a large alphabet. In *International Symposium on Algorithms and Computation, ISAAC'99*, volume 1741 of *Lecture Notes in Comput. Sci.*, pages 225–236. Springer, 1999. 162

[17] J. M. Steyaert and P. Flajolet. Patterns and pattern-matching in trees: an analysis. *Inform. and Control*, 58(1-3):19–58, 1983. 161, 167, 168

[18] M. Thorup. Efficient preprocessing of simple binary pattern forests. *J. Algorithms*, 20(3):602–612, 1996. 161

[19] K. Zhang and D. Shasha. Simple fast algorithms for the editing distance between trees and related problems. *SIAM J. Comput.*, 18(6):1245–1262, 1989. 160

Processing Text Files as Is: Pattern Matching over Compressed Texts, Multi-byte Character Texts, and Semi-structured Texts

Masayuki Takeda[1,2], Satoru Miyamoto[1], Takuya Kida[3], Ayumi Shinohara[1,2], Shuichi Fukamachi[4], Takeshi Shinohara[4], and Setsuo Arikawa[1]

[1] Department of Informatics, Kyushu University
Fukuoka 812-8581, Japan
{takeda,s-miya,ayumi,arikawa}@i.kyushu-u.ac.jp
[2] PRESTO, Japan Science and Technology Corporation (JST)
[3] Kyushu University Library
Fukuoka 812-8581, Japan
kida@lib.kyushu-u.ac.jp
[4] Department of Artificial Intelligence, Kyushu Institute of Technology
Izuka, 820-8502, Japan
{fukamati,shino}@ai.kyutech.ac.jp

Abstract. Techniques in processing text files "as is" are presented, in which given text files are processed without modification. The compressed pattern matching problem, first defined by Amir and Benson (1992), is a good example of the "as-is" principle. Another example is string matching over multi-byte character texts, which is a significant problem common to oriental languages such as Japanese, Korean, Chinese, and Taiwanese. A text file from such languages is a mixture of single-byte characters and multi-byte characters. Naive solution would be (1) to convert a given text into a fixed length encoded one and then apply any string matching routine to it; or (2) to directly search the text file byte after byte for (the encoding of) a pattern in which an extra work is needed for synchronization to avoid false detection. Both the solutions, however, sacrifice the searching speed. Our algorithm runs on such a multi-byte character text file at the same speed as on an ordinary ASCII text file, without false detection. The technique is applicable to *any* prefix code such as the Huffman code and variants of Unicode. We also generalize the technique so as to handle structured texts such as XML documents. Using this technique, we can avoid false detection of keyword even if it is a substring of a tag name or of an attribute description, without any sacrifice of searching speed.

1 Introduction

In the standard ASCII, alphabetic, numeric, and other special characters are represented in 7 bits and thus there are only 128 codewords. An extra 128 suffices to represent other characters for most western languages. However, an oriental

A.H.F. Laender and A.L. Oliveira (Eds.): SPIRE 2002, LNCS 2476, pp. 170–186, 2002.

language such as Japanese, Korean, Chinese, and Taiwanese, has often much more characters and multi-byte character code is therefore used to represent them. Since the ASCII characters are still expressed with a single byte for compatibility, there are single byte characters and multi-byte characters in one text file. For example, a text in Japanese Extended-Unix-Code (EUC) is a mixture of single byte characters and two byte characters. This destroys a comfortable property: one-to-one correspondence between the characters in a text string and the bytes in its representation.

Consider the classical string matching problem over such a text. One naive solution would be to convert a text file into a sequence of two byte codewords by padding each single byte codeword and then apply a favoured string matching algorithm. The method, however, requires an additional time for the conversion which is linearly proportional to the text length, and this is not desirable from the practical viewpoint despite the theoretical complexity does not get worse. We want to process a text file without modification. Another solution would be to directly search the text file for the encoding of a pattern by using a Boyer-Moore type string matching algorithm. An extra work for synchronization is needed to avoid false-detection. Simple and quick verification is possible for some specific codes. For example, we have only to go backward to find a byte in the range of 00h to 7fh, not used to represent multi-byte characters in the Japanese EUC. However, we do not adopt such approach by the following reasons: (1) A set of keywords should be simultaneously searched for. Although there are several multipattern variants of the BM algorithm (e.g. [12]), the performance gets worse if the keyword set contains at least one short keyword. (2) Keywords in Japanese are often of length two or three (as the number of characters is very large), and therefore they are represented by 4 or 6 bytes. (3) The above mentioned synchronization technique depends upon a code being used. In general, synchronization requires reading all of the symbols of a text encoded with a prefix code, and therefore it decelerates the over-all task even if we adopt a BM-type algorithm that allows skipping most of the symbols of the encoded text.

Our idea is to merge the synchronization and the string searching tasks into one. This enables us to perform string pattern matching over a multi-byte character text without sacrifices of searching speed. The method is to build a pattern matching machine by embedding a DFA recognizing the set of codewords into an ordinary Aho-Corasick machine and then make it run over a text file byte after byte. Although this synchronization technique has not been published yet, it was adopted as the main engine of the general purpose text database management system SIGMA [4], which has been exploited e.g. for literary analysis of whole volume of novel writers. Also, the technique can be generalized to handle *any* prefix code including the Huffman code, variants of Unicode, and so on. This technique can be generalized to handle *any* prefix code including the Huffman code, variants of Unicode, and so on.

Thus, researchers who must process such multi-byte character text files are forced to be aware of the difference between a text string and its representation. "Processing text files as is" has been one of the most important research topics for such researchers. The *compressed pattern matching problem*, which is first defined by Amir and Benson [2] and the aim of which is to efficiently perform string pattern matching over a compressed text without decompressing it, can be recognized as a topic along the "as-is" principle.

Here, we present another example along the "as-is" principle. In the query processing for XML documents, it is usual to convert each XML document into a tree structure and then process a user-specified query by node operations over the trees. However, this conversion often consumes much CPU time and a huge amount of memory. It is desirable to process XML documents without conversion, namely, "as is". The problems to be overcome are: (1) to avoid false-detection of keyword when it is a substring of a tag name or of attribute descriptions; and (2) to detect all occurrences of the start and the end tags even when many attribute descriptions are included in a start tag. A naive solution exists which requires an extra work to distinguish the inside and outside of a tag expression, but it sacrifices the searching speed. To resolve these problems, we generalize the synchronization technique so as to handle tag strings in structured texts such as XML documents. Using this method with a stack for storing tag names, we develop a fast pattern matching algorithm for structured texts. Experimental results show that it is approximately $7 \sim 10$ times faster than sgrep [5], an alternative tool for processing structured texts as strings.

2   Preliminaries

Let Σ be a finite set of characters, called an *alphabet*. A finite sequence of characters is called a *string*. The empty string is denoted by ε. Let Σ^* be the set of strings over Σ, and let $\Sigma^+ = \Sigma^* \backslash \{\varepsilon\}$. Strings x, y, and z are said to be a *prefix*, *factor*, and *suffix* of the string $u = xyz$, respectively. A prefix, factor, and suffix of a string u is said to be *proper* if it is not u. Let *Prefix*(u) be the set of prefixes of a string u, and let *Prefix*$(S) = \bigcup_{u \in S}$ *Prefix*(u) for a set S of strings.

2.1   Prefix Code

Definition 1. *A subset L of Σ^+ is said to have the* prefix property *if no string in L is a proper prefix of another string in L.*

Let Σ be a source alphabet and Δ be a code alphabet. The code alphabet Δ is usually a binary alphabet $\{0, 1\}$, but can be an arbitrary finite set of symbols. A mapping **code** : $\Sigma \to \Delta^+$ is called a *prefix code* if and only if:

1. For any $a, b \in \Sigma$, **code**$(a) = $ **code**(b) implies $a = b$.
2. The set **code**$(\Sigma) = \{$**code**$(a) \mid a \in \Sigma\}$ has the prefix property.

An element of **code**(Σ) is called a *codeword*. With a prefix code **code**, a string $a_1 \ldots a_n$ over the source alphabet Σ is encoded as concatenation of the codewords of characters $a_1, \ldots, a_n$, namely, **code**$(a_1 \ldots a_n) = $ **code**$(a_1) \ldots$ **code**(a_n).

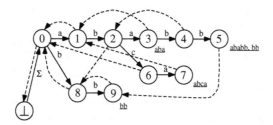

Fig. 1. Aho-Corasick machine for $\Pi = \{aba, ababb, abca, bb\}$. The circles denote states. The solid and the broken arrows represent the goto and the failure functions, respectively. The underlined strings adjacent to the states mean the outputs from them

The Huffman code is a typical example of prefix code, where the code alphabet is $\Delta = \{0, 1\}$. Multi-byte character encoding schemes for oriental languages such as Japanese, Korean, Chinese, and Taiwanese are also prefix codes, where the code alphabet is $\Delta = \{00, 01, \ldots, \text{ff}\}$, i.e., a set of one byte integers (represented here in hexadecimal) rather than the binary alphabet $\{0, 1\}$.

2.2   Aho-Corasick Pattern Matching Machine

The Aho-Corasick pattern matching machine (AC machine for short) [1] is a finite state machine which simultaneously recognizes all occurrences of multiple patterns in a single pass through a text. The AC machine for a finite set $\Pi \subseteq \Sigma^+$ of patterns consists of three functions: *goto, failure,* and *output.* Figure 1 displays the AC machine for the patterns $\Pi = \{aba, ababb, abca, bb\}$.

There is a natural one-to-one correspondence between the states of the AC machine and the pattern prefixes. For example, the initial state 0 corresponds to the empty string ε and the state 4 corresponds to the string $abab$ in Fig. 1. Based on this correspondence, the move of the AC machine is characterized as the following theorem.

Theorem 1 ([1]). *Let $a_1 \ldots a_n$ be the text $(n > 0)$. After reading a text prefix $a_1 \ldots a_j$ $(1 \leq j \leq n)$, the AC machine is in state corresponding to the string $a_i \ldots a_j$ $(1 \leq i \leq j)$ such that $a_i \ldots a_j$ is the longest suffix of $a_1 \ldots a_j$ that is also a prefix of some pattern in Π.*

3   Pattern Matching over Variable-Length Encoded Texts

Suppose we are given a text string encoded with a variable-length prefix code, and want to find a pattern within the text. One solution would be to apply a favoured string searching algorithm to find the encoded pattern, with performing an extra work to determine the beginning of codewords within the encoded text. This work can be done if we build a DFA that accepts the language

code$(\Sigma)^* \subseteq \Delta^*$ and make it run on the encoded text. An occurrence of the encoded pattern that begins at position i is a false match if the DFA is not in accepting state just after reading the $(i-1)$th symbol. However, even if we adopt a BM-type algorithm that allows skipping most symbols of the encoded text, the DFA reads all the symbols in it and therefore this decelerates the over-all task.

Klein and Shapira [6] proposed a probabilistic method: When the encoded pattern is found at index i, jump back by some constant number of symbols, say K, and make the DFA run on the substring of length K starting at the $(i-K)$th symbol. They showed that if K is large enough the probability of false match is low. However, the probability is not zero unless $K = i$.

Our idea is to merge the DFA and the AC machine into one pattern matching machine (PMM). This section illustrates the construction of such PMMs which never report false matches. The technique was originally developed for processing Japanese texts, and then generalized for prefix codes including variants of Unicode, other multi-byte encodings, and the Huffman code. However, the algorithm and its correctness proof have not been published yet. For this reason, the authors present the algorithm and give a correctness proof, together with presenting its applications.

3.1   PMM Construction Algorithm

Let us illustrate the algorithm with an example of the Huffman code. Suppose that the source alphabet $\Sigma = \{A, B, C, D, E\}$, the code alphabet $\Delta = \{0, 1\}$, and the encoding is given by the Huffman tree shown in Fig. 2. Let EC and CD be the patterns to be searched for. Their encodings are, respectively, **code**$(EC) = 1001$ and **code**$(CD) = 00101$. The AC machine for these bit strings is shown in Fig. 2. This machine, however, leads to false detection.

The way for avoiding false detection is quite simple. We build a DFA that accepts the set of codewords and then embed it into the AC machine. Such a DFA is called the *codeword DFA*. The smallest codeword DFA for the Huffman tree of Fig. 2 is shown in Fig. 3.

Proposition 1. *Let* $L \subseteq \Delta^+$ *be a regular language over* Δ*. If* L *has the prefix property, the smallest DFA accepting* L *has only one final state.*

From the proposition, if **code** is a prefix code, then the smallest codeword DFA has only one final state. The construction of the smallest codeword DFA is (1) building a codeword DFA as a trie representing the set **code**(Σ) and (2) then minimizing it. The minimization can be performed in only linear time with respect to the size of the codeword trie, by using the minimization technique [10].

We construct a PMM by embedding the codeword DFA into the ordinary AC machine. The algorithm is summarized as follows. (We omit the construction of the output function.)

Construction of the goto function.

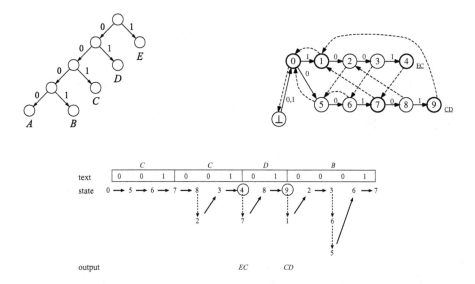

Fig. 2. On the upper-left a Huffman tree is displayed. On the upper-right the ordinary AC machine built from 1001 and 00101 that are the encodings of patterns EC and CD, respectively, is displayed. The move of this machine on the encoding 001001010001 of text $CCDB$ is illustrated on the lower, in which a false detection of pattern EC occurs

1. Build the smallest codeword DFA for **code**, which has a unique final state without outgoing edges. (See the DFA on the upper-left in Fig. 3.)
2. For the given pattern set $\Pi = \{w_1, \ldots, w_k\} \subseteq \Sigma^+$, build a trie for the set $\mathbf{code}(\Pi) = \{\mathbf{code}(w_1), \ldots, \mathbf{code}(w_k)\} \subseteq \Delta^+$. We call the trie *pattern trie.*
3. Replace the unique final state of the codeword DFA by the root node of the pattern trie. (See the state 0 of the PMM on the upper-right in Fig. 3.)

Construction of the failure function.

1. (Basis) Create a failure link from the root of the pattern trie to the initial state of the codeword DFA. (See the broken arrow from state 0 to state 10 in the PMM on the right in Fig. 3.)
2. (Induction Step) Consider a node s of depth $d > 0$ in the pattern trie. Assume the failure links are already computed for all nodes of depth less than d. Let r be the father of the node s and a be the label of the edge from r to s. Start from r and repeat failure transitions until a node r' is found that has an outgoing edge labeled a to some node s'. Create a new failure link from s to s'.

It should be noted that the induction step of the failure function construction is exactly the same as that of the original AC algorithm. The only difference is in the codeword DFA attached to the root node.

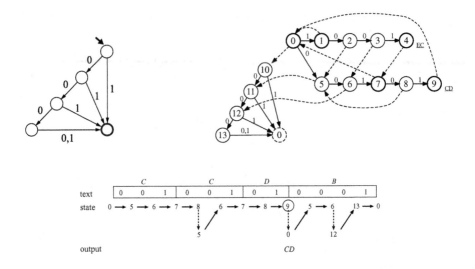

Fig. 3. On the upper-left the smallest DFA that accepts the set of codewords is shown. On the upper-right the PMM obtained by embedding this DFA into the AC machine of Fig. 2. The move of this PMM on the encoding 001001010001 of text $CCDB$ is displayed on the lower. No false detection occurs when using this PMM

3.2   Correctness of the Algorithm

Now, we give a characterization of the PMM constructed by the above mentioned algorithm. Let $\Pi \subseteq \Sigma^+$ be the given pattern set. Since there is a natural one-to-one correspondence between the nodes of the pattern trie for Π and the strings in $Prefix(\mathbf{code}(\Pi))$, a node of the pattern trie can be referred to as a string in $Prefix(\mathbf{code}(\Pi))$. A string u in $Prefix(\mathbf{code}(\Pi))$ can be specified by a pair of a string $x \in Prefix(\Pi)$ over Σ and a string $v \in \Delta^*$ such that $u = \mathbf{code}(x) \cdot v$. Such a reference pair $\langle x, v \rangle$ is said to be *canonical* if x is the longest one. Hereafter, we identify a canonical reference pair $\langle x, v \rangle$ with the corresponding node of the pattern trie, if no confusion occurs. For the pattern set $\Pi \subseteq \Sigma^+$, let denote by S_Π the set of canonical reference pairs to the nodes of the pattern trie for Π. Note that, for every $\langle x, v \rangle$ in S_Π, there exists a character a in Σ such that v is a proper prefix of the codeword $\mathbf{code}(a)$ for a.

Definition 2. *For any pair $\langle x, v \rangle \in S_\Pi$, let y be the longest proper suffix of x such that $\langle y, v \rangle \in S_\Pi$, and denote by $\Phi(x, v)$ the pair $\langle y, v \rangle$. If there is no such pair, let $\Phi(x, v) = nil$.*

The failure function computed by the above algorithm has the following property.

Lemma 1. *Let s be any node of the pattern trie for Π, and $\langle x, v \rangle$ be its canonical reference pair.*

1. If $\Phi(x, v) = \langle y, v \rangle$ is defined, the failure link from s goes to the node $\langle y, v \rangle$.
2. If $\Phi(x, v) = nil$, the failure link from s goes to the state of the codeword DFA to which the string v leads starting from the initial state.

Proof. By induction on the depth of the nodes in the pattern trie. When s is of depth 0, that is, $\langle x, v \rangle = \langle \varepsilon, \varepsilon \rangle$, then $\Phi(x, v) = nil$ and the lemma trivially holds. We now consider the nodes of depth > 0.

1. When $v \in \Delta^+$: The string v can be written as $v = wb$ with $w \in \Delta^*$ and $b \in \Delta$. Then, there is a sequence $x_0, x_1, \ldots, x_m \in \Sigma^*$ with $m \geq 0$ such that

$$x_0 = x; \qquad \langle x_i, w \rangle \in S_\Pi \quad (0 \leq i \leq m);$$
$$\Phi(x_{i-1}, w) = \langle x_i, w \rangle \quad (1 \leq i \leq m); \qquad \Phi(x_m, w) = nil.$$

   (a) If there is an integer ℓ $(0 < \ell \leq m)$ such that $\langle x_\ell, wb \rangle \in S_\Pi$, take ℓ as small as possible. By the definition of Φ, $\Phi(x, wb) = \langle x_\ell, wb \rangle$. By the induction hypothesis, for each $i = 1, \ldots, \ell$, the failure link from the node $\langle x_{i-1}, w \rangle$ goes to $\langle x_i, w \rangle$. By the construction of the failure function, the failure link from s goes to the node $\Phi(x, wb) = \langle x_\ell, wb \rangle$.
   (b) If there is no such integer ℓ, $\Phi(x, wb) = nil$. On the other hand, since $\Phi(x_m, w) = nil$, by the induction hypothesis, the failure link from the node $\langle x_m, w \rangle$ goes to the state of the codeword DFA to which the string w leads from the initial state. By the construction of the failure function, the failure link from s goes to the state of the codeword DFA to which the string $v = wb \in \Delta^+$ leads from the initial state.
2. When $v = \varepsilon$: If $x = \varepsilon$, s is the root of the pattern trie. This contradicts the assumption that s is of depth > 0. Hence we have $x \in \Sigma^+$. We can write x as $x'a$ with $x' \in \Sigma^*$ and $a \in \Sigma$. Since there uniquely exist $w \in \Delta^*$ and $b \in \Delta$ with $wb = \text{code}(a)$, we can prove this case in a way similar to 1.   □

Theorem 2. *Let $a_1 \ldots a_n$ be the text $(n > 0)$. After reading* **the encoding of** *a text prefix $a_1 \ldots a_j$ $(1 \leq j \leq n)$, PMM is in state corresponding to* **the en-** **coding of** *$a_i \ldots a_j$ $(1 \leq i \leq j)$ such that $a_i \ldots a_j$ is the longest suffix of $a_1 \ldots a_j$ that is also a prefix of some pattern in Π.*

The boldfaced portions are the difference in comparison with Theorem 1.

3.3   Applications

Searching in Multi-byte Character Texts. The ASCII (American Standard Code for Information Interchange) code, which is the basic character code in the world, represents characters with a 7-bit code. Variants of ISO646 such as BS4730 (England version), DIN66 003 (Germany version), and NF Z62-010 (France version) are also 7-bit codes. A string encoded with such a code is a sequence of bytes, and therefore people who use such codes are hardly conscious of the codeword boundaries. The boundaries, however, must be distinguished in multi-byte encoding scheme for oriental languages, such as Japanese, Korean, Chinese, and Taiwanese. The requirements of such a scheme are as follows.

1. Per byte encoding.
2. Single byte characters in range of 00h–7fh, which is compatible with ASCII.

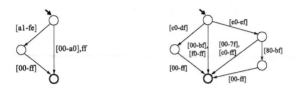

Fig. 4. The codeword DFAs for the Japanese EUC and for UTF-8 (Unicode) are shown on the left and on the right, respectively

3. Multi-byte characters do not begin with 00h-7fh.

The codes are therefore prefix codes.

For example, in the Japanese Extended-Unix-Code (EUC), both the bytes of each two-byte codeword fall into the range of a1h to feh. The smallest codeword DFA for the Japanese EUC is shown on the left of Fig. 4, where the code alphabet is $\Delta = \{00, \ldots, \text{ff}\}$. By using the codeword DFA, we can process Japanese EUC texts in a byte-by-byte manner. The DFA can also be used for CN-GB (Chinese), EUC-KR (Korean), and BIG5 (Taiwanese).

Both Unicode and ISO10646 are devised to put all the characters in the world into one coded character set. The former is a 16-bit code, and the latter is a 32-bit code. UCS-2 and UCS-4, which are respectively the encoding schemes of Unicode and ISO10646, are fixed-length encodings. Hence we can process texts encoded by such schemes byte after byte by using the codeword DFAs for them (although omitted here). UTF-8, an alternative encoding of Unicode is rather complex. The smallest codeword DFA for UTF-8 is shown on the right in Fig. 4.

Searching in Huffman Encoded Texts. The PMM for a Huffman code makes one state-transition per one bit of an encoded text, and such bit-wise processing is relatively slow. This problem can be overcome by converting PMM into a new one so that it runs in byte-by-byte manner, as shown in [9]. The new PMM runs on a Huffman encoded file faster than the AC machine on the original file. The searching time is reduced at nearly the same rate as the compression ratio.

Dividing a Codeword ([3]). Assume that the number of the states of PMM is ℓ. The size of a two-dimensional table storing the state transition function is then $|\Delta| \cdot \ell$. If a target text is encoded with a byte code, i.e., $\Delta = \{00, 01, \ldots, \text{ff}\}$, the table size becomes $256 \cdot \ell$. This space requirement could be unrealistic when a great deal of patterns are given. We can reduce the table size with the help of the syncronization technique. Consider dividing each byte of input text into two half bytes and replacing one state transition by two consecutive transitions. Namely, we use the code alphabet $\Delta = \{0, 1, \ldots, \text{f}\}$ instead of $\{00, 01, \ldots, \text{ff}\}$, and regard a text and a pattern as sequences of half bytes. The table size is reduced to 1/8, that is, it becomes $|\Delta| \cdot (2\ell) = 32\ell$ even in the worst case. False detection never occurs thanks to the syncronization technique.

3.4 Comparing with BM Algorithm Followed by Quick Verification

In Japanese EUC, bytes in the range of 00h to 7fh do not appear in the code-words representing two-byte characters. This provides us with a simple verification technique fast on the average: If an occurrence of the encoded pattern that begins at position i is found, start at the $(i-1)$th byte and go backward until a byte in the range of 00h to 7fh is found. The occurrence is false match if and only if the number of bytes not in the range is odd. For codes for which such a quick verification is possible, the "search-then-verify" method might be faster than the PMM-based method. Here, we compare the performance of the "search-then-verify" method with that of the PMM-based method.

We implemented a multipattern variant [12] of the BM algorithm so that the quick verification routine is invoked whenever the encoded pattern is found. On the other hand, the PMM was built from the encoded patterns and converted into a deterministic finite automaton by eliminating failure transitions as described in [1], and the state-transition function was implemented as a two-dimensional array, with the technique so-called *table-look-at* [7].

Our experiment was carried out on an AlphaStation XP1000 with an Alpha21264 processor at 667 MHz running Tru64 UNIX operating system V4.0F. The text file we used is composed of novels written by Soseki Natsume, a Japanese famous novelist, and of size 53.7Mb. The number k of patterns being searched for varied from 1 to 57. Each pattern set consists of uniform length patterns. The pattern length m varied from 2 to 10 bytes. The patterns were text substrings randomly chosen from the text file. For each combination of k and m, we generated 50 pattern sets and made the two algorithms run on the text file for each pattern set. The searching time reported in Fig. 3.4 is the average over the 50 runs. The solid lines show the total time, whereas the broken lines exclude the verification time. The verification time varies depending upon the number of occurrences of the encoded patterns and upon the expected number of bytes inspected in a single call of verification routine. The latter depends only on the nature of a text file. For the text file we used, this value was approximately 369 bytes. It should be stated that almost all occurrences of the single-byte characters in the file are those of the "newline" code. For this reason, almost every verification task for this file ended with encountering it.

Let us focus on the case of $m = 4$, which occurs frequently in Japanese language. The PMM-based method outperforms the "search-then-verify" method for $k > 2$. Even if we exclude the verification time, it is faster for $k > 10$. We observe that the "search-then-verify" method shows a good performance only when (1) all the patterns are relatively long and (2) the number of patterns is relatively small.

4   Generalization of Prefix Codes

The synchronization technique presented in the previous section is applicable to any prefix code. In this section, we generalize the scheme of prefix codes so as to allow the characters have one or more (possibly infinite) codewords. This may sound strange from the viewpoint of data compression, but has rich applications.

4.1 Generalized Prefix Codes

Recall that a prefix code to express the characters in a source alphabet Σ can be represented by a code tree in which every leaf is associated with a character a in the source alphabet Σ and the path from the root to the leaf spells out the codeword over Δ for a. See again the Huffman tree of Fig. 2. As a generalization of code tree, we consider a DFA called *code automaton* where:

1. there are exactly $|\Sigma|$ final states each corresponding to a character in Σ, and
2. every final state has no outgoing edge.

An example of the code automaton is shown on the left of Fig. 6, where the source alphabet is $\Sigma = \{A, B, C, D, E\}$ and the code alphabet is $\Delta = \{0, 1\}$.

Let denote by f_a the final state associated with a character a in Σ. For any $a \in \Sigma$, there can be more than one string in Δ^+ that leads to the state f_a starting at the initial state. Let such strings be the codewords to express the character a. Let **code** be the encoding determined by a code automaton. Then, **code** maps a character in Σ to a regular set over Δ. In the case of Fig. 6, it is easy to see that $\textbf{code}(A) = 01^*000$, $\textbf{code}(B) = 01^*001$, $\textbf{code}(C) = 01^*01 + 100$, $\textbf{code}(D) = 101$, and $\textbf{code}(E) = 11$. One of the encodings of text $ACED$ is $01000\,011101\,11\,101$. Since a prefix code is a special case where $|\textbf{code}(a)| = 1$ for all $a \in \Sigma$, this encoding scheme is a generalization of prefix codes. We call such a code *generalized prefix code*. The subgraph induced by the paths from the initial state to the final state f_a for $a \in \Sigma$ is called the *partial code automaton for a*, and denoted by $\textbf{PCA}(a)$. Similarly, we define $\textbf{PCA}(S)$ for a subset S of Σ. Note that $\textbf{PCA}(S)$ is a DFA that accepts the language $\textbf{code}(S) = \bigcup_{a \in S} \textbf{code}(a) \subseteq \Delta^+$.

Our algorithm for constructing PMMs can be extended to generalized prefix codes. The main difference is in the goto function construction.

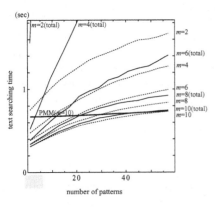

Fig. 5. Comparing the two methods. For the "search-then-verify" method, the solid lines show the total searching time, whereas the broken lines exclude the verification time. For the PMM-based method, we show the searching time only for $m = 10$

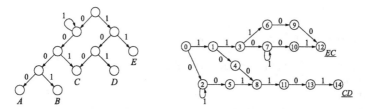

Fig. 6. An example of the code automaton is displayed on the left, and the pattern graph for patterns EC and CD is shown on the right, where the source alphabet is $\Sigma = \{A, B, C, D, E\}$ and the code alphabet is $\Delta = \{0, 1\}$

1. Create a pattern trie from a given pattern set Π.
2. Replace each edge of the pattern trie labeled a with the graph $\mathbf{PCA}(a)$. More precisely, if the node represented by a string $v \in \mathit{Prefix}(\Pi)$ has k outgoing edges labeled $a_1, \ldots, a_k \in \Sigma$, respectively, replace these edges with $\mathbf{PCA}(\{a_1, \ldots, a_k\})$. We call the obtained graph the *pattern graph*. The node corresponding to the root node of the pattern trie is referred to as the *source* node. (An example of the pattern graph is shown on the right in Fig. 6.)
3. Build the smallest codeword DFA that accepts the language $\mathbf{code}(\Sigma) \subseteq \Delta^+$. It can be obtained from the code automaton.
4. Replace the unique final state of the codeword DFA with the root node of the pattern graph.

The construction of the failure function is essentially the same as that for prefix codes.

4.2   Applications

One application is to make no distinction between some characters. People who use a western language might be often faced with the need for ignoring the distinction between upper-case and lower-case of alphabetic characters. More complex situation happens in the case of multi-byte encoding scheme for oriental languages. A two-byte character is usually twice of the width compared to single-byte characters. Wider characters are called "zen-kaku" - meaning full width, narrower characters are called "han-kaku" - meaning half width. The "zen-kaku" characters are usually fixed width. For the sake of proportion to multi-byte characters displayed in the "zen-kaku" form, there are "zenkaku" version of the ASCII characters such as alphabetic, numeric, and other special characters. Thus each of the characters has two representations of different length. Our technique described above is applicable in order to identify the two representations.

In the next section, we mention applications of our techniques to query processing for XML documents.

```
<db>
    <virus>
        <name> W32.Badtrans.B </name>
        <type> worm </type>
        <distribution> high </distribution>
    </virus>
    <virus>
        <name> W32.Zoek </name>
        <type> Trojan horse </type>
        <distribution> low </distribution>
    </virus>
</db>
```

Fig. 7. On the left an example of XML documents is displayed and on the right the tree structure it represents is shown

5   Applications to Query Processing for XML Documents

XML (Extensible Markup Language) is emerging as a standard format for data and documents on the Internet. An example of XML documents and the corresponding tree structure are displayed in Fig. 7.

Several query languages for XML have been proposed, e.g., XQL, Xquery, XPath. Most of them are based on the so-called *path expressions*. An example of the path expressions is "db/virus/type", where "db", "virus", and "type" are tag names which are node labels in the tree structure, and "/" means a direct descendant. We can also use "//" to indicate a descendant (not necessarily direct descendant). In processing path expression based queries, XML documents are usually converted into tree structures, and query processing is performed as node operations over the trees. Another approach stores all possible paths from the root in a tree structure into a relational database [13]. We shall adopt a different approach along our "as-is" principle.

5.1   XML Documents and What They Represent

A tag string in XML documents such as "<virus>" represents an "abstract" symbol. We shall put an explicit distinction between such abstract symbols and their representation. From this viewpoint, an XML document represents a string of abstract symbols, and this abstract string is generated by some unambiguous context-free grammar. The tree structure represented by an XML document is essentially the same as the parse tree of the abstract string.

Let Σ_0 be an alphabet. Let $\Gamma = \{\, [_1\,,\,]_1\,,\ldots,\, [_\ell\,,\,]_\ell \,\}$, where $[_i$ (resp. $]_i$) is the ith left (resp. right) bracket for $i = 1,\ldots,\ell$. Assume $\Sigma_0 \cap \Gamma = \emptyset$, and let $\Sigma = \Sigma_0 \cup \Gamma$ be the source alphabet. The elements of Σ are "abstract" symbols. Consider the context-free grammar $G = (\Sigma, N, P, A_1)$, where N is the set of nonterminals $A_1,\ldots,A_\ell$; A_1 is the start symbol; and P is the set of productions $A_1 \rightarrow [_1 \alpha_1]_1, \quad \cdots, A_\ell \rightarrow [_\ell \alpha_\ell]_\ell$, where α_i is a regular expression over $\Sigma_0 \cup N$.

An XML document is an encoding of some element of the language $L(G) \subseteq \Sigma^*$ generated by G. The encodings of the left brackets $[_i$ are called the *start tags*, and those of the right brackets $]_i$ the *end tags*. The start tags are enclosed by the angle brackets "<", ">", and the end tags are enclosed by "</" and ">". The symbols in Σ_0 are encoded with the standard ASCII (or its extension).

For example, consider the grammar with productions $S \rightarrow [_S A^*]_S, A \rightarrow [_A BCD]_A, B \rightarrow [_B \Sigma_0^*]_B, C \rightarrow [_C \Sigma_0^*]_C, D \rightarrow [_D \Sigma_0^*]_D$, where S, A, B, C, D are nonterminals and $[_S,]_S, [_A,]_A, [_B,]_B, [_C,]_C, [_D,]_D$ are four pairs of brackets. Suppose these bracket symbols are encoded as "<db>", "</db>", "<virus>", "</virus>", "<name>", "</name>", "<type>", "</type>", "<distribution>", "</distribution>", respectively. The XML document of Fig. 7 can then be seen as an encoding of some string generated by this grammar.

5.2   Processing XML Documents as Is

We process path expression based queries by using a PMM with stack. Namely, a PMM searches an XML document for tag strings as well as the keywords appearing in the queries. If a start tag is found, then push the corresponding nonterminal into the stack. If an end tag is found, then pop an element from the stack. The stack content is therefore the sequence of nonterminals on the path from the root node to the node corresponding to the current position within the XML document being processed. Path expressions can be regarded as limited regular expressions over the nonterminals, for which DFAs can be built only in linear time. We perform pattern matching of path expressions against the stack content using DFAs. In this way, we can process XML documents with recognizing its structure, without explicitly constructing tree structures.

We are faced with two difficulties in this approach. One is a problem of false-detections which occur when a keyword in the queries appears inside a tag. Of course, this problem is easily resolved if we keep a boolean value which indicates whether the current point is inside the tag enclosed with the angle brackets "<", ">". However, such an extra work requires an additional time. By using the synchronization technique mentioned in the previous section, we resolve the problem without sacrifices of running speed. Since we regard each tag string as an encoding of one symbol from the source alphabet $\Sigma = \Sigma_0 \cup \Gamma$, the above-mentioned false-detection never occurs.

The other difficulty is as follows. A start tag can contain descriptions of attribute values, e.g., as in "<section␣number="1.2">", where "␣" is a blank symbol. Even when we can omit the attribute values because of the irrelevance to the query, we have to identify the start tags with various attribute values whenever they have a unique tag name in common. One naive solution would be to eliminate all the attribute descriptions inside the tags. This, however, contradicts the "as-is" principle and sacrifices the processing speed. Let us recall that the generalized prefix coding scheme allows us to assign more than one codeword to each left-bracket symbol. With this scheme, for example, every string of the form "<section␣" · w · ">" can be regarded as one of the possible encodings of the left bracket represented simply as "<section>", where w is a string over $\Delta - \{<, >\}$. The difficulty is thus resolved by using the PMMs for generalized prefix codes presented in the previous section.

Moreover, we have only to distinguish the start tags appearing in the path expressions in the queries. The start tags not appearing in the path expressions should not necessarily distinguished. We can take them as encodings of one left bracket symbol. Similarly, the end tags irrelevant to the queries can be treated as different encodings of one right bracket symbol.

5.3   Experimental Results

First, we estimated the performance of PMM with synchronization technique in searching XML documents for keywords, in comparison with that of the ordinary AC machine with extra work for recognizing the inside/outside of a tag. We generated XML documents of various size by using the tool "XMLgen" (XML-benchmark project)[1]. The keywords were chosen from the XML documents. We performed this experiment on the AlphaStation XP1000 mentioned in Section 3.4. Although we omit here the detailed results for lack of space, they demonstrate that the PMM with synchronization runs approximately $1.2 \sim 1.5$ times faster than the ordinary AC machine with extra work.

Next, we implemented a prototype system for processing relatively simple path expression based queries for XML documents, based on the PMM with stack. We then compared its performance with that of sgrep [5]. This experiment was carried out on a Personal Computer with Celelon processor at 366 MHz running Kondara/MNU Linux 2.1 RC2. We used one of the XML documents generated with "XMLgen". It is of size 110 Mb and contains 77 different tag names. The corresponding tree is of height 21. The running times for each of the queries are shown in Table 1. We observe that our prototype system is approximately $7 \sim 10$ times faster than sgrep concerning these queries. Moreover a simultaneous processing of the three queries by our prototype system is only about 15% slower than single query case.

6   Conclusion

Along the "as-is" principle, we have presented a synchronization technique for processing multi-byte character text files efficiently, on the basis of Aho-Corasick pattern matching machine. The technique is applicable to any prefix code. We also generalize the scheme of prefix codes and then extend our algorithm to cope with text files encoded with the generalized scheme. One important application is query processing for XML documents. Experimental results demonstrate that our method is approximately $7 \sim 10$ times faster than sgrep in processing XML documents for some path expression based queries.

---

[1] http://monetdb.cwi.nl/xml/Benchmark/benchmark.html

Table 1. Running time for query processing (sec). We compared the two methods for the three queries shown in this table. The first query, for example, means "Find the tree nodes labeled `text` from which a text node containing an occurrence of the keyword `summers` is directly descended." We remark that the query language of sgrep is based on the region algebra, and therefore we translated the three queries appropriately

query	PMM with stack	sgrep
`//text/"summers"`	4.794	31.826
`//text//"summers"`	5.056	32.036
`/site/regions/africa/item/location/"United␣States"`	4.880	52.102
simultaneous processing of the three queries	5.614	—

The "as-is" principle also leads us to the question: Which form should be better in storing text? Shibata et al. [11] gave an answer to this question: they showed that a BM-type string pattern matching algorithm running over text files compressed by Byte-Pair Enconding (BPE) — which is a restricted version of Re-Pair [8] — is approximately $1.2 \sim 3.0$ times faster than that in the ASCII format. Namely, the BPE compressed format is one good format from the viewpoint of string pattern matching. Problems of representation of text strings from a viewpoint of processing speed thus attract special concerns.

References

[1] A. V. Aho and M. Corasick. Efficient string matching: An aid to bibliographic search. *Comm. ACM*, 18(6):333–340, 1975. 173, 179

[2] A. Amir and G. Benson. Efficient two-dimensional compressed matching. In *Proc. Data Compression Conference*, page 279, 1992. 172

[3] S. Arikawa and T. Shinohara. A run-time efficient realization of Aho-Corasick pattern matching machines. *New Generation Computing*, 2(2):171–186, 1984. 178

[4] S. Arikawa et al. The text database management syste SIGMA: An improvement of the main engine. In *Proc. of Berliner Informatik-Tage*, pages 72–81, 1989. 171

[5] J. Jaakkola and P. Kilpeläinen. A tool to search structured text. University of Helsinki. (In preparation). 172, 184

[6] S. T. Klein and D. Shapira. Pattern matching in Huffman encoded texts. In *Proc. Data Compression Conference 2001*, pages 449–458. IEEE Computer Society, 2001. 174

[7] D. E. Knuth. *The Art of Computer Programing, Sorting and Searching*, volume 3. Addison-Wesley, 1973. 179

[8] N. J. Larsson and A. Moffat. Offline dictionary-based compression. In *Proc. Data Compression Conference '99*, pages 296–305. IEEE Computer Society, 1999. 185

[9] M. Miyazaki, S. Fukamachi, M. Takeda, and T. Shinohara. Speeding up the pattern matching machine for compressed texts. *Transactions of Information Processing Society of Japan*, 39(9):2638–2648, 1998. (in Japanese). 178

[10] D. Revuz. Minimisation of acyclic deterministic automata in linear time. *Theoretical Computer Science*, 92(1):181–189, 1992. 174

[11] Y. Shibata, T. Matsumoto, M. Takeda, A. Shinohara, and S. Arikawa. A Boyer-Moore type algorithm for compressed pattern matching. In *Proc. 11th Ann. Symp. on Combinatorial Pattern Matching*, volume 1848 of *Lecture Notes in Computer Science*, pages 181–194. Springer-Verlag, 2000. 185

[12] N. Uratani and M. Takeda. A fast string-searching algorithm for multiple patterns. *Information Processing & Management*, 29(6):775–791, 1993. 171, 179

[13] M. Yoshikawa and T. Amagasa. XRel: a path-based approach to storage and retrieval of XML documents using relational databases. *ACM Transactions on Internet Technology*, 1(1):110–141, August 2001. 182

Pattern Matching over Multi-attribute Data Streams

Lilian Harada

Fujitsu Laboratories Ltd.
4-1-1 Kamikodanaka, Nakahara-ku, Kawasaki, Kanagawa 211-8588, Japan
lilian@flab.fujitsu.co.jp

Abstract. Recently a growing number of applications monitor the physical world by detecting some patterns and trends of interest. In this paper we present two algorithms that generalize string-matching algorithms for detecting patterns with complex predicates over data streams having multiple categorical and quantitative attributes. Implementation and evaluation of the algorithms show their efficiency when compared to the naive approach.

1 Introduction

In the database community, recently a great deal of attention has been driven towards a new class of applications: monitoring and notification applications that generate alerts or another "reaction" when pre-defined thresholds or patterns are detected over continuous data streams [1], as data feeds from sensor applications [2], performance measurements in network monitoring and traffic management, data from POS log or click streams in Web applications, to name a few. These data are mainly characterized by being continuously growing and so, their materialization with subsequent index construction, that is the usual approach used in database systems, is not feasible. On the other hand, some very efficient string matching algorithms preprocess the string pattern (and not the text) to find its occurrence in texts, being broadly used in textual information retrieval programs, in internet browsers and crawlers, in digital libraries and, more recently, in molecular biology where biological molecules can be seen as strings of nucleotides or amino acids [3].

Data streams in most monitoring and notification applications cited above are composed of records with multiple attributes that can be quantitative (e.g., temperature measured, amount sold) or categorical (e.g., sensor location, product brand). However, the ideas developed for string matching that deals with equality and inequality between characters can be extended for the pattern matching over data streams that require more complex relational comparison among their attributes. In [5], Sadri et al. introduce an algorithm that extends the KMP algorithm [3] to deal with patterns on sequential data with one unique quantitative attribute. In this paper we analyze the generalization of string matching algorithms for the more general case of pattern matching over data streams having multiple categorical and quantitative attributes, with details for two new algorithms – the R2L and L2R algorithms. Because of lack of space, here we don't present some details of the algorithms that are fully described in [4].

A.H.F. Laender and A.L. Oliveira (Eds.): SPIRE 2002, LNCS 2476, pp. 187-193, 2002.

2   Concepts and Notation

A stream is an ordered sequence of n records $r[0]$ ... $r[n-1]$ where each $r[i]$ can have z attributes $a[0]$ ... $a[z-1]$. An attribute can be quantitative or categorical. A pattern is an ordered list of m predicates $p[0]$ ... $p[j]$ ... $p[m-1]$ that we want to be satisfied by m consecutive records $r[i-j]$ ... $r[i]$ ... $r[i-j+m-1]$ of the data stream. Each pattern predicate $p[j]$ can specify conditions for any of the z attributes of a record stream, i.e.,

$$p[j] = f_{j0}(r[i].a[0]) \text{ AND } ... \text{ AND } f_{jt}(r[i].a[t]) \text{ AND } ... \text{ AND } f_{j(z-1)}(r[i].a[z-1]),$$

where $f_{jt}(r[i].a[t])$ can be a conjunction of inequalities involving attribute $a[t]$ of record $r[i]$ with a constant, or with the attribute $a[t]$ of another record $r[s]$. So each inequality can be of the form:

- $r[i].a[t]$ $op1$ C, in the case $a[t]$ is a categorical attribute; or
- $r[i].a[t]$ $op2$ C, in the case $a[t]$ is a quantitative attribute; or
- $r[i].a[t]$ $op2$ $r[s].a[t]$ $op3$ C, in the case $a[t]$ is a quantitative attribute,

where C is a constant, $op1 6 \{=, \neq\}$, $op2 6 \{<, 6 =, >, 6, \neq\}$ and $op3 6 \{+, \times\}$.

All the logical relations among pairs of pattern predicates can be represented using a positive precondition $\theta[j,k]$ and a negative precondition $\phi_q[j,k]$, such that:

$$\theta[j,k] = \begin{cases} 1 & \text{if } p[j] \Rightarrow p[k] \\ 0 & \text{if } p[j] \Rightarrow \overline{p[k]} \\ U & \text{otherwise} \end{cases} \qquad \phi_q[j,k] = \begin{cases} 1 & \text{if } \overline{p_q[j]} \Rightarrow p[k] \\ 0 & \text{if } \overline{p_q[j]} \Rightarrow \overline{p[k]} \\ U & \text{otherwise} \end{cases}$$

For the negative precondition $\phi_q[j,k]$, we first partition the inequalities on the z attributes of the conjunctive predicate into c clusters, so that q is defined for each combination of negative cluster inequalities. For example, let's suppose $a[0]$ is "level", and $a[1]$ is "temp" in a sensor data. Let's consider the two pattern predicates:

p[0] = r[i].level > r[i+1].level AND r[i].temp 6 r[i+1].temp
p[1] = r[i].level 6 r[i+1].level AND r[i].temp > r[i+1].temp.

For example, we find that the positive precondition $\theta[1,0] = 0$ (since $p[1] D \overline{p[0]}$). For the case $c=1$, that is, for the case of a unique cluster $c1$ for both conditions on level and temperature, we find that the negative precondition $\phi_{c1}[1,0] = U$. But for the case $c=2$ where $c1$ is a cluster for level, and $c2$ for temperature, we find that:

$\phi_{c1}[1,0] = 0$ (since $(\overline{r[i].level \ 6 \ r[i+1].level}$ AND $r[i].temp > r[i+1].temp) \ 6 \ \overline{p[0]}$),
$\phi_{c2}[1,0] = 0$ (since $(r[i].level \ 6 \ r[i+1].level$ AND $\overline{r[i].temp > r[i+1].temp}) 6 \ \overline{p[0]}$),
$\phi_{c1c2}[1,0] = 1$ (since $(\overline{r[i].level 6 \ r[i+1].level}$ AND $\overline{r[i].temp > r[i+1].temp}) 6 \ p[0]$).

3   Our Pattern Matching Algorithms

Our algorithms scan the data stream with the help of a window whose size is equal to m, the number of pattern predicates. We say that the window is associated with the position i in the stream when the window covers records $r[i]$ ... $r[i+m-1]$. The stream records in the window are checked against the pattern predicates from right-to-left for the R2L algorithm (similarly to the BM algorithm), and from left-to-right for the L2R algorithm (similarly to the KMP algorithm), as outlined in Fig. 1.

> The R2L Algorithm
> i = 0;
> while (i 6 n-m)
> $\qquad$ j = m-1;
> while (j 6 0 && p[j](r[i+j])) j--;
> $\qquad$ if (j < 0) find(i); i += shift$_q$[0];
> $\qquad$ else $\qquad$ i += shift$_q$[j];
>
> The L2R Algorithm
> j=0; i=0;
> while (j < m && i 6 n-m)
> $\qquad$ while (j < m && p[j](r[i+j])) j++;
> $\qquad$ if (j == m) find(i);
> i += shift$_q$[j];
> j = next$_q$[j];

Fig. 1. Algorithms R2L and L2R

$p[j](r[i+j])$ tests if $p[j]$ holds for record $r[i+j]$ of the stream. *Find(i)* outputs the stream records $r[i]$ ... $r[i+m-1]$ that fully match the pattern. *shift$_q$[j]* gives the number of positions to shift the window when the inequalities q of the pattern predicate $p[j]$ are not satisfied. For R2L, *shift$_q$* has m entries (0 to $m-1$), and *shift$_q$[0]* gives the shift distance when there is a mismatch at predicate $p[0]$ or when the pattern is fully matched. For L2R, *shift$_q$* has $m+1$ entries (0 to m). The last entry *shift$_q$[m]* gives the shift distance when the pattern is fully matched. For L2R, after the window shifts, the check begins at the predicate given by *next$_q$[j]*. This is because, as we will describe below, when $\theta[j,k]$ and $\phi_q[j,k]$ are U, that is, are undetermined at the preprocessing stage, there is the need to check the corresponding predicates at the search stage.

3.1   Precalculation for Algorithm R2L

When the matching process fails for the window at position i because predicate $p[j]$ (for $0 D j < m$) mismatches record $r[i+j]$, the window is shifted by k positions to the right, and the following three situations can occur:

(a) for $0 < k D j$, the new window entirely contains the sequence of records $r[i+j]$ ... $r[i+m-1]$ already checked in the previous window;
(b) for $j < k < m$, the new window contains only a partial sequence of records $r[i+k]$ ... $r[i+m-1]$ already checked in the previous window;
(c) for $k=m$, the new window has no overlap with records in the previous window.

Let's define $\alpha_q[j,k]$ and $\beta[k]$ for (a) and (b), respectively, as:

$\alpha_q[j,k] = \theta[m-1,m-k-1]\ D\ ...\ D\ \theta[j+1,j-k+1] 6\ \phi_q[j,j-k]$; and

$\beta[j,k] = \theta[m-1,m-k-1] D \ldots D\theta[k+1,1]6 \ \theta[k,0]$.

Analogously to the strong good-suffix rule of the BM algorithm, when there is a mismatch at $p[j]$ $(06 \ j<m)$, the window is shifted by:

$$\text{shift}_q[j] = m, \ \begin{cases} \text{if for any } 0<k<m, \ \alpha_q[j,k] = 0 \text{ and } \beta[j,k] = 0 \\ \min(\min(\{k \mid \alpha_q[j,k] \neq 0\}), \min(\{k \mid \beta[j,k] \neq 0\}), \text{otherwise} \end{cases}$$

Note that $\text{shift}_q[0]$ contains the shift distance when there is a mismatch at predicate $p[0]$ as well as when the pattern is fully matched.

3.2   Precalculation for Algorithm L2R

When the matching process fails for the window at position i because predicate $p[j]$ (for $0Dj<m$) mismatches record $r[i+j]$, the window is shifted by k positions to the right, and the following two situations can occur:

(a) for $0 < k \ D \ j$, the new window contains only a partial sequence of records $r[i+k] \ldots r[i+j]$ already checked in the previous window;
(b) for $k = j+1$, the new window has no overlap with any record checked in the previous window.

Let's define $\alpha_q[j,k]$ for (a) as:

$$\alpha_q[j,k] = \phi_q[j,j-k] \ 6 \ \theta[j-1,j-k-1] \ 6 \ldots 6 \ \theta[k,0].$$

Analogously to the KMP algorithm, when there is a mismatch at $p[j]$, we have that:

$$\text{shift}_q[j] = j + 1, \ \begin{cases} \text{if for any } 0<k \ 6 \ j, \ \alpha_q[j,k] = 0 \\ \min(\ \{k \mid \alpha_q[j,k] \neq 0 \ \}), \text{otherwise} \end{cases}$$

For case (b), the check begins with the first predicate $p[0]$, that is, $\text{next}_q[j] = 0$. For case (a), when $\alpha_q[j,k] = 1$, as in the KMP algorithm, $\text{next}_q[j] = j - \text{shift}_q[j] + 1$. However, when $\alpha_q[j,k] = U$, there is backtrack and the new window begins with the check of the leftmost predicate whose θ (or ϕ_q) $= U$ in the calculation of $\alpha_q[j,k] = U$ that determines $\text{shift}_q[j]$. Thus:

$$\text{next}_q[j] = \min(\ \{ t \mid 0 \ 6 \ t < j - \text{shift}_q[j] \ 6 \ \theta[\text{shift}_q[j] + t, t] = U \ \} \ 6$$
$$\{ j - \text{shift}_q[j] \mid \phi_q[j, j - \text{shift}_q[j]] \ = U \} \ )$$

For the case of full matching, the window is shifted by k positions to the right so that it contains only a partial sequence of records $r[i+k] \ldots r[i+m-1]$ already checked in the previous window. Let's define $\beta[k]$ as:

$$\beta[k] = \theta[m-1,m-k-1] D \ldots D\theta[k+1,1]6 \ \theta[k,0].$$

Analogously to the case of partial match, $\text{shift}_q[m]$ and $\text{next}_q[m]$ are given as:

$$\text{shift}_q[m] = m, \begin{cases} \text{if for any } 0<k<m, \ \beta[k] = 0 \\ \min(\ \{k \mid \beta[k] \neq 0 \ \}), \text{otherwise} \end{cases}$$

If $\beta[k] = 0$ for all $0<k<m$, then we have that $next_q[m] = 0$. Otherwise, if the minimum k with $\beta[k] \neq 0$ was in fact $\beta[k] = 1$, then $next_q[m] = m - shift_q[m]$. And if it was $\beta[k] = U$, then $next_q[m] = min(\{t \mid 06\ t<m-shift_q[m]\ 6\ \theta[shift_q[m]+ t, t] = U\})$.

4   Comparison Results

We have implemented R2L, L2R and the naive algorithm that shifts the window by one position whenever a mismatch or a full match occurs. In the following we present some evaluation results for the following 10 patterns.

P1: The water level remains in a range between –2 and +2 of its neighbor value for 7 consecutive measures.

P2: The water level goes up increasing in 7 consecutive measures.

P3: The water level goes down decreasing in 7 consecutive measures.

P4: The water level goes up increasing in the first half and then stabilizes or goes down decreasing in the last half of 7 consecutive measures.

P5: The water level has 3 consecutive spikes, that is, a sudden increase of more than 10 followed by a sudden decrease of more than 10 that repeats 3 times.

P6: The water level remains in a range between –2 and +2 of its neighbor value, while the temperature goes up increasing in 7 consecutive measures.

P7: The water level goes up increasing while the temperature goes down decreasing in 7 consecutive measures.

P8: The water level remains in a range between –2 and +2 of its neighbor value for 7 consecutive measures, while the temperature goes up increasing in the first half and then stabilizes or goes down decreasing.

P9: The water level remains in a range between –2 and +2 of its neighbor value, while the temperature has 3 consecutive spikes, that is, a sudden increase of more than 10 followed by a sudden decrease of more than 10 that repeats 3 times.

P10: The water level goes up increasing in 7 consecutive measures while the temperature has 3 consecutive spikes, that is, a sudden increase of more than 10 followed by a sudden decrease of more than 10 that repeats 3 times.

Fig. 2 presents the number of checks for the naive approach, L2R and R2L when a dataset of 100,000 records with randomly generated data was used. Patterns P1 to P5 have only predicate conditions on the water level and so $c=1$. For patterns P6 to P10 that have predicate conditions on both water level and temperature we show results for $c=1$, where the conditions on both attributes are considered in conjunction, and for $c=2$, where they are considered separately in the shift calculations.

From Fig. 2 we can see that both L2R and R2L need much fewer comparisons than the naive approach. The number of checks for L2R is almost the same or slightly higher than the total number of records in the data set, e.g., 100,000, meaning that there were no backtracks in most patterns processing. We can also see that for all the patterns, except P4 and P9 with $c=1$, R2L needs fewer checks than L2R. For patterns P8, P9 and P10, by increasing the number of clusters from $c=1$ to $c=2$, R2L shows a great reduction in the number of checks. This is because by taking the negative conditions for level and temperature attributes separately, R2L can determine the predicates compatibilities more precisely and so, determine some larger shift values.

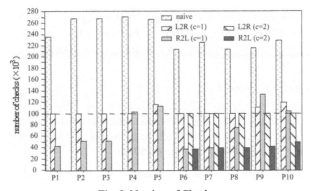

Fig. 2. Number of Checks

Fig. 3 compares the evolution of the values of positions i of the stream records, and j of the predicates of pattern P10, when the first 20 records of the dataset are checked. For algorithm L2R, backtracking episodes do not occur as in the naive approach. However, in L2R with $c=1$, mismatched records are sometimes re-checked (same i values for consecutive points), what does not occur with $c=2$ where the number of 20 checks equals the number of stream records. We can also see that for R2L with $c=1$ the recheck of the leftmost window record occurs frequently, but when longer partial matches occur the window shifts can be large, and many unnecessary checks are skipped. This occurs more frequently for $c=2$ that can more precisely determine predicates incompatibilities and so allow larger shifts with fewer checks.

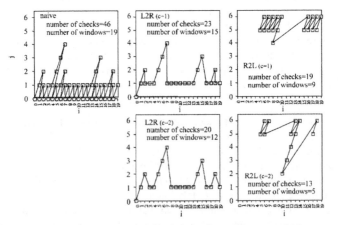

Fig. 3. Check of i-th record by j-th predicate for pattern P10

5   Conclusion

In this paper we describe two algorithms that generalize the classical BM and KMP string matching algorithms to detect complex patterns with conjunctions of inequalities on multiple attributes over data streams. We have implemented the proposed algorithms, and evaluation results showed that they could significantly outperform the naive approach. We are now interested in analyzing the feasibility of extending the many variants of these two classical string matching algorithms for the search of complex patterns over multi-attribute data streams.

References

[1]   Babu, S., Widom, J.: Continuous Queries over Data Streams. SIGMOD Record, Vol. 30, No. 3 (2001) 109-120

[2]   Bonnet, P., Gehrke J., Seshadri P.: Towards Sensor Database Systems. Mobile Data Management 2001 (2001) 3-14

[3]   Gusfield, D.: Algorithms on Strings, Trees, and Sequences: Computer Science and Computational Biology, Cambridge University Press (1997)

[4]   Harada, L.: Pattern Matching over Multi-Attribute Data Streams. Fujitsu Laboratories LTM2002-6843-302 (2002)

[5]   Sadri, R., Zaniolo, C., Zarkesh, A., Adibi, J.: Optimization of Sequence Queries in Database Systems. PODS2001 (2001) 71-81

Java MARIAN: From an OPAC
to a Modern Digital Library System

Marcos André Gonçalves, Paul Mather, Jun Wang, Ye Zhou, Ming Luo,
Ryan Richardson, Rao Shen, Liang Xu, and Edward A. Fox

Virginia Tech
Blacksburg VA 24061, USA
{mgoncalv,fox}@vt.edu

Abstract. This paper describes the Java MARIAN system, its implementation, and its evolution from a C++ Online Public Access Catalog (OPAC) to a modern and complete digital library system. We focus
on design, architectural, and implementation issues including: support
for storage, retrieval, and automatic generation of collections of semi-
structured digital objects; uniform and powerful representations based
on semantic networks, digital library specific datatypes, and weighted
sets; rich communities of searchers and fusion modules; and support for
distributed computation, multi-lingual retrieval, and personalization. We
present applications and some use statistics.

1 Introduction

Digital library (DL) systems provide rich services such as indexing, searching,
and browsing to interested communities over possibly large collections of digital
objects. Digital library collections, however, have several characteristic features
that make construction of such services difficult. DL collections are typically
very large and include heterogeneous kinds of digital objects (e.g., e-published
documents, images, hypertexts, videos, simulations, entire scientific databases)
with widely different formats and internal structure. Furthermore, they are typically in complex relationships with each other and with non-library objects such
as persons, institutions, and events.

Relationships are a common feature of traditional libraries in the form of "See
/ See also" pointers, hierarchical relationships among categories of classification
schemes, and relations between bibliographic and non-bibliographic objects such
as having an author or being on a subject. Binary relations (typically in the form
of directed links) are a common representational tool in computer science for
structures from trees and graphs to semantic networks. And the Web, and more
recently the "semantic web" [2], have made the construct of linked information
objects commonplace for millions. Despite this, relationships have rarely been
given "first-class" treatment in digital library collections or software (e.g., [13,
6, 5]).

MARIAN is a digital library system designed and built to: 1) support large
collections of diverse, semantically rich digital objects with explicit representations of internal and external relationships as networks of different sorts of links;

A.H.F. Laender and A.L. Oliveira (Eds.): SPIRE 2002, LNCS 2476, pp. 194–209, 2002.
© Springer-Verlag Berlin Heidelberg 2002

and 2) provide an extensible set of digital library services such as automatic collection building, indexing, searching, retrieving, browsing, and uniform presentation over such networked collections. This paper describes the evolution of the MARIAN system from a C++ Online Public Access Catalog (OPAC) [3] to a modern and complete Java digital library system. We focus on design, architectural, and implementation issues including support for storage, retrieval, and automatic generation of semi-structured collections and services; uniform and powerful representations based on semantic networks, digital library specific types and weighted sets; rich communities of searchers and fusion modules; and support for distributed computation and personalization. In the following discussion, we will use MARIAN to designate the Java version of the system when it is clear that we are not comparing it with the old C++ version.

This paper is organized as follows. Section 2 concentrates on the MARIAN design principles. Sections 3 and 4, which constitute the core of the paper, describe, respectively, the Java MARIAN digital library API, followed by the architecture and corresponding implementations. Section 5 outlines future work and concludes the paper.

2   Java MARIAN Design Principles

The proposed functionality of the MARIAN system is reflected in its design principles. Table 1 summarizes these principles, their objectives, the functionality they support, and examples of their applications.

Semantic networks, which are labeled directed graphs, are ideal to represent any kind of digital library structure including the internal structure of digital objects and metadata, and different kinds of relationships among objects or concepts [8]. In MARIAN, semantic networks are promoted to first-class objects.

In order to support IR-based services, nodes and links can be weighted. **Weights** are defined axiomatically to correspond to informal concepts of "similarity," "importance," "uncertainty," or "quality". With some additional axioms, weights also can be refined into probabilities. This is important when we consider weights derived from statistical and information-theoretic characteristics of the information represented in MARIAN semantic networks. Moreover, weights only have meaning in comparison to other weights. The seminal concept here is the weighted object set: a set of objects whose relationship to some external proposition is encoded in their decreasing weight within the set.

Nodes and links in the MARIAN semantic networks are further organized in **hierarchies of object-oriented classes**. Each class in a particular digital library collection is the responsibility of a class manager. Class managers store and maintain instance objects of their class, translate back and forth between object IDs and fully realized objects, and participate in the class hierarchy by collecting results from their subclasses and responding to requests from their superclasses. They also function as the search engines for the system.

A digital library built on the semantic network model could easily comprise hundreds of millions of objects and billions of links. Links and node classes

Table 1. MARIAN design principles, their objectives, and examples of use

Design principle	Objective	Examples of Use
Semantic networks	basic, unified representation of digital library structures	document and metadata internal structure; citation information; hierarchical relationships of classification systems; concept maps
Weighting schemes	support information retrieval operations and services; quantitative representation of qualitative properties such as similarity, uncertainty and quality	weighted links representing indexes (e.g., inverted lists); fusion of weighted sets in retrieval operations of multi-field, multi-word queries; representation of degree of semantic similarity among concepts in different ontologies
Object-oriented class system	provide common behavior, extensibility, and opportunity for improved performance	shared methods for matching different types of nodes (terms, controlled and free texts) and link topologies; extensible multilingual support and common presentation methods
Lazy evaluation	performance; management of large collections	Retrieval of customized, reduced number of search results; enhanced merging algorithms for weighted sets of searching results

can reduce the cognitive and the computational complexity of digital library operations by many orders of magnitude.

First, since the graph matching is done using the topology of the network of class managers, rather than instances, there is no longer any need to broadcast a query description throughout the whole network. Next, the cost of finding objects matching the description inside a particular class (e.g., person, abstract) is now determined by the interior structure of the class manager rather than the overt structure of the whole instance-level semantic network. Since the class manager is privy to the common structure of its instance nodes, it can more optimally implement search and matching functions. For simple objects like named persons, techniques such as hashing and B-trees suggest themselves; in more general applications, class managers can make use of sophisticated database techniques to optimize the search process. Any such algorithmic savings is a win over processing by distributed instance nodes.

Finally, the MARIAN class-level model gives support to the MARIAN fourth design principle, **lazy evaluation**, which is not feasible in the instance-level network. It is a well-known fact that users of web search engines and digital libraries normally get satisfied by examining a few results in a ranked list, but in arbitrary cases they may need to explore the result set to an arbitrarily deep level of match before the task is accomplished. In an instance-level system, link activation, i.e., the process whereby attention or focus on a set of nodes spreads to related nodes over intervening links, either occurs or does not occur. There

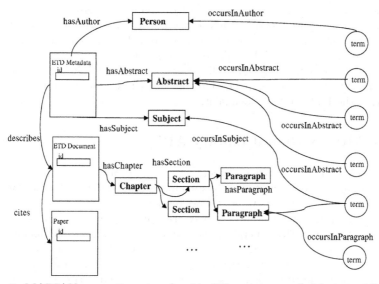

Fig. 1. MARIAN semantic network with different types of objects and links

is no easy way in such a system to defer activation until needed. In contrast, a class-level system needs only to develop as many candidate results as the user requests. In MARIAN this is accomplished by maintaining weighted object sets as abstract objects that are evaluated only as needed. The number of instances requested, and thus the transmission costs across the network and the amount of work done by different managers acting to solve a search request, are severely limited compared to the size of the sets they manage. In this way the class-level system exerts minimal energy to produce a presentation result set for the user. This sort of lazy evaluation is extremely important in a digital library environment, where different users have extremely different needs, from known-item search for a single work to in-depth research exploration, and where these needs cannot be distinguished based solely on overt user behavior.

Figure 1 shows a simple MARIAN semantic network with several different types of digital objects and links. All links, parts of documents and metadata, and terms are managed by specific class managers, most created as subclasses of the MARIAN digital library API (see Section 3). Descriptive and structural links such as hasAuthor, hasAbstract, and hasSubject for metadata records and HasChapter, has Section and hasParagraph for electronic theses and dissertations (ETDs) represent internal organization of semi-structured digital objects (e.g., MARC records, XML documents). Indexing information is represented by a bipartite network of weighted occursIn links connecting terms to specific parts of documents/metadata records. Several weighting schemas are possible. The popular term frequency-inverse document frequency (tf-idf) scheme is currently implemented, where the tf component is derived from statistical analysis of the distinct parts of the document, in a sort of "semantic passage" indexing, and the idf of a term node corresponds to the outdegree of the term node in the context of a specific link in the network topology. Finally, generic relationships (e.g., citation information, bibliographical relationships between metadata and documents) can be represented as illustrated by the "cites" link going from the ETD document to a generic paper and the "describes" from the ETD metadata record to the ETD fulltext document.

3   MARIAN Digital Library API

The Java MARIAN API is made of sets of reusable Java Packages and hierarchies of classes that compose most of the system functionality. Figure 2 shows the main hierarchy of class managers where arrows represent superclass relationships. The class hierarchy follows the Java classes used in the implementation. Interior classes in this hierarchy generally reflect significant common functionality, and have been given distinct Java implementations to encode this. Some of the points in this hierarchy are implemented with Java classes, some with interfaces.

Several generalizations apply across this hierarchy. Of particular interest are:

- Database / instance storage issues:
  If a class manager is responsible for storing the "raw form" of its instances, it needs some access to the underlying MARIAN databases. Different classes, depending on their semantics, have different database class managers as part of their attributes in order to manage those tasks. Each different type of table in the MARIAN database layer, as described in the following sections, is managed by a different class manager. However, subclasses of general API classes normally share the same inherited database manager static instance.

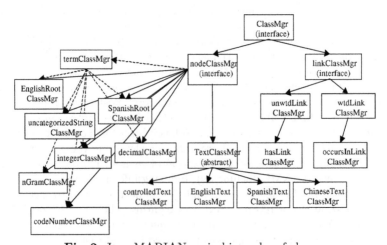

Fig. 2. Java MARIAN main hierarchy of classes

- Full ID genesis:
  Every object in Java MARIAN, whether an XML element, a MARC record attribute, a chunk of text, a unique term, etc., has a FullID, which is made of a class ID and an instance ID. ClassIDs for terms and controlled texts are normally pre-defined in some lexicon or authority file. The Java MARIAN EnglishTextClassMgr, for example, currently uses a lexicon of approximately 80,000 root terms extracted from the Collins English Dictionary improved with 16,000 geographic names extracted from the U.S census data. We have plans to incorporate a geographic lexicon with 5 million entries from the Alexandria project in future collections. ClassIDs for collection-dependent instances of nodes and links are created during collection building (see Section 5.1). Class managers are responsible for recognizing instances in raw form and for mapping back and forth between raw objects and FullIDs. There are several different methods for a class manager to find or create instanceIDs to fulfill this function.

Basic functionality to create, manage, and match portions of semantic networks is defined by the interfaces of the Link and Node class managers. Their subclasses implement and override those methods based on their specific semantics. Particular subclasses of nodeClassMgr implement match() methods which match graph queries, where the query root may match class instance nodes by the process of locating and enlisting surrounding linkClassMgrs to identify class instance nodes that match portions of the query graph. Types of nodes in MARIAN semantic networks include terms (termClassMgr), nodes of free text (TextClassMgr) or nodes for controlled text (ControlledTextClassMgr) such as people, geographic names, controlled vocabulary and codes from thesauri and classification schemes. The aspect of authority control in digital libraries is essential to guarantee quality of the information and services such as citation linking. Classes to support multi-lingual retrieval (EnglishTextClassMgr, SpanishTextClassMgr, ChineseTextClassMgr) also are implemented.

The TextClassManager, besides its methods for text matching and loading, this latter relying on specific database managers as explained earlier, also defines a general parse(Text) method which receives pieces of text for indexing or query matching and returns a weighted set of terms, the weight corresponding to the number and types of transformations necessary to produce a root for the term. Actually, the parse method of the TextClassManager is just a switch which, given a language parameter, passes the text to one of the language-based subclasses which apply their own overridden parse method, since parsing is a language-dependent task. Weighted sets of term FullIDs, however, provide a common cross-language representation to be used in all other operations. TermClassManager is a superclass constructed to contain all objects that can be components of text. As such it is a super class of language-based term roots, numbers, codes, etc.

Subclasses of linkClassManager include unwtdLinkClassManager and wtdLinkClassManager for respectively, unweighted and weighted links. Due to their common use for representing structural metadata and indexing information those classes are further subtyped in HasLinkClassManager and occursInClassManager. Collection dependent classes such as HasSubject and occursInAbstract are generated as subclasses of those general classes, inheriting all of their functionality.

Besides the main API a set of supporting APIs also are implemented in Java MARIAN. These include, as mentioned before, APIs for database management; for generic manipulation of FullIds, Weights and Weighted Sets; for tables, sequencers and fusion modules used in matching algorithms; and for generalized document presentation. In particular, the latter include methods to present short versions of documents in ranked lists with links to different views of full document presentations through XSL stylesheets. Some of those APIs will be further described in following sections.

4   Java MARIAN Architecture and Implementations

The Java MARIAN layered architecture is shown in Figure 3 with the respective services provided by each layer. The Database layer is responsible for persistently storing table versions of the DL semantic networks. It also provides a Database API that allows classes in the upper layers to manage their persistent instances, (e.g., to delete and insert new nodes and links and update weights). The Search layer, which carries most of the functionality of the system, is basically made of two complementary sub-layers: 1) one containing the main semantic network and digital library hierarchies of classes as described in the previous section; and 2) a community of searchers which implement the basic search functionalities, including fusion modules to combine multiple weighted sets for complex queries. The Webgate and User Information Layer deal with the end user. The Webgate functions as a session-based client to the system and can remotely communicate with several MARIAN servers besides providing extended DL logging capabilities for system evaluation. The User interaction layer provides personalization functions, such customization of several features of the system (e.g., maximum number of results to be retrieved, presentation styles, sorting rules), and keeps user's history of previous queries, which can be re-issued. Finally, a decoupled, additional layer provides functionality for automatic collection analysis and building. In the following, we describe in details each of the layers, including several aspects regarding implementation.

4.1   The Database Layer

The C++ Version of MARIAN used proprietary databases and files in a NeXT machine. Portability therefore was a problem. Also collection loading and indexing was done in a batch mode using special-purpose formatted files. In Java MARIAN the internal database schema was remodeled to be more flexible and implemented within a MySQL database. New database class managers also were implemented to support content loading. Dynamic incremental loading is an important characteristic in digital library environments such as union catalogs that periodically harvest Open Archives data providers [12]. Diagram 1 shows the MARIAN database-underlying schema.

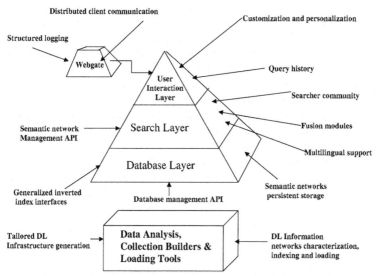

Fig. 3. Java MARIAN layered architecture

```
ClassMetadata:{ClassID|ClassName|tableName|nextInstID}
UnwtdLink:{linkClassID|sourceClassID|sourceInstID|sinkClassID|sinkInstID}
WtdLink:{linkClassID|sourceClassID|sourceInstID|sinkClassID|sinkInstID|weight}
NodeWeight:{NodeClassID|NodeInstID|LinkClassID|weight|isValid}
IndexedStr*:{ClassID|instID|str}
UnndexedStr*:{ClassID|instID|str}
```

Diagram 1. Java MARIAN general database schema

Information about class managers, their internal ClassIDs, type and expected size of instances, and next available instance ID to be assigned to a new incoming instance, are stored in the ClassMetadata table. For example, an entry (6029,AbstractClassManager, unindexedStrMedium, 9231) in the ClassMetadata table means that the ClassID for abstracts is 6029, abstract texts are not checked against a controlled vocabulary, they have a medium size (less than 5000 characters) and there are currently 9230 abstracts in the database. MARIAN node information, including instance IDs and their free or controlled text, are stored respectively in the indexedStr and unindexedStr tables. The asterisks in Diagram 1 mean that there are several types of these tables (e.g., indexedStrTiny, unindexedStrLong), depending on the expected size of its instances, using different SQL types for str columns to minimize storage and increase performance. For example, an entry (6029,670,"This dissertation describes a new system...") in the IndexedStrMedim table records the abstract text of the abstract no. 670. Similarly, MARIAN weighted and unweighted links are stored respectively in the tables wtdlink and unwtdlink. These tables record the classID of the particular type of link, the FullIDs of sources and sinks, and the weight of the link, if appropriate. For example if the entry (6004,6000,2305,6029,2304) is inserted in the unwtdlnk table, it means that a new link of the type HasAbstract (ClassID=6004) was created between a document (ClassID=6000), instance ID 2305 and a new abstract (ClassID=6029), instance ID 2304. Remember that each type of link is managed by a different OO class manager, therefore those classes are responsible for updating their respective databases, during loading time, and retrieve weighted sets of FullIDs during searching time by calling services of the corresponding database managers. Those services are implemented as methods that create and issue particular JDBC PreparedStatement SQL queries.

The NodeWeight table stores information about node weights (e.g., idf values) in the context of some specific link (linkClassID column). The isValid column is set to false if, during loading time, a piece of text including the specific term is inserted in the database, which will affect its outdegree and therefore weight. Invalid nodes are updated after the loading process is completed.

4.2   The Search Layer

Among their other functions, each MARIAN class manager implements one or more search methods. A search method is a mapping from abstract object descriptions to weighted sets of objects matching that description, where the weight of each object in the set functions as a measure of how well that object matches the description.

Any class in the MARIAN world can support search methods particular to itself. Two commonly used forms of searching are link activation and search within context. As an example, consider searching for library works with a certain person as author. In MARIAN's terms, this is a search for objects of class Work linked by one or more HasAuthor links to objects of class Person. The user puts together a description of a person. Identifying possible persons that match the description is a function of the Person class manager: the result of such a match is a weighted set of Person objects of decreasing similarity to the description. That set can be returned directly to the user, usually within some context for the Persons: books by them, books about them, and so forth. The user is more often interested, however, not in the persons themselves but in what they have written. Thus the weighted set of Person objects also can serve as input to a link class searching method, which returns a weighted set of works each linked to at least one person in the input set. In a more general case, link activation can proceed through arbitrary numbers of intermediate nodes and links before reaching objects of the desired class. In the most general case, entire patterns and topologies surrounding the desired objects may become activated. In this case, we say that the activated subgraph defines a context for the desired objects. Searching for an object in context thus becomes a process of searching through various link-node patterns in the network and then combining the intermediate results. This combination is the responsibility of MARIAN's searcher community.

The most commonly used types of searchers are the maximizing union and summative union. When combining sets coming from different link activations,

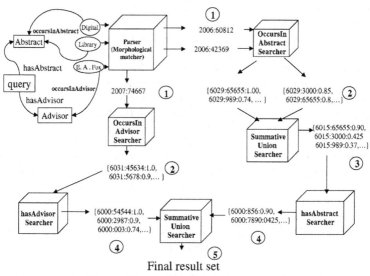

Fig. 4. Example of search processing

the maximizing union searcher keeps only the maximum value of weighted objects that occur in incoming sets. The current implementation of the summative union searcher calculates an average of the sums for incoming sets. Other weighting schemes such as Euclidian distance or sum-of-squares also can be used. Searchers for text and structured documents to combine multi-word, multi-field queries use summative union searchers.

Consider for example, a query for electronic theses and dissertations with the terms "digital library" in their abstracts and advisor "E. A. Fox" (see upper left of Figure 4). This is processed as follows:

1. each query term is fed to the morphological parser which returns a FullID (ClassID:InstanceID,e.g., "2006:60812") for each of them (yielding outputs shown as "1");
2. three weighted sets are produced by activating one occursInAbstract link for each term of the query (i.e., "Digital" and "Library") as well as the link occursInAdvisor (yielding outputs "2") [1];
3. the two weighted sets of FullIds for abstracts are combined using the summative union searcher, i.e., weights of FullIDs in the intersection of the two sets are summed, and, after that, all the weights are normalized by the number of incoming sets; in the case, two;

---

[1] Here, this is most likely a singleton, i.e., a set of one element, but that may not be true in the general case; variations of the advisor's name can be present in the knowledge base, whereupon all of those variations should be retrieved. This processing is responsibility of the match() algorithm of the Advisor class manager.

4. the weighted sets of FullIDs of abstracts and advisors are used as inputs to activate respectively the links hasAbstract and hasAdvisor; each link manager then computes a weighted set of FullIDs for metadata records linked to the abstracts and advisors in the respective weighted sets [2]; and finally
5. the two sets of metadata record FullIDs are fused using the same summative procedure as above and the resulting set returned as the answer of the query. The user then can browse through the ranked list of metadata records and ultimately retrieve the ETD fulltext by using the URL corresponding to the "describes" link from the metadata record to the ETD.

Searchers depend heavily on two software constructs: tables and sequencers. Tables maintain a short-term memory of elements seen to date, checking each new element against the table to tell whether or not it should be discarded. A sequencer is a software object that takes a set of incoming streams of weighted objects in weight order and produces a single output stream also in descending order. The output stream consists of the same elements and exactly the same weights as in the input streams, shuffled into a single non-increasing order by weight.

For performance purposes, MARIAN has a number of different implementations of tables and sequencers, the differences being in the particular data structures they use and combining algorithms they implement. For example, PriQueueSequencer is an implementation of a sequencer designed to be used for sequencing large numbers of component sets that are approximately the same with respect to the distribution of weights amongst them. Because of this, PriQueueSequencer uses a heap to merge items taken from the head of each component set in the sequencer. Small numbers of component sets, especially those whose weights drop off in a "stair step" fashion with respect to each other, are handled more efficiently by a different approach. Here, MergeSequencer uses a simple linear search to locate the component set with the highest weight, and also that with the next-highest weight, which is used as a trigger value. When sequencing, items are taken repeatedly from the highest-weighted set until the weight of the item falls below that of the trigger value. When this happens, the next-highest set becomes the highest-weighted, and a linear search is once again performed to determine a new trigger weight and set. For highly stair-stepped component sets, the number of linear searches is small. We are currently conducting extensive tests on the searcher performance to check if the actual performance matches with the predicted complexity [4].

4.3   Webgate and User Information Layer

The Webgate in Java MARIAN is basically a store-and-forward module, which maintains and manages all the information and flows for each end-user opera-

---

[2] Since hasAbstract and hasAdvisor are unweighted types of links, weights from the incoming sets are propagated to the FullIDs of the respective linked metadata records; for example, if an abstract matched the query with weight 0.90 this will be the weight of the metadata record linked to that abstract.

tion. It allows communications with multiple distributed MARIAN servers in a weakly-coupled manner and provides the functionality to log all the user information by using the MARIAN XML Log Manager, which implements a proposed rich XML standard for digital library logging [9]. Java MARIAN achieves the goal of distributed Client/Server architecture and loose-coupling by deploying an internal standard protocol called User Interaction Protocol (UIP) [14].

Beyond the enhancement of Webgate by adding the User Information Layer, there are several features shipped or ongoing, such as personalization and customization. For example, a Java MARIAN user can view, re-use, and manage the history of all the previous queries, select the preferred language, choose the maximum number of documents to be retrieved, sorting rule, query timeout, and so forth. Also, for performance reasons, the formit, a CGI module in Webgate that allowed Web access and had the overhead of starting a Java Virtual Machine (JVM) for every communication, has recently been replaced by a TomCat Servlet module.

4.4   Data Analysis, Collection Builders & Loading Tools

Automatic Collection Building: Java MARIAN uses a specific digital library generator to create tailored collections for specific community needs and requirements. The Java MARIAN digital library generator takes a description of digital library components in 5SL [7], a declarative language for digital library specification and generation, and produces: 1) all the necessary class managers, including those for structural and indexing information, and corresponding ClassIDs; 2) collection-dependent configuration and query processing classes; 3) the collection loader, a collection-dependent structural and content parser that takes collections of documents and incrementally loads them in Java MARIAN databases; and 4) collection-dependent search user interfaces and XSL stylesheets for document presentation. A portion of the 5SL code describing the ETD metadata records [1] and the metadata catalog is presented below.

```
<structural_model>
 <metadata_record name = "etdms_record">
    <stream_enumeration>
       <stream value = "etdms_text"/>
    </stream_enumeration>
    <structured_stream>
       <schema>etdms.xsd</schema>
    </structured_stream>
 </metadata_record>
 <catalog>
   <name>NDLTD</name>
   <description>Networked Digital Library of Theses and Dissertations
   </description>
   <creator>Virginia Tech</creator>
   <maintainer>mgoncalv@vt.edu</maintainer>
   <metadata_type>etdms_record</metadata_type>
 </catalog>
</structural_model>
```

The Java MARIAN dynamic collection loading process is shown in Figure 5 and works as follows. The generated collection loader receives a stream of incoming data and separates it into individual semi-structured documents. In case of XML documents, those are checked against an XML Schema and, if they are valid, the loading and inversion processes proceed. Currently, the loader is basically an automatically generated SAX event parser that knows how to parse and extract structuring and indexing information from valid documents of the specific collection, as described in the 5SL specifications. It works by registering events such as document and XML elements openings and closings and presence of textual information and by calling loading methods of the respective class managers at the occurrence of such events. Structural links are instantiated for each structural element found (e.g., ⟨subject⟩, ⟨description⟩). Textual information, including free text and controlled authorities, are stored in corresponding databases by calling Load(text) methods of the right generated class managers (e.g., AbstractClassManager). After database loading, texts are forwarded for inversion to the respective generated occursIn class managers (e.g., occursIn-Abstract). In the case of controlled texts, specified as such in the document description, authority control is ensured.

The text objects produced by the first step are indexed first by analyzing the texts into the terms that occur in them, then collecting the texts associated with unique terms. More specifically, each text is analyzed into a set of generated occursIn links, each connecting a unique term with a unique text of some structural element. While this is going on, weights are being computed that measure the strength of association between the terms and texts.

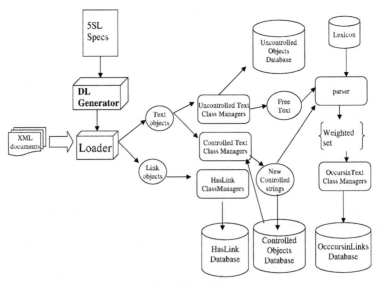

Fig. 5. Java MARIAN Collection Loading process in Spring 2002

Table 2. Statistics on Collection Loading

Collection/Statistics	Dirline	NDLTD	CITIDEL
Number Docs	9,233	3,753	4,379
Num of unweighted links	138,684	41,847	27,072
Num of wtdlinks	1,013,961	789,246	923,487
Words/Doc (mean)	110	210	210
Structural elements/Doc (mean)	15	11	6

Examples of Use and Evaluation Java MARIAN was released in Spring 2002, already in use in some prototype collections. Table 2 shows statistics for three collections: 1) Dirline, a U.S. National Library of Medicine's online digital library containing location and descriptive information about a wide variety of information resources including organizations and projects concerned with health and biomedicine; 2) the Union Archive of the Networked Digital Library of Theses and Dissertations (NDLTD); and 3) CITIDEL, a computing education collection (see www.citidel.org).

Current loading performance is acceptable for medium size collections but improvements need to be made for larger collections. Already, a 42x improvement over a naive implementation has resulted through: increasing MySQL buffer sizes, using BufferedStrings instead of static String objects, and reducing garbage collection through minimizing object creation.

5   Conclusions and Future Work

We have presented design, architecture and implementation details regarding Java MARIAN, a modern, "next-generation" digital library system that meets many of the complex and rich requirements of current digital library applications. Future work will proceed in many directions. We are incorporating support for harvesting and federated searching and we will be investigating new hybrid architectures that integrate both strategies [10]. We will incorporate other types of networks in the system, for example, belief networks [11] which allow combination of evidence from several sources for enhanced retrieval. New query languages and operators like generalized closure for multi-classification schemes browsing will be implemented. New interfaces for digital library modeling and generation will be incorporated. We will explore richer networks of relationships like citation linking and complex networks of multi-language relationships among terms. We are exploring the handling of concept maps in addition to full text and multimedia content, in addition to metadata records. And, at last, we will be investigating how to use caching with RAM as well as our VT-PetaPlex-1 system (a parallel machine with 2.5 terabytes of storage, 100 Pentium processors with 64M RAM, and high speed connectivity) as a storage system for MARIAN along with parallel information retrieval techniques to address issues of scalability and performance.

Acknowledgements

The MARIAN system and most of its ideas are a creation of our great friend Robert K. France who in Fall 2001 passed away. This paper is dedicated to his memory. We thank the National Library the Medicine for supporting this work. Thanks also are given for the support of NSF through its grants: IIS-9986089, IIS-0002935, IIS-0080748, IIS-0086227, DUE-0121679, DUE-0121741, and DUE-0136690.

References

[1] Anthony Atkins. Interoperability metadata standard for electronic theses and dissertations. http://www.ndltd.org/standards/metadata/current.html, 2001. 205

[2] T. Berners-Lee, J. Hendler, and O. Lassila. The Semantic Web. *Scientific American*, 284(5):34–43, May 2001. 194

[3] E. A. Fox, R. K. France, E. Sahle, A. Daoud, and B. E. Cline. Development of a modern OPAC: From REVTOLC to MARIAN. In *Proceedings of the Sixteenth Annual International ACM SIGIR Conference on Research and Development in Information Retrieval*, pages 248–259, 1993. 195

[4] Robert K. France. *Effective, Efficient Retrieval in a Network of Digital Information Objects*. Dissertation, Virginia Polytechnic Institute and State University, December 2001. 204

[5] Joe Futrelle, Su-Shing Chen, and Kevin C. Chang. NBDL: A CIS Framework for NSDL. In *Proceedings of the First ACM/IEEE-CS Joint Conference on Digital Libraries (JCDL'2001)*, pages 124–125, Roanoke, Virginia, June 24-28 2001. 194

[6] David A. Garza-Salazar. Phronesis. http://copernico.mty.itesm.mx/homedir tempo/Proyectos/, 2001. 194

[7] M. A. Gonçalves and E. A. Fox. 5SL – A Language for Declarative Generation and Specification of Digital Libraries . In *Proc. of the 2nd ACM/IEEE-CS Joint Conference on Digital Libraries (JCDL'2002)*, Portland, Oregon, July 14-18 2002. 205

[8] M. A. Gonçalves, E. A. Fox, L. T. Watson, and N. A. Kipp. Streams, Structures, Spaces, Scenarios and Societies (5S): A Formal Model for Digital Libraries. Technical Report TR-01-12, Virginia Tech, Blacksburg, VA, 2001. 195

[9] M. A. Gonçalves, M. Luo, R. Shen, M. F. Ali, and E. A. Fox. An XML Log Standard and Tool for Digital Library Logging. In *Proceedings of the 6th European Conference on Research and Advanced Technology for Digital Libraries*, Rome, Italy, 2002 (to appear). Springer. 205

[10] Marcos André Gonçalves, Robert K. France, and Edward A. Fox. MARIAN: Flexible Interoperability for Federated Digital Libraries. In *Proceedings of the 5th European Conference on Research and Advanced Technology for Digital Libraries*, pages 173–186, Darmsdadt, Germany, 2001. Springer. 207

[11] B. A. N. Ribeiro and R. Muntz. A belief network model for IR. In *Proc. of the 19th Annual Int. ACM SIGIR Conf. on Research and Development in Information Retrieval*, pages 253–260, 1996. 207

[12] H. Suleman, A. Atkins, M. A. Gonçalves, R. K. France, E. A. Fox, V. Chachra, M. Crowder, and J. Young. Networked Digital Library of Theses and Dissertations: Bridging the Gaps for Global Access – Part 2, Services and Research. *D-Lib Magazine*, 7(9), September 15, 2001. 200

[13] Ian H. Witten, Rodger J. McNab, Stefan J. Boddie, and David Bainbridge. Greenstone: A comprehensive open-source digital library software system. In *Proceedings of the Fifth ACM International Conference on Digital Libraries (ACM DL'2000)*, pages 113–121, San Antonio, TX, June 2-7 2000. 194

[14] Jianxin Zhao. *Making Digital Libraries Flexible, Scalable and Reliable: Reengineering the MARIAN System in JAVA*. Dissertation, Virginia Polytechnic Institute and State University, 1999. 205

A Framework for Generating Attribute Extractors for Web Data Sources

Davi de Castro Reis, Robson Braga Araújo, Altigran S. da Silva, and
Berthier A. Ribeiro-Neto

Department of Computer Science, Federal University of Minas Gerais
31270-901 - Belo Horizonte MG - Brazil
{braga,davi,alti,berthier}@dcc.ufmg.br

Abstract. To cope with the irregularities of typical semistructured Web
data, extraction tools usually break the extraction task in two phases:
an extraction phase, in which atomic attribute values are extracted from
Web pages, and an assembling phase, in which these atomic values are
grouped to form complex objects. As a consequence, the whole process
is highly dependent on the attribute values collected in the first phase.
All attribute values of interest should be properly recognized and spuri-
ous values should be discarded. Thus, attribute values extraction is an
important problem. In this paper, we propose a new framework for generating attribute value extractors. The main appeal of this framework is
that it can be adapted for dealing with specific types of data sources and
to incorporate distinct types of heuristics for achieving good extraction
performance. To demonstrate the feasibility of this proposal, we present
an implementation of this framework for data-rich Web pages and show
how a number of simple heuristics, some of them presented in the recent literature, can be incorporated into this framework. We also show
experimental results and, in most cases, our results are at least as good
as results previously presented in the literature.

1   Introduction

In the past few years, the number of sites and services available on the Web
that can be regarded as data "containers" has increased steadily. Such large
availability has opened the possibility of using these data in a variety of ways.
However, *data-rich* or *data-intensive* [6] Web sources most often provide only
HTML pages in which data of interest (e.g., data on featuring movies) appears
implicit. Its structure can be detected by virtual inspection but has not been
declared explicitly. In most cases, such data occur mixed inside Web page text
with markup tags, other strings, in-line code, etc. Further, the structure of the
data is only suggested by presentation features. Such a structure is often loose,
with the possibility that two similar items (e.g., entries on two distinct movies)
present structural variations between them. Because of this, data available in
Web sources is classified as being *semistructured* [1].

To exemplify, Figure 1 illustrates the excerpt of a Web page, obtained in response to the query "Paul McCartney" submitted to the *Amazon.com* Web site.

A.H.F. Laender and A.L. Oliveira (Eds.): SPIRE 2002, LNCS 2476, pp. 210–226, 2002.

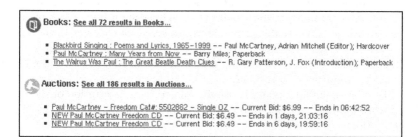

Fig. 1. An example Web page from Amazon.com

This page contains data about several distinct products related to the query, organized by sections that correspond to *Amazon.com* stores. To simplify our example, we consider only the stores *books* and *auctions*. Consider we are interested in extracting data on the stores and the products available on it. In the page excerpt of Figure 1, we can identify two *complex objects*: Books and Auctions. Both objects are of type Store. They are composed of an atomic value that identifies the store name and a list of Item objects, each of them being a complex object itself. Note that, for each store, the information on products is distinct. The information can be structured as an aggregation of attributes Item, AuthorList and BookType, for the Books store, and of attributes Item, Bid and Time, for the Auctions store.

A commonly adopted strategy for gaining access to implicit Web data is to build *wrappers* that extract the data of interest, uncover its semantics, and convert them to a suitable format such as relational tables or XML objects. These converted data can then be adequately processed according to specific application needs. Until recently, the most common approach for developing wrappers was to write them directly using general purpose languages such as *Perl* and *Java*. Developing wrappers manually has many well known shortcomings, mainly due to the difficulty in writing and maintaining them. More recently, several works in the literature have discussed approaches for semi-automatically generating wrappers for Web data [6, 11, 2].

Recent works in the literature propose the semiautomatic generation of wrappers by deriving the extraction rules w from a given set of examples of the objects to be extracted. According to this approach, given a set $E \subset O$ of example objects, taken from a subset $T_0 \subset T$ of a Web source S, a wrapper generation procedure g generates the extraction rules w. That is, $g(E, T_0) = w$.

In general, example-based approaches for generating wrappers use techniques from machine learning [14] or information retrieval [11]. Although one of the first works is this area [10] suggests the use of an "oracle" for providing examples, most of the research later developed rely on humans for this task [11].

To properly deal with the hierarchical and semistructured nature of the data to be extracted, state-of-art approach for Web data extraction divide the process in two distinct phases: an *extraction* phase and an *assembling* phase. In the extraction phase, atomic attribute values (e.g. names of authors, types of books, etc.) are identified and actually extracted from a given source page. In the *assembling* phase, the attribute values extracted in the previous phase are grouped to assemble complex objects. This two-phase approach is adopted by many recent works in the literature [5, 7, 8, 12, 13, 15, 14], because it provides for greater flexibility. The assembling phase is usually guided by a description of the target structure that is either implicitly assumed [8], obtained from a user [11, 13, 14, 15] or automatically inferred [5].

In this work we are particularly interested in the extraction phase, that is, our focus is on the the problem of extracting attribute values that compose complex semistructured objects. Indeed, this phase is critical for the whole extraction process to work properly.

We present an example-based framework for generating *attribute extractors*. Each such extractor can then be used by a wrapper for extracting values of a given attribute. Several works in the literature propose strategies for generating attribute extractors [8, 13, 15]. The main appeal of the framework we propose here is that it provides hooks that allow direct incorporation of several application-oriented heuristics, with no need of modifying the code of the framework itself. Using our framework, wrapper developers can customize the generation of attribute extractors for specific application needs and orient the extraction goals according to these needs.

Moreover, differently from most works in the field, the presented framework is very flexible. Actually, it is immediately ready for applications other than Web data extraction. By properly tuning the customizable components of the framework, called *delimiters tree* and *Guiders*, we can rapidly develop semi-automatic or automatic wrapper generation applications for several data sources, ranging from legacy proprietary database formats to web server log files.

To demonstrate the feasibility of our proposal, we present an implementation of this framework for data-rich Web pages [6] and show how simple heuristics can be incorporated into the framework. We also show experimental results achieved by using these heuristics individually and by combining them. Our results are at least as good as results previously presented in the literature.

The paper is organized as follows. Section 2 presents the notion of attribute extractors. Section 3 discuss PDS, the type of attribute extractors generated by our framework, while in Section 4 we present our strategy for obtaining a useful PDS. In Section 5 we describe how application-oriented heuristics can be incorporated to the framework. Section 6 describes an implementation of the

```
<HTML><BODY BGCOLOR=FFFFFF>
<B>The Catcher in The Rye</B> by <I>Sallinger, J.D.</I>
<B>Zen and The Art of Motorcycle Maintenance</B> by <I>Pirsig, R. M.</I>
</BODY></HTML>
```

Fig. 2. An example Web page

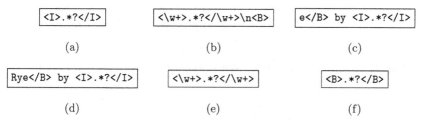

Fig. 3. Regular expressions for extracting author names from the Web page of Figure 2

framework targeted at Web pages and Section 7 presents experimental results obtained with this implementation. In Section 8, we briefly comment the related work. Finally, Section 9 presents our conclusions and comments on future work.

2 Attribute Extractors

This section presents the concept of an *Attribute Extractor*. Through the paper we use the term attribute to refer to atomic components of objects, similarly to what is done in databases.

Informally, we call attribute extractor a regular expression, grammar or finite-state automaton aimed at extracting from an input text (e.g., a Web page) values for a given attribute. Consider the HTML page shown in Figure 2. In this simple page, we can see a list of two books represented by their titles along with the names of their authors.

Suppose we are interested in extracting the names of the authors. For this, we build some regular expressions[1] as shown in Figure 3.

The regular expressions of Figures 3(a)–(e) can be considered as attribute extractors for author names, since all of them match strings corresponding to the name of an author in the page of Figure 2. The regular expression in Figure 3(f), however, does not match any author name and, thus, it is not an attribute extractor for author names.

There are two important properties a useful attribute extractor should have. First, it should be *sound*, that is, it should only match values in the domain of the attribute considered. Second, it should be *complete*, that is, it should match all values in the domain of the attribute considered, occurring in a given text or page.

To exemplify, the regular expressions of Figure 3(a)–(c) correspond to attribute extractors that are both sound and complete. Figure 3(d) correspond to an attribute extractors that is sound, but not complete, since it only extracts the value **Sallinger, J.D.**, while the regular expression in Figure 3(e) corresponds to an attribute extractor that is complete, but not sound, since it extracts strings that are not author names. These properties are formalized in Definition 1.

---

[1] We adopt here a usual notation for regular expressions similar to Perl, Grep, etc.

Fig. 4. Excerpt of a possible tokenization of the Web page in Figure 2

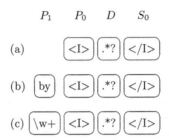

Fig. 5. Examples of attribute extractors

Definition 1. *Let τ be an attribute whose domain is D_τ, and let $D_\tau(g)$ be the set of strings in a Web page g that belong to D_τ. Let $\mathcal{E}_\tau$ be an attribute extractor for τ and L_ε be the language it denotes. We say that ε_τ is **sound** iff $D_\tau(g) \supseteq L_\varepsilon$. Also, we say that ε_τ is **complete** iff $D_\tau(g) \subseteq L_\varepsilon$.*

From our discussion, one can foresee that there are infinitely many possibilities for generating attribute extractors for a given domain, even if we limit ourselves to attribute extractors that are sound and complete.

To cope with such a complexity, a commonly adopted approach is to break the input document into *tokens*. For this, it is necessary to assume some tokenization policy. In Figure 4 we present an excerpt of a possible tokenization[2] of the page in Figure 2. Notice that we have adopted here a very simple tokenization policy.

By using tokenization, it is possible to construct attribute extractors that match tokens instead of single characters. Under this assumption, an attribute extractor is described as a sequence of *slots*, each slot matching a token in the input text. As an example, consider the three regular expressions presented in Figure 5. They correspond to attribute extractors for author names in Figure 2.

In the regular expression in Figure 5(a), the slot labeled D matches an author name, and the slots labeled P_0 and S_0 match respectively a token on the left and a token on the right of the author name. In the regular expression in Figures 5(b)–(c), an additional slot (P_1) was used.

Several recent works on Web data extraction adopt concepts similar to attribute extractors based on text tokenization. This is the case of the *AVP-Patterns* used in DEByE [11], the *Finite State Transducers* used in SoftMealy [8], the *Landscape Automata* used in Stalker [14], and the *DataFrames* used by Embley et. al. in their work [6].

---

[2] We represent blank spaces by •.

In this paper, our main goal is to investigate the design and implementation of a particular type of attribute extractor called *Prefix-Data-Suffix Extractor* or *PDS* extractor for short. The attribute extractors of Figure 5 are all examples of PDS extractors. A PDS extractor is composed of one *data* slot, one or more *prefix* slots (which occur on the left of the data slot), and one or more *suffix* slots (which occur on the right of the data slot). In the next section, PDS extractors are discussed in detail.

3   Prefix-Data-Suffix Extractors

Let us first introduce the notion of a *delimiters tree*. This notion is central to our ideas. Let $P_m, P_{m-1}, \ldots, P_1, P_0, D, S_0, S_1, \ldots, S_{n-1}, S_n$ be an attribute extractor for values of an attribute τ occurring in a Web page g. Each P_j or S_i is a slot (i.e., a regular expression) that matches a token in g, and D is any token that occurs between P_0 and S_0. For this attribute extractor to be useful, its slots must refer specifically to the tokens generated from the target input. Because of this, attribute extractors slots and tokens should be based on a same common tokenization policy. The structure responsible for this policy is what we call a *delimiters tree*.

Definition 2. *A **delimiters** tree D is a hierarchy (a tree) in which each node n is associated with a regular expression e_n over an alphabet Σ that denotes a language L_n, such that the following properties apply:*

- *Let r be the root of D, then $e_r = \Sigma^*$;*

- *Let r be the root of D and $\{c_1, \ldots, c_k\}$ be the set of its children, then $\bigcup_{i=1}^{k} L_{c_i} = L_r$.*

- *Let n be a node in D and $\{c_1, \ldots, c_k\}$ be the set of its children, then $\bigcup_{i=1}^{k} L_{c_i} \subseteq L_n$ and $\bigcap_{i=1}^{k} L_{c_i} = \emptyset$.*

The delimiters tree is used with two objectives. First, it guides the tokenization of the input document. The regular expressions in the second level of the delimiters tree are used to extract a sequence of tokens from the target page, assigning higher priority to the bigger tokens. Second, its nodes are used to compose the slots that form attribute extractors.

By building a delimiters tree, it is possible to specialize the framework to generate attribute extractors for a specific class of text documents. Implicitly, by defining such a tree the wrapper developer takes advantage of the structural elements typical of a documents class (e.g. HTML) to allow the construction of suitable attribute extractors. As an example, in Figure 6 we illustrate a delimiters tree built for specializing the framework for HTML documents.

Attribute extractors generated according to a delimiters tree are termed *Prefix-Data-Suffix Extractors* or *PDS extractors* for short. More formally, we have the following definition:

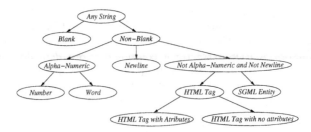

Fig. 6. A delimiters tree for HTML documents

Definition 3. *Let g be a Web page and e be a string in g. Also, let T be a delimiters tree and* $g_T = \ldots, p_m, \ldots, p_0, e, s_0, \ldots, s_n, \ldots$ *be a tokenization of g according to T, where e is a token in* g_T. *A* **Prefix-Data-Suffix Extractor** *or* **PDS extractor** *is an expression of the form:* $P_m, P_{m-1}, \ldots, P_1, P_0, D, S_0, S_1, \ldots, S_{n-1}, S_n$, *where D is a regular expression denoting* Σ^*, P_i *is the i-th token to the left of e in g, or a regular expression* ε_v, *where v is a node in the delimiters tree T that matches this token, and* S_j *is the j-th token to the right of e in g, or a regular expression* ε_u, *where u is a node in the delimiters tree T that matches this token.*

We notice that a given PDS extractor π, as any regular expression, denotes a language L_π. From the above definition, the matching portion D of any word belonging to L_π is the data the PDS extracts. A PDS π is said to be complete if the words in L_π contain all data to be extracted. Similarly, a PDS is said to be sound if all the words in L_π contain only valid data. Therefore, our ultimate purpose is to construct a PDS extractor that is sound and complete. The next session presents the strategy adopted in our framework for obtaining a suitable PDS extractor.

4   PDS Tree

In this section we describe our general strategy to obtain suitable PDS extractors for extracting attribute values from Web pages. As we shall see, this strategy consists in first generating a set of candidate PDS extractors and then using application-oriented heuristics to select from this set the most promising PDS extractor in terms of soundness and completeness.

Let g be a Web page and T be a delimiters tree used to generate a tokenization g_T of g. Given a token e, which is an *example* of a value of an attribute, say τ, it is possible to determine the set of all possible PDS extractors that match this token by using the regular expressions in T. For this, the tokens surrounding the example are turned into slots and combined in all possible ways. The set of these PDS extractors is called the *PDS candidate set*.

As the delimiters tree T defines an hierarchy over these regular expressions, it is also possible to define a hierarchy over the candidate PDS set. This results in a structure we call a *Candidate PDS Tree* or *PDS Tree*, for short.

Definition 4. *Let g be a Web page, T be a delimiters tree and $g_T = \dots, p_m, \dots, p_0, e, s_0, \dots, s_n, \dots$ be a tokenization of g according to T. We define a **PDS Tree** in g as follows:*

- *Each node in the tree is a PDS extractor of the form $P_m, \dots, P_0, D, S_0, \dots, S_n$, where D is a regular expression denoting σ^* and P_i (S_j) is either equal to p_i (s_j) or it is a regular expression in T that matches p_i (s_j);*
- *The root of the tree is the PDS p_0, D, s_0;*
- *If $P_m, \dots, P_0, D, S_0, \dots, S_n$ is a node in the tree, then*
  - *every PDS $P_{m+1}, P_m, \dots, P_0, D, S_0, \dots, S_n$ is a child of this node in the tree;*
  - *every PDS $P_m, \dots, P_0, D, S_0, \dots, S_n, S_{n+1}$ is a child of this node in the tree;*

Informally, a PDS Tree is generated for a token e, given as *example*, such that all PDS extractors in the tree are capable of extracting e and, possibly, other strings. The children of a given PDS extractor in a tree are those that have one more slot (to the left or to the right), being this slot the token (to the left or to the right) itself, or some equivalent regular expression obtained from the delimiters tree.

As an example, consider the example page of Figure 2, the delimiters tree of Figure 6, the tokenization of Figure 4 and the PDS extractor of Figure 5. In Figure 7 we illustrate an excerpt of a PDS Tree generated when the string `Sallinger, J.D.` is given as example. In the root of this subtree is the PDS labeled (a) formed using the tokens that occur immediately on the left and on the right of the string provided as example. Among the children of this PDS we find the PDS labeled (b), which adds a token to the left, and the PDS labeled (c), in which the token on the left (`by`) is replaced by a regular expression (`<\w+>`) taken from the delimiters tree of Figure 6.

Our next step consists in traversing the PDS Tree in search of a suitable PDS. A naive strategy to accomplish this would be to exhaustively traverse the whole tree, apply each PDS to the target page and use an oracle (e.g., a human user) to determine whether the PDS was able to correctly extract all values of interest and only those values. This strategy is not feasible for two main reasons. First, its not possible to guarantee that a sound and complete PDS exists, and, second, the complete traversal of the whole PDS Tree is unbearable in practice.

The tree-like organization of the structure comes in hand to solve this problem. We can see PDS tree as a decision tree, where each node is presented to the user as a possible solution. If the user is not satisfied with such solution, then he points the node that seems to be nearer to the optimal solution. As user feedback is a high cost resource, we will try to simulate it by means of decision making functions that encapsulate application-oriented heuristics. This functions are called *Guiders* and are discussed in the next section.

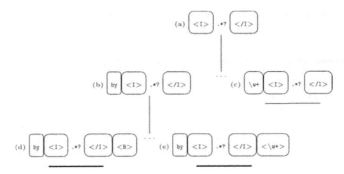

Fig. 7. Example of a PDS Tree

5   Guiders

Given a PDS tree as described above, consider an oracle[3] that is capable of telling for a given node n reached during the traversal: (1) whether the traversal must stop, meaning that n is "reasonable" PDS; or (2) which child of n is the "most promising" node for the traversal to continue. Such a traversal is describe by the PDS-Search algorithm in Figure 8.

```
1  PDS-Search(n : root of a subtree of a PDS Tree);
2
3  begin
4     if  Oracle.Stop(n)
5        then  Return n ;
6        else  c ← Oracle.ChooseChild(n) ;
7              PDS-Search(c) ;
9     fi
10 end
```

Fig. 8. The PDS-Search Algorithm

The Oracle described above is the second main component of the framework we propose in this paper. It is used to encapsulate a number of heuristics that can provide the two kinds of information required by the PDS-Search algorithm. In our framework, these heuristics are implemented by small functions called *Guiders*, since they have the role of guiding the traversal on the PDS Tree in the search for a "reasonable" PDS.

It should be noted that Guiders are meant to emulate the Guiders are invocated by the Oracle for each node traversed according to the PDS-Search

---

[3] This oracle is not related to oracles that can be used for automatically providing examples

algorithm. As a response, each guider must be capable of returning two values called *vote* and the *stop*. The *vote* value is used to choose one of the children of the current PDS as a next step. The *stop* value is used to know if this PDS is considered good enough so that the tree traversal can stop. Besides the *vote* and the *stop* value, guiders must return a *confidence level* associated to each of these values.

For each node n found in the traversal, the oracle must decide whether it must go on the traversal or not. If it takes the decision of going on, it must choose one of the children PDS of n. To make this decision, the oracle invokes all guiders available to evaluate each of the children. For each confidence level returned by the guiders, an average of the vote values for each child PDS is computed. Then, the oracle selects the child that received the highest vote average within the highest confidence level. In the case of a draw, the child that received the highest vote average within the second highest confidence level is selected and so on. The decision of stopping the traversal in node n is taken in a similar fashion. However, this is only taken if the highest average of stop values within the highest confidence level is greater than a predefined threshold. This is a very simple approach to combining evidences given by the guiders, but it showed to have enough power for our purposes.

Our framework allows guiders to have access to all information available during the process. That is, guiders have access to the example given, to the delimiters tree, to the target page and its tokenization, and, of course, to the PDS Tree. In addition, guiders may also receive parameters. Thus, guider developers are allowed to use any of these structures to compute votes and to establish their confidence levels. For instance, guiders can take the current PDS in the traversal, use it to extract from the input page and then cast its vote and confidence level based on the results of the extraction.

Guiders constitute, along with delimiters tree, the main customization resources within our framework. By properly building them, wrapper developers can introduce heuristics for dealing with specific type of text or with special kinds of data of their interest. They specify the biases of the wrapper induction system.

By making guiders properly declaring their confidence level, developers can prevent a guider that is too specific from compromising more generic guiders. For instance, a guider built to operate inside columns of an HTML table can declare a low confidence level when invoked outside an HTML table, so its vote is deprecated in favor of "more confident" guiders. Notice that we allow wrapper developers to choose only the guiders needed during a wrapper generation session, that is, it is not necessary to use all guiders available at once.

6   Putting All Together

To demonstrate the feasibility of the proposed framework, we created an implementation of it targeted to HTML documents. First, we built a delimiters tree similar to that presented at Figure 6 for exploiting the typical structural features of HTML documents. Next, we also created a few guiders to guide the traversal of the PDS Tree. Following, we briefly describe the guiders implemented.

- **Position Guider.** To evaluate a PDS, this guider bases its decision on the relative positions of the atomic values extracted by the PDS. For this, the guider uses the PDS to extract from the input page and verifies the standard deviation of the distances (in the page) between the atomic values obtained. PDS that result in small values for this metric are better evaluated. The heuristic implemented by this guider is similar to one of the heuristics used in [6].
- **Counter Guider.** This is an example of guider that receives a parameter. In this case, the guider takes from the user an estimate of the number of values of the attribute of interest in the input page. PDS extractors that extract nearly this number of atomic values are better evaluated. This guider emulates the heuristic use in [11].
- **HTML Tree Guider.** This guider takes advantage of the inherent structure of the HTML parse tree corresponding to the input page. When evaluating a given PDS, this guider determines, for each atomic value obtained by the PDS, the path in the parse where it is located. PDS that result in atomic values with similar paths are favored when evaluated by this guider. This guider provides a functionality similar to that of [4].
- **MSYFM Guider.** MSYFM (Make Sure You Find Me) is a guider that takes as parameters additional examples of values of the attribute of interest. This guider tries to ensure that all examples given are covered by the chosen PDS.

Concerning MSYFM Guider, it is worth noticing that some approaches in the literature [11] prefer to create distinct attribute extractor for different partitions of the set of attribute values and combine these attribute extractor using disjunctions. In our case, this can be easily accomplished by an application (i.e., a wrapper induction system) that uses our framework. The application can verify the failure of the MSYFM Guider, try new examples and create distinct PDS extractors, simulating the disjunction functionality. This is not an inherent part of the framework since we also support imperfect oracles [7] for providing examples.

In Figure 9 we present a diagram that illustrates the implemented framework. In summary, to generate a PDS for an attribute of interest, the framework takes an input page and one **Main Example** provided by the user. The **Tokenizer** then takes the **Input Page** and generates the **Tokenization** based on the **Delimiters Tree**. Next, the **PDS Tree Builder** takes the **Main Example**, the **Tokenization** and the **Delimiters Tree** and generates the **PDS Tree**. The **PDS Tree** is traversed by the **Oracle** relaying on the decisions taken by the guiders. We recall that, although not illustrated in Figure 9, the guiders have access to all structures manipulated by the framework during the process.

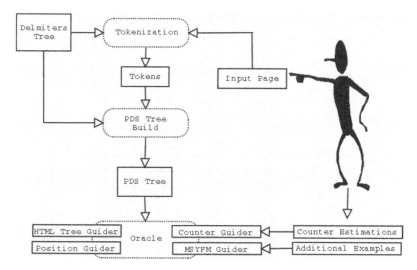

Fig. 9. Whole framework in action

7   Experimental Results

This section presents results from experiments we have carried out with the implemented framework described in Section 6. The experiments consist in generating sound and complete PDS extractors for extracting values of attributes of interest from typical data-rich Web pages. These Web pages were taken from several distinct Web sites, some of them previously used for experiments in other works in the literature [4, 11, 10].

Three guiders were used in the experiments: MSYFM, HTML Tree and Position. We do not use the Counter Guider, since we wanted to limit the role of users to simply providing examples. As for the remaining guiders, all extractions used the MSYFM Guider, and, for each site, we first tried the HTML Tree Guider and and the Position Guider separately and then tried both guiders together. For each attribute, we generate a single PDS. Notice that none of the guiders were specially tuned for a given page, and user feedback was not used.

The obtained results are shown in Table 1. In this table, column **Ex.** indicates the maximum number of examples used for each attribute. Column **Sound** shows whether the best final PDS extractor obtained among those generated is sound or not. The same applies to **Complete** column. Column **Tree** indicates whether the HTML Tree Guider individually was able to reach such result. The same applies to column **Pos** with respect to the Position Guider and to column **Both** with respect to the combined oracle of both guiders.

As Table 1 shows, in most of the 55 experiments our framework was able to generate PDS extractors that are sound and complete. In 4 cases (Attributes 6, 41, 45 and 46) the PDS extractors were neither sound nor complete. In 4 cases

Table 1. Results of the experiments

Source	#	Attribute	Ex.	Tree	Pos	Both	Sound	Complete
Bigbook	1	Address	1	x	x	x	x	x
	2	Business	2			x	x	x
	3	City	1	x		x	x	x
	4	Tel	1	x	x	x	x	x
ComputerESP	5	Price	1	x	x	x	x	x
	6	Product	2					
	7	Company	1	x			x	x
Altavista	8	Title	1	x	x	x	x	x
	9	Description	2	x	x	x	x	x
	10	URL	2	x	x	x	x	x
	11	Size	1	x	x	x	x	x
	12	Date	1	x		x	x	x
	13	Language	2	x	x	x		x
CineMachine	14	Movie Info	1		x	x	x	x
News.COM	15	Title	1	x			x	x
	16	Date	1	x		x	x	x
SiteSeeker	17	Site	1		x	x	x	x
	18	Description	1		x	x		x
Job Newsgroups	19	Headline	2	x			x	x
	20	Score	2		x	x	x	x
New Journal	21	Title	2	x				x
JOBS jobs Jobs	22	Job	2	x	x	x	x	x
	23	Date	1	x			x	x
Amazon - Cars	24	Car	2		x	x	x	x
	25	Price 1	1	x	x	x	x	x
	26	Price 2	1		x		x	x
	27	Company	1		x		x	x
Barnes E-books	28	Title	1		x	x	x	x
	29	Genre	1	x			x	x
	30	Price	1	x	x	x	x	x
	31	Author	1			x	x	x
	32	Description	1	x			x	x
Buy.com	33	Product	1		x	x	x	x
	34	Price	1		x		x	x
	35	Platform	1		x	x	x	x
	36	Midia	1		x	x	x	x
	37	Manufacturer	1	x	x	x	x	x
Travelocity	38	Zone	1	x				x
	39	Hotel	1		x		x	x
	40	Price	1	x			x	x
	41	Nights	1					
Restaurant	42	Restaurant	1	x			x	x
	43	Address	1	x			x	x
	44	Description	1	x	x		x	x
	45	Credit Card	1					
	46	Telephone	1					
Slashdot	47	Title	1	x	x	x	x	x
	48	Text	2		x		x	x
	49	Date	1	x	x	x	x	x
	50	Author	2	x	x	x	x	x
Freshmeat	51	Application	1		x		x	x
	52	About	1		x		x	x
	53	Changes	1		x	x	x	x
	54	Author	2	x	x	x	x	x
	55	Date	1		x		x	

(Attributes 13, 18, 21 and 38) they were just complete and in 1 case (Attribute 55) the obtained PDS extractor were just sound.

In most cases for which the generated PDS extractor were just complete, the values extracted incorrectly could be easily cleaned by using techniques like *Corroboration* [10] or ignored during the assembling of complex objects by using a technique like *Hot Cycles* [5]. The *date* attribute of *Freshmeat* was just sound, because there were some dates with a little different local context. A disjunction led us to the correct result.

The first attribute extraction that failed completely (Attribute 6), failed because the generated PDS tree had no sound or complete PDS extractor for it. When we properly extended the delimiters tree used, sound and complete PDS extractors were generated in the PDS tree and guiders were able to find it. For the case of Attribute 45, by using three distinct PDS extractors combined by disjunction, we successfully extracted the attribute values. For the two remaining cases (Attributes 41 and 46), the context was ambiguous and could not be described by a regular grammar such as the one used by PDS extractors.

8 Related Work

In the recent literature, a number of works on the generation of wrappers for Web data sources have been presented. A brief survey of these works can be found in [12].

Kushmerick et. al. [10] were the first to present formally the wrapper induction problem. Since then, several works [4, 11] tried to present specific wrapper induction systems for semistructured Web data extraction. Finally, [3] proposed an extensible architecture for creating wrapper induction systems.

SoftMealy [8], by Hsu et. al,. uses *finite-state transducers (FST)* for learning extractors. Their induction technique does not directly compare to our work, since we only deal with single attributes. Contextual rules, that constitute the edges connecting the FST states, are analogous to our PDS. SoftMealy relies on set-covering techniques to induce such rules. Our approach, based on guiders, is more flexible, still allowing to use the same techniques. SoftMealy is, however, more powerful in some cases. This is because contextual rules are reinforced by the current state information provided by the FST itself. To achieve the same level of expressiveness, we would need to extend the PDS extraction language to allow loops at a given slot, and null slots. With this change, our framework would provide a functionality closer to SoftMealy.

RoadRunner [4], by Crescenzi et. al., is a wrapper generation system targeted to HTML pages. It also has a fixed extraction language and fixed wrapper induction techniques. The main appeal of this tool is that it is able to automatically generate a Wrapper based only on a set of given sample pages. No user-provided examples are needed. On the contrary, our framework is based on examples. Indeed, relying on examples is considered safer in many situations [12]. However, we could use an automatic tool to provide the examples, such as [7]. Once more, our PDS extractor cannot cover all cases where is possible to generate a RoadRunner extractor. The same extensions to the language needed to reach SoftMealy expressiveness could be used to equalize both tools. The wrapper induction techniques used in RoadRunner could be reproduced by a guider taking as parameter additional sample pages. The HTML tree guider we have implemented introduces a few of the RoadRunner biases.

Stalker [14], by Muslea et. al., is a wrapper induction systems that uses *landscape automata*, a type of attribute extractor similar to PDS. It has a very powerful extraction language, and a fixed extractor inducing approach. Different from most works, Stalker heavily relies on disjunctions, that is, distinct extractors to deal with different partitions of the set of an attribute values in the target page. While it would be hard to change our framework to cover all extractors that can be created by Stalker, the same modifications proposed above could take PDS very near to Stalker's extraction language. Our framework do not support disjunction directly. In order to emulate Stalker bias, the application implementing the framework should introduce a guider that identifies the need of a disjunction, and then give the examples belonging to each partition separately to the framework, restarting the extractor inducing cycle.

To the best our knowledge, from the works in the literature, the Structured Wrapper Induction System [3] by Cohen et. al. is the one that most resembles our framework in terms of flexibility. Cohen relies on a single learning system and builders to define the bias of the system. Builders are analogous to our guiders, but they define extraction languages and are combined through specially hand-crafted functions, complying to a pre-defined interface. Our framework has a fixed extraction language, and guiders are combined either automatically, or through confidence levels definitions. This system can be tuned to work at very different targets, but requires a high effort and some expertise in the field in order to do so. We try to make guider construction a very simple task, and provides the possibility of applications automatically tuning their combination. While the Structured Wrapper Induction System is targeted at experts providing fast wrapper solutions, our framework is targeted at developers of wrapper induction systems for non-expert users.

From the above comparisons, we could see that the inherent extraction language of PDS is not the most powerful available. Its advantage is that it permits simple and efficient learning. More complex languages requires more complex learning systems. We chose to create good wrappers for a limited language. Further, the experimental results showed that a properly constructed PDS extractor is as good as any other extractor.

9   Conclusions and Future Work

We have presented an extensible framework for generating attribute extractors. The main appeal of this framework is that it can be adapted for dealing with specific types of data sources and to incorporate distinct types of heuristics for achieving good extraction performance. We have also demonstrated the feasibility of this proposal by implementing the framework along with a number of guiders that encapsulate simple heuristics to deal with Web pages. Experimental results we have presented demonstrate the effectiveness of the implemented framework with several typical Web data sources.

We recall that the main goal of our framework is to generate attribute extractors to be used by wrappers in the the extraction of atomic attribute values. The problem of grouping these values to compose complex objects is not addressed by our framework. It is the main subject of works such as [5] and [9].

In comparison to other wrapper generation systems, our framework can be considered one that requires *low effort for customization*. Empirical observation showed that: (1) the underlying PDS extraction language is expressive enough to address the majority of extractors needed; (2) guiders are able to introduce most of the biases or heuristics wrapper induction systems needs. Our framework takes these observations into account, and let as the only tasks for developers creating a delimiters tree that exploits the target document class structure and writing appropriate guiders to produce high quality extractors. The experimental results showed that a very simple implementation of the framework, with no special tuning, disjunction or user feedback was able to produce results comparable to those found in the related works, with very few examples.

The performance of the framework was not the main concern for the reference implementation, but still we achieved good results. The extractions sessions usually occur in small pages, and takes no more than a second in a standard desktop machine. Extraction from large repositories usually takes longer because of the cost of the tokenization process. For instance, extracting the City from the Bigbook Web source from a 3 MB page set took about 31 seconds. This can be considered as satisfactory, since the tokenization takes place just once for several attribute extractions. This result could be prohibitive for online systems, but they usually deal with small repositories. All processes in the framework have linear cost.

As future work, we intend to build a full-featured application that dynamically customizes the framework, and also let the user make manual customizations. Even an automatically delimiters tree generation seems possible, and we will try to accomplish this task. We intend to use these results in the next version of the DEByE Tool [11].

Finally, to verify the applicability of our framework for different document classes, we intend to build a delimiters tree and a set of guiders for extracting information from Postscript files. The main application would be to extract bibliographical information, abstracts and section titles from scientific articles available in this format.

References

[1] Serge Abiteboul, Peter Buneman, and Dan Suciu. *Data on the Web : From Relations to Semistructured Data and XML*. Morgan Kaufmann, San Francisco, 1999. 210

[2] Robert Baumgartner, Sergio Flesca, and Georg Gottlob. Visual web information extraction with lixto. In *Proceedings of the 27th International Conference on Very Large Data Bases (VLDB'01)*, pages 119–128, Rome, Italy, 2001. 211

[3] William W. Cohen and Lee S. Jensen. A structured wrapper induction system for extracting information from semi-structured documents. In *Proceedings of the IJCAI-2001 Workshop on Adaptive Text Extraction and Mining*, Seattle, Washington, 2001. 223, 224

[4] Valter Crescenzi, Giansalvatore Mecca, and Paolo Merialdo. RoadRunner: Towards automatic data extraction from large Web sites. In *Proceedings of the 26th International Conference on Very Large Data Bases*, pages 109–118, Rome, Italy, 2001. 220, 221, 223

[5] Altigran Soares da Silva. *Example-based Strategies for Extracting Semistructured Web Data*. PhD thesis, Deptartment of Computer Science, Federal University of Minas Gerais, 2002. 212, 222, 224

[6] David W. Embley, Douglas M. Campbell, Y. S. Jiang, Stephen W. Liddle, Yiu kai Ng, Dallan Quass, and Randy D. Smith. Conceptual-model-based data extraction

from multiple-record Web pages. *Data and Knowledge Engineering*, 31(3):227–251, 1999. 210, 211, 212, 214, 220

[7] Paulo B. Golgher, Altigran S. da Silva, Alberto H. F. Laender, and Berthier A. Ribeiro-Neto. Bootstrapping for Example-Based Data Extraction. In *Proceedings of the 2001 ACM CIKM International Conference on Information and Knowledge Management*, pages 371–378, Atlanta, GA, 2001. 212, 220, 223

[8] Chun-Nan Hsu and Chien-Chi Chang. Finite-state transducers for semi-structured text mining. In *Proceedings of IJCAI-99 Workshop on Text Mining: Foundations, Techniques and Applications*, pages 38–49, Stockholm, Sweden, 1999. 212, 214, 223

[9] Lee S. Jensen and William W. Cohen. Grouping extracted fields. In *Proceedings of the IJCAI-2001 Workshop on Adaptive Text Extraction and Mining*, Seattle, Washington, 2001. 224

[10] Nicholas Kushmerick, Daniel S. Weld, and Robert Doorenbos. Wrapper Induction for Information Extraction. In *Proceedings of the 15th International Joint Conference on Artificial Intelligence*, pages 729–737, Osaka, Japan, 1997. 211, 221, 222, 223

[11] Alberto H. F. Laender, Berthier Ribeiro-Neto, and Altigran S. da Silva. DEByE – Data Extraction by Example. *Data and Knowledge Engineering*, 40(2):121–154, 2002. 211, 212, 214, 220, 221, 223, 225

[12] Alberto Henrique Frade Laender, Berthier Ribeiro-Neto, Altigran Soares da Silva, and Juliana Santiago Teixeira. A Brief Survey of Web Data Extraction Tools. *SIGMOD Record*, 2002. To appear. 212, 223

[13] Ion Muslea, Steven Minton, and Craig Knoblock. An Hierarchical Approach to Wrapper Induction. In *Proceedings of the 3rd Annual Conference on Autonomous Agents*, pages 190–197, Seattle, WA, 1999. 212

[14] Ion Muslea, Steven Minton, and Craig Knoblock. Hierarchical wrapper induction for semistructured information sources. *Journal of Autonomous Agents and Multi-Agent Systems*, 4(1/2):93–114, 2001. 211, 212, 214, 223

[15] Berthier Ribeiro-Neto, Alberto Henrique Frade Laender, and Altigran Soares da Silva. Extracting semi-structured data through examples. In *Proceedings of the 1999 ACM CIKM International Conference on Information and Knowledge Management*, pages 94–101, Kansas City, MO, 1999. 212

Multiple Example Queries in Content-Based Image Retrieval

Seyed M. M. Tahaghoghi, James A. Thom, and Hugh E. Williams

School of Computer Science and Information Technology, RMIT University
GPO Box 2476V, Melbourne 3001, Australia
{stahagho,jat,hugh}@cs.rmit.edu.au

Abstract. Content-Based Image Retrieval (CBIR) is the practical class
of techniques used for information retrieval from large image collections.
Many CBIR systems allow users to specify their information need by providing an example image. This query-by-example paradigm can be extended to support multiple example images. In this work, we present
a large-scale experiment that shows the average performance of querying with multiple examples is significantly better than single-example
querying. We also investigate the effects of providing different numbers
of example images, the impact of example quality, and the relative performance of functions used to combine image features. Our experiments
indicate that three-example queries are more effective than other numbers of examples, and that the MINIMUM combining function is robust
for most query types.

1   Introduction

The ready availability of tools to create and publish digital images has led to
billions of images being produced. Unfortunately, the technology used to retrieve
these images has not kept up with that used to produce them. Most image
retrieval is still performed using well-known text information retrieval techniques
to match user-provided keywords against captions and other descriptive text.
This approach is not scalable, and depends on the annotator's impression and
choice of words. Moreover, machine recognition techniques are unsuitable for
general-purpose image collections, where the images are not limited to a specific
domain.

A practical solution for image retrieval from large, heterogeneous image collections is *content-based image retrieval* or CBIR. In CBIR, images are represented
by their features such as colour distribution, texture, and shape. These features
can then be used to estimate likely relevance of images to a query: by computing
the similarity of features provided by a user to those of images in a collection,
images can be ordered by decreasing similarity to the user's query, and a ranked
list of images returned to the user. An intuitive approach to querying is for the
user to provide a query image that represents their information need; this is
known as *Query-By-Example* (QBE).

A.H.F. Laender and A.L. Oliveira (Eds.): SPIRE 2002, LNCS 2476, pp. 227–241, 2002.
© Springer-Verlag Berlin Heidelberg 2002

A single-image QBE query may be insufficient to express an information need. For example, a user wishing to find images of a person standing in front of a building may pose a two-image query using two QBE examples: one of a building, and another of a person; suitably combined, the two examples can help find useful answers. While several CBIR systems use multiple examples—particularly in the context of iterative searches—it is not clear whether a multiple-example query is more effective than a single-example one.

In this paper, we investigate the performance of multiple-example queries in CBIR. Our focus is the relative accuracy of multiple-example and single-example queries. In multiple-example querying, the distance between each image in the collection and at least two query images must be calculated, and a combined result computed. We investigate the performance of three different *combining functions*, and examine the relationship between query images and the choice of combining function.

Overall, we have found that when using colour features, multiple-image queries are more accurate than single-image ones; using two examples can improve performance by around 3 percentage points on average. Using three examples is on average 10 percentage points better than using one example alone. However, performance does not improve linearly with added examples, and we show that the best performance is seen when using three examples. We also show that the distance between the query examples and their performance as single-example queries does not affect this result, although careful selection of the combining function can improve performance when using poor examples.

2   Background

Content-based image retrieval is becoming increasingly important as more images are stored online and must be retrieved in response to user queries. The attractiveness of CBIR is that it is automatic and scalable: as images are added to the collection, features are extracted without manual annotation or segmentation. Features that may be automatically extracted from images include colour and texture distributions, and shape representations [3, 19].

At query time, users express their requirements to the system, which estimates the likely relevance of images to the information need by calculating statistical similarity. This is determined by quantifying the distance between content features extracted from the images in a collection and those extracted from the query. The result is usually a list of all images in the collection, ordered by decreasing similarity to the query, in the same way as in conventional textual information retrieval [20, 31].

How users express their information need to the system is one of several popular CBIR research areas. Several methods of query specification have been proposed, including graphical description languages [14, 21], colour and texture selection tools [4], sketches [8], or the provision of example images [7]. The latter two methods form the class of *query-by-example* (QBE) techniques. Most CBIR systems support at least one form of QBE, where the query is posed by selecting, providing, or drawing an image that represents the information need. Systems that support QBE include CHITRA [18], MARS [17], MindReader [7], NETRA [9], QBIC [4, 5], Virage [6], and VisualSEEk [23].

2.1   Image Features and Distance Measures

In CBIR, the content of an image is represented through its *features* such as its colour, texture, and shape [3]. However, colour is the primary feature used in most CBIR systems. It provides a good estimate of the image content, and is robust because it is not significantly affected by occlusion or noise [3].

A colour space that is suitable for CBIR should separate the colour information (chrominance) from information about the lighting conditions (luminance); the better colour spaces also aim to be perceptually uniform, where incremental changes are uniformly perceptible across the range of values. We have found in preliminary experiments that the CIE[1] $L^*a^*b^*$ (LAB), CIE $L^*u^*v^*$ (LUV), and HSV colour spaces produce the best results [27]. Other colour features—such as red-green-blue (RGB), YC_bC_r, and the opponent colour space [1]—are more than 5 percentage points less accurate on average. We therefore experiment with only these selected colour features here.

The degree to which an image meets the user's information need is estimated by measuring the statistical similarity between the query and the candidate image. For this to be possible, a *similarity measure* or *distance measure* is required; while these terms are often used interchangeably in CBIR literature—and in this paper—this is not always strictly correct [16].

Statistical similarity can be measured by calculating the similarity between the feature data of the query, and that of the candidate image from the collection. One simple method frequently used in CBIR is to calculate the difference between the normalised frequency histograms of the feature for the two images [5, 15]. For example, if images are represented by the relative frequency of each possible colour, then the difference between the images can be calculated as the sum of the differences in the frequency of use of each colour. Using this method, two images that are predominantly red would have a small difference, while an image that is green and another that is red would have a large difference.

The similarity measurement is performed for every image in the collection, and a ranked list is presented to the user, with the image exhibiting the most similarity—the image having the least distance—ranked first.

Distance measures commonly used in CBIR include the Minkowski (of which the Manhattan or City-Block, and Euclidean are two cases), cumulative, quadratic, and histogram intersection [22, 25]. We have experimented with these distance measures on several image collections, and have found that overall, the Manhattan and cumulative Manhattan are consistently and significantly more accurate than the other measures. In most cases, the Manhattan measure outperformed the cumulative Manhattan.

---

[1] *Commission Internationale de l'Éclairage* - The International Commission on Illumination.

2.2 Multiple-Example Queries

Each example posed as a query is a representation of an information need. However, most images contain more than one object, and often express more than one concept. For example, a single photograph of a red rose may be used to specify the information need as red roses, red flowers, or roses of any colour. The difficulty, therefore, is determining which concept is specified using a single image query.

One possible partial solution to the problem of accurately specifying an information need is to permit the user to provide multiple images as examples. If two different examples are presented, commonality in the composition or structure of the images can be determined, and this information used to retrieve suitable images from the collection. However, multiple-example querying may also introduce ambiguity: the user may be specifying a low-level feature such as "red, similar to this tomato and this rose" or a high-level concept such as "flowers, similar to this violet and this daffodil". The ambiguity of the information need may therefore be compounded by multiple examples. However, as we show later, in general multiple-example querying improves retrieval effectiveness. Several CBIR projects support multiple-example queries; we describe these later.

Some prototypes also allow particular regions in an image to be selected, either automatically [2] or with user input [5, 11], and used for the query. This approach can be considered a form of multiple-example query. If the user is searching for images of a particular object, such as a car, the query item can be specified with greater precision than using the entire example picture, with its associated (and unwanted) background.

MindReader uses multiple user-provided examples to estimate the relative importance of the image attributes, based on the relationship between the examples [7]. In this scheme, each example is assigned a weighting to indicate its importance and the distance measure used in the calculations is then weighted accordingly. This is an iterative procedure, and good results are reported when using five examples. MARS allows the user to provide multiple examples, and uses relevance feedback methods to modify the query, adding positive examples and removing negative ones [17].

While iterative approaches are generally effective, most users expect relevant answers in the top ten or twenty retrieved images, and are likely to abandon the search if the first set of results is not promising [24]. We therefore restrict our attention to single-step queries, that is, where a query is evaluated once, and relevance feedback is not permitted. A further advantage of single-step, multiple-example querying over relevance feedback is that the former can be easily parallelised; the extra cost of processing multiple queries together will generally not be perceptible to the user, although the time required for the user to find and select the examples can not be ignored.

2.3 Combining Functions

Multiple example queries can be supported using one of two techniques:

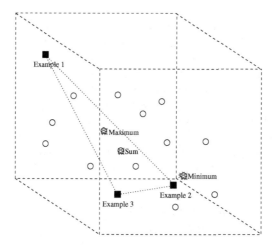

Fig. 1. With the three example images shown, different combining functions will evaluate the collection images differently; here, each combining function selects a different image as the "best" answer

- the examples are pre-processed and combined to form a single query—a weighted centroid—and this is then evaluated, or
- each query example is independently evaluated and the results combined.

Porkaew et al. refer to these techniques as the *Centroid Expansion Search* (CES), and *Multiple Expansion Search* (MES) [17] respectively; these are alternatively referred to as the Effective Nearest Neighbour (ENN) and the K-Nearest Neighbour (KNN) approaches [13]. It is generally agreed that the multiple expansion search is more effective [13, 17]; we use this method in our work.

With the multiple expansion search, the similarity of each collection image to the query is determined independently. The result is therefore an ordered list for each query image, and the lists must be combined to determine the final ranking of images. A *combining function* is therefore required to reduce multiple similarity values to a single value. When this reduction has been performed for all images in the collection, the user is presented with a list of the images, arranged in decreasing order of similarity.

In this work, we consider three simple combining functions: MINIMUM, MAXIMUM, and SUM. These determine the distance of a particular collection image from the specified multiple example images to be respectively the minimum, the maximum, and the sum of the distances to each example image.

Fig. 1 depicts a hypothetical three-dimensional feature space containing fifteen images, and three example images that form a query. When selecting the image that best matches the three examples, the SUM combining function chooses the image closest to the centroid of the examples. In contrast, MINIMUM chooses the image that is the closest to any example, in this case, to Example 2. MAX-

IMUM returns the image that is not too far from any one example, aiming to minimise overall dissimilarity.

The SUM and MINIMUM combining functions are likely to support accurate CBIR. We expect that the MAXIMUM function has less utility, since it gives (perhaps unwarranted) importance to outlying examples.

We have previously compared the performance of these combining functions for a collection using a more homogeneous set of query examples and relevance judgments [26]. We concluded that the SUM combining function produces better results than MINIMUM for multiple-example queries. Since the SUM combining function retrieves images near the centroid of the query points, this averaging behaviour will understandably produce good results for such collections. However, we expect that SUM is unlikely to perform so well for collections where the collection images and query examples are more varied.

In Sect. 4, we examine how these combining functions perform for multiple-example queries under various conditions.

3   Experiments

Unlike text retrieval, where researchers have access to the TREC text corpora [28], with a standard method of evaluating retrieval performance, no common test collection or ground truth assessment exists for CBIR. Although efforts are under way to address this problem [10, 12, 30], none have reached completion.

In our experiments, we used 2 500 images from volume twelve of the Corel® Photo CD collection. Each CD contains one hundred images of different scenes; the CDs have descriptive titles such as "Rural France", "English Country Gardens", and "Beautiful Bali". We selected 30% of the images at random and removed them to form a query set of 750 images, leaving 1 750 images as a test collection.

The Corel Photo CDs are designed for use with text-based image retrieval systems; the content of each image is described by keywords assigned by a human annotator. The metadata—which includes the file name, image caption, and keywords—for four images is shown below:

```
174008 - Flowering peach trees in Rhone Valley.
         (trees;orchard;fruit;blossoms;)

224015 - View from the Campanile, Florence.
         (buildings;city;clouds;sky;)

249085 - The Atomic Bomb Dome, Hiroshima.
         (building;tree;branches;sky;)

328010 - Handmade hats for sale, Port Antonio.
         (hats;market;merchandise;shop;)
```

In order to assess the effectiveness of multiple-example CBIR queries, we can use these keywords as a guide to the image content, and hence the relevance of the image to a query. We partition the images into categories using the keywords so that automated performance assessment is possible; as an image may have multiple keywords, it may be a member of several—possibly intersecting—concept sets.

We assume that information needs correspond to single keyword concepts, such as "building", and that any image with this keyword in the query set can be used as a query for this information need. Furthermore, any image in the test collection having this keyword is assumed to be relevant. As an example, for a query with the associated keyword "building", we assume that only images belonging to the "building" category in the test collection are relevant. By making this assumption, we can measure the approximate retrieval performance of our techniques using the retrieval measures we describe later in this section.

We manually stemmed the keywords by removing suffixes. For example, the "buildings" and "building" sets were merged. Inspection of the individual sets also led to the "women" set being merged with the "woman" set, although sets such as "path" and "pathway" were preserved as separate categories. We then constructed a set of actual queries and corresponding relevant answers. As we were to experiment with up to five examples per query, categories having less than five query images were removed; next, the categories were standardised to five randomly chosen query images each.

We used only those keywords that had associated images in both the query and the test sets, that is, for each query there is at least one relevant answer in the test collection. After following these steps, we had 97 query categories, each category containing 5 query images[2]. Other researchers have used similar approaches to evaluate retrieval performance, though with varying levels of keyword filtering [30]. Sample one- and two-example queries for the information need represented by the keyword "rooftop" are shown in Fig. 2.

We measure the accuracy of multiple- and single-example querying using the well-known measures of precision and recall [31]. Precision represents the fraction of retrieved answers that are relevant, while recall measures the fraction of all relevant answers that have been retrieved. To quantify recall, we therefore require that each image in the database be classified as either "relevant" or "not relevant" to each query. As discussed above, we approximate relevance by assuming that only images that are members of the same category set as the query are relevant to that query. In the example shown in Fig. 2, the relevant images as determined by the keyword category are marked with a tick.

Interpolated precision is often used to discuss average effectiveness. The interpolated precision at a given recall level—for example, after 20% of answers have been seen—is the maximum actual precision that occurs at any recall level equal to or greater than that level. Thus, the interpolated precision at 0% recall is the highest precision obtained at any recall value. Interpolated precision is commonly presented for the eleven 10% increments of recall, and we report interpolated precision values throughout this paper.

---

[2] The query and test sets and keyword queries we used for both collections can be found at http://www.cs.rmit.edu.au/~stahagho/Research/CBIR/SPIRE2002

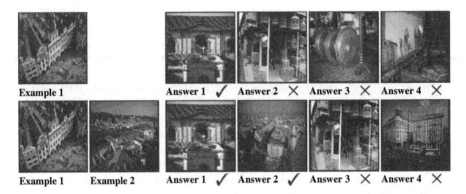

Fig. 2. Sample one- and two-example queries for "rooftop"; retrieved images associated with this keyword are marked with a tick ($\sqrt{}$), while the others are marked with a cross ($\times$). Here, adding a second example to the query doubles retrieval effectiveness over the top four ranked answers

4   Results

As discussed earlier, we use the HSV, LAB, and LUV colour features in our experiments. We represent each feature as a colour histogram, where the number of elements for each feature dimension in the feature vector is 512 for HSV, 16 384 for LAB, and 128 for LUV. We found in other experiments that these values afford the best performance in each scheme for single-example queries [27]. Similarity is measured as the Manhattan distance of the feature vectors, that is, the simple histogram distance is used to rank images in response to a query. All results presented are statistically significant at greater than a 90% confidence interval.

As described in the previous section, each query category has five images. To compare the performance of single- and multiple-example queries, we used the first image in each query set as a single-example query, and recorded the retrieval performance for this query. Next, the second query was paired with the first to form a two-example query and the performance recorded. We repeated this process for three-, four-, and five-example queries.

As Fig. 3 shows, multiple-example querying improves average retrieval performance. We present in this figure the average precision of the 97 one-example queries, the average precision of the 97 two-example queries, and so forth; the MINIMUM combining function and the HSV colour space are used, and we discuss the choice of these parameters later.

Our results show that adding a second example improves the average interpolated precision at 0% recall from 23.2% to 26.6%. However, we have found that a greater improvement occurs when three example images are used, with the precision at this point rising to 33.91%. This increase in performance does not continue for four- and five-example queries; indeed, the performance of four- and five-example queries is slightly worse than that of three-example queries. The

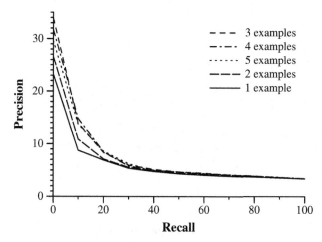

Fig. 3. Adding more examples to the query improves performance; beyond three examples, however, the improvement is more modest, and unlikely to be worth the effort in procuring the examples, and the additional processing involved. The HSV colour feature is used with the Manhattan distance measure and the MINIMUM combining function

eleven-point average interpolated precision rises correspondingly, from 6.53% for 1-example queries, to 8.31% for 3-example queries (using the HSV colour feature and the Manhattan combining function).

Adding additional examples has two opposite effects: on the one hand it may increase the likelihood of including a very good example that improves retrieval significantly; on the other hand, it may increase noise, causing poor retrieval. Our experiments indicate that the optimum number of examples from a retrieval effectiveness viewpoint is three.

There were 97 concepts in our experiments. For each concept, a particular query type was most effective. We show in Fig. 4 the number of cases where each query mode was the best for queries using the HSV colour feature, the Manhattan distance measure, and the MINIMUM combining function. For example, the left-most bar shows that in 19 out of 97 cases, single-example queries were best. In 27 out of the 97 queries, a three-example query was most effective. In addition, 70 of the 97 information needs were best met by multiple-example queries.

Three-example queries also offer an excellent trade-off between improved performance and user effort in procuring example images; we conclude that three-example queries should be used in preference to lesser or greater numbers of examples. We have therefore investigated three-example queries further.

Table 1 shows the average performance of three-example and single-example queries using three colour spaces and the three combining functions. Our results show that the HSV colour space is marginally less effective for single-example querying than LAB, but that it is the most effective feature at low recall levels

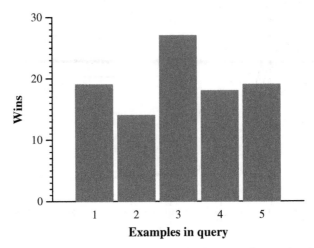

Fig. 4. For the great majority of queries, multiple-example queries, in particular three-example queries, produced the best result. The values shown are for the HSV colour feature, Manhattan distance measure, and the MINIMUM combining function

for three-example queries with the MINIMUM combining function. The MINIMUM combining function is best overall; we discuss this further later in this section.

We did not experiment with more than five examples. We argue that it is unreasonable to expect the user to have access to more than a five examples that express an information need. Indeed, the reason the user is querying is to find relevant images from the collection.

We found that on average, the MINIMUM combining function performs better overall than SUM; the opposite is true for selected cases and we discuss counter examples later. As expected, the MAXIMUM combining function performance is poor. The overall trend is shown in Fig. 5. High-precision results for the three combining functions are also shown in Table 1. Porkaew et al. [17] have found similarly that a balanced (non-weighted) search using the MES approach—the MINIMUM combining function—produces better results than CES; the SUM combining function is identical to using a non-weighted centroid as the effective query point.

The MINIMUM function works well when an image collection is heterogeneous because images are highly ranked if they are close to any of the three examples. In contrast, the SUM combining function highly ranks images that are near a centroid between the example images and, in a heterogeneous collection, this is less effective than MINIMUM, since the centroid is less representative of any individual example. Indeed, we have found in experiments on a small, homogeneous image collection that the SUM function is more effective than MINIMUM [26].

We have also examined the relationship between performance, combining functions, and the similarity of the images used in two-example queries. We

Table 1.   Average retrieval effectiveness of 97 one-image and three-image queries. Interpolated precision is shown for for 0%, 10%, and 20% recall, and the HSV, LAB, and LUV colour features. The last row shows the 11-point average interpolated precision for the three features. For three-image queries, results of the MINIMUM, MAXIMUM, and SUM combining functions are shown. The Manhattan distance function is used for distance calculation

Recall (%)	Feature	One image (% Precision)	Three images (% Precision)		
			MINIMUM	SUM	MAXIMUM
	HSV	23.23	33.91	24.48	18.21
0	LAB	24.69	29.34	23.31	14.21
	LUV	22.06	29.38	21.21	15.13
	HSV	8.76	13.95	9.87	9.03
10	LAB	8.90	12.86	10.70	7.80
	LUV	8.62	11.79	9.31	6.98
	HSV	6.91	8.35	7.20	6.33
20	LAB	6.24	7.97	7.60	6.37
	LUV	6.32	7.22	6.89	5.89
11-point	HSV	6.53	8.31	7.02	6.05
average	LAB	6.65	7.79	6.95	5.61
precision	LUV	6.41	7.60	6.62	5.56

ranked the examples in each query category by decreasing performance as single-example queries, and then paired the queries and measured the performance of each possible two-example pairing. For each of the 97 query categories, there are ten possible unique pairings of five images, giving 970 different two-example queries overall. We found that the MINIMUM combining function has the best performance overall, and that multiple-example querying is more effective than single-example querying.

However, when both examples have poor single-example performance, MAXIMUM performs better than SUM, and SUM performs better than MINIMUM. In addition, for such poor-performing individual examples, querying with multiple examples is less effective than querying with the best single-example query alone. This result is not surprising: using better examples in queries is always desirable. We have also carried out this analysis with three-example queries and observed similar trends.

To confirm the validity of our results, we repeated our experiments on another image collection derived from the University of Washington annotated groundtruth database [29]; at the time we accessed the collection, only 697 of the approximately 2 500 images had associated annotations, and were thus useful for our purpose. Since no explicit keywords exist for these images, query keywords were derived by parsing the annotations, stemming plurals, and stopping abstract words such as "on", "north", and "partly". A similar process to that

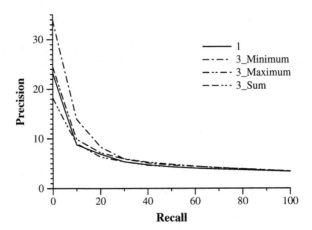

Fig. 5. Comparison of combining functions using the HSV colour space, three examples, and the Manhattan distance measure

described in Sect. 3 was carried out for this collection, resulting in a query set of 200 images, a test set of 497 images, and 37 concept queries.

We found that for this collection, too, using three examples with the MINIMUM combining function was better than using a single example alone. For the HSV colour space and the Manhattan distance measure, the precision at 0% recall improved from 47.6% to 52.8%; applying the Manhattan distance to cumulative histograms led to an increase from 61.9% to 78.1%. The corresponding rises in the 11-point average precision were 22.80% to 27.14%, and 35.73% to 44.43%.

5   Conclusion and Future Work

Many CBIR systems have adopted multiple-example querying to improve retrieval performance. This is often used in relevance feedback, where the user is able to refine the query by adding and removing example images. However, users expect good results at the first attempt. We have investigated whether using multiple examples leads to better results than using a single query example when only one iteration is allowed. We have shown that when using the HSV colour feature, multiple example querying with three examples images can improve precision by up to 10 percentage points over using a single example alone.

This trend is similarly observed with other colour and texture features. In other experiments, not reported here, we have found similar behaviour for texture and wavelet features.

We also investigated the relationship between multiple query examples and the effectiveness of the query. We found that a MINIMUM combining function is robust for most multiple-example queries, except where multiple poorly-performing examples are posed as a query. We conclude that in general, multiple-example querying improves the effectiveness of content-based image retrieval.

Multiple-example querying has synergies with relevance feedback. The former can be easily parallelised, with processing overhead that is imperceptible to the user; the latter has been shown to produce significant improvements in retrieval performance. We hope to investigate how the two approaches may be integrated.

We also aim to apply the multiple example approach to searching for images on the Web; current image search engines make use of the text surrounding an image to decide on relevance. We believe that multiple examples will improve performance in this context as well.

Acknowledgments

This work was supported by the Australian Research Council.

References

[1] D. H. Ballard and C. M. Brown. *Computer Vision*. Prentice Hall, 1982. 229

[2] C. Carson, S. Belongie, H. Greenspan, and J. Malik. Region-based image querying. In *Proceedings of the IEEE Workshop on Content-Based Access of Image and Video Libraries*, 1997. 230

[3] A. Del Bimbo. *Visual Information Retrieval*. Morgan Kaufmann Publishers Inc., 1999. 228, 229

[4] C. Faloutsos, R. Barber, M. Flickner, J. Hafner, W. Niblack, D. Petkovic, and W. Equitz. Efficient and effective querying by image content. *Journal of Intelligent Information Systems*, 3(3/4):231–262, 1994. 228, 229

[5] M. Flickner, H. Sawhney, W. Niblack, J. Ashley, Q. Huang, B. Dom, M. Gorkani, J. Hafner, D. Lee, D. Petkovic, and D. Steele. Query by image and video content: The QBIC system. *IEEE Computer Magazine*, 28(9):23–32, 1995. 229, 230

[6] A. Gupta. Visual information retrieval: A Virage perspective. Technical report, Virage Inc., 1996. 229

[7] Y. Ishikawa, R. Subramanya, and C. Faloutsos. Mindreader: Querying databases through multiple examples. In *Proceedings of 24rd International Conference on Very Large Data Bases (VLDB'98)*, pages 218–227, 1998. 228, 229, 230

[8] C. E. Jacobs, A. Finkelstein, and D. H. Salesin. Fast multiresolution image querying. *Computer Graphics*, 29(Annual Conference Series):277–286, 1995. 228

[9] W. Y. Ma and B. S. Manjunath. NETRA: A toolbox for navigating large image databases. In *Proceedings of the IEEE International Conference on Image Processing*, pages 568–571, 1997. 229

[10] M. Markkula, M. Tico, B. Sepponen, K. Nirkkonen, and E. Sormunen. A test collection for the evaluation of content-based image retrieval algorithms - a user and task-based approach. *Information Retrieval*, pages 275–294, 2001. 232

[11] B. Moghaddam, H. Biermann, and D. Margaritis. Defining image content with multiple regions of interest. In *Proceedings of the IEEE Workshop on Content-Based Access of Image and Video Libraries*, pages 89–93, 1999. 230

[12] H. Müller, W. Müller, D. M. Squire, S. Marchand-Maillet, and T. Pun. Automated benchmarking in content-based image retrieval. In *Proceedings of the 2001 IEEE International Conference on Multimedia and Expo (ICME2001)*, 2001. 232

[13] S. Nepal and M. V. Ramakrishna. Single feature query by multi examples in image databases. In *Proceedings of SPIE (SPIE Photonic East International Symposium on Voice, Data and Communications)*, volume 4210, pages 424–435, 2000. 231

[14] S. Nepal, M. V. Ramakrishna, and J. A. Thom. A fuzzy object query language (FOQL) for image databases. In *Proceedings of the Sixth International Conference on Database Systems for Advanced Applications, Hsinchu, Taiwan*, pages 117–124, 1999. 228

[15] V. E. Ogle and M. Stonebraker. Chabot: Retrieval from a relational database of images. *IEEE Computer Magazine*, 28(9):40–48, 1995. 229

[16] W. Pearson and W. Miller. Dynamic programming algorithms for biological sequence comparison. *Methods in Enzymology*, 210:575–601, 1992. 229

[17] K. Porkaew, S. Mehrotra, M. Ortega, and K. Chakrabarti. Similarity search using multiple examples in MARS. In *International Conference on Visual Information Systems, VISUAL'99*, pages 68–75, 1999. 229, 230, 231, 236

[18] M. V. Ramakrishna, S. Nepal, S. Sumanasekara, and S. M. M. Tahaghoghi. Design of a CBIR system supporting high level concepts. In *Proceedings of the Information Resources Management Association International Conference*, pages 1164–1167, 2001. 229

[19] Y. Rui, T. S. Huang, and S.-F. Chang. Image retrieval: Past present and future. *Journal of Visual Communication and Image Representation*, 10:1–23, 1999. 228

[20] G. Salton. *Automatic Text Processing: the transformation, analysis, and retrieval of information by computer.* Addison Wesley, 1989. 228

[21] U. Shaft and R. Ramakrishnan. Data modeling and querying in the PIQ image DBMS. *Bulletin of the IEEE Computer Society Technical Committee on Data Engineering*, pages 28–36, 1996. 228

[22] J. R. Smith and S.-F. Chang. Tools and techniques for color image retrieval. In *Proceedings of the SPIE; Storage and Retrieval for Image and Video Databases*, volume 2670, pages 426–437, 1996. 229

[23] J. R. Smith and S.-F. Chang. VisualSEEk: A fully automated content-based image query system. In *Proceedings of ACM International Conference on Multimedia*, pages 87–98, 1996. 229

[24] A. Spink, D. Wolfram, B. J. Jansen, and T. Saracevic. Searching the Web: The public and their queries. *Journal of the American Society for Information Science*, 52(3):226–234, 2001. 230

[25] M. Stricker and M. Orengo. Similarity of color images. In *Proceedings of the SPIE; Storage and Retrieval for Image and Video Databases*, volume 2420, pages 381–392, 1995. 229

[26] S. M. M. Tahaghoghi, J. A. Thom, and H. E. Williams. Are two pictures better than one? In *Proceedings of the 12th Australasian Database Conference (ADC2001)*, volume 23:3, pages 138–144, 2001. 232, 236

[27] S. M. M. Tahaghoghi, J. A. Thom, and H. E. Williams. Colour features in content-based image retrieval. Technical Report TR-01-5, RMIT University, School of Computer Science and Information Technology, 2001. 229, 234

[28] Text REtrieval Conference (TREC). URL: http://trec.nist.gov. 232

[29] Annotated groundtruth database, Department of Computer Science and Engineering, University of Washington, 1999. URL: http://www.cs.washington.edu/research/imagedatabase/groundtruth/. 237

[30] L. Wenyin, Z. Su, S. Li, Y. Sun, and H. Zhang. A performance evaluation protocol for content-based image retrieval algorithms/systems. In *Proceedings of the CVPR Workshop on Empirical Evaluation in Computer Vision*, 2001. 232, 233

[31] I. H. Witten, A. Moffat, and T. C. Bell. *Managing Gigabytes: Compressing and Indexing Documents and Images*. Morgan Kaufmann Publishers Inc., second edition, 1999. 228, 233

Focussed Structured Document Retrieval

Gabrialla Kazai, Mounia Lalmas, and Thomas Roelleke

Department of Computer Science, Queen Mary University of London
London E1 4NS, England
{gabs,mounia,thor}@dcs.qmul.ac.uk
http://qmir.dcs.qmul.ac.uk

Abstract. Focussed structured document retrieval aims at retrieving best entry points from where users can browse to access relevant document components in the document structure. In this paper, we report on the development, implementation and evaluation of best entry point retrieval strategies derived from user studies designed to elicit what constitutes a best entry point.

1   Introduction

With the rapid adoption of the XML markup language on the Web and in digital libraries there is more scope and need to exploit the structural knowledge of documents for the purpose of their retrieval. Numerous studies (e.g. [3,5,7]) have highlighted that indexing structured documents based on combined structure and content knowledge can improve retrieval effectiveness. In addition, this combination makes it possible to retrieve relevant document components of varying granularity, for example, a document component when only that component is relevant, a group of components, when all the components in the group are relevant, or the document itself, when the entire document is relevant. The retrieval result of structured document retrieval is then a ranked list of pointers to relevant document components, which may be "related" to each other, e.g. a component and its sub-components. According to the ranking algorithm these related components may be displayed at distant locations in the result. This can waste user time and lead to user disorientation [1]. By exploiting structural knowledge these relationships can be made explicit to the user.

In this paper, we develop an approach that allows to *focus retrieval* to the so-called *best entry points* (BEPs), which correspond to document components from which users can browse to access relevant document components. Returning BEPs, and not merely relevant document components, is a means to capture relationships between retrieved document components. The approach defines the representation of a document component as the *aggregated* representation of its own content and the content of its structurally related components. Using the aggregated representation of document components, BEPs are selected based on criteria elicited from user studies.

The rest of this paper is organised as follows. In Section 2, we describe our approach for obtaining aggregated representations of document components and select-

A.H.F. Laender and A.L. Oliveira (Eds.): SPIRE 2002, LNCS 2476, pp. 241–247, 2002.

ing BEPs. In Section 3, we describe a test collection of structured documents based on XML that was built to evaluate our approach. Section 4 describes a number of experiments that were carried out to evaluate the effectiveness of both the aggregation strategies and BEP selection algorithms. We conclude in Section 5.

2   The Approach

We are concerned with document structure that can be viewed as a tree whose nodes are components of the document and whose edges represent the relationships between the connected nodes. A document component can be either a leaf or a composite node. Leaf nodes are document components that correspond to the last elements of hierarchical relationship chains. All other nodes are composite nodes. Both leaf and composite nodes can contain raw data (text), referred to as the node's own content (in this paper we use the terms "node" and "component" interchangeably).

Best Entry Points. For the focussed retrieval of structured documents, we first determine what constitutes a BEP. Based on two user studies [2,4], we adopt the following two criteria: (C1) a super-node is retrieved instead of its sub-nodes if *many* of the sub-nodes have been estimated relevant to the query; otherwise the sub-nodes are retrieved individually. (C2) Only the *first* node in a linear sequence of closely related nodes that have been retrieved according to C1 is returned as a result. To implement C1, the estimation of relevance, i.e. the retrieval status value (RSV) of a super-node, is based on a content description that is derived from its own content and the content of its sub-nodes. For this purpose, we aggregate the content of a super-node with that of its sub-nodes taking into account their so-called *accessibility*, which reflects the extent to which a sub-node's content should contribute to the super-node's aggregated representation. [6]. The aggregation process is applied to the whole document structure, starting with the leaf nodes, where no aggregation is performed.

Aggregated Representations. Consider a super-node p composed of m sub-nodes $c_1,...,c_m$. Let $P(term(t,p))$ be the probability of the event $term(t,p)$ that term t describes the own content of p, $P(term(t,c_k))$ be the probability of the event $term(t,c_k)$ that term t describes the own content of the k-th sub-node, and $P(term^*(t,c_k))$ the probability of the event $term^*(t,c_k)$ that term t describes the aggregated representation of the k-th sub-node, for $k=1...m$. For a leaf node c_k, $P(term^*(t,c_k)) = P(term(t,c_k))$. Let $P(acc(p,c_k))$ be the probability of the event $acc(p,c_k)$ that the k-th sub-node is accessed from p. We define the aggregated representation of term t in p, $P(term^*(t,p))$, as a probabilistic disjunction of the events $term(t,p)$, $term^*(t,c_1) \wedge acc(p,c_1)$, ..., $term^*(t,c_m) \wedge acc(p,c_m)$. To reduce complexity, we assume independence over the events, and therefore calculate $P(term^*(t,p))$ as:

$$P\big(term^*(t,p)\big)=1-\big(1-P(term(t,p))\big)\prod_{k=1}^{m}\big(1-P\big(acc(p,c_k)\big)\big)P\big(term^*(t,c_k)\big)$$

Estimating the Probabilities. $P(term(t,p))$ and $P(term(t,c_k))$ can be estimated using standard term weighing schemes. The probability $P(acc(p,c_k))$, referred to as the *accessibility function*, is estimated in the following ways:

(a) $\dfrac{1}{m}$ (b) $\dfrac{1}{m^2}$ (c) $\dfrac{1}{m^{0.5}}$ (d) $\dfrac{1}{d_{ck}}$ (e) fixed values of 0.2, 0.4, 0.6 and 0.8

In (a), $P(acc(p,c_k))$ is viewed as the probability of a user, randomly browsing the structure of a document, arriving in node c_k from node p. (b) and (c) are based on the findings in [6] and allow to emphasise or de-emphasise the effect of the number of sub-nodes in the aggregation. (d) is motivated by the findings of the user study in [4], which suggests that users generally prefer to retrieve more specific, smaller contexts to general, larger contexts. The "depth" d_{ck} is measured as the distance between the sub-node c_k and the last element of the longest structural chain that c_k is an element of. Finally, (e) uses fixed values of 0.2, 0.4, 0.6, and 0.8.

Retrieval Strategies. During retrieval, a query is matched against the aggregated representation of the document components, where the probability of relevance of a document component a_node to the query q is calculated as follows.

$$P(a\_node \text{ is relevant to } q) = 1 - \prod_{t \in q}(1 - P(term^*(t, a\_node)))$$

We refer to this strategy as our baseline retrieval (BR). We also investigated several recall-enhancing retrieval strategies exploiting the structural nature of the XML data in order to increase retrieval performance and allowing us to observe the behavior of the BEP selection algorithms. These strategies are specific to the collection used to evaluate our approach, but can be adapted for other collections of structured documents. The strategies are:

- Cascaded Retrieval (CR): retrieves the sibling nodes of a relevant Speaker elements. This strategy aims to compensate for the Speech-Speaker semantic relationship being expressed as parent-child elements in the collection instead of Speaker being an attribute of Speech.
- Enforced Retrieval (ER): enforces the retrieval of all descendant elements of relevant Speech elements.
- Cascaded Enforced Retrieval (CER): applies first the CR strategy then the ER strategy.
- United (UNT): performs retrieval using the CR and ER strategies independently and then joins their result sets.

With CER sub-nodes of Speech elements containing relevant Speaker elements are elevated to higher ranks, whereas UNT will only increase the RSV of those sub-nodes of a Speech that contain both relevant Line and Speaker elements.

Focussed Retrieval Algorithms. The results of the above retrieval strategies are ordered lists of document components that may be structurally related. The ranking of the document components varies depending on the applied aggregation strategy. To return only the BEPs to the user, we remove *redundant* nodes from the result list using the two criteria C1 and C2. With respect to C1, redundant nodes are those components in the ranking, which are hierarchically related to BEPs with a *higher* RSV. Two nodes, *n1* and *n2*, are hierarchically related if *n1* lies on *n2*'s path and vice versa. This is implemented in an algorithm referred to as R1. With respect to C2, every node, but the first, in a linearly related chain is considered redundant. To implement this, the algorithm R2 selects the first element of a linearly connected chain of nodes, where two nodes are linearly connected if they are no further away from each other than a preset threshold value (derived from our user study [4]).

3   Structured Test Collection

To evaluate the effectiveness of our approach, we constructed a test collection, which consists of a set of structured documents, queries, "standard" relevance assessments (the document components that are relevant to a given query), and "best entry point" relevance assessments (the BEPs for each query). The test collection was based on the Shakespeare plays marked up in XML by Jon Bosak (http://www.ibiblio.org/bosak/). The queries, relevance assessments and BEPs were obtained from 11 English and Drama students who were experts in Shakespeare's works. The test collection consists of 37 plays, with an average of 30,600 words per play, a total 180,000 retrievable elements, 25 queries, with an average of 4 words per query, and an average of 124 relevant elements and 12 BEPs per query. The relevance assessments were obtained at leaf node level. The relevance of higher structural levels was then computed automatically as follows: a composite element was judged relevant if at least one of its child elements was marked relevant. The maximum depth of nested XML tags is 6 (Play, Act, Scene, Speech, Line, StageDir (stage direction)). These correspond to retrieval elements of varying complexity. The test collection is available at http://qmir.dcs.qmul.ac.uk/Focus/resources.htm.

Analysis of the collected BEPs [4] showed that users preferred to retrieve smaller, more specific contexts to larger, more general components. Another result of the study was that users preferred to see the context within which relevant elements occurred, but priority was given to having their attention directed at the relevant components. The algorithm R1 applied to the aggregated representations of document components reflects this finding. Regarding the linear relationship between relevant nodes, the first node of a linear chain was in most cases selected as BEP. The BEP selection algorithm R2 relates directly to this finding.

4   Experiments and Results

We designed our experiments with the aim to identify which combinations of aggregation and BEP algorithms produce the best retrieval performance. We indexed the document components' content using *idf* weighting (here, inverse node frequency) after stopword removal and stemming. We implemented our aggregation method using the eight different accessibility functions (denoted *acc*). We performed retrieval on the aggregated representations using the five retrieval strategies. We then implement the algorithms R1 and R2 to remove redundant nodes from the obtained ranked lists. We evaluated our retrieval results with respect to the retrieval effectiveness of relevant nodes and BEPs.

Retrieval of Relevant Document Components. Table 1 shows the precision values (in percentage) for retrieving relevant nodes using the eight *acc* functions, averaged over the 11 recall points and the 25 queries. The best performances for each strategy are highlighted in bold. The results show that all recall-enhancing strategies outperform the baseline retrieval method. The best retrieval performance is achieved by the CER strategy, which produces the highest precision values for seven of the eight *acc* functions, including the highest overall precision for $P(acc(p,c_k))=0.2$. One finding is the performance difference between the *acc* functions of $1/m$, $1/m^{0.5}$ and $1/m^2$ using the baseline strategy. Another conclusion is that although all eight of the *acc* functions produce similar precision values, those employing fixed *acc* functions tend to outperform those based on structure-dependant *acc* functions.

Table 1. Average precision of retrieval of relevant nodes

acc	BR	CR	ER	CER	UNT
$1/m$	9.64	20.90	26.96	28.91	29.75
$1/m^{0.5}$	13.36	21.51	25.63	31.53	28.95
$1/m^2$	9.81	21.55	25.81	29.12	28.77
$1/d_{ck}$	16.56	24.97	26.21	28.67	27.47
0.2	12.46	24.50	**29.55**	**31.67**	29.98
0.4	15.19	25.21	29.27	31.05	**29.99**
0.6	15.72	25.51	28.84	31.41	29.20
0.8	**17.08**	**26.31**	27.20	31.52	27.61

Retrieval of Best Entry Points. Table 2 lists the average precision values calculated against the BEP relevance set before removing redundant nodes from the result set. With the baseline retrieval the highest average precision is only 10%. The recall percentage of retrieved relevant BEPs were, however, comparable for all *acc* methods (75%), so the low precision values are due to BEPs being retrieved at lower ranks. This indicates that the applied *acc* functions do not push BEPs high enough in the result set.

Looking at the effect of the recall-enhancing strategies, the improved effectiveness achieved when retrieving relevant nodes is not reflected in the retrieval of BEPs (average improvement over the baseline is 19% for CR, 32% for ER, -4% for CER and 23% for UNT). It can be inferred that although these particular strategies proved to be effective for the retrieval of relevant components, they are less suitable for the retrieval of BEPs. Although they have an overall positive effect, they tend to retrieve too many non-BEP elements, particularly at higher ranks. This could be explained by the fact that as recall-enhancing strategies, CR and ER retrieve additional elements (with equal RSV), which "dilute" the result set, and lead to BEPs being retrieved at lower ranks. Furthermore, the CER strategy, which proved the most successful for the retrieval of relevant components, produces the worst performance values for the retrieval of BEPs. The best overall performance is achieved by the *acc* functions using $P(acc(p,c_k))=1/d_{ck}$, $P(acc(p,c_k))=0.4$ and $P(acc(p,c_k))=1/m^{0.5}$.

Table 2. Average precision of retrieving BEPs

acc	BR	CR	ER	CER	UNT
$1/m$	5.17	5.07	4.45	2.06	3.76
$1/m^{0.5}$	7.21	9.78	10.77	9.67	11.52
$1/m^2$	4.82	3.92	3.81	1.90	3.06
$1/d_{ck}$	**10.09**	11.46	11.88	8.97	**12.99**
0.2	6.90	11.78	11.44	7.77	11.16
0.4	9.05	**12.10**	13.28	**10.62**	11.50
0.6	8.48	9.48	10.49	9.70	10.82
0.8	7.19	7.63	**13.52**	9.00	10.16

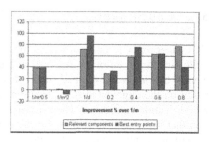

Fig. 1. Relative baseline performance of *acc* functions to $1/m$

Figure 1 shows the relative performance of the different *acc* functions in retrieving relevant document components and BEPs compared against $P(acc(p,c_k))=1/m$. It can be seen that the relative performance of most *acc* functions for retrieving BEPs is similar to the relative performance of retrieving relevant document components when compared against $P(acc(p,c_k))=1/m$. The main difference is the relative improved performance of $P(acc(p,c_k))=1/d_{ck}$. Also notable, is the relative performance drop of $P(acc(p,c_k))=0.8$, which produced the highest improvement of 77% for the retrieval of relevant components, but exhibits only 39% improvement in retrieving BEPs over $P(acc(p,c_k))=1/m$ using baseline retrieval. Meanwhile $P(acc(p,c_k))=1/d_{ck}$ shows 95% improvement when retrieving BEPs, compared with 72% when retrieving relevant components.

Effects of R1 and R2. The difference in retrieval effectiveness between the results obtained in the previous section, and the results after applying R1 alone and R1 followed by R2 are shown in Figures 2 and 3, respectively. Algorithm R1 leads to a performance decrease, which suggests that BEPs are being removed by R1. The function $P(acc(p,c_k))=0.8$ suffers the worst performance drop across all retrieval strategies and $P(acc(p,c_k))=0.6$ and $P(acc(p,c_k))=0.4$ are also greatly affected. The functions least affected, and even improved, by R1 are $P(acc(p,c_k))=1/m^2$ and $P(acc(p,c_k))=1/m^{0.5}$, which assign higher RSV to BEPs. $P(acc(p,c_k))=0.2$ and $P(acc(p,c_k))=1/d_{ck}$, also show tendencies of retrieving BEPs with higher RSV. The overall best performing *acc* function is $P(acc(p,c_k))=1/m^{0.5}$. With respect to R2, we can observe that there is an improvement of up to 35% for structure-dependant *acc* functions, whereas the performance of fixed-valued *acc* functions reduces by up to 74%. This indicates that R2 seems a promising BEP selection strategy.

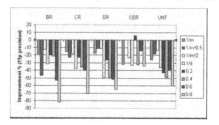

Fig. 2. Effect of R1 on average precision

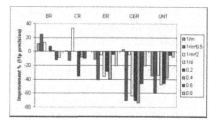

Fig. 3. Effect of R1+R2 on average precision

5   Conclusions

This paper reported on an approach for the focussed retrieval of structured documents. Following from various theoretical and empirical studies regarding structured document retrieval, we developed, implemented and evaluated document representations based on the aggregated representation of their components, retrieval strategies, and BEP selection algorithms. The evaluation was done using the Shakespeare test collection that was specifically built for the purpose. Our experiments showed that the aggregation of document component representations as well as retrieval strategies reflecting user conceptions of relevance in our test collection led to effective retrieval of relevant nodes. However, these same user conceptions led to poor performance with respect to the selection of BEPs. We also observed that recall-enhancing strategies, although successful in improving the effectiveness of retrieving relevant nodes, are harmful for retrieving BEPs. We believe that the nature of the data set used in our experiments, with its specific characteristics, also had strong implications. We are currently investigating the evaluation of our approach with other test collections of structured documents.

Acknowledgements

This work has been carried out in the framework of the EPSRC Project GR/N37612 and the British Council ARC Project 1162.

References

[1]   Y Chiaramella. Browsing and querying: two complementary approaches for multimedia information retrieval. *Hypermedia - Information Retrieval - Multimedia*, pp 9-26, 1997.

[2]   M Hertzum, M Lalmas and E Frokjer. How Are Searching and Reading Intertwined during Retrieval from Hierarchically Structured Documents?, *INTERACT 2001*, pp 537-544, 2001.

[3]   E Kotsakis. Structured Information Retrieval in XML documents. *17th ACM Symposium on Applied Computing*, pp 663-667, 2002.

[4]   M Lalmas, J Reid and M Hertzum. Information-seeking Behaviour in the Context of Structured Documents, 2002 (Submitted for Publication).

[5]   S Myaeng, DH Jang, MS Kim and ZC Zhoo. A flexible model for retrieval of SGML documents. *ACM-SIGIR Conference on Research and Development in Information Retrieval*, pp 138-145, 1998.

[6]   T Roelleke, M Lalmas, G Kazai, I Ruthven and S Quicker. The Accessibility Dimension for Structured Document Retrieval, *European Colloquium on Information Retrieval Research*, pp 284-302, 2002.

[7]   R Wilkinson. Effective Retrieval of Structured Documents. *ACM-SIGIR Conference on Research and Development in Information Retrieval*, pp 311-317, 1994.

Towards a More Comprehensive Comparison of Collaborative Filtering Algorithms

Cristina N. González-Caro[1], Maritza L. Calderón-Benavides[1],
José de J. Pérez-Alcázar[1], Juan C. García-Díaz[1], and Joaquin Delgado[2]

[1] Laboratorio de Computo Especializado, Universidad Autónoma de Bucaramanga
Calle 48 No 39 - 234, Bucaramanga, Colombia
{cgonzalc,mcalder1,jperez,jgarcia}@bumanga.unab.edu.co
[2] TripleHop Technologies
45 West 25th Street, 9th Floor, New York, NY 10010
joaquin@triplehop.com

Abstract. The basic objective of a Collaborative Filtering (CF) algorithm is to suggest items to a particular user based on his/her preferences and users with similar interests. Although, there is an apparently strong demand for CF techniques, and many algorithms have been recently proposed, very few articles comparing these techniques can be found. Our paper is oriented towards the study of a sample of algorithms to representing differents stages in the evolutive process of CF.

Experiments were conducted on two datasets with different characteristics, using two protocols and three evaluation metrics for the different algorithms. The results indicate that, in general, the Online-Learning (WMA, MWM) and the Support Vector Machines algorithms have a better performance that the other algorithms, on both datasets. Considering the amount of information, the less sparse such information is, the higher the coverage and accuracy of general models tend to be; however, the behavior under sparse data is closer to what is observed in a real system if we have in mind that users usually rate an amount of records much smaller than the total available.

Keywords: Collaborative Filtering; Online learning; Memory-based models; Dependency Networks; Aspect model; Support Vector Machines.

1 Introduction

The basic objective of a Collaborative Filtering [15] (CF) algorithm is to suggest items to a particular user based on his/her preferences and users with similar interests. The user can, then, become interested in items he did not previously know [8].

Although, there is an apparently strong demand for CF techniques, and many algorithms have been recently proposed, very few articles comparing these techniques can be found. Among such works, it is worth to mention those by Breese et al. [3], Herlocker et al. [11] and Fisher et al. [8]. Contrary to the mentioned

A.H.F. Laender and A.L. Oliveira (Eds.): SPIRE 2002, LNCS 2476, pp. 248–253, 2002.

works, we included new and important models such as On-line learning [7], Aspect Model [12] and Dependency Networks [10]. Our work is oriented towards the study of a sample of algorithms widely reported in the literature; these algorithms represent different approaches in the evolutive process of CF. In this way a current vision allowing a better dimensioning of such technology can be shown.

The paper is organized as follows: in Section 2 we describe the methods used in our comparison; in Section 3, we evaluate empirically the accuracy of these CF algorithms in order to establish a comparison of them; in Section 4, we reviews the results; and Section 5 gathers some concluding remarks.

2   Collaborative Filtering Algorithms

In this section we show the methods included in our study and describe briefly how they were implemented.

- **Memory-based Algorithms (MB)** [15]. The algorithms were in-house implemented in the Java language.
- **Dependency-Networks Algorithm (DN)** [10]. Decision trees for each node were generated using the algorithm J48 as part of the public-domain WEKA system [17].
- **Aspect Model Algorithm (AM)** [12]. A simulated annealing type Expectation Maximization (EM) algorithm variant called Tempered EM was used. For training the AM, the software PennAspect was used [16].
- **On-line Learning Algorithms.** Two algorithms were used: Weighted Majority (WMA) [13, 7] and Memory-based Weighted Majority (MWM) [7]. To conduct the experiments, the possible state of the database at the time when the prediction will be made, was simulated. Then, the chronological order in which the rates are received was considered for the learning process. The algorithms were in-house implemented in the Java language.
- **Support Vector Machines (SVM)** [1, 5, 4] The LIBSVM Java Version [6] was used for obtaining the SVM classifiers.

3   Experimental Procedure

Next, we describe, briefly, some characteristics of the experiments.

- **Data sets.** Currently, there exist few input data sets available for CF. This work was conducted on two of the most popular data sets which are available to researchers: Eachmovie [14] and Jester [9]. We classified the numerical values from the data sets into two classes: Like and Dislike following Billsus and Pazzani [1].
- **Methodology for evaluation.** One of the main aspects to have in mind when analyzing CF algorithms is their behavior under different quantities of votes for making a prediction. Hence, we chose evaluation methods which

emphasize the variation of information quantities available for making rating calculations.

As done in [3], two protocols were used for running tests: "All but one" and "Given X". We tested with "Given 20, 10 and 5".

Out of the 2000 users selected from each set, 30% of them were randomly selected as test data; the remaining 70% were training data.

The run of a protocol with each of the chosen data sets was denoted as an experiment. Thus, having in mind the number of data sets and protocols, the total number of tests was 8 experiments per algorithm. For each experiment, a training data set and a test data set were randomly selected. Different algorithms were run on the same data for each experiment. Results from these runs are discussed later in Section 4[1].

- **Metrics.** Researchers on recommendation systems have used different methods to measure quality of predictions. We used the most popular ones: the mean absolute error (MAE) which measures the average absolute deviation between predicted and real ratings for a given user [11]; ROC (Receiver Operating Characteristic) Sensitivity, whose purposes are to evaluate how effectively the predictions help a user to select high quality items from a group of items and to measure the power of decision making in a filtering system [11]; and coverage defines as the measure of the percentage of items for which a recommendation system can provide predictions [11].

Finally, we used as a reference for measuring the quality of a CF algorithm, the base case (BC). In our BC, the prediction of each vote of a user is calculated through the average number of votes given by her/him in the training set.

4   Results

The results (Table 1) indicate that, in general, the Online-Learning (WMA, MWM) and the SVM algorithms have a better performance than the other algorithms, on both datasets. Such algorithms behave well under the different quantities of available information. Specific characteristics of the used datasets must be considered in analyzing the results; for instance, EachMovie exhibits a higher sparseness than Jester. Hence, most of the algorithms present a better prediction behavior with Jester; an evidence is the results obtained with MB using the AllButOne protocol where the predictions were pretty good.

That SVM shows a good behavior in binary classification scenarios is a well known fact. This is confirmed in our study: the obtained results were very positive; the model found an appropriate scenario, becoming one of the best options, even if a small amount of information is available.

Comparing with the other algorithms, the prediction behavior of the WMA is, in practical terms homogeneous, offering acceptable results. If we consider the

---

[1] The conducted tests were run on Pentium IV - 1.6 GHz personal computers with 128 MB of RAM, working under the Windows 2000 operating system.

Table 1. Obtained results from the EachMovie and Jester datasets

	Given 5		Given 10		Given 20		All but one	
EACHMOVIE								
	MAE	ROC	MAE	ROC	MAE	ROC	MAE	ROC
BC	0.41	0.57	0.43	0.59	0.44	0.60	0.41	0.64
WMA	0,31	0.64	0,32	0.64	0,33	0.64	0,27	0.65
MWM	0,37	0.50	0,38	0.52	0,39	0.53	0,29	0.61
SVM	0.38	0.57	0.35	0.61	0.35	0.62	0.30	0.60
DN	0.38	0.52	0.39	0.55	0.43	0.54	0.33	0.58
AM	0.64	0.63	0.62	0.65	0.60	0.68	0.69	0.65
MB	0.43	0.62	0.41	0.67	0.41	0.67	0.36	0.74
JESTER								
	Given 5		Given 10		Given 20		All but one	
	MAE	ROC	MAE	ROC	MAE	ROC	MAE	ROC
BC	0.41	0.67	0.40	0.70	0.41	0.71	0.41	0.71
WMA	0,38	0.60	0,37	0.60	0,38	0.60	0,38	0.61
MWM	0,40	0.60	0,36	0.63	0,35	0.65	0,34	0.64
SVM	0.36	0.64	0.32	0.66	0.30	0.68	0.27	0.72
DN	0.49	0.52	0.45	0.55	0.42	0.57	0.38	0.57
AM	0.45	0.64	0.43	0.67	0.45	0.69	0.43	0.71
MB	0.44	0.64	0.41	0.70	0.40	0.74	0.04	1

different data quantities offered by each protocol and the different sparseness in each dataset, the sensitivity and error rates show very little variation.

MWM follows a pattern, which is very similar to WMA. Their results do not show a high variation from protocol to protocol; however, there exist some particular jumps such as the transition from Given 20 to AllButOne in Each-Movie, or the transition from Given 5 to Given 10 in Jester. This sensitivity to a higher amount of available information reflects their relationship with classical Memory-Based.

Online-Learning algorithms also show a better performance with EachMovie than Jester, but this behavior is a result of the characteristics of each dataset. EachMovie stores the date when the items where rated; thus it is possible to consider the chronological order in which the rates are received for the learning process. This feature allows a better performance of these algorithms [2].

As expected, the DN based algorithm improves its results as we move from the Given 20 to the All But One scenario. In the Given 20 there is a very low availability of data; the resulting decision tree has a low number of nodes and branches; in other words, the tree will contain very few referenced items. For an active user, many of the items rated by him will not be found in the tree; hence they will not be considered in the prediction. Such is the main reason for the high error. Meanwhile, in the All But One scenario, decision trees are more populated; most (or all) of the active user's ratings can be considered in the prediction. This is a rather disencouraging feature of dependency networks for doing recommendations in very disperse data bases.

Likewise other models, regarding the ROC sensitivity, the behavior of AM reflects better results under low sparseness conditions. Results obtained for MAE in AM are obvious since the obtained probability values are extremely low from a logical point of view (figures between 0.1×10^{-5} and $0.x10^{-282}$); to find a threshold to normalize such figures on a 0 -1 scale would lessen the reliability of results. Thus, we calculated the MAE deviations using values with a scale which is very different from the other models; using such measurement for comparison would be unrealistic.

A characteristic of the values obtained in the BC is their dependence on the standard deviation of the votes in the analyzed dataset; this deviation shows a correlation with the information domain. For instance, ratings of users for movies (in EachMovie) tend to be very diverse; hence, the vote average is not a good indicator of final predictions; however, this characteristic is not common in the information domain handled by Jester (jokes), where the standard deviation is lower.

Coverage for most of the models was 100% except in very few cases (such as the MB model when an item which is not rated by any user is found); that is, nearly all the models offered the expected amount of predictions according to the information from each protocol.

5   Conclusions

In this article, we compared six CF algorithms, which deal with the problem of recommending items to users from different perspectives. The obtained results show that Online-Learning and SVM algorithms make better predictions for data with both high and low sparseness.

We observed that although the new trends become good alternatives, the classical algorithms (MB) or those based on their philosophy (MWM) still keep offering good results in specific scenarios and direct solutions to the CF problem.

The fact that the dataset's conditions or characteristics influence heavily the obtained results is confirmed. Under low sparseness conditions, algorithms tend to offer better results.

Finally, the comparison of techniques with so diverse characteristics allows us to establish a framework where we can observe the growth of the set of alternatives for giving solution to the information overload through collaborative filtering. From that framework we can also notice that new methods showing good and efficient solutions to a variety of scenarios are proposed constantly.

References

[1] D. Billsus and M. Pazzani. Learning collaborative information filters. In *Proceedings of the Fifteenth International Conference on Machine Learning*, pages 43–52, 1998.   249

[2] Avrim Blum. Empirical support for winnow and weighted-majority algorithms: Results on a calendar scheduling domain. *Proc. 12th International Conference on Machine Learning*, (240):265–23, 1997.   251

[3] J. S. Breese, D. Heckerman, and C. Kadie. Empirical analysis of predictive algorithms for collaborative filtering. In *Proceedings of the 14th Conference on Uncertainty in Artificial Intelligence, Madison, WI*, pages 43–52. Morgan Kaufman Eds., 1998. 248, 250

[4] M. Brown, W. Grundy, D. Lin, N. Cristianini, C. Sugnet, M. Ares, and D. Haussler. Support vector machine classification of microarray gene expression data. Technical report UCSC-CRL99 -09, Department of Computer Science, University of California, Santa Cruz, 1999. 249

[5] C. Burgues. *A tutorial on Support Vector Machines for Pattern Recognition.* Kluwer Academic Publishers, Boston, 1998. 249

[6] C. Chang and C. Lin. Libsvm: a library for support vector machines (version 2.33). Technical report, Department of Computer Science and Information Engineering, National Taiwan University. 249

[7] J. Delgado and N. Ishii. Memory-based weighted-majority prediction for recommender systems. In *Proceedings of the ACM SIGIR-99, Recommender Systems Workshop, August 1999, UC Berkeley*, pages 1–5, 1999. 249

[8] D. Fisher, K. Hildrum, J. Hong, M. Newman, M. Thomas, and R. Vuduc. Swami (poster session): a framework for collaborative filtering algorithm development and evaluation. In *Proceedings of the 22nd Annual International ACM SIGIR, 2000, Athens, Greece*, pages 366 – 368. ACM, 2000. 248

[9] K. Goldberg, T. Roeder, D. Gupta, and C. Perkins. Eigentaste: A constant time collaborative filtering algorithm. Technical report m00/41., University of California, Berkeley, 2000. 249

[10] D. Heckerman, D. Chickering, C. Meek, R. Rounthwaite, and C. Kadie. Dependency networks for inference, collaborative filtering and data visualization. *Journal of Machine Learning Research*, 1:49–75, 2000. 249

[11] J. L. Herlocker, J. A. Konstan, A. Borchers, and J. Riedl. An algorithmic framework for performing collaborative filtering. In *Proceedings of the 22nd Annual International ACM SIGIR, August 15-19, 1999, Berkeley, CA, USA*, pages 230–237. ACM, 1999. 248, 250

[12] T. Hofmann and J. Puzicha. Latent class model from collaborative filtering. In *Proceedings of the Sixteenth International Joint Conference on Artificial Intelligence.* Morgan Kaufman Eds., 1999. 249

[13] N. Littelstone and M. K. Warmuth. The weighted-majority algorithm. *Information and Computation*, 108(2):212–261, 1994. 249

[14] P. McJonese. Eachmovie collaborative filtering data set. DEC Systems Research Center., 1997. 249

[15] P. Resnick, N. Iacovou, M. Suchak, P. Bergstorm, and J. Riedl. GroupLens: An Open Architecture for Collaborative Filtering of Netnews. In *Proceedings of ACM 1994 Conference on Computer Supported Cooperative Work*, pages 175–186, Chapel Hill, North Carolina, 1994. ACM. 248, 249

[16] A. Shein and L. Popescul, A.and Ungar. Pennaspect: A two-way aspect model implementation. Technical Report MS-CIS-01-25, The University of Pennsylvania., 2001. 249

[17] I. Witten and E. Frank. *Data Mining, Practical Machine Learning Tools and Techniques with Java Implementations.* Morgan Kaufmann Publishers, 2000. 249

Fully Dynamic Spatial Approximation Trees*

Gonzalo Navarro[1] and Nora Reyes[2]

[1] Center for Web Research, Dept. of Computer Science, University of Chile
Blanco Encalada 2120, Santiago, Chile
gnavarro@dcc.uchile.cl
[2] Depto. de Informática, Universidad Nacional de San Luis
Ejército de los Andes 950, San Luis, Argentina
nreyes@unsl.edu.ar

Abstract. The Spatial Approximation Tree (*sa-tree*) is a recently proposed data structure for searching in metric spaces. It has been shown that it compares favorably against alternative data structures in spaces of high dimension or queries with low selectivity. Its main drawbacks are: costly construction time, poor performance in low dimensional spaces or queries with high selectivity, and the fact of being a static data structure, that is, once built, one cannot add or delete elements. These facts rule it out for many interesting applications.

In this paper we overcome these weaknesses. We present a dynamic version of the *sa-tree* that handles insertions and deletions, showing experimentally that the price of adding dynamism is rather low. This is remarkable by itself since very few data structures for metric spaces are fully dynamic. In addition, we show how to obtain large improvements in construction and search time for low dimensional spaces or highly selective queries. The outcome is a much more practical data structure that can be useful in a wide range of applications.

1 Introduction

The concept of "approximate" searching has applications in a vast number of fields. Some examples are non-traditional databases (e.g. storing images, fingerprints or audio clips, where the concept of exact search is of no use and we search instead for similar objects); text searching (to find words and phrases in a text database allowing a small number of typographical or spelling errors); information retrieval (to look for documents that are similar to a given query or document); machine learning and classification (to classify a new element according to its closest representative); image quantization and compression (where only some vectors can be represented and we code the others as their closest representable point); computational biology (to find a DNA or protein sequence in a database allowing some errors due to mutations); and function prediction (to

---

* This work has been partially supported CYTED VII.19 RIBIDI Project (both authors) and Millenium Nucleus Center for Web Research, Grant P01-029-F, Mideplan, Chile (first author).

A.H.F. Laender and A.L. Oliveira (Eds.): SPIRE 2002, LNCS 2476, pp. 254–270, 2002.
© Springer-Verlag Berlin Heidelberg 2002

search for the most similar behavior of a function in the past so as to predict its probable future behavior).

All those applications have some common characteristics. There is a universe $\mathbb{U}$ of *objects*, and a nonnegative *distance function* $d : \mathbb{U} \times \mathbb{U} \longrightarrow \mathbb{R}^+$ defined among them. This distance may (and ideally does) satisfy the three axioms that make the set a *metric space*: strict positiveness ($d(x,y) = 0 \Leftrightarrow x = y$), symmetry ($d(x,y) = d(y,x)$) and triangle inequality ($d(x,z) \leq d(x,y) + d(y,z)$). The smaller the distance between two objects, the more "similar" they are. We have a finite *database* $S \subseteq \mathbb{U}$, which is a subset of the universe of objects and can be preprocessed (to build an index, for example). Later, given a new object from the universe (a *query q*), we must retrieve all similar elements found in the database. There are two typical queries of this kind:

Range query: Retrieve all elements within distance r to q in S. This is, $\{x \in S , d(x,q) \leq r\}$.

Nearest neighbor query (k-NN): Retrieve the k closest elements to q in S. That is, a set $A \subseteq S$ such that $|A| = k$ and $\forall x \in A, y \in S - A, d(x,q) \leq d(y,q)$.

The distance is considered expensive to compute (think, for instance, in comparing two fingerprints). Hence, it is customary to define the complexity of the search as the number of distance evaluations performed, disregarding other components such as CPU time for side computations, and even I/O time. Given a database of $|S| = n$ objects, queries can be trivially answered by performing n distance evaluations. The goal is to structure the database such that we perform less distance evaluations.

A particular case of this problem arises when the space is a set of D-dimensional points and the distance belongs to the Minkowski L_p family: $L_p = (\sum_{1 \leq i \leq D} |x_i - y_i|^p)^{1/p}$. For example $p = 2$ yields Euclidean distance. There are effective methods to search in D-dimensional spaces [4, 1]. However, for roughly 20 dimensions or more those structures cease to work well. We focus in this paper on general metric spaces, although the solutions are well suited also for D-dimensional spaces. It is interesting to notice that the concept of "dimensionality" can be translated to metric spaces as well: the typical feature in high dimensional spaces with L_p distances is that the probability distribution of distances among elements has a very concentrated histogram (with larger mean as the dimension grows), making the work of any similarity search algorithm more difficult [2, 3]. We say that a general metric space is high dimensional when its histogram of distances is concentrated.

For general metric spaces, there exist a number of methods to preprocess the database in order to reduce the number of distance evaluations [3]. All those structures work on the basis of discarding elements using the triangle inequality, and most use the classical divide-and-conquer approach (which is not specific of metric space searching).

The Spatial Approximation Tree (*sa-tree*) is a recently proposed data structure of this kind [5, 6], based on a novel concept: rather than dividing the search space, approach the query spatially, that is, start at some point in the space and get closer and closer to the query. Apart from being algorithmically interesting by itself, it has been shown that the *sa-tree* gives better space-time tradeoffs than the other existing structures on metric spaces of high dimension or queries with low selectivity, which is the case in many applications.

The *sa-tree*, however, has some important weaknesses. The first is that, compared to other indexes, it is relatively costly to build in low dimensions (it is harder to build in high dimensions, but in this case the competing indexes are even more costly). The second is that, in low dimensions or for queries with high selectivity (small r or k), its search performance is poor when compared to simple alternatives. The third is that it is a static data structure: once built, it is hard to add/delete elements to/from it. These weaknesses make the *sa-tree* unsuitable for important applications such as multimedia databases.

Overcoming these drawbacks is the aim of this paper. We present a dynamic version of the *sa-tree* that handles insertions and deletions. We show that the dynamic *sa-tree* can be built incrementally (i.e., by successive insertions) at the same cost of its static version, and that the search performance is unaffected. We also show that one can remove elements from the structure at about the same cost of an insertion, with a very small penalty in the search performance.

Full dynamism is not so common in metric data structures [3]. While permitting efficient insertions is quite usual, deletions are rarely handled. In several indexes one can delete some elements, but there are selected elements that cannot be deleted at all. This is particularly problematic in the metric space scenario, where objects could be very large (e.g., images) and deleting them physically may be mandatory. Our algorithms permit deleting any element from a *sa-tree*. This is remarkable on a data structure whose original conception was markedly static [5].

In addition to the above achievement, we find out how to obtain large improvements in construction and search time for low dimensional spaces or highly selective queries. The method consists of limiting the tree arity and involves new algorithmic insights on this data structure. The lower the arity, the cheaper to build the tree. However, at search time, the best arity depends on the dimension and the query selectivity. In particular, for low dimensions, we obtain improved construction and search time simultaneously.

The outcome is a much more practical data structure that can be useful in a wide range of applications. We expect the dynamic *sa-tree* to replace the static version in the developments to come.

This work builds over [7], where it was shown that insertions on the *sa-tree* could be reasonably handled. We improve their insertion algorithm and also permit deletions, thus obtaining a fully dynamic data structure. In addition, we capture in the tree arity the parameter that permits adapting it better to different dimensions. The original *sa-tree* adapts itself to the dimension, but not optimally.

For the experiments of this paper we have selected two metric spaces. The first is a dictionary of 69,069 English words. The distance is the edit distance, that is, the minimum number of character insertions, deletions and replacements to make the strings equal. The second space is the real unitary cube in dimension 15 using Euclidean distance, where we generated 100,000 random points with uniform distribution.

In both cases, we built the indexes with 90% of the points and used the other 10% (randomly chosen) as queries. For the experiments with deletions in an index of n elements, we select at random a fraction of those n elements and delete them from the index. The results on these two spaces are representative of those on several other metric spaces we tested: NASA images, dictionaries in other languages, Gaussian distributions, other dimensions, etc.

2   The Spatial Approximation Tree

We describe briefly in this section the static *sa-tree* data structure. It needs $O(n)$ space, $O(n \log^2 n / \log \log n)$ construction time, and sublinear search time: $O(n^{1-\Theta(1/\log \log n)})$ in high dimensions and $O(n^\alpha)$ $(0 < \alpha < 1)$ in low dimensions. It is experimentally shown to offer better space-time tradeoffs than other data structures when the dimension is high or the query radius is large. For more details see the original work [5, 6].

2.1   Construction

We select a random element $a \in S$ to be the root of the tree. We then select a suitable set of neighbors $N(a)$ satisfying

Condition 1: (given a, S) $\forall x \in S,\ x \in N(a) \Leftrightarrow \forall y \in N(a) - \{x\},\ d(x,y) > d(x,a)$.

That is, the neighbors of a form a set such that any neighbor is closer to a than to any other neighbor. The "only if" ($\Leftarrow$) part of the definition guarantees that if we can get closer to any $b \in S$ then an element in $N(a)$ is closer to b than a, because we put as direct neighbors all those elements that are not closer to another neighbor. The "if" part ($\Rightarrow$) aims at putting as few neighbors as possible.

Notice that the set $N(a)$ is defined in terms of itself in a non-trivial way and that multiple solutions fit the definition. For example, if a is far from b and c and these are close to each other, then both $N(a) = \{b\}$ and $N(a) = \{c\}$ satisfy the definition.

Finding the smallest possible set $N(a)$ seems to be a nontrivial combinatorial optimization problem, since by including an element we need to take out others (this happens between b and c in the example of the previous paragraph). However, simple heuristics which add more neighbors than necessary work well. We begin with the initial node a and its "bag" holding all the rest of S. We first sort the bag by distance to a. Then, we start adding nodes to $N(a)$ (which is initially empty). Each time we consider a new node b, we check whether it is

---

BuildTree (Node a, Set of nodes S)
1. $N(a) \leftarrow \emptyset$ // neighbors of a
2. $R(a) \leftarrow 0$ // covering radius
4. For $v \in S$ in increasing distance to a Do
5. $R(a) \leftarrow \max(R(a), d(v,a))$
6.   If $\forall b \in N(a), \ d(v,a) < d(v,b)$ Then $N(a) \leftarrow N(a) \cup \{v\}$
7. For $b \in N(a)$ Do $S(b) \leftarrow \emptyset$
8. For $v \in S - N(a)$ Do
9. $c \leftarrow \text{argmin}_{b \in N(a)} d(v,b)$
10. $S(c) \leftarrow S(c) \cup \{v\}$
11. For $b \in N(a)$ Do BuildTree (b, $S(b)$)

Fig. 1. Algorithm to build the *sa-tree*

closer to some element of $N(a)$ than to a itself. If that is not the case, we add b to $N(a)$.

At this point we have a suitable set of neighbors. Note that Condition 1 is satisfied thanks to the fact that we have considered the elements in order of increasing distance to a. The "only if" part of Condition 1 is clearly satisfied because any element not satisfying it is inserted in $N(a)$. The "if" part is more delicate. Let $x \neq y \in N(a)$. If y is closer to a than x then y was considered first. Our construction algorithm guarantees that if we inserted x in $N(a)$ then $d(x,a) < d(x,y)$. If, on the other hand, x is closer to a than y, then $d(y,x) > d(y,a) \geq d(x,a)$ (that is, a neighbor cannot be removed by a new neighbor inserted later).

We now must decide in which neighbor's bag we put the rest of the nodes. We put each node not in $\{a\} \cup N(a)$ in the bag of its closest element of $N(a)$ (*best-fit* strategy). Observe that this requires a second pass once $N(a)$ is fully determined.

We are done now with a, and process recursively all its neighbors, each one with the elements of its bag. Note that the resulting structure is a tree that can be searched for any $q \in S$ by spatial approximation for nearest neighbor queries. The reason why this works is that, at search time, we repeat exactly what happened with q during the construction process (i.e. we enter into the subtree of the neighbor closest to q), until we reach q. This is is because q is present in the tree, i.e., we are doing an exact search after all.

Finally, we save some comparisons at search time by storing at each node a its covering radius, i.e., the maximum distance $R(a)$ between a and any element in the subtree rooted by a. The way to use this information is made clear in Section 2.2.

Figure 1 depicts the construction process. It is first invoked as BuildTree($a, S - \{a\}$) where a is a random element of S. Note that, except for the first level of the recursion, we already know all the distances $d(v,a)$ for every $v \in S$ and hence do not need to recompute them. Similarly, some of the

$d(v, c)$ distances at line 9 is already known from line 6. The information stored by the data structure is the root a and the $N()$ and $R()$ values of all the nodes.

2.2   Searching

Of course it is of little interest to search only for elements $q \in S$. The tree we have described can, however, be used as a device to solve queries of any type for any $q \in \mathbb{U}$. We consider first range queries with radius r.

The key observation is that, even if $q \notin S$, the answers to the query are elements $q' \in S$. So we use the tree to pretend that we are searching for an element $q' \in S$. We do not know q', but since $d(q, q') \leq r$, we can obtain from q some distance information regarding q': by the triangle inequality it holds that for any $x \in \mathbb{U}$, $d(x, q) - r \leq d(x, q') \leq d(x, q) + r$.

Hence, instead of simply going to the closest neighbor, we first determine the closest neighbor c of q among $\{a\} \cup N(a)$. We then enter into *all* neighbors $b \in N(a)$ such that $d(q, b) \leq d(q, c) + 2r$. This is because the virtual element q' sought can differ from q by at most r at any distance evaluation, so it could have been inserted inside any of those b nodes. In the process, we report all the nodes q' we found close enough to q. (A more sophisticated search scheme is given in [6], but it cannot be applied to our dynamic version, so we prefer to omit it.)

Finally, the covering radius $R(a)$ is used to further prune the search, by not entering into subtrees such that $d(q, a) > R(a) + r$, since they cannot contain useful elements.

Figure 2 illustrates the search process on the left, starting from the tree root p_{11}. Only p_9 is in the result, but all the bold edges are traversed. On the right, we give the search algorithm, initially invoked as RangeSearch(a,q,r), where a is the tree root. Note that in the recursive invocations $d(a, q)$ is already computed.

We can also perform nearest neighbor searching by simulating a range search where the search radius is reduced as we proceed. We have a priority queue of subtrees sorted by the known lower bound distance between the subtree and q.

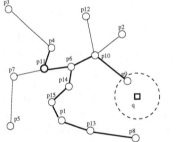

RangeSearch (Node a, Query q,
Radius r)
1. If $d(a, q) \leq R(a) + r$ Then
2.   If $d(a, q) \leq r$ Then Report a
3. $d_{min} \leftarrow \min \{d(c, q), \ c \in \{a\} \cup N(a)\}$
4.   For $b \in N(a)$ Do
5.   If $d(b, q) \leq d_{min} + 2r$ Then
6.   RangeSearch (b,q,r)

Fig. 2. On the left, an example of the search process. On the right, the algorithm to search for q with radius r in a *sa-tree*

Initially, we insert the *sa-tree* root in the data structure. Iteratively, we extract the (as far as it is known) closest subtree, process its root, and insert all its subtrees in the queue. This is repeated until the queue gets empty or the lower bound distance is larger than r. For lack of space we omit further details.

3   Incremental Construction

The construction of the *sa-tree* needs to know all the elements of S in advance. In particular, it is difficult to add new elements once the tree is already built. To insert a new element x, we should go down the tree by the closest neighbor until x must become a neighbor of the current node a, that is, until x is closer to a than to any $b \in N(a)$ (Condition 1). All the subtree rooted at a must be rebuilt from scratch, since some nodes that went into another neighbor could prefer now to get into the new neighbor x.

Several insertion alternatives have been previously considered [7, 6]. The best me-thods turned out to be the so-called "timestamping" and "insertion at the fringe". We propose here a novel technique based on ideas from these two methods.

Timestamping permits inserting an element with a technique very similar to that of the static construction, by recording the time every element was inserted. Remarkably, this technique obtained a performance very similar to that of the static version, by avoiding any reconstruction. Insertion at the fringe, on the other hand, limits the maximum tree size where a new element can be inserted, with the aim of reconstructing only small subtrees. The technique permits us avoiding insertion at the point where Condition 1 would require it, delaying it to a point downwards the tree. Surprisingly, this technique even *improved* the performance in low dimensions, so there was a factor largely compensating the cost of the reconstructions. Where this factor came from was not clear at that time [7].

We have pursued this line and determined that the key fact is that these trees have a reduced arity. Moreover, the main reason of the poor performance of the *sa-tree* in low dimensional spaces is its excessively high arity (the tree automatically adapts its arity to the dimension, but not optimally). Hence we decided to focus directly on the maximum permitted arity and made it a tuning parameter. The same delaying technique used to limit the tree size to rebuild is now used to limit the tree arity. Moreover, by merging this technique with timestamping, we have no reconstruction cost to compensate, so we get the best of both worlds.

Observe that one of the nice features of the original *sa-tree* was that it had no parameter to set, so any non-expert could just use it. Our new parameter does not harm in this sense, because it can be set to ∞ to obtain the same performance of the original *sa-tree*. On the other hand, very large improvements can be obtained in low dimensions by appropriately setting the maximum tree arity. We get into the details now.

3.1   Insertion

To construct the *sa-tree* incrementally we fix a maximum tree arity, and also keep a timestamp of the insertion time of each element. When inserting a new element x, we add it as a neighbor at the appropriate point a (Condition 1) only if the arity of node a is not already maximal. Otherwise, even when x is closer to a than to any $b \in N(a)$, we force x to choose the closest neighbor in $N(a)$ and keep walking down the tree, until we reach a node a where Condition 1 is satisfied (x is closer to a than to any $b \in N(a)$) and the arity of node a is not maximal (this eventually occurs at a tree leaf). At this point we add x at the end of the list $N(a)$, put the current timestamp to x and increment the current timestamp.

Note that by reading neighbors from left to right we have increasing timestamps. It also holds that the parent is always older than its children. Note also that now it is not sure anymore that a new inserted element x is a neighbor of the first node a that satisfies Condition 1 in its path. It may be that the arity of a was maximal and x was forced to choose a neighbor of a. This has implications in the search process that will be considered soon.

Figure 3 illustrates the insertion process. We follow only one path from the tree root to the parent of the inserted element. The function is invoked as Insert(a,x), where a is the tree root and x is the element to be inserted. The *sa-tree* can now be built by starting with a first single node a where $N(a) = \emptyset$ and $R(a) = 0$, and then performing successive insertions.

Figure 4 compares the cost of incremental construction using our technique against static construction for increasing subsets of the database. We show arities 4, 8, 16 and 32. In both cases, the construction performance improves as we reduce the tree arity, being by far better than the static construction (twice as fast on strings and four times faster on vectors). Note that if we permit a sufficiently large arity (e.g., 32 on strings) the incremental version becomes somewhat worse than the static version (whose arity is unlimited). This shows that the reduced arity is a key factor in lowering construction costs. This is clear, as the insertion cost with arity A is $A \log_A n$. On unlimited arity the average arity

---

```
Insert (Node a, Element x)
1.    R(a) ← max(R(a), d(a, x))
2.    c ← argmin_{b∈N(a)} d(b, x)
3.    If d(a, x) < d(c, x) ∧ |N(a)| < MaxArity Then
4.        N(a) ← N(a) ∪ {x}
5.        N(x) ← ∅,  R(x) ← 0
6.        time(x) ← CurrentTime
7.    Else Insert (c, x)
```

Fig. 3. Insertion of a new element x into a dynamic *sa-tree* with root a. *MaxArity* is the maximum tree arity and *CurrentTime* is the current time, incremented in each insertion

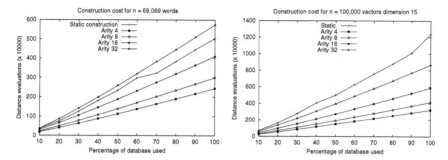

Fig. 4. Static versus dynamic construction costs

is $A = O(\log n)$, so the construction cost per element is $O(\log^2 n / \log \log n)$ [6]. We consider next how a reduced arity affects search time.

3.2   Searching

At search time we have to consider two facts. The first is that, at the time an element x was inserted, a node a in its path may not have been chosen as its parent because its arity was already maximal. So instead of choosing the closest to x among $\{a\} \cup N(a)$, we may have chosen only among $N(a)$. This means that we have to remove $\{a\}$ from the minimization of line 3 in Figure 2. The second fact to consider is that, at the time x was inserted, elements with higher timestamp were not present in the tree, so x could choose its best neighbor only among elements older than itself.

Hence, we consider the neighbors $\{b_1, \ldots, b_k\}$ of a from oldest to newest, disregarding a, and perform the minimization as we traverse the list. This means that we enter into the subtree of b_i if $d(q, b_i) \leq \min(d(q, b_1), \ldots, d(q, b_{i-1})) + 2r$. That is, we always enter into b_1; we enter into b_2 if $d(q, b_2) \leq d(q, b_1) + 2r$; and so on. Let us stress again the reason: between the insertion of b_i and b_{i+j} there may have appeared new elements that chose b_i just because b_{i+j} was not yet present, so we may miss an element if we do not enter into b_i because of the existence of b_{i+j}.

Up to now we do not really need the exact timestamps but just to keep the neighbors sorted by timestamp. We can make better use of the timestamp information in order to reduce the work done inside older neighbors. Say that $d(q, b_i) > d(q, b_{i+j}) + 2r$. We have to enter into the subtree of b_i anyway because b_i is older. However, only the elements with timestamp smaller than that of b_{i+j} should be considered when searching inside b_i; younger elements have seen b_{i+j} and they cannot be interesting for the search if they are inside b_i. As parent nodes are older than their descendants, as soon as we find a node inside the subtree of b_i with timestamp larger than that of b_{i+j} we can stop the search in that branch, because all its subtree is even younger.

RangeSearch (Node a, Query q, Radius r, Timestamp t)
1. If $time(a) < t \ \wedge \ d(a,q) \leq R(a) + r$ Then
2.   If $d(a,q) \leq r$ Then Report a
3. $d_{min} \ \leftarrow \ \infty$
4.   For $b_i \in N(a)$ in increasing timestamp order Do
5.   If $d(b_i, q) \leq d_{min} + 2r$ Then
6. $k \leftarrow \min \ \{j > i, \ d(b_i, q) > d(b_j, q) + 2r\}$
7.   RangeSearch $(b_i, q, r, time(b_k))$
8. $d_{min} \leftarrow \min\{d_{min}, d(b_i, q)\}$

Fig. 5. Searching q with radius r in a dynamic *sa-tree*

Figure 5 shows the search algorithm, initially invoked as RangeSearch(a,q,r,∞), where a is the tree root. Note that $d(a,q)$ is always known except in the first invocation. Despite of the quadratic nature of the loop implicit in lines 4 and 6, the query is of course compared only once against each neighbor.

Figure 6 compares this technique against the static one. In the case of strings, the static method provides slightly better search time compared to the dynamic technique. In vector spaces of dimension 15, arities 16 and 32 improve (by a small margin) the static performance. We have also included an example in dimension 5, showing that in low dimensions small arities largely improve the search time of the static method. The best arity for searching depends on the metric space, but the rule of thumb is that low arities are good for low dimensions or small search radii.

The percentage retrieved in the space of strings for search radius 1 is 0.003%, for 2 is 0.037%, for 3 is 0.326% and for 4 is 1.757% aproximately.

We consider the number of distance evaluations instead of the CPU time because the CPU overhead over the number of distance evaluations is negligible in the *sa-tree*, unlike other structures.

It is important to notice that we have obtained dynamism and also have improved the construction performance. In some cases we have also (largely) improved the search performance, while in other cases we have paid a small price for the dynamism. Overall, this turns out to be a very convenient choice. This technique can be easily adapted to nearest neighbor searching with the same results.

4 Deletions

To delete an element x, the first step is to find it in the tree. Unlike most classical data structures, doing this is not equivalent to simulating the insertion of x and seeing where it leads us to in the tree. The reason is that the tree was different at the time x was inserted. If x were inserted again, it could choose to enter a different path in the tree, which did not exist at the time of its first insertion.

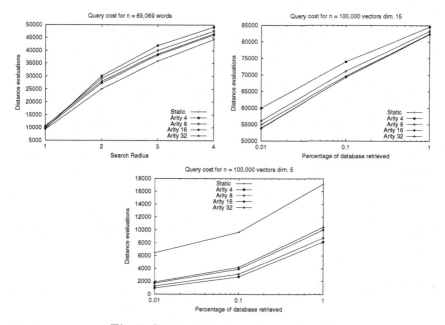

Fig. 6. Static versus dynamic search costs

An elegant solution to this problem is to perform a range search with radius zero, that is, a query of the form $(x, 0)$. This is reasonably cheap and will lead us to all the places in the tree where x could have been inserted.

On the other hand, whether this search is necessary is application dependent. The application could return a handle when an object was inserted into the database. This handle can contain a pointer to the corresponding tree node. Adding pointers to the parent in the tree would permit to locate the path for free (in terms of distance computations). Hence, in which follows, we do not consider the location of the object as part of the deletion problem, although we have shown how to proceed if necessary.

We have studied several alternatives to delete elements from a dynamic *sa-tree*. From the beginning we have discarded the trivial option of marking the element as deleted without actually deleting it. As explained, this is likely to be unacceptable in most applications. We assume that the element has to be physically deleted. We may, if desired, keep its node in the tree, but not the object itself.

It should be clear that a tree leaf can always be removed without any complication, so we focus on how to remove internal tree nodes.

4.1   Fake Nodes

Our first alternative to delete element x is to leave its node in the tree (without content) and mark it as deleted. We call these nodes *fake*. Although cheap and simple at deletion time, we must now figure out how to carry out a consistent search when some nodes do not contain an object.

Basically, if node $b \in N(a)$ is fake, we do not have enough information to avoid entering into the subtree of b once we have reached a. So we cannot include b in the minimization and have to enter always its subtree (except if we can use the timestamp information of b to prune the search).

The search performed at insertion time, on the other hand, has to follow just one path in the tree. In this case, one is free to choose inserting the new element into any fake neighbor of the current node, or into the closest non-fake neighbor. A good policy is, however, trying not to increase the size of subtrees rooted at fake nodes, as eventually they will have to be rebuilt (see later).

Hence, although deletion is simple, the search process degrades its performance.

4.2   Reinserting Subtrees

A widespread idea in the Euclidean range search community is that reinserting the elements of a disk page may be benefical because, with more elements in the tree, the space can be clustered better. We follow this principle now to obtain a method with costly deletions but good search performance.

When node x is deleted, we disconnect the subtree rooted at x from the main tree. This operation does not affect the correctness of the remaining tree, but we have now to reinsert the subtrees rooted at the nodes of $N(x)$. To do this efficiently we try to reinsert complete subtrees whenever possible.

In order to reinsert a subtree rooted at y, we follow the same steps as for inserting a fresh object y, so as to find the insertion point a. The difference is that we have to assume that y is a "fat" object with radius $R(y)$. That is, we can choose to put the whole subtree rooted at y as a new neighbor of a only if $d(y, a) + R(y)$ is smaller than $d(y, b)$ for any $b \in N(a)$. Similarly, we can choose to go down by neighbor $c \in N(a)$ only if $d(y, c) + R(y)$ is smaller than $d(y, b)$ for any $b \in N(a)$. When none of these conditions hold, we are forced to split the subtree rooted at y into its elements: one is a single element y, and the others are the subtrees rooted at $N(y)$. Once we split the subtree, we continue the insertion process with each constituent separately.

Every time we insert a node or a subtree, we pick a fresh timestamp for the node or the root of the subtree. The elements inside the subtree should get fresh timestamps while keeping the relative ordering among the subtree elements. The easiest way to do this is to assume that timestamps are stored relative to those of their parent. In this way, nothing has to be done. We need, however, to store at each node the maximum differential time stored in the subtree, so as to update *CurrentTime* appropriately when a whole subtree is reinserted. This is easily done at insertion time and omitted in the pseudocode for simplicity.

```
Reinsert (Node a, Node y)
 1.   If |N(a)| < MaxArity Then M ← {a} ∪ N(a)   Else  M ← N(a)
 2.   c₁ ← argmin_{b∈M} d(b, y)
 3.   c₂ ← argmin_{b∈M−{c₁}} d(b, y)
 4.   If d(c₁, y) + R(y) ≤ d(c₂, y) Then // keep subtree together
 5.       R(a) ← max(R(a), d(a, y) + R(y))
 6.       If c₁ = a Then // insert it here
 7.           N(a) ← N(a) ∪ {y}
 8.           time(y) ← CurrentTime // subtree shifts automatically
 9.       Else Reinsert (c₁, y) // go down
10.   Else // split subtree
11.       For z ∈ N(y) Do Reinsert (a, z)
12.       N(y) ← ∅, R(y) ← 0
13.       Reinsert (a, y)
```

Fig. 7. Simple algorithm to reinsert a subtree with root y into a dynamic *sa-tree* with root a

During reinsertion, we also modify the covering radii of the tree nodes a traversed. When inserting a whole subtree we have to add $d(y, a) + R(y)$, which may be larger than necessary. This involves at search time a price for having reinserted a whole subtree in one shot.

Note that it may seem that, when searching the place to reinsert the subtrees of a removed node x, one could save some time by starting the search at the parent of x. However, the tree has changed since the time the subtree of x was created, and new choices may exist now.

Figure 7 shows the algorithm to reinsert a tree with root y into a dynamic *sa-tree* rooted at a. The deletion of a node x is done by first locating it in the tree (say, $x \in N(b)$), then removing it from $N(b)$, and finally reinserting every subtree $y \in N(x)$ using `Reinsert(a,y)`.

Optimization. A further optimization to the subtree reinsertion process makes a more clever use of timestamps. Say that x will be deleted, and let $A(x)$ be the set of ancestors of x, that is, all the nodes in the path from the root to x. For each node c belonging to the subtree rooted at x we have $A(x) \subset A(c)$. So, when node c was inserted, it was compared against all the neighbors of every node in $A(x)$ whose timestamp was lower than that of c. Using this information we can avoid evaluating distances to these nodes when revisiting them at the time of reinserting c. That is, when looking for the neighbor closest to c, we know that the one in $A(x)$ is closer to c than any older neighbor, so we have to consider only newer neighbors. Note that this is valid as long as we reenter the same path where c was inserted previously.

The average cost of subtree reinsertion is as follows. Assume that we just reinsert the elements one by one. Assuming that the tree has always arity A and that it is perfectly balanced, the average size of a randomly chosen subtree turns out to be $\log_A n$. As every (re)insertions costs $A \log_A n$, the average deletion cost is $A \log_A^2 n$. This is much more costly than an insertion.

4.3   Combining Both Methods

We have two methods. Fake nodes delete elements for free but degrade the search performance of the tree. Subtree reinsertion make a costly subtree reinsertion but try to maintain the search quality of the tree. Note that the cost of reinserting a subtree would not be much different if it contained fake nodes, so we could remove all the fake nodes with a single subtree reinsertion, therefore amortizing the high cost of the reinsertion over many deletions.

Our idea is to ensure that every subtree has at most a fraction α of fake nodes. We say that such subtrees are "balanced". When we mark a new node x as fake, we check if we have not unbalanced it. In this case, x is discarded and its subtrees reinserted. The only difference is that we never insert a subtree whose root is fake, rather, we split the subtree and discard the fake root.

A complication is that removing the subtree rooted at x may unbalance several ancestors of x, even if x is just a leaf that can be directly removed, and even if the ancestor is not rooted at a fake node. As an example, consider a unary tree of height $3n$ where all the nodes at distance $3i$ from the root, $i \geq 0$, are fake. The three is balanced for $\alpha = 1/3$, but removing the leaf or marking as fake its parent unbalances every node.

We opt for a simple solution. We look for the lowest ancestor of x that gets unbalanced and reinsert all the subtree rooted at x. Because of this complication, we reinsert whole subtrees only when they have no fake nodes.

This technique has a nice performance property. Even if we reinserted the elements one by one (instead of whole subtrees), we would have the guarantee that we would reinsert a subtree only when a fraction α of its elements were fake. This would mean that if the size of the subtree to rebuild were m, we would pay $m(1 - \alpha)$ reinsertions for each αm deletions made in the subtree. Hence the amortized cost of a deletion would be at most $(1 - \alpha)/\alpha$ times the cost of an insertion, that is, $(1 - \alpha)/\alpha \ A \log_A n$. Asymptotically, the tree would work as if we permanently had a fraction α of fake nodes. Hence, we can control the tradeoff between deletion and search cost. Note that pure fake nodes corresponds to $\alpha = 1$ and pure subtree reinsertion to $\alpha = 0$.

4.4   Experimental Comparison

Let us now compare the three methods to handle deletions on the space of words using arity 16. Figure 8 shows the deletion cost for the first 10% (left) or 40% (right) of the database. On the left we have shown the case of full subtree reinsertion (that is, reinserting the subtrees after each deletion), with and without the final optimization proposed. As it can be seen, we save about 50% of the deletion cost with the optimization. We also show that one can only rarely insert whole subtrees, as reinserting the elements one by one has almost the same cost. Hence the algorithms could be simplified without sacrificing much.

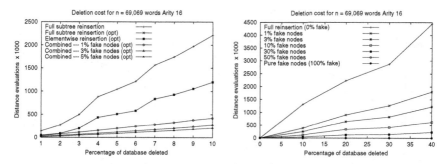

Fig. 8. Deletion costs using different methods

We also show the combined method with $\alpha = 1\%$, 3% and 5%. On the right we have shown much larger values of α, from 0% (full reinsertion) until 100% (pure fake nodes), as well as larger percentages of deletions (only the optimized version of reinsertions is used from now on).

We compare the methods deleting different percentages of the database to make appreciable not only the deletion cost per element but also to show the cumulative effect of deletions over the structure.

It can be seen that, even with full reinsertion, the individual deletion cost is not so high. For example, the average insertion cost in this space is about 58 distance computations per element. With the optimized method, each deletion costs about 173 distance computations, i.e., 3 times the cost of an insertion. The combined method largely improves over this: using α as low as 1% we have a deletion cost of 65 distance computations, which is close to the cost of insertions, and with $\alpha = 3\%$ this reduces to 35.

Let us now consider how the search costs are affected by deletions. We search on an index built on half of the elements of the database. This half is built by inserting more elements and then removing enough elements to leave 50% of the set in the index. So we compare the search on sets of the same size where a percentage of the elements has been deleted in order to leave the set in that size. For example, 30% deletions means that we inserted 49,335 elements and then removed 14,800, so as to leave 34,534 elements (half of the set).

Figure 9 shows the results. As it can be seen, even with full reinsertions ($\alpha = 0\%$) the search quality degrades, albeit hardly noticeably and non-monotonically with the number of deletions made. As α grows, the search costs increase because of the need to enter every children of fake nodes. The difference in search cost ceases to be reasonable as early as $\alpha = 10\%$, and in fact it is significant even for $\alpha = 1\%$. So one has to choose the right tradeoff between deletion and search cost depending on the application. A good tradeoff for strings is $\alpha = 1\%$.

Figure 10 shows the same data in a way that permits comparing the change in search cost as α grows.

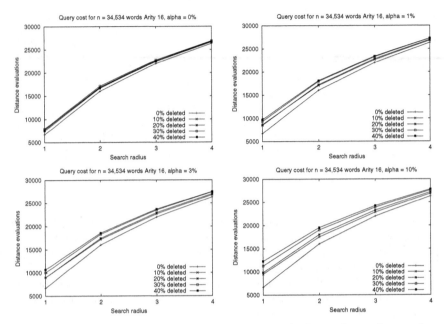

Fig. 9. Search costs using different deletion methods. In reading order we show the cases of $\alpha = 0\%$, 1%, 3% and 10%

5   Conclusions

We have presented a dynamic version of the *sa-tree* data structure, which is able of handling insertions and deletions efficiently without affecting its search quality. Very few data structures for searching metric spaces are fully dynamic. Furthermore, we have shown how to improve the behavior of the *sa-tree* in low dimensional spaces, both for construction and search costs.

The *sa-tree* was a promising data structure for metric space searching, with several drawbacks that prevented it from being practical: high construction cost in low dimensional spaces, poor search performance in low dimensional spaces or queries with high selectivity, and unability to accommodate insertions and deletions.

We have addressed all these weaknesses. Our new dynamic *sa-tree* stand out as a practical and efficient data structure that can be used in a wide range of applications, while retaining the good features of the original data structure.

As an example to give an idea of the behavior of our dynamic *sa-tree*, let us consider the space of vectors in dimension 15 using arity 16. We save 52.63% of the static construction cost, and improve the search time by 0.91% on average. A deletion with full element reinsertion costs on average 143 distance evaluations, which is 2.43 times the cost of an insertion. If we allow 10% of fake nodes in the

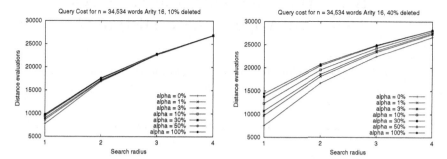

Fig. 10. Search costs using different deletion methods, comparing α. On the left we have deleted 10% of the database, on the right, 40%

structure, then the cost of a deletion drops to 17 and the search time becomes 3.04% worse than the static version.

We are currently pursuing in the direction of making the *sa-tree* work efficiently in secondary memory. In that case both the number of distance computations and disk accesses are relevant.

References

[1] C. Böhm, S. Berchtold, and D. Keim. Searching in high-dimensional spaces: Index structures for improving the performance of multimedia databases. *ACM Computing Surveys*, 33(3):322–373, September 2001. 255

[2] S. Brin. Near neighbor search in large metric spaces. In *Proc. 21st Conference on Very Large Databases (VLDB'95)*, pages 574–584, 1995. 255

[3] E. Chávez, G. Navarro, R. Baeza-Yates, and J. Marroquín. Searching in metric spaces. *ACM Computing Surveys*, 33(3):273–321, September 2001. 255, 256

[4] V. Gaede and O. Günther. Multidimensional access methods. *ACM Computing Surveys*, 30(2):170–231, 1998. 255

[5] G. Navarro. Searching in metric spaces by spatial approximation. In *Proc. String Processing and Information Retrieval (SPIRE'99)*, pages 141–148. IEEE CS Press, 1999. 255, 256, 257

[6] G. Navarro. Searching in metric spaces by spatial approximation. *The VLDB Journal*, 2002. To appear. 255, 257, 259, 260, 262

[7] G. Navarro and N. Reyes. Dynamic spatial approximation trees. In *Proc. XXI Conference of the Chilean Computer Science Society (SCCC'01)*, pages 213–222. IEEE CS Press, 2001. 256, 260

String Matching with Metric Trees
Using an Approximate Distance

Ilaria Bartolini, Paolo Ciaccia, and Marco Patella

DEIS - CSITE-CNR
University of Bologna, Italy
{ibartolini,pciaccia,mpatella}@deis.unibo.it

Abstract. Searching in a large data set those strings that are more similar, according to the *edit distance*, to a given one is a time-consuming process. In this paper we investigate the performance of metric trees, namely the M-tree, when they are extended using a cheap approximate distance function as a filter to quickly discard irrelevant strings. Using the *bag distance* as an approximation of the edit distance, we show an improvement in performance up to 90% with respect to the basic case. This, along with the fact that our solution is independent on both the distance used in the pre-test and on the underlying metric index, demonstrates that metric indices are a powerful solution, not only for many modern application areas, as multimedia, data mining and pattern recognition, but also for the string matching problem.

1 Introduction

Many modern real world applications, as text retrieval, computational biology, and signal processing, require searching in a huge string database for those sequences that are more similar to a given *query* string. This problem, usually called *approximate string matching*, can be formally defined as follows: Let Σ be a finite alphabet of symbols, let $\mathcal{O} \subseteq \Sigma^*$ be a database of finite length strings over the Σ alphabet, let $q \in \Sigma^*$ be a string, and let d_{edit} be the edit distance function, find the strings in $\mathcal{O}$ which are sufficiently similar to q, up to a given threshold. The edit distance $d_{edit}(X, Y)$ between two strings $X, Y \in \Sigma^*$ counts the minimum number of atomic edit operations (insertions, deletions, and substitutions of one symbol) needed to transform X in Y. As an example, the distance between the strings "spire" and "peer" is 4, $d_{edit}(\text{"spire"}, \text{"peer"}) = 4$, because to transform "spire" in "peer" we need at least 4 edit operations, i.e. 1 substitution (replace i with e), 2 deletions (s and e), and 1 insertion (e).

In the *online* version of the problem [13], the query string can be preprocessed, but the database cannot, thus the best algorithms are at least linear in the database size. An alternative approach, first proposed in [2], considers the strings to be searched as points in a metric space: A metric index is then built on the strings to reduce the number of distance computations needed to solve a query. Metric indices organize strings using relative distances and are able to consistently improve search performance over the simple sequential scan, since

A.H.F. Laender and A.L. Oliveira (Eds.): SPIRE 2002, LNCS 2476, pp. 271–283, 2002.
© Springer-Verlag Berlin Heidelberg 2002

only a fraction of database strings has to be compared against q. In some cases, however, response times are still unsatisfactory, particularly in the case of long strings, due to the fact that computing $d_{edit}(X, Y)$ using dynamic programming is $O(|X| \cdot |Y|)$, where $|X|$ (resp. $|Y|$) is the length of string X (resp. Y) [19]. To overcome such limitation, we propose the use of an approximate and cheap distance function to quickly discard objects that cannot be relevant for the query. We then show how, using a simple "bag distance", whose complexity is $O(|X| + |Y|)$, performance of metric trees can be improved up to 90%. Moreover, our results can also be applied to other approximate distances, thus making metric trees a powerful solution also for the text application domain, a fact that only in recent times has been considered [2, 14].

The paper is organized as follows: In Section 2 we give background information on solving similarity queries with metric trees. Section 3 presents our approach, and Section 4 contains results obtained from experimentations with real data sets. Finally, in Section 5 we conclude and discuss about possible extensions for our work.

2   Background

Metric trees are access methods that are able to efficiently solve range and k-nearest neighbor queries over general metric spaces. A metric space is a pair $(\mathcal{U}, d)$, where $\mathcal{U}$ is a set of objects and $d : \mathcal{U} \times \mathcal{U} \to \Re^+$ is a symmetric binary function that also satisfies the triangle inequality: $d(O_i, O_j) \leq d(O_i, O_k) + d(O_k, O_j)$, $\forall O_i, O_j, O_k \in \mathcal{U}$. Given a data set $\mathcal{O} = \{O_1, \ldots, O_N\}$, an object $q \in \mathcal{U}$, and a value $r \in \Re^+$, a range query selects all the objects O in $\mathcal{O}$ whose distance d from q is not higher than r. A k-nearest neighbor query, k being a natural number, retrieves the k objects in $\mathcal{O}$ having the minimum distance d from q. This general view of the problem is shared by many application domains (e.g. image databases [15], computational biology [8], and pattern recognition [3]).

To reduce the number of distance evaluations needed to solve a query, a number of index structures has been recently introduced for the general case of metric spaces [6, 5, 4, 9]. Among them, metric trees, like the M-tree [9] and the Slim-tree [17], are secondary memory structures whose goal is to reduce both CPU and I/O times for solving queries over very large data sets, that cannot fit into main memory.

A characteristic shared by all metric trees is that they partition the data space $\mathcal{U}$ into regions and assign each region to a node n stored on a disk page, whereas data objects are stored into leaf nodes [7]. In detail, at index-construction time, a hierarchical subdivision of the space is performed, such that each region of a node in a sub-tree is enclosed within the region associated to the root of the tree (thus, the root of a sub-tree is a coarser description of its descendant nodes).

Even if metric trees can be used to solve both range and k-nearest neighbors queries, in the following we will concentrate on the former type, since the latter can be built over range queries by using a priority search on the tree [9, 7]. At query time, the index is explored downwards, and distances between the query

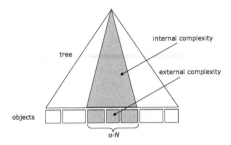

Fig. 1. Internal and external complexity when querying a tree

object q and objects in internal nodes are computed in order to prune away subtrees that cannot lead to any qualifying object, since their regions are disjoint from the query region. At the leaf level, objects that have not been filtered out, which are called *candidate objects*, are directly compared to the query to check if they should be included in the result (for a candidate object O this happens if $d(q, O) \leq r$). Following the terminology introduced in [7], the cost for determining the candidate objects is named *internal complexity*, while the cost for checking all candidates is referred as *external complexity* (see Figure 1).

Usually, the internal complexity is (much) lower than the external complexity. For a given range query, with query object q and radius r, let $\alpha_q(r) \cdot N$ be the number of candidate objects, N being the cardinality of the data set and $\alpha_q(r) \in [0, 1]$ being the *selectivity factor* of the tree with respect to the query. Although the definition of $\alpha_q(r)$ depends on both q and r, we can eliminate the dependency on q by simply averaging $\alpha_q(r)$ over a sample of query objects. Moreover, let $cost_d$ be the average cost of computing d.[1] The external complexity needed to solve a range query is therefore:

$$\alpha(r) \cdot N \cdot cost_d \tag{1}$$

The goal of metric trees, therefore, is to (consistently) reduce the external complexity, i.e. access only the objects relevant to the query, by (slightly) increasing the internal complexity (for the sequential scan, the internal complexity is 0 and the external complexity is $N \cdot cost_d$).

2.1 The M-tree

The M-tree is a paged, dynamic, and balanced metric tree. Each node n corresponds to a *region* of the indexed metric space $(\mathcal{U}, d)$, defined as $Reg(n) = \{O \in \mathcal{U} | d(O^{[n]}, O) \leq r^{[n]}\}$, where $O^{[n]}$ is called the *routing object* of node n and $r^{[n]}$

---

[1] Note that this is a simplification, since, in the general case, the cost of a single distance does depend on the objects for which it is computed, e.g. this is the case for the edit distance.

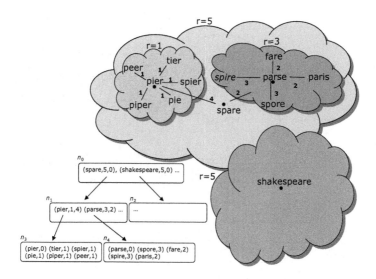

Fig. 2. An example of an M-tree and regions associated to each node. For each entry in an internal node, the routing object, the covering radius, and the distance from the parent object are shown, whereas entries in leaf nodes only contain a data string and its distance to the routing object

is its *covering radius*. All the objects in the sub-tree rooted at n are then guaranteed to belong to $Reg(n)$, thus their distance from $O^{[n]}$ does not exceed $r^{[n]}$. Both $O^{[n]}$ and $r^{[n]}$ are stored, together with a pointer to node n, $ptr(n)$, in an entry of the parent node of n. In order to save distance computations, the M-tree also stores pre-computed distances between each object and its parent. Thus, if n_p is the parent node of n, the entry for n in node n_p also includes the value of $d(O^{[n_p]}, O^{[n]})$.

When the metric space is the space of strings over an alphabet Σ equipped with d_{edit}, each object corresponds to a string. Figure 2 shows an example of (a part of) an M-tree indexing strings: Strings in each node are connected to the routing string of that node with a line whose length is proportional to the edit distance between them.

Given a query string q and a search radius r, the M-tree is recursively descended and sub-trees are accessed iff the region associated with their root node overlaps the query region (see Figure 3). For a given node n with routing object $O^{[n]}$ and covering radius $r^{[n]}$, this amounts to check if $d(q, O^{[n]}) \leq r + r^{[n]}$ holds, since from the triangle inequality it follows:

$$d(q, O^{[n]}) > r + r^{[n]} \implies d(q, O) > r \qquad \forall O \in Reg(n) \tag{2}$$

In the example of Figure 3, where $q = $ "spire" and $r = 1$, node n_3 can be pruned since it is $d_{edit}($"spire", "pier"$) = 3 > r + r^{[n_3]} = 1 + 1 = 2$. The dis-

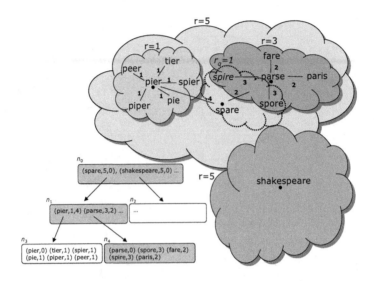

Fig. 3. Solving a range query with an M-tree: Highlighted nodes are those accessed during the search. Nodes n_2 and n_3 are pruned since their regions do not overlap the query region

tance $d(O^{[n_p]}, O^{[n]})$ can be used to prune out nodes without actually computing $d(q, O^{[n]})$, since the triangle inequality guarantees that:

$$|d(q, O^{[n_p]}) - d(O^{[n_p]}, O^{[n]})| > r + r^{[n]} \implies d(q, O) > r \quad \forall O \in Reg(n) \quad (3)$$

Note that, since the tree is recursively descended, $d(q, O^{[n_p]})$ has been already calculated, thus in Equation 3 no new distance is computed. In the example of Figure 3, we can avoid to compute $d_{edit}(\texttt{"spire"}, \texttt{"pier"})$, since it is $|d_{edit}(\texttt{"spire"}, \texttt{"spare"}) - d_{edit}(\texttt{"spare"}, \texttt{"pier"})| = |1 - 4| = 3 > 1 + 1 = 2$. Thus, the internal complexity for solving the query with the given tree is $3 \cdot cost_{d_{edit}}$, since we have to compare $\texttt{"spire"}$ with the routing strings $\texttt{"spare"}$, $\texttt{"shakespeare"}$, and $\texttt{"parse"}$, whereas the external complexity is $4 \cdot cost_{d_{edit}}$, since candidate strings are those contained in node n_4, except for $\texttt{"parse"}$ which can again be eliminated using Equation 3. Result strings are $\texttt{"spire"}$ and $\texttt{"spore"}$.[2]

3   Proposed Solution

The internal complexity for solving range queries with metric indices is usually very low. On the other hand, when using the edit distance, the external complexity, expressed by Equation 1, can be too high due to $cost_{d_{edit}}$. Thus, to reduce

---

[2] Note that routing objects do not necessarily belong to the data set [9], as it is the case for $\texttt{"spare"}$ in Figure 2.

the external complexity, we need a way to decrease the number of strings for which d_{edit} has to be computed. The solution we propose here is to use another distance d_c, which approximates d_{edit}, to quickly filter out candidates. All the strings remaining after this filtering phase are then checked, using d_{edit}, against q to see if they qualify for the result. The test to filter out a candidate string X is:

$$d_c(q, X) > r \tag{4}$$

All the strings satisfying Equation 4 are discarded without further processing. In order to guarantee that no string which should be included in the result is filtered out (no *false dismissals* are allowed), we need a constraint over d_c:

$$d_c(X, Y) \le d_{edit}(X, Y) \qquad \forall X, Y \in \Sigma^* \tag{5}$$

i.e. d_c should be a lower bound for d_{edit}. If this is not the case, in fact, it could be $d_{edit}(q, X) \le r$, thus X satisfies the query, yet $d_c(q, X) > r$, thus X is filtered out by d_c.

In order to keep costs low, d_c should be also very cheap to compute. A good candidate for approximating d_{edit} is the "bag distance" (also called "counting filter" in [12]), which is defined as follows.

Definition 1 (Bag Distance). *Given a string X over an alphabet Σ, let $x = ms(X)$ denote the multiset (bag) of symbols in X. For instance, $ms(\texttt{"peer"}) = \{\{e, e, p, r\}\}$. The following can be easily proved to be a metric on multisets:*

$$d_{bag}(x, y) = \max\{|x - y|, |y - x|\}$$

where the difference has a bag semantics (e.g. $\{\{a, a, a, b\}\} - \{\{a, a, b, c, c\}\} = \{\{a\}\}$), and $|\cdot|$ counts the number of elements in a multiset (e.g. $|\{\{a, a\}\}| = 2$). In practice, $d_{bag}(x, y)$ first "drops" common elements, then takes the maximum considering the number of "residual" elements. For instance:

$$d_{bag}(\{\{a, a, a, b\}\} - \{\{a, a, b, c, c\}\}) = \max\{|\{\{a\}\}|, |\{\{c, c\}\}|\} = 2$$

It is immediate to observe that $d_{bag}(X, Y) \le d_{edit}(X, Y), \forall X, Y \in \Sigma^*$.[3] Further, since computing $d_{bag}(X, Y)$ is $O(|X| + |Y|)$, d_{bag} can indeed be effectively used to quickly filter out candidate strings.[4] In the example of Figure 3, the filtering step would exclude the candidate string `"fare"` since it is $d_{bag}(\texttt{"spire"}, \texttt{"fare"}) = 3$, whereas the string `"paris"` cannot be excluded since $d_{bag}(\texttt{"spire"}, \texttt{"paris"}) = 1$. Thus, $d_{edit}(\texttt{"spire"}, \texttt{"paris"}) = 4$ has to be computed to exclude the string from the result. The external complexity now is $4 \cdot cost_{d_{bag}} + 3 \cdot cost_{d_{edit}}$.

---

[3] For the sake of brevity, here and in the following, we will replace the bag $ms(X)$ of symbols in a string with the string X itself, with a slight abuse of notation.

[4] Other distances can be used to approximate d_{edit} [11]; d_{bag} has, however, the advantage that it does not require further processing of strings and is very fast to compute.

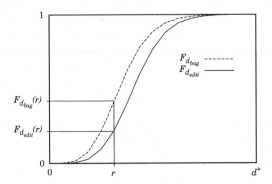

Fig. 4. Distance distributions for d_{bag} and d_{edit}

3.1   How Much Do We Save?

In order to compute the reduction in the external complexity obtained by using d_{bag}, we need to know the probability that the filter condition of Equation 4 succeeds for a string X. To this end, we use the *distance distribution* of objects, which has been profitably adopted several times to predict performance of metric structures [10, 16, 7, 17]. Formally, for a generic distance d over a domain $\mathcal{U}$, we denote with $F_{\mathbf{d}}(\cdot)$ the distance distribution of d, that is:

$$F_{\mathbf{d}}(x) = \Pr\{d(\mathbf{O_i}, \mathbf{O_j}) \leq x\} = \Pr\{\mathbf{d} \leq x\} \qquad x \in [0, d^+]$$

where $\mathbf{O_i}$ and $\mathbf{O_j}$ are randomly chosen objects of $\mathcal{U}$, d^+ is a finite upper bound on distance values, and $\mathbf{d} = d(\mathbf{O_i}, \mathbf{O_j})$ is a random variable with distribution $F_{\mathbf{d}}(\cdot)$. Figure 4 shows two sample distance distributions. Of course, since $d_{bag}(X, Y) \leq d_{edit}(X, Y)$, $\forall X, Y \in \Sigma^*$, it is also $F_{\mathbf{d_{bag}}}(x) \geq F_{\mathbf{d_{edit}}}(x)$, $\forall x \in [0, d^+]$.

The probability that a random string $\mathbf{X}$ is not filtered away by d_{bag} can be, therefore, computed as:

$$\Pr\{d_{bag}(q, \mathbf{X}) \leq r\} = F_{\mathbf{d_{bag}}}(r) \tag{6}$$

We are now ready to compute the overall cost for solving a query. For each candidate string X, $d_{bag}(q, X)$ has to be computed, with a cost of $cost_{d_{bag}}$. Only if the test of Equation 4 fails, which happens with probability given by Equation 6, we have to compute $d_{edit}(q, X)$, paying $cost_{d_{edit}}$. The overall external complexity is therefore given as:

$$\alpha(r) \cdot N \cdot cost_{d_{bag}} + F_{\mathbf{d_{bag}}}(r) \cdot \alpha(r) \cdot N \cdot cost_{d_{edit}} \tag{7}$$

Comparing Equation 7 with Equation 1, we obtain a saving in search time whenever it is:

$$\alpha(r) \cdot N \left(cost_{d_{bag}} + F_{\mathbf{d_{bag}}}(r) \cdot cost_{d_{edit}}\right) \leq \alpha(r) \cdot N \cdot cost_{d_{edit}}$$

that is when:

$$F_{d_{bag}}(r) \leq 1 - \frac{cost_{d_{bag}}}{cost_{d_{edit}}} \qquad (8)$$

The saving S in search time can be computed as:

$$S \approx \frac{\alpha(r) \cdot N \cdot cost_{d_{edit}} - \left(\alpha(r) \cdot N \cdot cost_{d_{bag}} + F_{d_{bag}}(r) \cdot \alpha(r) \cdot N \cdot cost_{d_{edit}}\right)}{\alpha(r) \cdot N \cdot cost_{d_{edit}}} =$$

$$= 1 - F_{d_{bag}}(r) - \frac{cost_{d_{bag}}}{cost_{d_{edit}}} \qquad (9)$$

where the approximation is due to the fact that, in Equation 9, the internal complexity is ignored.[5] Finally, if $F_{d_{bag}}$ is invertible, we can obtain the maximum search radius r_{max} for which it is convenient to use d_{bag}:

$$r_{max} = F_{d_{bag}}^{-1}\left(1 - \frac{cost_{d_{bag}}}{cost_{d_{edit}}}\right) \qquad (10)$$

3.2   Generalizing the Approach

In the previous Section we showed how we can reduce the external complexity for solving a query by filtering out objects using an approximate distance. In line of principle, nothing would prevent to use not only a single distance, but several ones. However, one should consider the fact that each filtering step requires the computation of some distances. As an example, consider the case where two approximate distances, d_{c_1} and d_{c_2}, are present, with $d_{c_1}(X,Y) \leq d_{c_2}(X,Y) \leq d_{edit}(X,Y)$. We can first use d_{c_1} to prune out some candidate strings, and then use d_{c_2} to discard some of the remaining ones. Finally, $d_{edit}(q,X)$ is computed for strings not filtered out by the second step. The external complexity for this solution can be computed as (see Figure 5):

$$\alpha(r) \cdot N \left(cost_{d_{c_1}} + F_{d_{c_1}}(r) \cdot cost_{d_{c_2}} + F_{d_{c_2}}(r) \cdot cost_{d_{edit}}\right) \qquad (11)$$

Now, one can compare the cost obtained from Equation 11 with that given by Equation 7 (by replacing d_{bag} with either d_{c_1} or d_{c_2}) to choose whether it is convenient to use both distances or only one of them. Of course, it can be expected that $cost_{d_{c_1}} < cost_{d_{c_2}}$, since d_{c_2} is a better approximation of d_{edit}.

It is now easy to generalize the above discussion to the case where m distances, $d_{c_1}, \ldots, d_{c_m}$, each lower-bounding d_{edit}, are present. Possible relations existing among the d_{c_i}s allow for a variety of scenarios:

- If it is $d_{c_i}(X,Y) \leq d_{c_{i+1}}(X,Y)$ $(i = 1, \ldots, m-1)$, then each distance can be used to filter out a fraction of candidate objects. Equation 11 can be easily extended to deal with m different distances, obtaining:

$$\alpha(r) \cdot N \left(cost_{d_{c_1}} + F_{d_{c_1}}(r) \cdot cost_{d_{c_2}} + \ldots + F_{d_{c_m}}(r) \cdot cost_{d_{edit}}\right) \qquad (12)$$

---

[5] We will experimentally validate this assumption in Section 4.

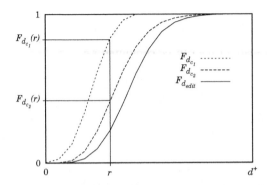

Fig. 5. Distance distributions for d_{c_1}, d_{c_2}, and *edit*

- A second scenario is obtained whenever it is $d_{c_i}(X, Y) \leq d_{c_{i+1}}(X, Y)$, yet $d_{c_{i+1}}(X, Y)$ can be incrementally obtained from $d_{c_i}(X, Y)$. As an example, this is the case we get considering the bag distance as computed only on the first i symbols of the Σ alphabet: This can be easily obtained starting from the distance computed considering only the first $i-1$ symbols. Of course, in computing $cost_{d_{c_{i+1}}}$, we should not take into account the cost already payed for computing $cost_{d_{c_i}}$.
- The more general case is obtained when it is $d_{c_i}(X, Y) \leq d_{edit}(X, Y)$, yet $d_{c_i}(X, Y) \not\leq d_{c_j}(X, Y), i \neq j$. In this case, the external complexity can still be computed from Equation 12, but now an important optimization issue regards the order in which the m distances should be considered.

It has to be noted that, even if in this paper we only use d_{bag} to approximate the edit distance, *any* function that lower bounds d_{edit} can do the job, since it is not required that d_c is a metric, but only that Equation 5 holds.

4   Experimental Results

In this Section we experimentally evaluate the solution proposed in Section 3. To this purpose, we provide results obtained from the following *real* data sets:

BibleWords: This data set consists of all the 12,569 distinct words occurring in the English King James version of the Holy Bible (as provided by [1]).
BibleLines: The 74,645 variable-length lines of the Holy Bible.
BibleLines20: We took the Holy Bible and segmented it into lines of length 20, which resulted in a total of 161,212 lines.

For each data set, we used a sample of the data (approximately 1% of the whole data set in size) as query objects and built the tree using the remaining strings. In order to predict the time saving when using d_{bag}, in Figure 6 distance

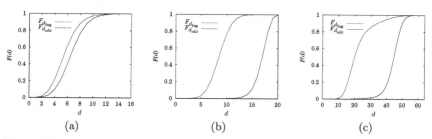

Fig. 6. Distributions of d_{edit} and d_{bag} for the `BibleWords` (a), `BibleLines20` (b), and `BibleLines` (c) data sets

distributions for the three data sets are shown, whereas Table 1 presents the average time needed to compute d_{bag} and d_{edit} for the three data sets.

We ran all the experiments on a Linux PC with a Pentium III 450 MHz processor, 256 MB of main memory, and a 9 GB disk. The node size of the M-tree was set to 8 Kbytes. In Figure 7, we show average search times for solving a range query as a function of the query radius r. The graphs indeed demonstrate that search times rapidly increase for long strings (see Figures 7 (b) and (c)), but also that, for a sufficiently wide interval of query radius values, the use of an approximate distance is very effective in reducing search costs. In particular, for the `BibleLines` data set, when $r = 10$ (0.1% of the data set is retrieved), the average search time when d_{bag} is not used is 64 seconds, which obviously makes this solution unaffordable, whereas the cost can be reduced to less than 8 seconds by using d_{bag}.

In Figure 8 we compare the saving in search time obtained through the experiments with the value predicted using Equation 9. As the graphs show, the actual searching performance can be very well estimated. The accuracy of Equation 9 is only slightly reduced for low values of the query radius, i.e. when the internal complexity for searching in the M-tree cannot be neglected wrt the external complexity. In Figure 8 the maximum search radius for which is convenient to use d_{bag}, obtained through Equation 10, is also shown. In particular, using values for distance computation times in Table 1 and the corresponding distance distributions (Figure 6), we obtain:

Table 1. Distance computation times for data sets used in the experiments

Data set	$cost_{d_{bag}}$ (s)	$cost_{d_{edit}}$ (s)
`BibleWords`	7.78×10^{-6}	26.1×10^{-6}
`BibleLines20`	17.7×10^{-6}	231.6×10^{-6}
`BibleLines`	66.1×10^{-6}	1300×10^{-6}

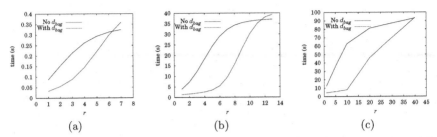

Fig. 7. Search times when d_{bag} is used or not for the BibleWords (a), BibleLines20 (b), and BibleLines (c) data sets

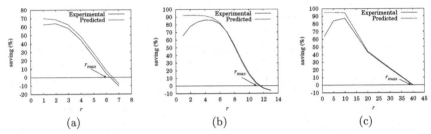

Fig. 8. Real and predicted time saving for the BibleWords (a), BibleLines20 (b), and BibleLines (c) data sets. Also shown are the r_{max} values which limit the usefulness of using d_{bag}

- $r_{max}(\texttt{BibleWords}) = F_{d_{bag}}^{-1}(1 - 7.78/26.1) \approx F_{d_{bag}}^{-1}(0.703) \approx 6,$
- $r_{max}(\texttt{BibleLines20}) = F_{d_{bag}}^{-1}(1 - 17.7/232) \approx F_{d_{bag}}^{-1}(0.924) \approx 11,$ and
- $r_{max}(\texttt{BibleLines}) = F_{d_{bag}}^{-1}(1 - 66.1/1300) \approx F_{d_{bag}}^{-1}(0.949) \approx 39.$

The graphs indeed demonstrate the accuracy of Equation 10 that can, therefore, be used to reliably predict whether, for a given query, it is worth using an approximate distance or not. The values of r_{max} are high enough to allow efficient search performance over a wide interval of values of the query radius.

It is also worth noting that even if, for the BibleLines20 and the BibleLines data sets, d_{edit} is not very well approximated by d_{bag} (see Figure 6), we can still obtain significant performance improvements (see Figure 8). This is due to the fact that, in such cases, d_{bag} is very cheap to compute compared to d_{edit}, because of the increased strings length (see Table 1), and this indeed allows to reduce search times, as also demonstrated by Equation 9.

5   Conclusions

In this paper we considered the problem of searching in a string database for those strings which are similar, according to the *edit distance*, to a given one.

Metric trees, as the M-tree [9], can be used to efficiently reduce the time needed to solve such queries. However, metric trees do not always succeed in consistently reducing the number of strings that have to be directly compared to the query, a fact that can indeed abate search performance, particularly when long strings are used. To solve this problem we proposed the use of the approximate and cheap *bag distance*, to quickly get rid of irrelevant strings. We also used the distribution of distances to predict the effectiveness of this pre-filtering step, showing how the saving in search times can be analytically computed, thus one can decide in advance if it is worth to use an approximate distance. Experimental results with large real data sets demonstrate that our approach achieves savings up to 90% with respect to the case when the approximate distance is not used, and that analytical predictions are very accurate.

Even if in this paper we concentrated on the M-tree, our solution and results apply to any other metric index, e.g. the recent Slim-tree [17] or the main memory structures considered in [2]. Moreover, we would also point out that our approach allows different functions to be used for approximating the edit distance, since we only require the former to lower bound the latter. Together, these two facts indeed broaden the applicability of our approach.

An issue not covered in this work is that of *local string alignment*, where the longest common substrings between a query and a database string are searched [11]. Since, however, such problem can be reduced to that of string matching, we believe that the use of a cheap function to approximate the edit distance can be effective also in this case. We leave this research topic as future work.

Finally, we would like to point out that in this paper we did not consider other techniques that are commonly used to reduce the complexity of the online problem, e.g. cutoff heuristics that can reduce the complexity of computing the edit distance to $O(r \cdot |X|)$ [18], where r is the query radius and $|X|$ is the length of a string in the data set. We plan to investigate in the future how such techniques can be embedded in our approach to further improve its efficiency. Moreover, we also plan to compare our approach with other state-of-the-art main memory solutions [13].

References

[1] Project Gutenberg official home site. http://www.gutenberg.net/. 279
[2] R. Baeza-Yates and G. Navarro. Fast approximate string matching in a dictionary. In *Proceedings of the 5th String Processing and Information Retrieval Symposium (SPIRE'98)*, Santa Cruz, Bolivia, Sept. 1998. 271, 272, 282
[3] S. Berretti, A. Del Bimbo, and P. Pala. Retrieval by shape similarity with perceptual distance and effective indexing. *IEEE Transaction on Multimedia*, 2(4):225–239, Dec. 2000. 272
[4] T. Bozkaya and M. Özsoyoglu. Indexing large metric spaces for similarity search queries. *ACM Transactions on Database Systems*, 24(3):361–404, Sept. 1999. 272
[5] S. Brin. Near neighbor search in large metric spaces. In *Proceedings of the 21st International Conference on Very Large Data Bases (VLDB'95)*, pages 574–584, Zurich, Switzerland, Sept. 1995. 272

[6] W. A. Burkhard and R. M. Keller. Some approaches to best-match file searching. *Communications of the ACM*, 16(4):230–236, Apr. 1973. 272

[7] E. Chávez, G. Navarro, R. Baeza-Yates, and J. L. Marroquín. Proximity searching in metric spaces. *ACM Computing Surveys*, 33(3):273–321, Sept. 2001. 272, 273, 277

[8] W. Chen and K. Aberer. Efficient querying on genomic databases by using metric space indexing techniques. In *1st International Workshop on Query Processing and Multimedia Issues in Distributed Systems (QPMIDS'97)*, Toulouse, France, Sept. 1997. 272

[9] P. Ciaccia, M. Patella, and P. Zezula. M-tree: An efficient access method for similarity search in metric spaces. In *Proceedings of the 23rd International Conference on Very Large Data Bases (VLDB'97)*, pages 426–435, Athens, Greece, Aug. 1997. 272, 275, 282

[10] P. Ciaccia, M. Patella, and P. Zezula. A cost model for similarity queries in metric spaces. In *Proceedings of the 16th ACM SIGACT-SIGMOD-SIGART Symposium on Principles of Database Systems (PODS'98)*, pages 59–68, Seattle, WA, June 1998. 277

[11] T. Kahveci and A. K. Singh. An efficient index structure for string databases. In *Proceedings of the 27th International Conference on Very Large Data Bases (VLDB 2001)*, pages 351–360, Rome, Italy, Sept. 2001. 276, 282

[12] G. Navarro. Multiple approximate string matching by counting. In *Proceedings of the 4th South American Workshop on String Processing (WSP'97)*, pages 125–139, Valparaiso, Chile, Nov. 1997. 276

[13] G. Navarro. A guided tour to approximate string matching. *ACM Computing Surveys*, 33(1):31–88, Mar. 2001. 271, 282

[14] G. Navarro, R. Baeza-Yates, E. Sutinen, and J. Tarhio. Indexing methods for approximate string matching. *IEEE Data Engineering Bulletin*, 24(4):19–27, Dec. 2001. Special Issue on Text and Databases. 272

[15] S. Santini. *Exploratory Image Databases: Content-Based Retrieval*. Series in Communications, Networking, and Multimedia. Academic Press, 2001. 272

[16] C. Traina Jr., A. J. M. Traina, and C. Faloutsos. Distance exponent: A new concept for selectivity estimation in metric trees. In *Proceedings of the 16th International Conference on Data Engineering (ICDE 2000)*, page 195, San Diego, CA, Mar. 2000. 277

[17] C. Traina Jr., A. J. M. Traina, C. Faloutsos, and B. Seeger. Fast indexing and visualization of metric data sets using Slim-trees. *IEEE Transactions on Knowledge and Data Engineering*, 14(2):244–260, Mar. 2002. 272, 277, 282

[18] E. Ukkonen. Finding approximate patterns in strings. *Journal of Algorithms*, 6(1):132–137, Mar. 1985. 282

[19] R. A. Wagner and M. J. Fischer. The string-to-string correction problem. *Journal of the ACM*, 21(1):168–173, Jan. 1974. 272

Probabilistic Proximity Searching Algorithms Based on Compact Partitions*

Benjamin Bustos[2] and Gonzalo Navarro[1,2]

[1] Center for Web Research
[2] Departamento de Ciencias de la Computación, Universidad de Chile
Blanco Encalada 2120, Santiago, Chile
{bebustos,gnavarro}@dcc.uchile.cl

Abstract. The main bottleneck of the research in metric space searching is the so-called curse of dimensionality, which makes the task of searching some metric spaces intrinsically difficult, whatever algorithm is used. A recent trend to break this bottleneck resorts to probabilistic algorithms, where it has been shown that one can find 99% of the elements at a fraction of the cost of the exact algorithm. These algorithms are welcome in most applications because resorting to metric space searching already involves a fuzziness in the retrieval requirements. In this paper we push further in this direction by developing probabilistic algorithms on data structures whose exact versions are the best for high dimensions. As a result, we obtain probabilistic algorithms that are better than the previous ones. We also give new insights on the problem and propose a novel view based on time-bounded searching.

1 Introduction

The concept of proximity searching has applications in a vast number of fields, for example: multimedia databases, machine learning and classification, image quantization and compression, text retrieval, computational biology, function prediction, etc. All those applications have in common that the elements of the database form a *metric space* [6], that is, it is possible to define a positive real-valued function d among the elements, called *distance* or *metric*, that satisfies the properties of *strict positiveness* $(d(x,y) = 0 \Leftrightarrow x = y)$, *symmetry* $(d(x,y) = d(y,x))$, and *triangle inequality* $(d(x,z) \leq d(x,y) + d(y,z))$. For example, a *vector space* is a particular case of metric space, where the elements are tuples of real numbers and the distance function belongs to the L_s family, defined as $L_s\left((x_1, \ldots, x_k),(y_1, \ldots, y_k)\right) = \left(\sum_{1 \leq i \leq k} |x_i - y_i|^s\right)^{1/s}$. For example, L_2 is the *Euclidean distance*.

One of the typical queries that can be posed to retrieve similar objects from a database is a *range query*, which retrieves all the elements within distance r to a query object q. An easy way to answer range queries is to make an exhaustive

---

* Work supported by the Millenium Nucleus Center for Web Research, Grant P01-029-F, Mideplan, Chile.

A.H.F. Laender and A.L. Oliveira (Eds.): SPIRE 2002, LNCS 2476, pp. 284–297, 2002.
© Springer-Verlag Berlin Heidelberg 2002

search on the database, but this turns out to be too expensive for real-world applications, because the distance d is considered expensive to compute. Think, for example, of a biometric device that computes the distance between two fingerprints.

Proximity searching algorithms build an *index* of the database and perform range queries using this index, avoiding the exhaustive search. Many of these algorithms are based on dividing the space in *partitions* or *zones* as compact as possible. Each zone stores a representative point, called the *center*, and a few extra data that permit quickly discarding the entire zone at query time, without measuring the actual distance from the elements of the zone to the query object, hence saving distance computations. Other algorithms are based in the use of *pivots*, which are distinguished elements from the database and are used together with the triangle inequality to filter out elements of the database at query time.

An inherent problem of proximity searching in metric spaces is that the search becomes more difficult when the "intrinsic" dimension of the metric space increases, which is known as the *curse of dimensionality*. The intrinsic dimension of a metric space is defined in [6] as $\mu^2/2\sigma^2$, where μ and σ^2 are the mean and the variance of the distance histogram of the metric space. This is coherent with the usual vector space definition. Analytical lower bounds and experiments [6] show that all proximity searching algorithms degrade their performance systematically as the dimension of the space grows. For example, in the case of vector space there is no technique that can reasonably cope with dimension higher than 20 [6]. This problem is due to two possible reasons: high dimensional metric spaces have a very concentrated distance histogram, which gives less information for discarding elements at query time; on the other hand, in order to retrieve a fixed fraction of the elements of the space it is necessary to use a larger search radius, because in high dimensional spaces the elements are "far away" from each other.

Probabilistic algorithms are acceptable in most applications that need to search in metric spaces, because in general the modelization as a metric space already carries some kind of relaxation. In most cases, finding some close elements is as good as finding all of them.

There exists a pivot-based probabilistic proximity searching algorithm which largely improves the search time at the cost of missing few elements [5]. On the other hand, it is known that compact partitioning algorithms perform better than pivot-based algorithms in high dimensional metric spaces [6] and they have lower memory requirements.

In this paper we present several probabilistic algorithms for proximity searching based on compact partitions, which alleviate in some way the curse of the dimensionality. We also present experimental results that show that these algorithms perform better than probabilistic algorithms based on pivots, and the latter needs much more memory space to beat the former when the dimension of the space is very high.

2   Basic Concepts

Let $(\mathbb{X}, d)$ be a metric space and $\mathbb{U} \subseteq \mathbb{X}$ the set of objects or database, with $|\mathbb{U}| = n$. There are two typical proximity searching queries:

- *Range query.* A range query (q, r), $q \in \mathbb{X}$, $r \in \mathbb{R}^+$, reports all elements that are within distance r to q, that is $(q, r) = \{u \in \mathbb{U}, d(u, q) \leq r\}$.
- *k nearest neighbors (k-NN).* Reports the k elements from $\mathbb{U}$ closer to q, that is, returns the set $\mathbb{C} \subseteq \mathbb{U}$ such that $|\mathbb{C}| = k$ and $\forall x \in \mathbb{C}, y \in \mathbb{U} - \mathbb{C}, d(x, q) \leq d(y, q)$.

The volume defined by (q, r) is called the *query ball*, and all the elements inside it are reported. Nearest neighbors queries can be implemented using range queries.

There exist two classes of techniques used to implement proximity searching algorithms: based on pivots and based on compact partitions.

2.1   Pivot-Based Algorithms

These algorithms select a number of "pivots", which are distinguished elements from the database, and classify all the other elements according to their distance to the pivots.

The canonical pivot-based algorithm is as follows: given a range query (q, r) and a set of k pivots $\{p_1, \ldots, p_k\}, p_i \in \mathbb{U}$, by the triangle inequality it follows for any $x \in \mathbb{X}$ that $d(p_i, x) \leq d(p_i, q) + d(q, x)$, and also that $d(p_i, q) \leq d(p_i, x) + d(x, q)$. From both inequalities it follows that a lower bound on $d(q, x)$ is $d(q, x) \geq |d(p_i, x) - d(p_i, q)|$. The elements $u \in \mathbb{U}$ of interest are those that satisfy $d(q, u) \leq r$, so one can exclude all the elements that satisfy $|d(p_i, u) - d(p_i, q)| > r$ for some pivot p_i (exclusion condition), without actually evaluating $d(q, u)$.

The index consists of the kn distances $d(u, p_i)$ between every element and every pivot. Therefore, at query time it is necessary to compute the k distances between the pivots and the query q in order to apply the exclusion condition. Those distance calculations are known as the *internal complexity* of the algorithm, and this complexity is fixed if there is a fixed number of pivots. The list of elements $\{u_1, \ldots, u_m\} \subseteq \mathbb{U}$ that cannot be excluded by the exclusion condition, known as the *element candidate list*, must be checked directly against the query. Those distance calculations $d(u_i, q)$ are known as the *external complexity* of the algorithm. The total complexity of the search algorithm is the sum of the internal and external complexity, $k + m$. Since one increases and the other decreases with k, it follows that there is an optimum k^* that depends on the tolerance range r of the query. In practice, however, k^* is so large that one cannot store the k^*n distances, and the index uses as many pivots as space permits.

Examples of pivot-based algorithms [6] are *BK-Tree, Fixed Queries Tree (FQT), Fixed-Height FQT, Fixed Queries Array, Vantage Point Tree (VPT), Multi VPT, Excluded Middle Vantage Point Forest, Approximating Eliminating Search Algorithm (AESA)* and *Linear AESA.*

2.2   Algorithms Based on Compact Partitions

These algorithms are based on dividing the space in *partitions* or *zones* as compact as possible. Each zone stores a representative point, called the *center*, and a few extra data that permit quickly discarding the entire zone at query time, without measuring the actual distance from the elements of the zone to the query object. Each zone can be partitioned recursively into more zones, inducing a *search hierarchy*. There are two general criteria for partitioning the space: *Voronoi partition* and *covering radius*.

Voronoi partition criterion. A set of m centers is selected, and the rest of the elements are assigned to the zone of their closest center. Given a range query (q, r), the distances between q and the m centers are computed. Let c be the closest center to q. Every zone of center $c_i \neq c$ which satisfies $d(q, c_i) > d(q, c) + 2r$ can be discarded, because its Voronoi area cannot have intersection with the query ball. Figure 1 (left) shows an example of the Voronoi partition criterion. For q_1 the zone of c_4 can be discarded, and for q_2 only the zone of c_3 must be visited.

Covering radius criterion. The covering radius $cr(c)$ is the maximum distance between a center c and an element that belongs to its zone. Given a range query (q, r), if $d(q, c_i) - r > cr(c_i)$ then zone i cannot have intersection with the query ball and all its elements can be discarded. In Figure 1 (right), the query ball of q_1 does not have intersection with the zone of center c, thus it can be discarded. For the query balls of q_2 and q_3, the zone cannot be discarded, because it intersects these balls.

   Generalized-Hyperplane Tree [14] is an example of an algorithm that uses the Voronoi partition criterion. Examples of algorithms that use the covering radius criterion are *Bisector Trees (BST)* [11], *Monotonous BST* [13], *Voronoi Tree* [8], *M-Tree* [7] and *List of Clusters* [4]. Also, there exist algorithms that use both criteria, for example *Spatial Approximation Tree (SAT)* [12] and *Geometric*

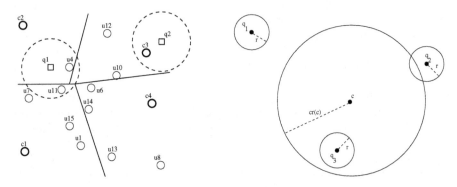

Fig. 1. Voronoi partition criterion (left) and covering radius criterion (right)

Near-neighbor Access Tree [2]. Of all these algorithms, two of the most efficient are SAT and List of Clusters, so now we explain briefly how these algorithms work.

2.3   Spatial Approximation Tree

The *SAT* [12] is based on approaching the query spatially rather than dividing the search space, that is, start at some point in the space and get closer to the query, which is done only via "neighbors". The SAT uses both compact partition criteria for discarding zones, it needs $O(n)$ space, reasonable construction time $O(n \log^2(n)/\log(\log(n)))$ and sublinear search time $O(n^{1-\Theta(1/\log(\log(n)))})$ in high dimensional spaces.

Construction of SAT is as follows: an arbitrary object $a \in \mathbb{U}$ is chosen as the root node of the tree (note that since there exists only one object per node, we use both terms interchangeably in this section). Then, we select a suitable set of neighbors $N(a)$ such that $\forall u \in \mathbb{U}, u \in N(a) \Leftrightarrow \forall v \in N(a) - \{u\}, d(u,v) > d(u,a)$. Note that $N(a)$ is defined in terms of itself in a non-trivial way, and that multiple solutions fit the definition. In fact, finding the minimal set of neighbors seems to be a hard combinatorial optimization problem [12]. A simple heuristic that works well in most cases considers the objects in $\mathbb{U} - \{a\}$ in increasing order of their distance from a, and adds an object x to $N(a)$ if x is closer to a than to any object already in $N(a)$. Next, we put each node in $\mathbb{U} - N(a)$ into the bag of it closest element of $N(a)$. Also, for each subtree $u \in N(a)$ we store its covering radius $cr(u)$. The process is repeated recursively in each subtree using the elements of its bag. Figure 2 (left) shows an example of a SAT.

This construction process ensures that if we search for an object $q \in \mathbb{U}$ by spatial approximation, we will find that element in the tree because we are repeating exactly what happened during the construction process, i.e., we enter into the subtree of the neighbor closest to q, until we reach q (in fact, in this case we are doing an exact search because q is present in the tree). For general range queries (q, r), instead of simply going to the closest neighbor, we first determine the closest neighbor c of q among $\{a\} \cup N(a)$. Then, we enter into all neighbors $b \in N(a)$ such that $d(q, b) \leq d(q, c) + 2r$. During the search process, all the nodes x such that $d(q, x) \leq r$ are reported. The search algorithm can be improved a bit more: when we search for an element $q \in \mathbb{U}$ (exact search), we follow a single path from the root to q. At any node a' in this path, we choose the closest to q among $\{a'\} \cup N(a')$. Therefore, if the search is currently at tree node a, we have that q is closer to a than to any ancestor a' of a and also any neighbor of a'. Hence, if we call $A(a)$ the set of ancestors of a (including a), we have that, at search time, we can avoid entering any element $x \in N(a)$ such that $d(q, x) > 2r + \min\{d(q, c), c \in \{a'\} \cup N(a'), a' \in A(a)\}$. This condition is a stricter version of the original Voronoi partition criterion. The covering radius stored for all nodes during the construction process can be used to prune the search further, by not entering into subtrees such that $d(q, b) - r > cr(b)$.

2.4   List of Clusters

The *List of Clusters* [4] is a list of "zones". Each zone has a center and stores its covering radius. A center $c \in \mathbb{U}$ is chosen at random, as well as a radius rp, whose value depends on whether the number of elements per compact partition is fixed or not. The *center ball* of (c, rp) is defined as $(c, rp) = \{x \in \mathbb{X}, d(c, x) \leq rp\}$. We then define $I = \mathbb{U} \cap (c, rp)$ as the bucket of "internal" objects lying inside (c, rp), and $E = \mathbb{U} - I$ as the rest of the elements (the "external" ones). The process is repeated recursively inside E. The construction process returns a list of triples (c_i, rp_i, I_i) (center, radius, internal bucket), as shown in Figure 2 (right).

This data structure is asymmetric, because the first center chosen has preference over the next centers in case of overlapping balls, as shown in Figure 2 (right). With respect to the value of the radius rp of each compact partition and the selection of the next center in the list, there exist many alternatives. In [4] it is shown experimentally that the best performance is achieved when the compact partition has a fixed number of elements, so rp becomes simply $cr(c)$, and the next center is selected as the element which maximizes the distance sum to the centers previously chosen. The brute force algorithm for constructing the list takes $O(n^2/m)$, where m is the size of the compact partition, but it can be improved using auxiliary data structures to build the partitions. For high dimensional metric spaces, the optimal m is very low (we used $m = 5$ in our experiments).

For a range query (q, r), $d(q, c)$ is computed, reporting c if it is within the query ball. Then, we search exhaustively inside I only if $d(q, c) - cr(c) \leq r$ (covering radius criterion). E is processed only if $cr(c) - d(q, c) < r$, because of the asymmetry of the data structure. The search cost has a form close to $O(n^\alpha)$ for some $0.5 < \alpha < 1.0$ [4].

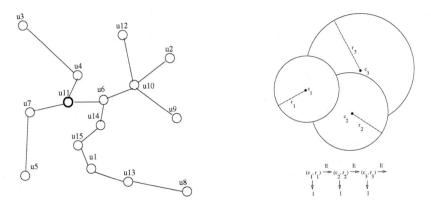

Fig. 2. Example of SAT (left) and List of Clusters (right)

3   Probabilistic Algorithms for Proximity Searching

All the algorithms seen in the previous section are *exact algorithms*, which retrieve exactly the elements of $\mathbb{U}$ that are within the query ball of (q, r). In this work we are interested in *probabilistic algorithms*, which relax the condition of delivering the exact solution. As explained before, this is acceptable in most applications.

In [5] they present a probabilistic algorithm based on "stretching" the triangle inequality. The idea is general, but they applied it to pivot based algorithms. Their analysis shows that the net effect of the technique is to reduce the search radius by a factor β, and that that reduction is larger when the search problem becomes harder, i.e., the intrinsic dimension of the space becomes high. Even with very little stretching, they obtain large improvements in the search time with low error probability. The factor β can be chosen at search time, so the index can be built beforehand and later one can choose the desired level of accurateness and speed of the algorithm. As the factor is used only to discard elements, no element closer to q than r/β can be missed during the search. In practice, all the elements that satisfy $|d(p_i, u) - d(p_i, q)| > r/\beta$ for some p_i are discarded. Figure 3 illustrates how the idea operates. The exact algorithm guarantees that no relevant element is missed, while the probabilistic one stretches both sides of the ring and can miss some elements.

4   Our Approach

We focus in probabilistic algorithms for high dimensional metric spaces, where for exact searching it is very difficult to avoid the exhaustive search regardless of the index and search algorithm used.

It is well known that compact partition algorithms perform better than pivot-based algorithms in high dimensional metric spaces [6], and that the latter need

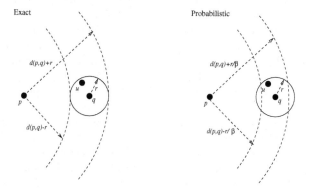

Fig. 3. How the probabilistic algorithm based on pivots works

more space requirements, i.e., many pivots, to reach the performance of the former. For this reason, it is interesting to develop probabilistic algorithms based on compact partitions, with the hope that these algorithms could have at least the same performance than pivot-based probabilistic algorithms, with less memory requirements. It is worth noting that the index data structure used with the probabilistic search algorithm is the same used with the exact search algorithm.

We propose two techniques: the first based on incremental searching and the last based on ranking zones.

4.1   Probabilistic Incremental Search

This technique is an adaptation of the *incremental nearest neighbor search* algorithm [10]. This incremental search traverses the search hierarchy defined by the index (whatever it be) in a "best-first" manner. At any step of the algorithm, it visits the "element" (zone or object) with the smallest distance from the query object among all unvisited elements in the search hierarchy. This can be done by maintaining a priority queue of elements organized by their maximum lower bound distance known to the query object at any time.

In [10] is proved that this search is *range-optimal*, that is, it obtains the kth nearest neighbor, o_k, after visiting the same search hierarchy elements as would a range query with radius $d(q, o_k)$ implemented with a top-down traversal of the search hierarchy.

The incremental nearest neighbor search can be adapted to answer range queries. We report all objects u that satisfy $d(q, u) \leq r$, but we stop when it is dequeued an element with lower bound $l > r$ (*global stopping criterion*). It is not possible to find another object within the query ball among the unexplored elements, because we have retrieved them ordered by their lower bounded distances to q. An equivalent method is to enqueue elements only if they have a lower bound $l \leq r$, in which case the queue must be processed until it gets empty.

The idea of the probabilistic technique based on the incremental search is to fix in advance the number of distance computations allowed to answer a range query. Using the adapted incremental search for range queries, if the search is pruned after we make the maximum number of distance computations allowed, then we obtain a probabilistic algorithm in the sense that some relevant elements can be missed. However, as the search is performed range-optimally, one can presume that the allotted distance computations are used in an efficient way.

Figure 4 depicts the general form of the probabilistic incremental search. *Index* is the data structure that indexes $\mathbb{U}$, q is the query object, e is an element of the index and $d_{LB}(q, e)$ is a lower bound of the real distance between q and all the elements rooted in the search hierarchy of e, where $d_{LB}(q, e) = d(q, e)$ if e is an object of $\mathbb{U}$, and $d_{LB}(q, e) \geq d_{LB}(q, e')$ if e' is an ancestor of e in the hierarchy. For example, in the List of Clusters, if e is a child of a and belongs to the zone of center c then $d_{LB}(q, e) = \max(d(q, c) - cr(c), d_{LB}(q, a))$; in SAT if e is a child of a then $d_{LB}(q, e) = \max(d(q, a) - cr(a), (d(q, e) - \min\{d(q, c), c \in \{a'\} \cup N(a'), a' \in A(a)\})/2, d_{LB}(q, a))$. The maximum number of distance computations allowed to perform the search is denoted by *quota*. Once *quota* has been reached, no more elements are enqueued. Note that the only stopping criterion of the algorithm is that the queue gets empty, even if the work quota has been reached, because for all the objects enqueued their distance to q are already known. The syntax of the enqueue procedure is `Enqueue(queue, element, lower bound distance)`. The dequeue procedure recovers the element e and its lower bound distance. Variable *cost* indicates the number of distance computations needed to process the children of element e in the search hierarchy. In SAT, *cost* is equal to $N(e)$; in List of Clusters, *cost* is equal to m.

4.2 Ranking of Zones

The probabilistic incremental search aims at quickly finding elements within the query ball, before the work quota gets exhausted. As the maximum number of distance computations is fixed, the total search time is also bounded. This technique can be generalized to what we call *ranking of zones*, where the idea is to sort the zones in order to favor the most promising and then to traverse the list until we use up the quota. The probabilistic incremental search can be seen as a ranking method, where we first rank all the zones using $d_{LB}(q, e)$ and then work until we use up the quota. However, this ranking does not have to be the best zone ranking criterion.

The sorting criterion must aim at quickly finding elements that are close to the query object. As the space is partitioned into zones, we must sort these zones in a promising search order using the information given by the index data structure. For example, in List of Clusters the only information we have is the distances from q to each center and the covering radius of each zone. One not

---

```
ProbIncrSearch(q, Index, quota)

 1. Queue ← ∅ // Priority queue
 2. e ← root of Index
 3. counter ← 0 // Number of distances computed
 4. Enqueue(Queue, e, 0)
 5. while not IsEmpty(Queue) do
 6.    (e, d_LB(q,e)) ← Dequeue(Queue)
 7.    if e is an object then report e
 8.    else
 9.       cost ← cost to process children of e
10.       if counter + cost ≤ quota
11.          for each child element e' of e do
12.             Compute d_LB(q,e')
13.             if d_LB(q,e') ≤ r then
14.                Enqueue(Queue, e', max(d_LB(q,e), d_LB(q,e')))
15.          counter ← counter + cost
```

Fig. 4. Probabilistic incremental search algorithm

only would like to search first the zones closer to the query, but also to search first the zones that are more compact, that is, the zones which have "higher element density". In spite of the fact that it is very difficult to define the volume of a zone in a general metric space, we assume that if the zones have the same number of elements, as in the best implementation of List of Clusters, then the zones with smaller covering radii have higher element density than those with larger covering radii.

We have tested several zone ranking criteria:

- the distance from q to each zone center, $d(q, c)$, closest first.
- the covering radius of each zone, $cr(c)$, in increasing order.
- $d(q, c) + cr(c)$, the distance from q to the farthest element in the zone.
- $d(q, c) \cdot cr(c)$.
- $d(q, c) - cr(c)$, the distance from q to the closest element in the zone.
- $\beta(d(q, c) - cr(c))$.

The first two techniques are the simplest ranking criteria. The next two techniques aim to search first in those zones that are closer to q and also are compact. The next technique, $d(q, c) - cr(c)$, is equivalent to the incremental search technique. The last technique is equivalent to reducing the search radius by a factor β as in [4], where $1/\beta \in [0..1]$.

If factor β is fixed, then this technique is equivalent to the probabilistic incremental search, because the ordering is the same in both cases. However, instead of using a constant factor $\beta \in [0..1]$, we can use a *dynamic factor* of the form $\beta = 1/(1.0 - \frac{cr(c)}{mcr})$, where mcr is the maximum size of the covering radius of all zones. This implies that we reduce more the search radius as the covering radius of a particular zone is greater. A special case is when $cr(c) = mcr$. In this case we define $d_{LB}(q, e) = \infty$ for all objects in the zone of center c.

Note that $d(q, c) - cr(c)$ is the only criterion that can be used with the incremental search technique, because only with this criterion is guaranteed that $d_{LB}(q, e) \geq d_{LB}(q, e')$ for any element e' ancestor of e.

5   Experimental Results

We use the SAT and List of Clusters to implement the probabilistic techniques described in Section 4, but with SAT we only implement the probabilistic incremental search because in this data structure every node is a center, so it takes $O(n)$ time to compute the distances between the query and every center. We have tested the probabilistic techniques on a synthetic set of random points in a k-dimensional vector space treated as a metric space, that is, we have not used the fact that the space has coordinates, but treated the points as abstract objects in an unknown metric space. The advantage of this choice is that it allows us to control the exact dimensionality we are working with, which is very difficult to do in general metric spaces. The points are uniformly distributed in the unitary cube, our tests use the L_2 (Euclidean) distance, the database size is $n = 10,000$

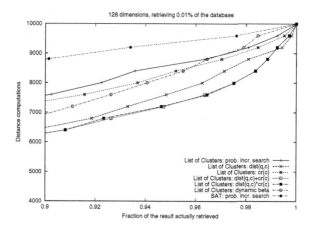

Fig. 5. Probabilistic List of Clusters and SAT in a vector space of dimension 128

and we perform range queries returning 0.01% of the total database size, taking an average from 1,000 queries. The techniques were tested using a space of dimension 128, where no known exact algorithm can avoid an exhaustive search to answer useful range queries.

Figure 5 shows the results of the probabilistic List of Clusters and SAT. The best technique, in this case, is the ranking zone method with criterion $d(q,c) + cr(c)$.

Figure 6 shows a comparison of the probabilistic List of Clusters and the probabilistic pivot-based algorithm, implemented in its canonical form (see Section 2.1 and 3). In this experiment, the probabilistic List of Clusters performs almost equal than the pivot-based algorithm with 256 pivots when more than 97% of the result is actually retrieved. The pivot-based techniques are slightly better when the pivots are selected using the "good pivots" criterion [3]. However, the size of the List of Clusters index (0.12 Mb) is about 82 times less than the size of the pivot-based index with 256 pivots (9.78 Mb) and about 5 times less than the size of the pivot-based index with 16 pivots (0.62 Mb). Experiments with different search radius and database size obtained similar results to those presented here.

One of the most clear applications of metric space techniques to Information Retrieval is the task of finding documents relevant to a query (which can be a set of terms or a whole document itself) [1]. Documents (and queries) are seen as vectors, where every term is a coordinate whose value is the weight of the term in that document. The distance between two documents is the angle between their vectors, so documents sharing important terms are seen as more similar. Documents closer to a query are considered to be more relevant to the query. Hence the task is to find the elements of this metric space of documents which are closest to a given query.

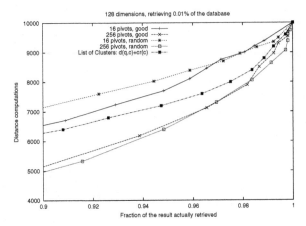

Fig. 6. Comparison among probabilistic algorithms in a vector space of dimension 128

Despite of this clear link, metric space techniques have seldom been used for this purpose. One reason is that the metric space of documents has a very high dimension, which makes any exact search approach unaffordable. This is a case where probabilistic algorithms would be of great value, since the definition of relevance is fuzzy and it is customary to permit approximations. Figure 7 shows a result on a subset of the TREC-3 collection [9], comparing the pivot-based algorithm with the ranking zone method using the dynamic beta criterion ($m = 10$ for the List of Clusters, retrieving on average 0.035% of the database per query). The result shows that our probabilistic algorithms can handle better this

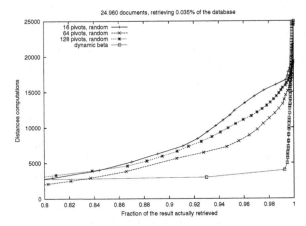

Fig. 7. Comparison among probabilistic algorithms in a document space

space, retrieving more than 99% of the relevant objects and traversing merely a 17% of the database, using much less memory, approximately 16 times less than the index with 64 pivots, hence becoming for the first time a feasible metric space approach to this long standing problem.

6 Conclusions

We have defined a general probabilistic technique based on the incremental nearest search, that allows us to perform time-bounded range search queries in metric spaces with a high probability of finding all the relevant elements. Our experimental results show in both synthetic and real-world examples that our technique performs better than the pivot-based probabilistic algorithm in high dimensional metric spaces, as the latter needs much more memory space to be competitive.

Future work involves testing more zone ranking criteria. Also, we are interested in finding a formal model that allows us to predict how well will perform an arbitrary index with our probabilistic techniques.

References

[1] R. Baeza-Yates and B. Ribeiro-Neto. *Modern Information Retrieval.* Addison-Wesley, 1999. 294

[2] S. Brin. Near neighbor search in large metric spaces. In *Proc. 21st Conference on Very Large Databases (VLDB'95)*, pages 574–584, 1995. 288

[3] B. Bustos, G. Navarro, and E. Chávez. Pivot selection techniques for proximity searching in metric spaces. In *Proc. of the XXI Conference of the Chilean Computer Science Society (SCCC'01)*, pages 33–40. IEEE CS Press, 2001. 294

[4] E. Chávez and G. Navarro. An effective clustering algorithm to index high dimensional metric spaces. In *Proc. 7th South American Symposium on String Processing and Information Retrieval (SPIRE'00)*, pages 75–86. IEEE CS Press, 2000. 287, 289, 293

[5] E. Chávez and G. Navarro. A probabilistic spell for the curse of dimensionality. In *Proc. 3rd Workshop on Algorithm Engineering and Experiments (ALENEX'01)*, LNCS 2153, pages 147–160, 2001. 285, 290

[6] E. Chávez, G. Navarro, R. Baeza-Yates, and J. Marroquín. Proximity searching in metric spaces. *ACM Computing Surveys*, 33(3):273–321, 2001. 284, 285, 286, 290

[7] P. Ciaccia, M. Patella, and P. Zezula. M-tree: an efficient access method for similarity search in metric spaces. In *Proc. of the 23rd Conference on Very Large Databases (VLDB'97)*, pages 426–435, 1997. 287

[8] F. Dehne and H. Noltemeier. Voronoi trees and clustering problems. *Information Systems*, 12(2):171–175, 1987. 287

[9] D. Harman. Overview of the Third Text REtrieval Conference. In *Proc. Third Text REtrieval Conference (TREC-3)*, pages 1–19, 1995. NIST Special Publication 500-207. 295

[10] G. Hjaltason and H. Samet. Incremental similarity search in multimedia databases. Technical Report TR 4199, Department of Computer Science, University of Maryland, November 2000. 291

[11] I. Kalantari and G. McDonald. A data structure and an algorithm for the nearest point problem. *IEEE Transactions on Software Engineering*, 9(5):631–634, 1983. 287

[12] G. Navarro. Searching in metric spaces by spatial approximation. *The Very Large Databases Journal (VLDBJ)*, 2002. To appear. Earlier version in SPIRE'99, IEEE CS Press. 287, 288

[13] H. Noltemeier, K. Verbarg, and C. Zirkelbach. Monotonous Bisector* Trees – a tool for efficient partitioning of complex schenes of geometric objects. In *Data Structures and Efficient Algorithms*, LNCS 594, pages 186–203. Springer-Verlag, 1992. 287

[14] J. Uhlmann. Satisfying general proximity/similarity queries with metric trees. *Information Processing Letters*, 40:175–179, 1991. 287

t-Spanners as a Data Structure
for Metric Space Searching*

Gonzalo Navarro[1], Rodrigo Paredes[1], and Edgar Chávez[2]

[1] Center for Web Research, Dept. of Computer Science, University of Chile
Blanco Encalada 2120, Santiago, Chile
{gnavarro,raparede}@dcc.uchile.cl
[2] Escuela de Ciencias Físico-Matemáticas, Univ. Michoacana
Morelia, Mich. México
elchavez@zeus.ccu.umich.mx.

Abstract. A *t-spanner*, a subgraph that approximates graph distances within a precision factor t, is a well known concept in graph theory. In this paper we use it in a novel way, namely as a data structure for searching metric spaces. The key idea is to consider the t-spanner as an approximation of the complete graph of distances among the objects, and use it as a compact device to simulate the large matrix of distances required by successful search algorithms like AESA [Vidal 1986]. The t-spanner provides a time-space tradeoff where full AESA is just one extreme. We show that the resulting algorithm is competitive against current approaches, e.g., 1.5 times the time cost of AESA using only 3.21% of its space requirement, in a metric space of strings; and 1.09 times the time cost of AESA using only 3.83 % of its space requirement, in a metric space of documents. We also show that t-spanners provide better space-time tradeoffs than classical alternatives such as pivot-based indexes. Furthermore, we show that the concept of t-spanners has potential for large improvements.

1 Introduction

The concept of "approximate" searching has applications in a vast number of fields. Some examples are non-traditional databases (where the concept of exact search is of no use and we search for similar objects, e.g. databases storing images, fingerprints or audio clips); machine learning and classification (where a new element must be classified according to its closest existing element); image quantization and compression (where only some vectors can be represented and those that cannot must be coded as their closest representable point); text retrieval (where we look for words in a text database allowing a small number of errors, or we look for documents which are similar to a given query or document); computational biology (where we want to find a DNA or protein sequence

---

* This work has been supported in part by the Millenium Nucleus Center for Web Research, Grant P01-029-F, Mideplan, Chile (1st and 2nd authors), CYTED VII.19 RIBIDI Project (all authors), and AT&T LA Chile (2nd author).

A.H.F. Laender and A.L. Oliveira (Eds.): SPIRE 2002, LNCS 2476, pp. 298–309, 2002.

in a database allowing some errors due to typical variations); function prediction (where we want to search the most similar behavior of a function in the past so as to predict its probable future behavior); etc.

All those applications have some common characteristics. There is a universe $\mathbb{X}$ of *objects*, and a nonnegative *distance function* $d : \mathbb{X} \times \mathbb{X} \longrightarrow \mathbb{R}^+$ defined among them. This distance satisfies the three axioms that make the set a *metric space*

$$d(x, y) = 0 \quad \Leftrightarrow \quad x = y$$
$$d(x, y) = d(y, x)$$
$$d(x, z) \leq d(x, y) + d(y, z)$$

where the last one is called the "triangle inequality" and is valid for many reasonable similarity functions. The smaller the distance between two objects, the more "similar" they are. This distance is considered expensive to compute (think, for instance, in comparing two fingerprints). We have a finite *database* $\mathbb{U} \subseteq \mathbb{X}$, which is a subset of the universe of objects and can be preprocessed (to build an index, for instance). Later, given a new object from the universe (a *query q*), we must retrieve all similar elements found in the database. There are two typical queries of this kind:

(a) Retrieve all elements which are within distance r to q.
   This is, $\{x \in \mathbb{U} \ / \ d(x, q) \leq r\}$.
(b) Retrieve the k closest elements to q in $\mathbb{U}$.
   This is, $A \subseteq \mathbb{U}$ such that $|A| = k$ and $\forall x \in A, y \in \mathbb{U} - A, d(x, q) \leq d(y, q)$.

Given a database of $|\mathbb{U}| = n$ objects, all those queries can be trivially answered by performing n distance evaluations. The goal is to structure the database such that we perform less distance evaluations. Since the distance is usually expensive to compute, we take the number of distance evaluations as the measure of the search complexity. This is the approach we take in this paper.

A particular case of this problem arises when the space is $\mathbb{R}^k$. There are effective methods for this case, such as kd-trees, R-trees, X-trees, etc. [6]. However, for roughly 20 dimensions or more those structures cease to work well. We focus in this paper in general metric spaces, although the solutions are well suited also for k-dimensional spaces. It is interesting to notice that the concept of "dimensionality" can be translated to metric spaces as well: the typical feature in high dimensional spaces is that the probability distribution of distances among elements has a very concentrated histogram (with larger mean as the dimension grows), difficulting the work of any similarity search algorithm [4]. We say that a general metric space is high dimensional when its histogram of distances is concentrated.

There are a number of methods to preprocess the set in order to reduce the number of distance evaluations. All them work by discarding elements with the triangle inequality. See [4] for a recent survey.

By far, the most successful technique for searching metric spaces ever proposed is AESA [10]. Its main problem is that it requires precomputing and storing a matrix with all the $O(n^2)$ distances among the objects of $\mathbb{U}$. This high space requirement has prevented it from being seriously considered except in very small domains.

On the other hand, the concept of a t-spanner is well known in graph theory [9]. Let G be a connected graph $G(V, E)$ with a nonnegative cost function $d(e)$ assigned to its edges $e \in E$, and $d_G(u, v)$ be the cost of the cheapest path between $u, v \in V$. Then, a t-spanner of G is a subgraph $G'(V, E')$ where $E' \subseteq E$ and $\forall u, v \in V$, $d_{G'}(u, v) \leq t \cdot d_G(u, v)$. (It should be clear that $d_G(u, v) \leq d_{G'}(u, v)$ also holds because G' is a subgraph of G.) Several algorithms to build t-spanners are known [5, 7], and we have proposed some specific construction algorithms for our present metric space application [8] (complete G, metric costs, and $t < 2$). The naive construction algorithm is $O(n^4)$ time. On euclidean spaces, this drops to $O(n \log n)$. Our construction complexity [8] for general metric spaces is around $O(n^{2.2})$ in practice.

Our main idea is to combine both concepts so as to use the t-spanner as a controlled approximation to the full AESA distance matrix, so as to obtain a competitive space-time tradeoff. We show experimentally that t-spanners provide competitive performance as simple replacements of AESA. At the end, we argue that they give us tools for several improvements that are under study.

We apply the idea to approximate dictionary searching under the edit distance, which is a common problem in text databases. As an example, if we search permitting one error, a 1.4-spanner (needing only a 3.2% of the memory of AESA) needs only 26% distance evaluations over AESA. If we permit two errors the overhead in distance computations is 15%, and 46% for three errors. A classical pivot-based technique using the same amount of memory needs much more distance evaluations.

We also apply the idea to approximate document retrieval form textual database using the cosine distance. As an example, if we use a 2.0-spanner we need only a 3.8% of the memory of AESA for the index. With the 2.0-spanner index, we need only 9% distance evaluations over AESA in order to retrieve 1 document on average, and 8% distance evaluations over AESA to retrieve 10 documents on average.

2   Previous Work

Different data structures have been proposed to filter out elements at search time based on the triangle inequality [4]. In this paper we will focus on a particular class of algorithms called "pivot-based". These algorithms select a set of pivots $\{p_1 \ldots p_k\} \subseteq \mathbb{U}$ and store a table of kn distances $d(p_i, u)$, $i \in \{1 \ldots k\}$, $u \in \mathbb{U}$. To solve a range query (q, r), we measure $d(q, p_1)$ and use the fact that, because of the triangle inequality,

$$d(q, u) \geq |d(q, p) - d(u, p)|,$$

so we can discard every $u \in \mathbb{U}$ such that $|d(q, p_1) - d(u, p_1)| > r$, as this implies $d(q, u) > r$. Once we are done with p_1 we try to discard elements from the

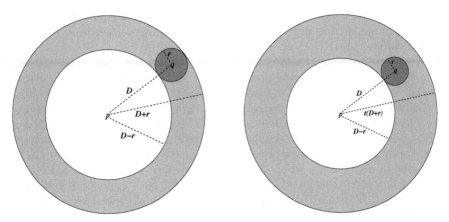

Fig. 1. On the left, the ring of elements not discarded by pivot p. On the right, the relaxed ring used when using a t-spanner. We denote as D the (real or approximated) distance between p and q

remaining set using p_2 and so on until we use all the k pivots. The elements u that still cannot be discarded at the end are directly compared against q. Fig. 1 (left) shows the concept graphically.

In AESA [10] this idea is taken to the extreme $k = n$, that is, every element is a potential pivot and hence we need a matrix with all the $n(n-1)/2$ distances precomputed. Since we are free to choose any pivot, the "next" pivot is chosen from the remaining set of elements, which improves locality and the search cost. Additionally, as it is well known that pivots closer to the query are much more effective, candidates to pivots u are sorted according to the sum of their lower bound distances to q up to now. That is, if we have used pivots $\{p_1 \dots p_i\}$ and want to choose pivot p_{i+1}, we choose the element u minimizing

$$SumLB(u) \;\; = \;\; \sum_{j=1}^{i} |d(p_j, q) - d(p_j, u)| \qquad (1)$$

AESA is experimentally shown to have almost constant cost as a function of n. The problem is that storing $O(n^2)$ distances is unrealistic for most applications. This has restricted an excellent algorithm to the few applications where n is small. Our goal in this paper is to overcome this weakness.

3   Our Proposal

Our main idea is to use t-spanners as low memory replacement of the full distance matrix, allowing a controlled approximation to the true distances. Let us assume we have a complete graph $G(\mathbb{U}, \mathbb{U} \times \mathbb{U})$, where $d(u, v) = d_G(u, v)$ is the metric space distance between elements u and v. A t-spanner $G'(\mathbb{U}, E)$ of G would permit us estimate the distance between every pair of objects within a factor t, without the need to store $O(n^2)$ distances but only $|E|$ edges. We note that, for every $u, v \in \mathbb{U}$,

$$d(u,v) \; \leq \; d_{G'}(u,v) \; \leq \; t \cdot d(u,v) \qquad (2)$$

which permits us adapting AESA to this approximated distance.

Let us return to the condition to discard an element u with a pivot p. The condition to be outside the ring can be rewritten as

$$d(p,u) \; < \; d(p,q) - r \quad \text{or} \quad d(p,u) \; > \; d(p,q) + r \; . \qquad (3)$$

If we only know $d_{G'}(p,u)$, we can use Eqs. (2) and (3) to obtain a new condition that implies Eq. (3) and hence guarantees that $d(q,u) > r$:

$$d_{G'}(p,u) \; < \; d(p,q) - r \quad \text{or} \quad d_{G'}(p,u) \; > \; t \cdot (d(p,q) + r) \; . \qquad (4)$$

Therefore, a pivot p can discard every element outside the ring $d_{G'}(p,u) \in [d(p,q) - r \, , \, t \cdot (d(p,q) + r)]$. Fig. 1 (right) illustrates.

What we have obtained is a relaxed version of AESA, which requires less memory ($O(|E|)$ instead of $O(n^2)$) and, in exchange, discards less element per pivot. As t tends to 1, our approximation becomes better but we need more and more edges. Hence we have a space-time tradeoff where the full AESA is just one extreme.

Since we have only an approximation to the distance, we cannot directly use Eq. (1). To compensate the effect of the precision factor t, we define α_t, and rewrite Eq. (1) as follows:

$$sumLB'(u) = \sum_{i=0}^{k-1} \left| d(p_i,q) - d_{G'}(p_i,u) \cdot \alpha_t \right|, \qquad \alpha_t = \frac{2/t + 1}{3} \qquad (5)$$

Our search algorithm is as follows. We start with a set of candidate nodes C, which is initially $\mathbb{U}$. Then, we choose a node $p \in C$ minimizing $SumLB'$ (Eq. (5)) and remove it from C. We measure $D = d(p,q)$ and report p if $D \leq r$. Now, we run Dijkstra's shortest path algorithm in the t-spanner starting at p, until the last node v whose distance to p gets computed satisfies $d_{G'}(v,p) > t(D+r)$. (Since Dijkstra's algorithm gives the distances to p in increasing order, we know that all the remaining nodes will be farther away.) By Eq. (4), we keep from C only the nodes u such that $D - r \leq d_{G'}(p,u) \leq t(D+r)$. We repeat these steps until $C = \emptyset$. Fig. 2 depicts the algorithm.

The analysis is similar to that of AESA. Let n_i be the number of pivots we have to consider before we can remove node u_i from C (it may be necessary to finally compare q against u_i directly). Then the number of distance computations made by AESA is $\max_{i=1...n} n_i$ and its extra CPU cost is $\sum_{i=1...n} n_i$ (which is between $O(n)$ and $O(n^2)$). In practice it is shown that the number of distance evaluations is close to $O(1)$ and the extra CPU time to $O(n)$ [10].

In our case, however, we have the additional cost of running Dijkstra. Albeit we are interested only in the nodes belonging to C, we need to compute the

```
Search (Query q, Radius r, t-Spanner G')

C ← 𝕌
α_t ← (2/t + 1)/3
for p ∈ C do SumLB(p) ← 0
while C ≠ ∅ do
    p ← argmin_{c∈C} SumLB'(c)
    C ← C − {p}
    D ← d(q,p)
    if D ≤ r then Report p
    d_{G'} ← Dijkstra(G', p, t(D + r))
    for u ∈ C do
        if d_{G'}(p,u) ∉ [D − r, t(D + r)] then
            C ← C − {u}
        else SumLB'(u) ← SumLB'(u) + |D − d_{G'}(p,v) · α_t|
```

Fig. 2. Search algorithm. Dijkstra(G', p, x) computes the distances from p in G' for all nodes up to distance x, and marks the remaining ones as "farther away"

distances to all the others to obtain the ones we need. We remark that this algorithm works only up to the point where the next closest element it extracts is far enough. Overall, this can be as bad as $O(n|E|\log n)$ or $O(n^3)$ depending on the version of Dijkstra we use. On the other hand, if we assume that we work to obtain little more than the distances we preserve in C, the overall cost is only that of AESA multiplied by $O(\log n)$. In any case, we remind that we are focusing on applications where the cost to compute d dominates even heavy extra CPU costs.

4   Experimental Results

We have tested our *t-spanner* on two real-world metric spaces. The first is a string metric space using the edit distance (a discrete function that measures the minimum number of character insertions, deletions and replacements needed to make them equal). The strings form an English dictionary, where we index a subset of $n = 23{,}023$ words. The second is a space of 1,215 documents under the Cosine distance, which is used to retrieve documents with higher rank with respect to a query (i.e., closer to the query point under Cosine distance) [1]. Both spaces are of interest to Information Retrieval applications.

As our index data structure we use *t*-spanners with precision factors $t \in [1.4, 2.0]$, and compare them against AESA. Since *t*-spanners offer a time-space tradeoff and AESA does not, we consider also pivot-based indexes with varying number of pivots. For every t value, we measure the size of the resulting *t*-spanner and build a pivot-based index using the same amount of memory (pivots are chosen at random). This way we compare *t*-spanners against the classical space-

Table 1. t-Spanner index size and distance evaluations at query time. Every edge needs two machine words of storage

t	$|E'|$	$r = 1$	$r = 2$	$r = 3$
1.4	8,507,720	27.66	98.54	723.20
1.5	3,740,705	34.55	135.59	944.13
1.6	2,658,556	39.00	167.36	1188.44
1.7	1,861,260	42.53	185.24	1205.32
1.8	1,249,313	56.15	267.22	1581.68
1.9	901,577	62.79	293.80	1763.81
2.0	626,266	96.25	471.35	2306.07

Table 2. AESA structure size and distance evaluations at query time. Every cell entry needs one machine word of storage

$n(n-1)/2$	$r = 1$	$r = 2$	$r = 3$
265,017,753	21.83	85.05	495.05

time alternative tradeoff. Note that AESA needs more than 250 millions of cells (1 gigabytes of memory) even for the relatively small example of strings.

Since in some cases the pivots were too many compared to the average number of candidates to eliminate, we decided to stop using the pivots when the remaining set of candidates was smaller than the remaining set of pivots to use. This way we never pay more for having more pivots available than necessary. Also, it turns out that even the smallest number of pivots shown is beyond the optimal sometimes. In these cases we show also the result with less pivots until we reach the optimum.

4.1   Strings under Edit Distance

In the space of strings, we select 100 queries randomly from dictionary words not included in the index, and search with radii $r = 1, 2, 3$, which return 0.0041%, 0.036% and 0.29% of the database, respectively. Tables 1, 2 and 3 show the size of the index structures tested, as well as the distance evaluations required for searching.

As seen in Tables 1 and 2, our indexes are competitive against AESA and use only a fraction of its space (e.g., only 3.21% for $t = 1.4$). With respect to pivots (Tables 1 and 3), in almost every case the corresponding t-spanners use the space better.

Figures 3, 4 and 5 present the results graphically. We have chosen to draw a line to represent AESA, although, since it permits no space-time tradeoffs, a point would be the correct representation. The position of this point in the x axis would be 132.5, far away from the right end of the plot.

Table 3. Pivot table structure and distance evaluations at query time. Every table cell needs one machine word. We have computed the amount of pivots that corresponds to the *t*-spanner size for every *t*

t	equivalent # of pivots	*r* = 1	*r* = 2	*r* = 3
1.4	739	539.48	642.65	1251.15
1.5	325	248.13	318.57	1685.52
1.6	230	181.80	268.40	2129.34
1.7	161	132.13	256.17	2845.85
1.8	108	86.75	321.08	3956.21
1.9	78	64.26	465.84	5047.14
2.0	54	49.29	748.81	6082.60

4.2 Documents under Cosine Distance

In the space of documents, we select 50 queries randomly from the document database not included in the index, and search with radii chosen to retrieve 1 or 10 documents per query ($r = 0.1325, 0.167$ respectively). Tables 4, 5 and 6 show the size of the index structures tested, as well as the distance evaluations required for searching.

As seen in Tables 4 and 5, our indexes are very competitive against AESA and use only a fraction of its space (e.g., only 3.84% for $t = 2.0$). With respect to pivots (Tables 4 and 6), in all cases the corresponding *t*-spanners use the space better.

Figures 6 and 7 present the results graphically. We have chosen to draw a line to represent AESA.

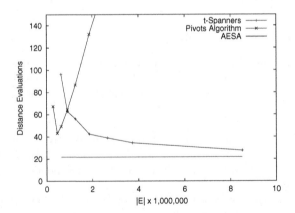

Fig. 3. Distance evaluations, search radius $r = 1$

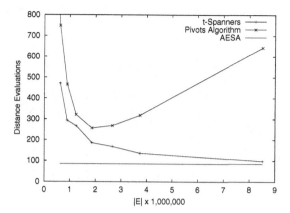

Fig. 4. Distance evaluations, search radius $r = 2$

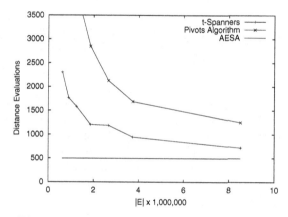

Fig. 5. Distance evaluations, search radius $r = 3$

5   Conclusions

We have presented a new approach to metric space searching, which is based on using a t-spanner data structure as an approximate map of the space. This permits us trading space for query time. We have shown experimentally that the alternative is competitive against existing solutions. In particular we have shown that t-spanners are specially competitive in applications of interest to Information Retrieval: strings under edit distance and documents under cosine distance. For example, in an approximate string matching scenario typical of text databases, we show that t-spanners provide better space-time tradeoffs compared to the classical pivot-based solutions. It also permits approximating AESA, which is an unbeaten index, within 50% of extra time using only about 3% of the space it requires. This becomes a feasible approximation to AESA, which in its

Table 4. *t*-Spanner index size and distance evaluations at query time. Every edge needs two machine words of storage

t	$|E'|$	retrieving 1 document	retrieving 10 documents
1.4	266,590	191.60	210.84
1.5	190,145	193.04	212.78
1.6	125,358	195.14	212.30
1.7	109,387	194.96	215.30
1.8	87,618	197.20	216.38
1.9	43,336	201.76	218.98
2.0	28,239	205.60	223.02

Table 5. AESA structure size and distance evaluations at query time. Every cell entry needs one machine word of storage

$n(n-1)/2$	retrieving 1 document	retrieving 10 documents
737,505	187.32	206.26

original form cannot be implemented in practice because of its quadratic memory requirements. Furthermore, for document retrieval in a textual database, we need a 9% extra time over AESA, using only 4% of its memory requirement.

On the other hand, *t*-spanners have a large potential for improvements we are pursuing. A first one is that we do not really need the same precision *t* for all the edges. Shorter edges are more important than longer edges, as Dijkstra

Table 6. Pivot table structure and distance evaluations at query time. Every table cell needs one machine word. We have computed the amount of pivots that corresponds to the *t*-spanner size for every *t*

t	equivalent # of pivots	retrieving 1 document	retrieving 10 documents
1.4	438	256.54	288.54
1.5	312	273.80	281.28
1.6	206	281.98	307.46
1.7	180	275.42	319.20
1.8	144	279.48	307.04
1.9	71	251.30	269.70
2.0	46	232.98	252.20

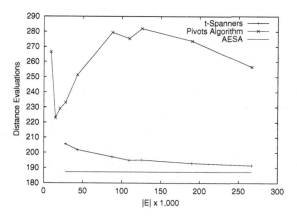

Fig. 6. Distance evaluations, search radius $r = 0.1325$, retrieving 1 document

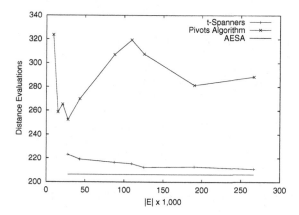

Fig. 7. Distance evaluations, search radius $r = 0.167$, retrieving 10 documents

tends to use shorter edges to build the shortest paths. Using a t that depends on the distance to estimate may give us better space-time tradeoffs.

Another idea is that we can build a t-spanner and use it as a t'-spanner, for $t' < t$. This may lose some relevant elements but improves the search time. The result is a probabilistic algorithm, which is a new successful trend in metric space searching [3, 2]. In particular, we have observed that in order to build a t-spanner, many distances are estimated better than t times the real one, so this idea seems promising. For example, a preliminary experiment in the string metric space shows that, with a 2.0-spanner and using $t' = 1.9$, we need only 53% of the distance computations to retrieve the 92% of the result.

Finally, another idea is to use the t-spanner as a navigational device. A pivot is much more effective if it is closer to the query, as the ball of candidate elements has much smaller volume. We can use the *t*-spanner edges to start at a random node and approach the query by neighbors.

References

[1] R. Baeza-Yates and B. Ribeiro-Neto. *Modern Information Retrieval*. Addison-Wesley, 1999. 303

[2] B. Bustos and G. Navarro. Probabilistic proximity searching algorithms based on compact partitions. In *Proc. 9th International Symposium on String Processing and Information Retrieval (SPIRE 2002)*, LNCS. Springer, 2002. To appear. 308

[3] E. Chávez and G. Navarro. A probabilistic spell for the curse of dimensionality. In *Proc. 3rd Workshop on Algorithm Engineering and Experiments (ALENEX'01)*, LNCS 2153, pages 147–160, 2001. 308

[4] E. Chávez, G. Navarro, R. Baeza-Yates, and J. L. Marroquin. Proximity searching in metric spaces. *ACM Computing Surveys*, 33(3):273–321, September 2001. 299, 300

[5] E. Cohen. Fast algorithms for constructing *t*-spanners and paths with stretch *t*. *SIAM J. on Computing*, 28:210–236, 1998. 300

[6] V. Gaede and O. Günther. Multidimensional access methods. *ACM Computing Surveys*, 30(2):170–231, 1998. 299

[7] J. Gudmundsson, C. Levcopoulos, and G. Narasimhan. Improved greedy algorithms for constructing sparse geometric spanners. In *Proc. 7th Scandinavian Workshop on Algorithm Theory (SWAT 2000)*, LNCS v. 1851, pages 314–327, 2000. 300

[8] G. Navarro and R. Paredes. Practical construction of metric *t*-spanners. Technical Report TR/DCC-2002-4, Dept. of Computer Science, Univ. of Chile, July 2002. 300

[9] D. Peleg and A. Schaffer. Graph spanners. *Journal of Graph Theory*, 13(1):99–116, 1989. 300

[10] E. Vidal. An algorithm for finding nearest neighbors in (approximately) constant average time. *Patt. Recog. Lett.*, 4:145–157, 1986. 299, 301, 302

Compact Directed Acyclic Word Graphs for a Sliding Window

Shunsuke Inenaga[1], Ayumi Shinohara[1,2], Masayuki Takeda[1,2], and Setsuo Arikawa[1]

[1] Department of Informatics, Kyushu University
33, Fukuoka 812-8581, Japan
[2] PRESTO, Japan Science and Technology Corporation (JST)
{s-ine,ayumi,takeda,arikawa}@i.kyushu-u.ac.jp

Abstract. The *suffix tree* is a well-known and widely-studied data structure that is highly useful for string matching. The suffix tree of a string w can be constructed in $O(n)$ time and space, where n denotes the length of w. Larsson achieved an efficient algorithm to maintain a suffix tree for a sliding window. It contributes to *prediction by partial matching* (*PPM*) style statistical data compression scheme. The *compact directed acyclic word graph* (*CDAWG*) is a more space-economical data structure for indexing a string. In this paper we propose a linear-time algorithm to maintain a CDAWG for a sliding window.

1 Introduction

String matching is one of the central tasks in data compression. A straightforward method for matching strings would be to construct an index structure for the full text to be compressed. It is, however, easy to imagine that indexing the whole string requires too much space for the storage. This fact implies that an index structure needs to be *dynamic* in order to be suitable for *processing part of the text*.

The *suffix tree* is a highly efficient data structure for string matching, therefore being extensively studied [18, 15, 1, 17, 5, 8]. $STree(w)$ represents all factors of w and can be constructed in linear time and space. The on-line algorithm by Ukkonen [17] processes a given string w from left to right, and at each j-th phase it maintains $STree(w[1:j])$, where $w[1:j]$ denotes the prefix of w of length j. Larsson [13] modified Ukkonen's algorithm so as to maintain $STree(w[i:j])$ with $0 \leq i \leq j \leq |w|$, for any factor of length $j - i + 1 = M$. The width M of indexed factors is called the *window size*. That is, Larsson presented an algorithm to maintain a suffix tree for a *sliding window* mechanism where the values of i and j are incremented.

An application of a suffix tree for a sliding window is the *prediction by partial matching* (*PPM*) style statistical data compression model [4, 3, 16]. PPM* [3] is an improvement that allows unbounded context length. PPM* employs a tree structure called the *context trie*, which supports indexes of the input string.

A.H.F. Laender and A.L. Oliveira (Eds.): SPIRE 2002, LNCS 2476, pp. 310–324, 2002.
© Springer-Verlag Berlin Heidelberg 2002

The drawback of PPM* is, however, its too much computational resources in both time and space, which weakens its practical usefulness. In particular, the context trie occupies major part of the space requirement. Larsson's suffix tree for a sliding window offered a variant of PPM*, feasible in practice since its space requirement is bounded by the window size M and the running time is linear in the length of the input string w.

In this paper, we take another approach to reduce the space requirement in PPM*-style statistical compression. We propose an algorithm to maintain a *compact directed acyclic word graph* (*CDAWG*) for a sliding window, which performs in linear time and space. CDAWGs require less space than suffix trees in both theory and practice [2, 6]. In our previous work [11], we presented an on-line algorithm that constructs $CDAWG(w)$ in linear time and space. Moving the rightmost position of a sliding window can be accomplished by the algorithm. In case of a suffix tree, it is also rather straightforward to advance the leftmost position of a sliding window: basically we have only to remove the leaf node and its in-coming edge corresponding to the longest suffix. However, since a CDAWG is a graph, the matter is much more complex and technically difficult. Thus more detailed and precise discussions are necessary. In addition, we have to ensure that no edge labels refer to positions outside a sliding window. To guarantee it, Larsson utilized the technique of *credit issuing* first introduced in [7], which takes amortized constant time. We introduce an extended version of credit issuing that is modified to be suitable for treating CDAWGs.

2   Compact Directed Acyclic Word Graphs

2.1   Definitions

Let Σ be an *alphabet*. An element of Σ^* is called a *string*. The length of a string w is denoted by $|w|$. Strings x, y, and z are said to be a *prefix*, *factor*, and *suffix* of string $w = xyz$, respectively. The sets of the prefixes, factors, and suffixes of a string w are denoted by $Prefix(w)$, $Factor(w)$, and $Suffix(w)$, respectively. The empty string is denoted by ε, that is, $|\varepsilon| = 0$. Let $\Sigma^+ = \Sigma^* - \{\varepsilon\}$. The factor of a string w that begins at position i and ends at position j is denoted by $w[i:j]$ for $1 \leq i \leq j \leq |w|$. For convenience, let $w[i:j] = \varepsilon$ for $j < i$. Let $S \subseteq \Sigma^*$. The cardinality of S is denoted by $|S|$. For any string $x \in \Sigma^*$, $Sx^{-1} = \{u \mid ux \in S\}$ and $x^{-1}S = \{u \mid xu \in S\}$. We define equivalence relations $\equiv_w^L$ and $\equiv_w^R$ on Σ^* by

$$x \equiv_w^L y \Leftrightarrow Prefix(w)x^{-1} = Prefix(w)y^{-1},$$
$$x \equiv_w^R y \Leftrightarrow x^{-1}Suffix(w) = y^{-1}Suffix(w),$$

respectively. Let $[x]_w^L$ and $[x]_w^R$ denote the equivalence classes of a string $x \in \Sigma^*$ under $\equiv_w^L$ and $\equiv_w^R$, respectively. The longest elements in the equivalence classes $[x]_w^L$ and $[x]_w^R$ for $x \in Factor(w)$ are called their *representatives* and denoted by $\overrightarrow{x}^w$ and $\overleftarrow{x}^w$, respectively. For any string $x \in Factor(w)$, there uniquely exist strings $\alpha, \beta \in \Sigma^*$ such that $\overrightarrow{x}^w = x\alpha$ and $\overleftarrow{x}^w = \beta x$.

We now introduce a relation X_w over Σ^* such that

$$X_w = \{(x, xa) \mid x \in Factor(w) \text{ and } a \in \Sigma \text{ is unique such that } xa \in Factor(w)\},$$

and let $\equiv_w'^L$ be the equivalence closure of X_w, i.e., the smallest superset of X_w that is symmetric, reflexive, and transitive. It can be readily shown that $\equiv_w^L$ is a refinement of $\equiv_w'^L$, namely, every equivalence class under $\equiv_w'^L$ is a union of one or more equivalence classes in $\equiv_w^L$. For a string $x \in Factor(w)$, let $\overrightarrow{x}$ denote the longest string in the equivalence class to which x belongs under the equivalence relation $\equiv_w'^L$.

Note that $\overset{w}{\overrightarrow{x}}$ and $\overset{w}{\overrightarrow{\overrightarrow{x}}}$ are not always equal. For example, consider the case that $w = \mathsf{abab}$ and $x = \mathsf{ab}$, where $\overset{w}{\overrightarrow{x}} = \mathsf{ab}$ but $\overset{w}{\overrightarrow{\overrightarrow{x}}} = \mathsf{abab}$. More formally:

Proposition 1 ([10]). *Let $w \in \Sigma^*$. For any string $x \in Factor(w)$, $\overset{w}{\overrightarrow{x}}$ is a prefix of $\overset{w}{\overrightarrow{\overrightarrow{x}}}$. If $\overset{w}{\overrightarrow{x}} \neq \overset{w}{\overrightarrow{\overrightarrow{x}}}$, then $\overset{w}{\overrightarrow{\overrightarrow{x}}} \in Suffix(w)$.*

In the following, we define the suffix tree and the CDAWG of w, denoted by $STree(w)$ and $CDAWG(w)$, respectively. We define them as edge-labeled graphs (V, E) with $E \subseteq V \times \Sigma^+ \times V$ where the second component of each edge represents its label. We also give definitions of the *suffix links*, frequently used for time-efficient construction of the structures [18, 15, 17, 2, 6, 11, 9].

Definition 1. *$STree(w)$ is the tree (V, E) such that*

$$V = \{\overset{w}{\overrightarrow{x}} \mid x \in Factor(w)\},$$

$$E = \{(\overset{w}{\overrightarrow{x}}, a\beta, \overset{w}{\overrightarrow{xa}}) \mid x, xa \in Factor(w), a \in \Sigma, \beta \in \Sigma^*, \overset{w}{\overrightarrow{xa}} = xa\beta, \overset{w}{\overrightarrow{x}} \neq \overset{w}{\overrightarrow{xa}}\},$$

and its suffix links are the set

$$F = \{(\overset{w}{\overrightarrow{ax}}, \overset{w}{\overrightarrow{x}}) \mid x, ax \in Factor(w), a \in \Sigma, \overset{w}{\overrightarrow{ax}} = a \cdot \overset{w}{\overrightarrow{x}}\}.$$

Definition 2. *$CDAWG(w)$ is the dag (V, E) such that*

$$V = \{[\overset{w}{\overrightarrow{x}}]_w^R \mid x \in Factor(w)\},$$

$$E = \{([\overset{w}{\overrightarrow{x}}]_w^R, a\beta, [\overset{w}{\overrightarrow{xa}}]_w^R) \mid x, xa \in Factor(w), a \in \Sigma, \beta \in \Sigma^*, \overset{w}{\overrightarrow{xa}} = xa\beta, \overset{w}{\overrightarrow{x}} \neq \overset{w}{\overrightarrow{xa}}\},$$

and its suffix links are the set

$$F = \{([\overset{w}{\overrightarrow{ax}}]_w^R, [\overset{w}{\overrightarrow{x}}]_w^R) \mid x, ax \in Factor(w), a \in \Sigma, \overset{w}{\overrightarrow{ax}} = a \cdot \overset{w}{\overrightarrow{x}}, [\overset{w}{\overrightarrow{x}}]_w^R \neq [\overset{w}{\overrightarrow{ax}}]_w^R\}.$$

One can see that $CDAWG(w)$ is the "minimization" of $STree(w)$ due to "the $[(\cdot)]_w^R$ operation".

The nodes $[\overset{w}{\overrightarrow{\varepsilon}}]_w^R = [\varepsilon]_w^R$ and $[\overset{w}{\overrightarrow{w}}]_w^R = [w]_w^R$ are called the *source* node and the *sink* node of $CDAWG(w)$, respectively. For any $x \in Factor(w)$ such that

$x = \overrightarrow{x}^w$, x is said to be represented by the *explicit* node $[\overrightarrow{x}^w]_w^R$. If $x \neq \overrightarrow{x}^w$, x is said to be on an *implicit* node. The implicit node is represented by a *reference pair* $([\overrightarrow{z}^w]_w^R, y)$ such that $z \in Prefix(x)$, $y \in \Sigma^*$ and $\overrightarrow{z}^w \cdot y = x$. When $|y|$ is minimum, the pair $([\overrightarrow{z}^w]_w^R, y)$ is called the *canonical* reference pair of x. Note that an explicit node can also be represented by a reference pair.

Proposition 1 implies that, for a string $x \in Factor(w)$, $\overrightarrow{x}^w$ is not always represented on an explicit node in $CDAWG(w)$. Actually, in $CDAWG(\text{coco})$ displayed at Fig. 1, string $\overrightarrow{\text{co}}^w = \text{co}$ is on an implicit node, where $w = \text{coco}$.

To implement $CDAWG(w)$ using only $O(|w|)$ space, labels of edges are represented by two integers indicating their beginning and ending positions in w, respectively. Suppose that $([\overrightarrow{x}^w]_w^R, y, [\overrightarrow{z}^w]_w^R)$ is an edge of $CDAWG(w)$. Then the edge label y is actually represented by a pair (i, j) of integers such that $w[i : j] = y$. A reference pair can be represented in a similar way.

2.2   On-Line Algorithm to Construct CDAWGs

We here recall the on-line algorithm to construct $CDAWG(w)$, introduced in our previous work [11]. The algorithm is based on Ukkonen's on-line suffix tree construction algorithm [17]. It constructs $CDAWG(wa)$ from $CDAWG(w)$ by inserting suffixes of wa into $CDAWG(w)$ in decreasing order of their length. Let z be the longest string in $Factor(w) \cap Suffix(wa)$. Then z is called the *longest repeated suffix* of wa and denoted by $LRS(wa)$. Let $z' = LRS(w)$. Let $|wa| = l$ and $u_1, u_2, \ldots, u_l, u_{l+1}$ be the suffixes of wa ordered in their length, that is, $u_1 = wa$ and $u_{l+1} = \varepsilon$. We categorize these suffixes into the following three groups.

(Group 1) $u_1, \ldots, u_{i-1}$
(Group 2) $u_i, \ldots, u_{j-1}$ where $u_i = z'a$
(Group 3) $u_j, \ldots, u_{l+1}$ where $u_j = z$

Note all suffixes in Group 3 have already been represented in $CDAWG(w)$. Let $v_1, \ldots, v_{i-1}$ be the suffixes of w such that, for any $1 \leq k \leq i - 1$, $v_k a = u_k$. Then we can insert all the suffixes of Group 1 into $CDAWG(w)$ by appending the character a at the end of edges leading to the sink node. Moreover, we can update those edges in constant time, by setting the ending position of the labels so to refer to a global variable e indicating the length of the scanned part of the input string. In this case, $e = l$. It therefore results in that we have only to care about those in Group 2. We start from the locus corresponding to $z' = v_i$ in $CDAWG(w)$, which is called the *active point*. If the active point is on an edge, a new explicit node is created and from there a new edge labeled by a is inserted leading to the sink node. The locus of v_{i+1} can be found by following the suffix link and possibly some downward edges. Assume v_{i+1} is also on an edge when it is found. Sometimes the edge can be *redirected* to the node created when u_i was inserted. For the detailed condition to examine whether the edge should be

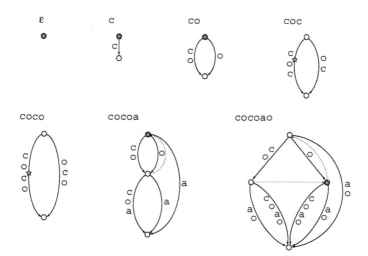

Fig. 1. The on-line construction of $CDAWG(w)$ with $w = $ cocoao. The dotted lines represent the suffix links. The gray star indicates the active point of each step

merged or not, see [11]. After the last suffix u_{j-1} is inserted to the CDAWG, all suffixes of wa are represented in the CDAWG. We now pay attention to $LRS(wa) = z = u_j$. Consider the case that $\overrightarrow{u_j}^{wa} = u_j$, that is, the case that u_j is now represented in an explicit node. Then we have to check whether or not u_j is the representative of $[u_j]_{wa}^R$. If not, the explicit node is *separated* into two explicit nodes $[x]_{wa}^R$ and $[u_j]_{wa}^R$, where $x \in [u_j]_w^R$ and $x \neq u_j$. The on-line construction of $CDAWG(w)$ with $w = $ cocoao is shown in Fig. 1.

Theorem 1 ([11]). *For any string $w \in \Sigma^*$, $CDAWG(w)$ can be constructed on-line and in $O(|w|)$ time and space.*

3   Suffix Trees for a Sliding Window

In [13], Larsson introduced an algorithm for maintaining a suffix tree for a *sliding window*, whose width is $M > 0$. Let i (resp. j) be the leftmost (resp. rightmost) position of the window sliding in w, that is, $j - i + 1 = M$. To move the sliding window ahead, we need to increment i and j. Incrementing j can be accomplished by Ukkonen's on-line algorithm. On the other hand, incrementing i means to delete the leftmost character of the currently scanned string, that is, to convert $STree(bu)$ into $STree(u)$ with some $b \in \Sigma$ and $u, bu \in Factor(w)$. We focus on the path of $STree(bu)$ which spells out bu from the root node. This path is called the *backbone* of $STree(bu)$. Let x be the longest string in $Prefix(bu) - \{bu\}$ such that $\overrightarrow{x}^{bu} = x$. The locus of x in $STree(bu)$ is called the *deletion point* and denoted by

$DelPoint(bu)$. On the other hand, let z be the longest string in $Prefix(bu) - \{bu\}$ such that $\overset{bu}{\Longrightarrow} = z$. The string z is called the *last node* in the backbone and denoted by $LastNode(bu)$.

When $DelPoint(bu) = LastNode(bu)$, there is an explicit node representing the string x in $STree(bu)$. Then there exists an edge $(\overset{bu}{\Rightarrow}, y, \overset{bu}{\Rightarrow})$ in $STree(bu)$ where $xy = bu$. Only by removing this edge, we can obtain $STree(u)$.

When $DelPoint(bu) \neq LastNode(bu)$, it follows from Proposition 1 that $x \in Suffix(bu)$. Moreover, $x = LRS(bu)$, as to be proven by Lemma 3 in Section 4.1. Namely, the active point is on the locus for x in $STree(bu)$. Let $(\overset{bu}{\Rightarrow}, y, \overset{bu}{\Rightarrow})$ be the edge on which x is represented. Let $\overset{bu}{\Rightarrow} \cdot t = x$, where $t \in Prefix(y)$. We *shorten* the edge to $(\overset{u}{\Rightarrow}, t, \overset{u}{\Rightarrow})$, and move the active point to the locus for the one-character shorter suffix of x.

Theorem 2 ([13]). *Let $w \in \Sigma^*$ and M be the window size. Larsson's algorithm runs in $O(|w|)$ time using $O(M)$ space.*

4   CDAWGs for a Sliding Window

In this section, we consider the maintenance of a CDAWG for a sliding window. Advancing the rightmost position of the window can be done by the on-line algorithm recalled in Section 2.2. Thus the matter is to move ahead the leftmost position of the window.

4.1   Edge Deletion

Given $CDAWG(w)$, we also focus on its backbone, the path spelling out w from the source node. Let $x = DelPoint(w)$. If $DelPoint(w) = LastNode(w)$, we remove the edge $([\overset{w}{\Rightarrow}]^R_w, y, [\overset{w}{\Rightarrow}]^R_w)$ such that $xy = w$. However, notice that this method might remove other suffixes of w from the CDAWG. More precise arguments follow.

Lemma 1. *Let $w \in \Sigma^+$, $x = DelPoint(w)$, and $z = LastNode(w)$. Assume $x = z$. Let s be any string in $[\overset{w}{\Rightarrow}]^R_w = [\overset{w}{\Rightarrow}]^R_w$. Then there uniquely exists a string $y \in \Sigma^+$ such that $sy \in Suffix(w)$.*

Proof. Since $x = DelPoint(w)$, there uniquely exists a character $a \in \Sigma$ such that $xa \in Factor(w)$ and $\overset{w}{\overrightarrow{xa}} = w$. Let y be the string such that $xy = w$ with $y \in \Sigma^+$, where the first character of y is a. Let s be an arbitrary element in $[x]^R_w$. Since $x \in Prefix(w)$, $\overset{w}{\overleftarrow{x}} = x$. Thus $s \in Suffix(x)$, which implies $sy \in Suffix(w)$.   □

For the case that $DelPoint(w) \neq LastNode(w)$, we have the following.

Lemma 2. *Let* $w \in \Sigma^+$, $x = DelPoint(w)$, *and* $z = LastNode(w)$. *Assume* $x \neq z$. *Let* s *be any string in* $[\overset{w}{\overrightarrow{z}}]_w^R$. *Then there uniquely exist strings* $t, u \in \Sigma^+$ *such that* $st \in Suffix(x)$ *and* $stu \in Suffix(w)$.

Proof. Since $\overset{w}{\overrightarrow{z}} = z$, $\overset{w}{\overrightarrow{z}} = z$. By the assumption that $z \neq x$, we have $z \in Prefix(x)$. Since $x = DelPoint(w)$, there uniquely exists a character $a \in \Sigma$ such that $\overset{w}{\overrightarrow{za}} = x$. Thus there is a unique string $t \in \Sigma^+$ such that $zt = x$. Since $z \in Prefix(w)$, $z = \overset{w}{\overleftarrow{z}}$. Therefore, for any string $s \in [z]_w^R$ it holds that $st \in Suffix(x)$. Moreover, there uniquely exists a character $b \in \Sigma$ such that $\overset{w}{\overrightarrow{xb}} = w$. Let $u \in \Sigma^+$ be the string satisfying $\overset{w}{\overrightarrow{xb}} = xu$. Now we have $ztu = w$, and for any $s \in [z]_w^R$, it holds that $stu \in Suffix(w)$. $\square$

Lemma 3. *Let* $w \in \Sigma^+$, $x = DelPoint(w)$, *and* $z = LastNode(w)$. *Assume* $x \neq z$. *Then* $x = LRS(w)$.

Proof. Since $x \neq z$, $\overset{w}{\overrightarrow{x}} \neq \overset{w}{\overrightarrow{x}}$. Hence $\overset{w}{\overrightarrow{x}} = x \in Suffix(w)$ by Proposition 1. It is not difficult to show that x occurs in w just twice. Let $y = ax$ with $a \in \Sigma$, such that $y \in Suffix(w)$. Assume, for a contradiction, $y = LRS(w)$. On the assumption, y appears in w at least twice. If $y \notin Prefix(w)$, y must also occur in w as neither a prefix nor a suffix of w. It turns out that x appears three times in w: a contradiction. If $y \in Prefix(w)$, x is of the form a^ℓ. Then $y = DelPoint(w)$, which contradicts the assumption that $x = DelPoint(w)$. Consequently, $x = LRS(w)$. $\square$

According to the above three lemmas, we obtain the following theorem.

Theorem 3. *Let* $w \in \Sigma^+$, $x = DelPoint(w)$, *and* $z = LastNode(w)$. *Let* $k = |[\overset{w}{\overrightarrow{z}}]_w^R|$. *Suppose* $u_1, u_2, \ldots, u_k$ *be the suffixes of* w *arranged in decreasing order of their length, where* $u_1 = w$.

1. *When* $x = z$: *Let* $xy = w$. *Assume that the edge* $([\overset{w}{\overrightarrow{x}}]_w^R, y, [\overset{w}{\overrightarrow{w}}]_w^R)$ *is deleted from* $CDAWG(w)$.

2. *When* $x \neq z$: *Let* $zt = x$ *and* $ztu = w$. *Assume that the edge* $([\overset{w}{\overrightarrow{z}}]_w^R, tu, [\overset{w}{\overrightarrow{w}}]_w^R)$ *of* $CDAWG(w)$ *is shortened into the edge* $([\overset{w}{\overrightarrow{z}}]_w^R, t, [\overset{w}{\overrightarrow{x}}]_w^R)$.

In both cases, the suffixes $u_1, \ldots, u_k$ *are removed from the CDAWG.*

What the above theorem implies is that after deleting or shortening the last edge in the backbone of $CDAWG(w)$, the leftmost position of a sliding window "skips" k characters at once. Let $DelSize(w) = k$. The next question is the exact upper bound of $DelSize(w)$. Fortunately, we achieve a reasonable result such that $DelSize(w)$ is at most about half of $|w|$. A more precise evaluation will be performed in Section 4.4.

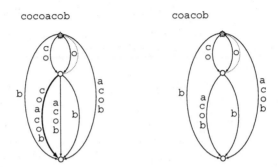

Fig. 2. On the left, $CDAWG(\texttt{cocoacob})$ is shown. The thick edge is to be deleted. The resulting structure is $CDAWG(\texttt{coacob})$, shown on the right. The gray star indicates the active point for each

Can't we delete only the leftmost character of w in (amortized) constant time? We strongly believe the answer is "No". The reason is as follows. Let $|w| = n$ where $w \in \Sigma^*$. Let $u_1, u_2, \ldots, u_{n+1}$ be all the suffixes of w arranged in decreasing order of their length. In [12], it has been proven that the total number of nodes necessary to keep $CDAWG(u_i)$ for every $1 \le i \le n+1$ is $\Theta(n^2)$, even if we minimize the CDAWGs so to share as many nodes and edges as possible. Therefore, the amortized time complexity to delete the leftmost character of w would be proportional to n.

4.2   Maintaining the Structure of CDAWG

Suppose the last edge of the backbone of $CDAWG(w)$ is deleted or shortened right now. Let $k = DelSize(w)$. Let $u = w[k + 1 : n]$ where $n = |w|$. We sometimes need to modify the structure of the current graph, so that it exactly becomes $CDAWG(u)$. The *out-degree* of a node v is denoted by $OutDeg(v)$. Let $x = DelPoint(w)$ of $CDAWG(w)$.

Firstly, we consider when $OutDeg([\overrightarrow{x}]_w^R) \ge 3$ in the first cast of Theorem 3. In this case, $\overrightarrow{x}^u = x$ and $OutDeg([\overrightarrow{x}^u]_u^R) \ge 2$. It does not contradict Definition 2, and thus no more maintenance is required. An example of the case is shown in Fig. 2.

Secondly, we consider when $OutDeg([\overrightarrow{x}^w]_w^R) = 2$ in the first case of Theorem 3. Let $([\overrightarrow{r}^w]_w^R, s, [\overrightarrow{x}^w]_w^R)$ be an arbitrary in-coming edge of the node $[\overrightarrow{x}^w]_w^R$ in $CDAWG(w)$. Assume $\overrightarrow{r}^w = r$, that is, $rs \in Suffix(x)$. Let $([\overrightarrow{x}^w]_w^R, t, [\overrightarrow{w}^w]_w^R)$ be the edge which is to be the sole remaining out-going edge of the node $[\overrightarrow{x}^w]_w^R$ after the deletion. Notice that, however, $\overrightarrow{x}^u = u$. Thus the edge $([\overrightarrow{r}^w]_w^R, s, [\overrightarrow{x}^w]_w^R)$ is

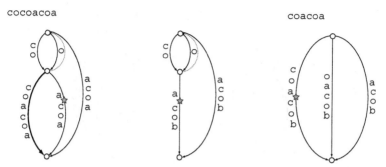

Fig. 3. On the left, $CDAWG(\text{cocoacoa})$ is shown, where the thick edge is to be deleted. The center is the intermediate structure in which the edge is deleted. After the modifications, we obtain $CDAWG(\text{coacoa})$, shown on the right. The gray star indicates the active point for each

modified to $([\overset{u}{\overrightarrow{r}}]_u^R, st, [\overset{u}{\overrightarrow{u}}]_u^R)$. The total time required in the operations is proportional to the number of in-coming edges of the node $[\overset{w}{\overrightarrow{x}}]_w^R$ in $CDAWG(w)$. It is bounded by $DelSize(w)$.

Moreover, we might need a maintenance of the active point. Let $v = LRS(w)$. Supposing that $v \in Prefix(xt)$, v is represented on the edge $([\overset{w}{\overrightarrow{x}}]_w^R, t, [\overset{w}{\overrightarrow{w}}]_w^R)$ in $CDAWG(w)$. The active point is actually referred to as the pair $([\overset{w}{\overrightarrow{x}}]_w^R, p)$, where $p \in Prefix(t)$ and $xp = v$. The reference pair is modified to $([\overset{u}{\overrightarrow{r}}]_u^R, sp)$ in $CDAWG(u)$. Note that $\overset{u}{\overleftarrow{r}} \cdot sp = v$. An example of the case is shown in Fig. 3.

Thirdly, we consider the second case in Theorem 3. In this case, the last edge in the backbone, $([\overset{w}{\overrightarrow{z}}]_w^R, tu, [\overset{w}{\overrightarrow{u}}]_w^R)$, is shortened into $([\overset{u}{\overrightarrow{z}}]_u^R, t, [\overset{u}{\overrightarrow{x}}]_u^R) = ([\overset{u}{\overrightarrow{z}}]_u^R, t, [\overset{u}{\overrightarrow{u}}]_u^R)$ in $CDAWG(u)$. It implies that $x \neq LRS(u)$, although $x = LRS(w)$. The active point of $CDAWG(w)$ is represented by $([\overset{w}{\overrightarrow{z}}]_w^R, t)$, since $zt = x$ (by Lemma 3). Let $SufLink([\overset{w}{\overrightarrow{z}}]_w^R) = [\overset{w}{\overrightarrow{s}}]_w^R$. Assuming $\overset{w}{\overrightarrow{s}} = s$, s is the longest string such that $s \in Suffix(z)$ and $s \notin [\overset{w}{\overrightarrow{z}}]_w^R$. Notice that $LRS(u) = st$. Hereby, the reference pair of the active point is changed to $([\overset{u}{\overrightarrow{s}}]_u^R, t)$. If $[\overset{u}{\overrightarrow{s}}]_u^R$ is the explicit parent node nearest the locus of st, we are done. If not, the reference pair is canonized to $([\overset{u}{\overrightarrow{r}}]_u^R, p)$ such that $s \in Prefix(\overset{u}{\overrightarrow{r}})$, $st = \overset{u}{\overrightarrow{r}} \cdot p$, and $|p|$ is minimum. An example of the case is shown in Fig. 4.

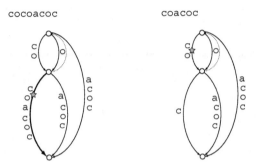

Fig. 4. On the left, $CDAWG(\texttt{cocoacoc})$ is shown. The thick edge is to be shortened. The resulting structure is $CDAWG(\texttt{coacoc})$, shown on the right. The gray star indicates the active point for each

4.3   Detecting $DelPoint(u)$

Suppose that after the edge deletion or shortening of $CDAWG(w)$, we got $CDAWG(u)$, where $u \in Suffix(w)$. The problem is how to locate $DelPoint(u)$ in $CDAWG(u)$. A naive solution is to traverse the backbone of $CDAWG(u)$ from the source node. However, it takes $O(|u|)$ time, which leads to quadratic time complexity in total.

Our approach is to keep track of the *advanced point* that corresponds to the locus of $w[1 : n - 1]$, where $n = |w|$. Let $x = LastNode(w)$ and $xy = w$, that is, $([\overset{w}{\overrightarrow{x}}]^R_w, y, [\overset{w}{\overrightarrow{w}}]^R_w)$ is the edge for deletion or shortening. The canonical reference pair for the advanced point is $([\overset{w}{\overrightarrow{x}}]^R_w, t)$, where $t \in Prefix(y)$ and $\overset{w}{\overrightarrow{x}} \cdot t = w[1 : n - 1]$. We move to node $[\overset{w}{\overrightarrow{s}}]^R_w = SufLink([\overset{w}{\overrightarrow{x}}]^R_w)$. Suppose $CDAWG(w)$ has already been converted to $CDAWG(u)$. Assume $[\overset{u}{\overrightarrow{s}}]^R_u = [\overset{w}{\overrightarrow{s}}]^R_w$. Since $\overset{u}{\overrightarrow{s}} \cdot t = u[1 : m - 1]$ where $m = |u|$, $([\overset{u}{\overrightarrow{s}}]^R_u, t)$ is a reference pair of the next advanced point, and then it is canonized. Let $([\overset{u}{\overrightarrow{s'}}]^R_u, t')$ be the canonical reference pair of the advanced point. Then $\overset{u}{\overrightarrow{s'}} = LastNode(u)$. If $LastNode(u) \notin Prefix(LRS(u))$, that is, if the active point is not on the longest out-going edge from the node $[\overset{u}{\overrightarrow{s'}}]^R_u$, $DelPoint(u) = LastNode(u)$. Otherwise, $DelPoint(u) = LRS(u)$. In the case that $[\overset{u}{\overrightarrow{s}}]^R_u \neq [\overset{w}{\overrightarrow{s}}]^R_w$, we perform the same procedure from its closest parent node (see Fig. 3). If Σ is fixed, the cost of canonizing the reference pair is only proportional to the number of nodes included in the path. The amortized number of such nodes is constant.

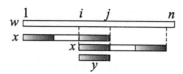

Fig. 5. The case $j > \frac{n}{2}$. x occurs at least twice in w, and the overlap y is in fact both a prefix and a suffix of x

4.4   On Buffer Size

The main theorem of this section shows an exact estimation of the upperbound of $DelSize(w)$. For an alphabet Σ and an integer n, we define $MaxDel_\Sigma(n) = \max\{DelSize(w) \mid w \in \Sigma^*, |w| = n\}$.

Theorem 4. *If* $|\Sigma| \geq 3$, $MaxDel_\Sigma(n) = \lceil \frac{n}{2} \rceil - 1$.

By this theorem, edge deletion or edge shortening can shrink the window size upto the half of the original size. Therefore, in order to keep the window size at least M, a buffer of size $2M + 1$ is necessary and sufficient.

We will prove the above theorem in the sequel.

Lemma 4. *Let* $w \in \Sigma^*$. *For any string* $x \in Factor(w)$, *let* $SufLink([\overset{w}{\overrightarrow{x}}]^R_w) = [\overset{w}{\overrightarrow{s}}]^R_w$. *Then* $|[\overset{w}{\overrightarrow{x}}]^R_w| = |\overset{w}{\overrightarrow{x}}| - |\overset{w}{\overrightarrow{s}}|$.

Proof. $|[\overset{w}{\overrightarrow{x}}]^R_w| = |Suffix(\overset{w}{\overrightarrow{x}})| - |Suffix(\overset{w}{\overrightarrow{s}})| = (|\overset{w}{\overrightarrow{x}}|+1) - (|\overset{w}{\overrightarrow{s}}|+1) = |\overset{w}{\overrightarrow{x}}| - |\overset{w}{\overrightarrow{s}}|$. $\qquad\square$

Lemma 5. *Let* $w \in \Sigma^*$ *and* $n = |w|$. *For any* $x \in Prefix(w) - \{w\}$ *with* $\overset{w}{\overrightarrow{x}} = x$, $|[\overset{w}{\overrightarrow{x}}]^R_w| \leq \lceil \frac{n}{2} \rceil - 1$.

Proof. Let $j = |x| = |\overset{w}{\overrightarrow{x}}|$. Let $SufLink([\overset{w}{\overrightarrow{x}}]^R_w) = [\overset{w}{\overrightarrow{s}}]^R_w$. We have the following three cases.

(1) When $j < \frac{n}{2}$: Since j is an integer, $j \leq \lceil \frac{n}{2} \rceil - 1$, and $|[\overset{w}{\overrightarrow{x}}]^R_w| = |\overset{w}{\overrightarrow{x}}| - |\overset{w}{\overrightarrow{s}}| \leq \lceil \frac{n}{2} \rceil - 1$ by Lemma 4.

(2) When $j > \frac{n}{2}$: (See Fig. 5.) The equivalences $x = w[1 : j]$ and $\overset{w}{\overrightarrow{x}} = x$ imply that $x = w[i : i + j - 1]$ for some $i \geq 2$ and $i + j - 1 \leq n$. Then $i - j \leq n - 2j + 1 < 1$, that is, $i \leq j$. Let $y = w[i : j]$. Its length is $|y| = j - i + 1 \geq 1$, and $y = x[i : j] \in Suffix(x)$. Since $\overset{w}{\overrightarrow{x}} = x$ and $y \in Suffix(x)$, $\overset{w}{\overrightarrow{y}} = y$. On the other hand, $y = w[i : j] = x[1 : j-i+1] = w[1 : j - i + 1] \in Prefix(w)$, which implies $\overset{w}{\overleftarrow{y}} = y$. Thus y is the longest element of $[\overset{w}{\overrightarrow{y}}]^R_w$. Since $|x| > |y|$, $x \notin [\overset{w}{\overrightarrow{y}}]^R_w$. Therefore $|\overset{w}{\overrightarrow{s}}| \geq |y|$, which yields

$$|[\overrightarrow{x}]_w^R| = |\overrightarrow{x}| - |\overrightarrow{s}| \leq |x| - |y| = j - (j - i + 1) = i - 1 \leq n - j < n - \tfrac{n}{2} = \tfrac{n}{2}.$$

Thus $|[\overrightarrow{x}]_w^R| \leq \lceil \tfrac{n}{2} \rceil - 1$.

(3) When $j = \tfrac{n}{2}$: Since $\overrightarrow{x} = x$, x occurs in w at least twice. If $x = w[i : i + j - 1]$ for some i with $2 \leq i \leq j$, we can show the inequality holds in the same way as (2). Otherwise, $x = w[j + 1 : 2j] = w[j + 1 : n] = w[1 : j]$, that is $w = xx$. Then $\overrightarrow{x} = w \neq x$, which does not satisfy the precondition of the lemma.

In any cases, we have got the result. $\square$

We are ready to prove the upperbound of $MaxDel_\Sigma(n)$.

Lemma 6. $MaxDel_\Sigma(n) \leq \lceil \tfrac{n}{2} \rceil - 1$ for any Σ and any $n \geq 3$.

Proof. Let $x = DelPoint(w)$ and $z = LastNode(w)$. First we consider the case $x = z$. Since $\overrightarrow{x} = x$ and $x \in Prefix(w) - \{w\}$, $DelSize(w) = |[\overrightarrow{z}]_w^R| = |[\overrightarrow{x}]_w^R| \leq \lceil \tfrac{n}{2} \rceil - 1$ by Lemma 5.

We now assume $x \neq z$. Then $z \in Prefix(x)$, and $x = DelPoint(w)$ implies that $x \in Prefix(w) - \{w\}$, which yields $z \in Prefix(w) - \{w\}$. Thus by Lemma 5,

$$DelSize(w) = |[\overrightarrow{z}]_w^R| \leq \lceil \tfrac{n}{2} \rceil - 1.$$ $\square$

On the other hand, the lowerbound is given by the following lemma.

Lemma 7. If $|\Sigma| \geq 3$, $MaxDel_\Sigma(n) \geq \lceil \tfrac{n}{2} \rceil - 1$ for any $n \geq 1$.

Proof. For each $1 \leq n \leq 4$, the inequality trivially holds since $\lceil \tfrac{n}{2} \rceil - 1 \leq 1$. Let a, b, c be distinct symbols in Σ. For each odd $n \geq 5$, let $w_n = a^k b a^k b c$, where $k = \tfrac{n-3}{2}$. Remark that $DelPoint(w_n) = a^k b$. Let $x = a^k b$. We can see that any suffix of x except ε belongs to $[\overrightarrow{x}]_w^R$, so that $SufLink(x) = \varepsilon$. Thus $DelSize(w_n) = |x| - |\varepsilon| = |a^k b| - 0 = k + 1 = \tfrac{n-1}{2} = \lceil \tfrac{n}{2} \rceil - 1$, since n is odd. For each even $n \geq 6$, let $w_n' = a^{k-1} b a^k b c$, where $k = \tfrac{n}{2} - 1$, and we can verify that $DelSize(w_n') = \lceil \tfrac{n}{2} \rceil - 1$ similarly. $\square$

Consequently, Theorem 4 is proved by Lemma 6 and Lemma 7. We note that for a binary alphabet $\Sigma = \{a, b\}$, two series of the strings $a^k b a^k bab$ and $a^{k-1} b a^k bab$ give the lowerbound $MaxDel_\Sigma(n) \geq \lceil \tfrac{n-3}{2} \rceil$.

On the on-line algorithm of [11], each node $[\overrightarrow{x}]_w^R$ of $CDAWG(w)$ stores the value of $|\overrightarrow{x}|$. By Lemma 4, it is guaranteed that we can calculate $DelSize(w)$ in constant time with no additional information.

4.5   Keeping Edge Labels Valid

As mentioned previously, an edge label is actually represented by a pair of integers indicating its beginning and ending positions in input string w, respectively.

We must ensure that no edge label becomes "out of date" after the window slides, e.g., that no integer refers to a position outside the sliding window. In case of a suffix tree, when a new edge is created, we can guarantee the above regulation by traversing from the leaf node toward the root node while updating all edge labels encountered. However, this would yield quadratic time complexity in the aggregate. Larsson [13, 14] utilized *credit issuing*, an update-number-restriction technique, originally proposed in [7], which takes in total $O(|w|)$ time and space. In the following, we introduce an extended credit issuing technique for CDAWGs. Our basic strategy is to show that we can handle the credit issuing as well as in case of suffix trees.

We assign each internal node s of $CDAWG(w)$ a binary counter called *credit*, denoted by $Cred(s)$. This credit counter is initially set to zero when s is created. When a node s receives a credit, we update the labels of in-coming edges of s. Then, if $Cred(s) = 0$, we set it to one, and stop. If $Cred(s) = 1$, after setting it to zero, we let the node s issue a credit to its parent nodes.

When s is newly created, $Cred(s) = 0$. The creation of the new node s implies that a new edge is to be inserted from s to the sink node. When the new edge is created leading to the sink node, the sink node *issues* a credit to the parent node s. Assume the new edge is labeled by pair (i, j) where i, j are some integers with $i < j$. Let ℓ be the length of the label of the in-coming edge of s. After s received a credit from the sink node, we reset its in-coming edge label to $(i - \ell, i - 1)$. Remember the edge redirection happening in the construction of a CDAWG (see Section 2.2 or [11]). If some edge is actually redirected to node s, its label is updated as well. Note that we need not change the value of $Cred(s)$ again.

Suppose a node r has right now received a credit from one of its child nodes. Assume $Cred(r)$ is currently one. We need to update all in-coming edge labels of r. We store a list in r to maintain its in-coming edges arranged in the order of the length of the path they correspond to. The maintenence of the list is an easy matter, since the on-line algorithm of [11] inserts edges to r in such order. Let t be an arbitrary parent node of r. Let k be the number of the in-coming edges of r connected from t. One might wonder that r must issue k credits to t, but there is the following time-efficient method. In case k is even, $Cred(t)$ need not to be changed because it is a *binary* counter. Contrarily, in case k is odd, we always change the value of $Cred(t)$. If $Cred(t)$ was one, we also have to update the in-coming edge of t. To do it, we focus on the *shortest* in-coming edge of r connected from t, which is in turn the shortest out-going edge of t leading to r. In updating the in-coming edges of t, we should utilize the label of the shortest edge, since the label corresponds to the possibly newest occurrence of the factors represented in node t. We continue updating edge labels by traversing the reversed graph rooted at r in width-first manner while issuing credits.

Recall the node separation in constructing a CDAWG (see Section 2.2 or [11]). Assume a node r has right now been created owing to the separation of a node s. The subgraph rooted at r is currently the same as the one rooted at s, since r was created as a clone of s. Thus we simply set $Cred(r) = Cred(s)$.

Now consider a node u to be deleted, corresponding to the second case of Section 4.2. It might have received a credit from its newest child node (that is not deleted), which has not been issued to its parent node yet. Therefore, when a node u is scheduled for deletion and $Cred(u) = 1$, node u issues credits to its parent nodes. However, this complicates the update of edge labels: several waiting credits may aggregate, causing nodes upper in the CDAWG to receive a credit *older* than the one it has already received from its another child node. Therefor, before updating an edge label, we compare its previous value against the one associated with the received credit, and refer to the newer one. As well as the case of edge insertion mentioned in the above paragraph, we traverse the reversed graph rooted at u in width-first fashion to update edge labels. In the worst case, the updating cost is proportional to the number of paths from the source node to node u. Nevertheless, it is bounded by $DelSize(w)$.

By analogous arguments to [7, 13, 14], we can establish the following lemma.

Lemma 8. *All edge labels of a CDAWG can be kept valid in a sliding window, in linear time and space with respect to the length of an input string.*

As a conclusion of Section 4, we finally obtain the following.

Theorem 5. *Let $w \in \Sigma^*$ and M be the window size. The proposed algorithm runs in $O(|w|)$ time using $O(M)$ space.*

5   Conclusion

We introduced an algorithm to maintain CDAWGs for a sliding window, which runs in linear time and space. It can be an alternative of Larsson's suffix tree algorithm in [13]. Moreover, CDAWGs are known to be more space-economical than suffix trees [2, 6], and thus our algorithm seems to contribute to reducing the space requirement in PPM*-style data compression scheme. We are currently implementing our algorithm to experimentally evaluate its efficiency in both time and space.

Acknowledgment

We wish to thank Ricardo Garcia and Veli Mäkinen who suggested us to apply our previous work [11] to the sliding window mechanism. We also appreciate Ricardo Garcia's fruitful comments and suggestions in the early stage of this work.

References

[1] A. Apostolico. The myriad virtues of subword trees. In A. Apostolico and Z. Galil, editors, *Combinatorial Algorithm on Words*, volume 12 of *NATO Advanced Science Institutes, Series F*, pages 85–96. Springer-Verlag, 1985. 310

[2] A. Blumer, J. Blumer, D. Haussler, R. McConnell, and A. Ehrenfeucht. Complete inverted files for efficient text retrieval and analysis. *J. ACM*, 34(3):578–595, 1987. 311, 312, 323

[3] J. G. Cleary, W. J. Teahan, and I. H. Witten. Unbounded length contexts for PPM. In *Proc. Data Compression Conference '95 (DCC'95)*, pages 52–61. IEEE Computer Society, 1995. 310

[4] J. G. Cleary and I. H. Witten. Data compression using adaptive coding and partial string matching. *IEEE Trans. Commun.*, 32(4):396–402, 1984. 310

[5] M. Crochemore and W. Rytter. *Text Algorithms*. Oxford University Press, New York, 1994. 310

[6] M. Crochemore and R. Vérin. On compact directed acyclic word graphs. In J. Mycielski, G. Rozenberg, and A. Salomaa, editors, *Structures in Logic and Computer Science*, volume 1261 of *Lecture Notes in Computer Science*, pages 192–211. Springer-Verlag, 1997. 311, 312, 323

[7] E. R. Fiala and D. H. Greene. Data compression with finite windows. *Commun. ACM*, 32(4):490–505, 1989. 311, 322, 323

[8] D. Gusfield. *Algorithms on Strings, Trees, and Sequences*. Cambridge University Press, New York, 1997. 310

[9] S. Inenaga, H. Hoshino, A. Shinohara, M. Takeda, and S. Arikawa. Construction of the CDAWG for a trie. In *Proc. The Prague Stringology Conference '01 (PSC'01)*. Czech Technical University, 2001. 312

[10] S. Inenaga, H. Hoshino, A. Shinohara, M. Takeda, and S. Arikawa. On-line construction of symmetric compact directed acyclic word graphs. In *Proc. 8th International Symposium on String Processing and Information Retrieval (SPIRE'01)*, pages 96–110. IEEE Computer Society, 2001. 312

[11] S. Inenaga, H. Hoshino, A. Shinohara, M. Takeda, S. Arikawa, G. Mauri, and G. Pavesi. On-line construction of compact directed acyclic word graphs. In A. Amir and G. M. Landau, editors, *Proc. 12th Annual Symposium on Combinatorial Pattern Matching (CPM'01)*, volume 2089 of *Lecture Notes in Computer Science*, pages 169–180. Springer-Verlag, 2001. 311, 312, 313, 314, 321, 322, 323

[12] S. Inenaga, A. Shinohara, M. Takeda, H. Bannai, and S. Arikawa. Space-economical construction of index structures for all suffixes of a string. In *Proc. 27th International Symposium on Mathematical Foundations of Computer Science (MFCS'02)*, Lecture Notes in Computer Science. Springer-Verlag, 2002. (to appear). 317

[13] N. J. Larsson. Extended application of suffix trees to data compression. In *Proc. Data Compression Conference '96 (DCC'96)*, pages 190–199. IEEE Computer Society, 1996. 310, 314, 315, 322, 323

[14] N. J. Larsson. *Structures of String Matching and Data Compression*. PhD thesis, Lund University, 1999. 322, 323

[15] E. M. McCreight. A space-economical suffix tree construction algorithm. *J. ACM*, 23(2):262–272, 1976. 310, 312

[16] A. Moffat. Implementing the PPM data compression scheme. *IEEE Trans. Commun.*, 38(11):1917–1921, 1990. 310

[17] E. Ukkonen. On-line construction of suffix trees. *Algorithmica*, 14(3):249–260, 1995. 310, 312, 313

[18] P. Weiner. Linear pattern matching algorithms. In *Proc. 14th Annual Symposium on Switching and Automata Theory*, pages 1–11, 1973. 310, 312

Indexing Text Using the Ziv-Lempel Trie

Gonzalo Navarro

Dept. of Computer Science, Univ. of Chile
Blanco Encalada 2120, Santiago, Chile gnavarro@dcc.uchile.cl
Partially supported by Fondecyt Grant 1-020831

Abstract. Let a text of u characters over an alphabet of size σ be compressible to n symbols by the LZ78 or LZW algorithm. We show that it is possible to build a data structure based on the Ziv-Lempel trie that takes $4n \log_2 n(1 + o(1))$ bits of space and reports the R occurrences of a pattern of length m in worst case time $O(m^2 \log(m\sigma) + (m+R) \log n)$.

1 Introduction

Modern text databases have to face two opposed goals. On the one hand, they have to provide fast access to the text. On the other, they have to use as little space as possible. The goals are opposed because, in order to provide fast access, an *index* has to be built on the text. An index is a data structure built on the text and stored in the database, hence increasing the space requirement. In recent years there has been much research on *compressed text databases*, focusing on techniques to represent the text and the index in succinct form, yet permitting efficient text searching.

Let our text $T_{1...u}$ be a sequence of characters over an alphabet Σ of size σ, and let the search pattern $P_{1...m}$ be another (short) sequence over Σ. Then the text search problem consists of finding all the occurrences of P in T.

Despite that there has been some work on succinct inverted indexes for natural language for a while [24, 21], until a short time ago it was believed that any general index for string matching would need $\Omega(u)$ space. In practice, the smaller indexes available were the suffix arrays [17], requiring $u \log_2 u$ bits to index a text of u characters, which required $u \log_2 \sigma$ bits to be represented, so the index is in practice larger than the text (typically 4 times the text size).

In the last decade, several attempts to reduce the space of the suffix trees [2] or arrays have been made by Kärkkäinen and Ukkonen [10, 13], Kurtz [15] and Mäkinen [16], obtaining reasonable improvements, albeit no spectacular ones (at best 9 times the text size). Moreover, they have concentrated on the space requirement of the data structure only, needing the text separately available.

Grossi and Vitter [8] presented a suffix array compression method for binary texts, which needed $O(u)$ bits and was able to report all the R occurrences of P in T in $O\left(\frac{m}{\log u} + (R+1) \log^\varepsilon u\right)$ time. However, they need the text as well as the index in order to answer queries.

Following this line, Sadakane [22] presented a suffix array implementation for general texts (not only binary) that requires $u \left(\frac{1}{\varepsilon} H_0 + 8 + 3 \log_2 H_0\right) (1 +$

A.H.F. Laender and A.L. Oliveira (Eds.): SPIRE 2002, LNCS 2476, pp. 325–336, 2002.

$o(1)) + \sigma \log_2 \sigma$ bits, where H_0 is the zero-order entropy of the text. This index can search in time $O(m \log u + R \log^\varepsilon u)$ and contains enough information to reproduce the text: any piece of text of length L is obtained in $O(L + \log^\varepsilon u)$ time. This means that the index *replaces* the text, which can hence be deleted. This is an *opportunistic* scheme, i.e., the index takes less space if the text is compressible. Yet there is a minimum of $8u$ bits of space which has to be paid independently of the entropy of the text.

Ferragina and Manzini [5] presented a different approach to compress the suffix array based on the Burrows-Wheeler transform and block sorting. They need $5uH_k + O\left(u \frac{\log\log u + \sigma \log \sigma}{\log u}\right)$ bits and can answer queries in $O(m + R \log^\varepsilon u)$ time, where H_k is the k-th order entropy and the formula is valid for any constant k. This scheme is also opportunistic. However, there is a large constant $\sigma \log \sigma$ involved in the sublinear part which does not decrease with the entropy, and a huge additive constant larger than σ^σ. (In a real implementation [6] they removed these constants at the price of a not guaranteed search time.)

However, there are older attempts to produce succinct indexes, by Kärkkäinen and Ukkonen [12, 11]. Their main idea is to use a suffix tree that indexes only the beginnings of the blocks produced by a Ziv-Lempel compression(see next section if not familiar with Ziv-Lempel). This is the only index we are aware of which is based on this type of compression. In [11] they obtain a range of space-time trade-offs. The smallest indexes need $O\left(u\left(\log \sigma + \frac{1}{\varepsilon}\right)\right)$ bits, i.e., the same space of the original text, and are able to answer queries in $O\left(\frac{\log \sigma}{\log u} m^2 + m \log u + \frac{1}{\varepsilon} R \log^\varepsilon u\right)$ time. Note, however, that this index is not opportunistic, as it takes space proportional to the text, and indeed needs the text besides the data of the index.

In this paper we propose a new index on these lines. Instead of using a generic Ziv-Lempel algorithm, we stick to the LZ78/LZW format and its specific properties. We do not build a suffix tree on the strings produced by the LZ78 algorithm. Rather, we use the very same LZ78 trie that is produced during compression, plus other related structures. We borrow some ideas from Kärkkäinen and Ukkonen's work, but in our case we have to face additional complications because the LZ78 trie has less information than the suffix tree of the blocks. As a result, our index is smaller but has a higher search time. If we call n the number of blocks in the compressed text, then our index takes $4n \log_2 n(1 + o(1))$ bits of space and answers queries in $O(m^2 \log(m\sigma) + (m+R) \log n)$. It is shown in [14, 7] that Ziv-Lempel compression asymptotically approaches H_k for any k. Since this compressed text needs at least $n \log_2 n$ bits of storage, we have that our index is opportunistic, taking at most $4uH_k$ bits, for any k. There are no large constants involved in the sublinear part.

This representation, moreover, contains the information to reproduce the text. We can reproduce a text context of length L around an occurrence found (and in fact any sequence of blocks) in $O(L \log \sigma)$ time, or obtain the whole text in time $O(u \log \sigma)$. The index can be built in $O(u \log \sigma)$ time. Finally, the time can be reduced to $O(m^2 \log(m\sigma) + m \log n + R \log^\varepsilon n)$ provided we pay $O\left(\frac{1}{\varepsilon} n \log n\right)$ space.

About at the same time and independently of us [7], Ferragina and Manzini have proposed another idea combining compressed suffix arrays and Ziv-Lempel compression. They achieve optimal $O(m + R)$ search time at the price of $O(uH_k \log^\varepsilon u)$ space. Moreover, this space includes two compressed suffix arrays of the previous type [5] and their large constant terms. It is interesting that they share, like us, several ideas of previous work on sparse suffix trees [12, 11].

What is unique in our approach is the reconstruction of the occurrences using a data structure that does not record full suffix information but just of text substrings, thus addressing the problem of reconstructing pattern occurrences from these pieces information.

2 Ziv-Lempel Compression

The general idea of Ziv-Lempel compression is to replace substrings in the text by a pointer to a previous occurrence of them. If the pointer takes less space than the string it is replacing, compression is obtained. Different variants over this type of compression exist, see for example [3]. We are particularly interested in the LZ78/LZW format, which we describe in depth.

The Ziv-Lempel compression algorithm of 1978 (usually named LZ78 [25]) is based on a dictionary of blocks, in which we add every new block computed. At the beginning of the compression, the dictionary contains a single block b_0 of length 0. The current step of the compression is as follows: if we assume that a prefix $T_{1...j}$ of T has been already compressed in a sequence of blocks $Z = b_1 \ldots b_r$, all them in the dictionary, then we look for the longest prefix of the rest of the text $T_{j+1...u}$ which is a block of the dictionary. Once we have found this block, say b_s of length ℓ_s, we construct a new block $b_{r+1} = (s, T_{j+\ell_s+1})$, we write the pair at the end of the compressed file Z, i.e $Z = b_1 \ldots b_r b_{r+1}$, and we add the block to the dictionary. It is easy to see that this dictionary is prefix-closed (i.e. any prefix of an element is also an element of the dictionary) and a natural way to represent it is a trie.

LZW [23] is just a coding variant of LZ78, so we will focus in LZ78 in this paper, understanding that the algorithms can be trivially ported to LZW.

An interesting property of this compression format is that every block represents a different text substring. The only possible exception is the last block. We use this property in our algorithm, and deal with the exception by adding a special character "$" (not in the alphabet) at the end of the text. The last block will contain this character and thus will be unique too.

Another concept that is worth reminding is that a set of strings can be lexicographically sorted, and we call the *rank* of a string its position in the lexicographically sorted set. Moreover, if the set is arranged in a trie data structure, then all the strings represented in a subtree form a lexicographical interval of the universe. We remind that, in lexicographic order, $\varepsilon \le x$, $ax \le by$ if $a < b$, and $ax \le ay$ if $x \le y$, for any strings x, y and characters a, b.

3   Basic Technique

We now present the basic idea to search for a pattern $P_{1...m}$ in a text $T_{1...u}$ which has been compressed using the LZ78 or LZW algorithm into $n + 1$ blocks $T = B_0 \ldots B_n$, such that $B_0 = \varepsilon$; $\forall k \neq \ell$, $B_k \neq B_\ell$; and $\forall k \geq 1$, $\exists \ell < k, c \in \Sigma$, $B_k = B_\ell \cdot c$.

3.1   Data Structures

We start by defining the data structures used, without caring for the exact way they are represented. The problem of their succinct representation, and consequently the space occupancy and time complexity, is considered in the next section.

1. *LZTrie* : is the trie formed by all the blocks $B_0 \ldots B_n$. Given the properties of LZ78 compression, this trie has exactly $n+1$ nodes, each one corresponding to a string. *LZTrie* stores enough information so as to permit the following operations on every node x:
   (a) $id_t(x)$ gives the node identifier, i.e., the number k such that x represents B_k;
   (b) $leftrank_t(x)$ and $rightrank_t(x)$ give the minimum and maximum lexicographical position of the blocks represented by the nodes in the subtree rooted at x, among the set $B_0 \ldots B_n$;
   (c) $parent_t(x)$ gives the tree position of the parent node of x; and
   (d) $child_t(x, c)$ gives the tree position of the child of node x by character c, or *null* if no such child exists.
   Additionally, the trie must implement the operation $rth_t(rank)$, which given a rank r gives the r-th string in $B_0 \ldots B_n$ in lexicographical order.
2. *RevTrie* : is the trie formed by all the reverse strings $B_0^r \ldots B_n^r$. For this structure we do not have the nice properties that the LZ78/LZW algorithm gives to *LZTrie*: there could be internal nodes not representing any block. We need the same operations for *RevTrie* than for *LZTrie*, which are called id_r, $leftrank_r$, $rightrank_r$, $parent_r$, $child_r$ and rth_r.
3. *Node* : is a mapping from block identifiers to their node in *LZTrie*.
4. *Range* : is a data structure for two-dimensional searching in the space $[0 \ldots n] \times [0 \ldots n]$. The points stored in this structure are $\{(revrank(B_k^r), rank(B_{k+1})), k \in 0 \ldots n - 1\}$, where *revrank* is the lexicographical rank in $B_0^r \ldots B_n^r$ and *rank* is the lexicographical rank in $B_0 \ldots B_n$.

3.2   Search Algorithm

Let us now consider the search process. We distinguish three types of occurrences of P in T, depending on the block layout (see Figure 1):

LZ78 block numbers

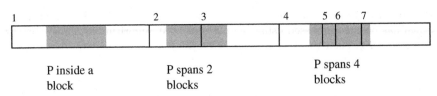

Fig. 1. Different situations in which P can match inside T

(a) the occurrence lies inside a single block;
(b) the occurrence spans two blocks, B_k and B_{k+1}, such that a prefix $P_{1...i}$ matches a suffix of B_k and the suffix $P_{i+1...m}$ matches a prefix of B_{k+1}; and
(c) the occurrence spans three or more blocks, $B_k \ldots B_\ell$, such that $P_{i...j} = B_{k+1} \ldots B_{\ell-1}$, $P_{1...i-1}$ matches a suffix of B_k and $P_{j+1...m}$ matches a prefix of B_ℓ.

Note that each possible occurrence of P lies exactly in one of the three cases above. We explain now how each type of occurrence is found.

Occurrences lying inside a single block.

Given the properties of LZ78/LZW, every block B_k containing P is formed by a shorter block B_ℓ concatenated to a letter c. If P does not occur at the end of B_k, then B_ℓ contains P as well. We want to find the shortest possible block B in the referencing chain for B_k that contains the occurrence of P. This block B finishes with the string P, hence it can be easily found by searching for P^r in *RevTrie*.

Hence, in order to detect all the occurrences that lie inside a single block we do as follows:

1. Search for P^r in *RevTrie*. We arrive at a node x such that every string stored in the subtree rooted at x represents a block ending with P.
2. Evaluate $leftrank_r(x)$ and $rightrank_r(x)$, obtaining the lexicographical interval (in the reversed blocks) of blocks finishing with P.
3. For every rank $r \in leftrank_r(x) \ldots rightrank_r(x)$, obtain the corresponding node in *LZTrie*, $y = Node(rth_r(r))$. Now we have identified the nodes in the normal trie that finish with P and have to report all their extensions, i.e., all their subtrees.
4. For every such y, traverse all the subtree rooted at y and report every node found. In this process we can know the exact distance between the end of P and the end of the block. Note that a single block containing several occurrences will report them several times, since we will report a subtree that is contained in another subtree reported. To avoid this we keep track of the last m characters that the current node represents. When this string

equals P, we have arrived at another node that has been or will be reported elsewhere so we stop that branch. The equality condition can be tested in constant time using a KMP-like algorithm.

Occurrences spanning two blocks.

We do not know the position where P has been split, so we have to try them all. The idea is that, for every possible split, we search for the reverse pattern prefix in $RevTrie$ and the pattern suffix in $LZTrie$. Now we have two ranges, one in the space of reversed strings (i.e., blocks finishing with the first part of P) and one in that of the normal strings (i.e. blocks starting with the second part of P), and need to find the pairs of blocks $(k, k+1)$ such that k is in the first range and $k+1$ is in the second range. This is what the range searching data structure is for. Hence the steps are:

1. For every $i \in 1 \ldots m - 1$, split P in $pref = P_{1\ldots i}$ and $suff = P_{i+1\ldots m}$ and do the next steps.
2. Search for $pref^r$ in $RevTrie$, obtaining x. Search for $suff$ in $LZTrie$, obtaining y.
3. Search for the range $[leftrank_r(x) \ldots rightrank_r(x)] \times [leftrank_t(y) \ldots rightrank_t(y)]$ using the $Range$ data structure.
4. For every pair $(k, k+1)$ found, report k. We know that P_i is aligned at the end of B_k.

Occurrences spanning three blocks or more.

We need one more observation for this part. Recall that the LZ78/LZW algorithm guarantees that every block represents a different string. Hence, there is at most one block matching $P_{i\ldots j}$ for each choice of i and j. This fact severely limits the number of occurrences of this class that may exist.

The idea is, first, to identify the only possible block that matches every substring $P_{i\ldots j}$. We store the block numbers in m arrays A_i, where A_i stores the blocks corresponding to $P_{i\ldots j}$ for all j. Then, we try to find concatenations of successive blocks B_k, B_{k+1}, etc. that match contiguous pattern substrings. Again, there is only one candidate (namely B_{k+1}) to follow an occurrence of B_k in the pattern. Finally, for each maximal concatenation of blocks $P_{i\ldots j} = B_k \ldots B_\ell$ contained in the pattern, we determine whether B_{k-1} finishes with $P_{1\ldots i-1}$ and $B_{\ell+1}$ starts with $P_{j+1\ldots m}$. If this is the case we can report an occurrence. Note that there cannot be more than $O(m^2)$ occurrences of this type. So the algorithm is as follows:

1. For every $1 \le i \le j \le m$, search for $P_{i\ldots j}$ in $LZTrie$ and record the node x found in $C_{i,j} = x$, as well as add $(id_t(x), j)$ to array A_i. The search is made for increasing i and for each i value we increase j. This way we perform a single search in the trie for each i. If there is no node corresponding to $P_{i\ldots j}$ we store a null value in $C_{i,j}$ and don't modify A_i. At the end of every i-turn, we sort A_i by block number. Mark every $C_{i,j}$ as *unused*.

2. For every $1 \leq i \leq j < m$, for increasing j, try to extend the match of $P_{i...j}$ to the right. We do not extend to the left because this, if useful, has been done already (we mark used ranges to avoid working on a sequence that has been tried already from the left). Let S and S_0 denote $id_t(C_{i,j})$, and find $(S+1, r)$ in A_{j+1}. If r exists, mark $C_{j+1,r}$ as *used*, increment S and repeat the process from $j = r$. Stop when the occurrence cannot be extended further (no such r is found).

   (a) For each maximal occurrence $P_{i...r}$ found ending at block S, check whether block $S + 1$ starts with $P_{r+1...m}$, i.e., whether $leftrank_t(Node(S + 1)) \in leftrank_t(C_{r+1,m}) \ldots rightrank_t(C_{r+1,m})$. Note that $leftrank_t(Node(S + 1))$ is the exact rank of node $S + 1$, since every internal node is the first among the ranks of its subtree. Note also that there cannot be an occurrence if $C_{r+1,m}$ is null.

   (b) If block $S + 1$ starts with $P_{r+1...m}$, check whether block $S_0 - 1$ finishes with $P_{1...i-1}$. For this sake, find $Node(S_0 - 1)$ and use the $parent_t$ operation to check whether the last $i - 1$ nodes, read backward, equal $P^r_{1...i-1}$.

   (c) If this is the case, report node $S_0 - 1$ as the one containing the beginning of the match. We know that P_{i-1} is aligned at the end of this block.

Note that we have to make sure that the occurrences reported span at least 3 blocks.

Figure 3.2 depicts the whole algorithm. Occurrences are reported in the format $(k, offset)$, where k is the identifier of the block where the occurrence starts and $offset$ is the distance between the beginning of the occurrence and the end of the block.

If we want to show the text surrounding an occurrence $(k, offset)$, we just go to $LZTrie$ using $Node(k)$ and use the $parent_t$ pointers to obtain the characters of the block in reverse order. If the occurrence spans more than one block, we do the same for blocks $k + 1$, $k + 2$ and so on until the whole pattern is shown. We also can show larger block numbers as well as blocks $k - 1$, $k - 2$, etc. in order to show a larger text context around the occurrence. Indeed, we can recover the whole text by repeating this process for $k \in 0 \ldots n$.

4   A Succinct Index Representation

We show now how the data structures used in the algorithm can be implemented using little space.

Let us first consider the tries. Munro and Raman [19] show that it is possible to store a binary tree of N nodes using $2N + o(N)$ bits such that the operations $parent(x)$, $leftchild(x)$, $rightchild(x)$ and $subtreesize(x)$ can be answered in constant time. Munro et al. [20] show that, using the same space, the following operations can also be answered in constant time: $leafrank(x)$ (number of leaves to the left of node x), $leafsize(x)$ (number of leaves in the subtree rooted at x), $leftmost(x)$ and $rightmost(x)$ (leftmost and rightmost leaves in the subtree rooted at x).

Search $(P_{1...m}, LZTrie, RevTrie, Node, Range)$
1.   /* Lying inside a single block */
2. $x \leftarrow$ search for P^r in $RevTrie$
3.   **For** $r \in leftrank_r(x) \ldots rightrank_r(x)$ **Do**
4. $y \leftarrow Node(rth_r(r))$
5.   **For** z in the subtree rooted at y not containing P again **Do**
6.   Report $(id_t(z), m + depth(y) - depth(z))$
7.   /* Spanning two blocks */
8.   **For** $i \in 1 \ldots m - 1$ **Do**
9. $x \leftarrow$ search for $P^r_{1...i}$ in $RevTrie$
10. $y \leftarrow$ search for $P_{i+1...m}$ in $LZTrie$
11.   Search for $[leftrank_r(x) \ldots rightrank_r(x)]$
                    $\times [leftrank_t(y) \ldots rightrank_t(y)]$ in $Range$
12.   **For** $(k, k+1)$ in the result of this search **Do** Report (k, i)
13.   /* Spanning three or more blocks */
14.   **For** $i \in 1 \ldots m$ **Do**
15. $x \leftarrow$ root node of $LZTrie$
16. $A_i \leftarrow \emptyset$
17.   **For** $j \in i \ldots m$ **Do**
18.   **If** $x \neq null$ **Then** $x \leftarrow child_t(x, P_j)$
19. $C_{i,j} \leftarrow x$
20. $used_{i,j} \leftarrow$ FALSE
21.   **If** $x \neq null$ **Then** $A_i \leftarrow A_i \cup (id_t(x), j)$
22.   **For** $j \in 1 \ldots m$ **Do**
23.   **For** $i \in i \ldots j$ **Do**
24.   **If** $C_{i,j} \neq null$ AND $used_{i,j} =$ FALSE **Then**
25. $S_0 \leftarrow id_t(C_{i,j})$
26. $S \leftarrow S_0 - 1, \ r \leftarrow j - 1$
27.   **While** $(S + 1, r') \in A_{r+1}$ **Do** /* always exists the 1st time */
28. $used_{r+1,r'} \leftarrow$ TRUE
29. $r \leftarrow r', \ S \leftarrow S + 1$
30. $span \leftarrow S - S_0 + 1$
31.   **If** $i > 1$ **Then** $span \leftarrow span + 1$
32.   **If** $r < m$ **Then** $span \leftarrow span + 1$
33.   **If** $span \geq 3$ AND $C_{r+1,m} \neq null$ **Then**
34.   **If** $leftrank_t(Node(S+1)) \in leftrank_t(C_{r+1,m}) \ldots$
                                      $rightrank_t(C_{r+1,m})$ **Then**
35. $x \leftarrow Node(S_0 - 1), \ i' \leftarrow i - 1$
36.   **While** $i' > 0$ AND $parent_t(x) \neq null$
                                      AND $x = child(parent_t(x), P_{i'})$ **Do**
37. $x \leftarrow parent_t(x), \ i' \leftarrow i' - 1$
38.   **If** $i' = 0$ **Then** Report $(S_0 - 1, i - 1)$

Fig. 2. The search algorithm. The value $depth(y) - depth(z)$ is determined on the fly since we traverse the whole subtree of z

In the same paper [20] they show that a trie can be represented using this same structure by representing the alphabet Σ in binary. This trie is able to point to an array of identifiers, so that the identity of each leaf can be known. Moreover, path compressed tries (where unary paths are compressed and a skip value is kept to indicate how many nodes have been compressed) can be represented without any extra space cost, as long as there exists a separate representation of the strings stored readily available to compare the portions of the pattern skipped at the compressed paths.

We use the above representation for $LZTrie$ as follows. We do not use path compression, but rather convert the alphabet to binary and store the $n + 1$ strings corresponding to each block, in binary form, into $LZTrie$. For reasons that are made clear soon, we prefix every binary representation with the bit "1". So every node in the binary $LZTrie$ will have a path of length $1 + \log_2 \sigma$ to its real parent in the original $LZTrie$, creating at most $1 + \log_2 \sigma$ internal nodes. We make sure that all the binary trie nodes that correspond to true nodes in the original $LZTrie$ are leaves in the binary trie. For this sake, we use the extra bit allocated: at every true node that happens to be internal, we add a leaf by the bit "0", while all the other children necessarily descend by the bit "1".

Hence we end up with a binary tree of $n(1 + \log_2 \sigma)$ nodes, which can be represented using $2n(1 + \log_2 \sigma) + o(n \log \sigma)$ bits. The identity associated to each leaf x will be $id_t(x)$. This array of node identifiers is stored in order of increasing rank, which requires $n \log_2 n$ bits, and permits implementing rth_t in constant time.

The operations $parent_t$ and $child_t$ can therefore be implemented in $O(\log \sigma)$ time. The remaining operations, $leftrank(x)$ and $rightrank(x)$, are computed in constant time using $leafrank(\ leftmost(x))$ and $leafrank(rightmost(x))$, since the number of leafs to the left corresponds to the rank in the original trie.

For $RevTrie$ we have up to n leaves, but there may be up to u internal nodes. We use also the binary string representation and the trick of the extra bit to ensure that every node that represents a block is a leaf. In this trie we do use path compression to ensure that, even after converting the alphabet to binary, there are only n nodes to be represented. Hence, all the operations can be implemented using only $2n + o(n)$ bits, plus $n \log_2 n$ bits for the identifiers. Searching in $RevTrie$ has the same cost as in $LZTrie$.

It remains to explain how we store the representation of the strings in the reverse trie, since in order to compress paths one needs the strings readily available elsewhere. Instead of an explicit representation, we use the same $LZTrie$: given the target node x of an edge we want to traverse, we obtain using $Node(rth_r(leftrank_r(x)))$ a node in $LZTrie$ that represents a binary string whose (reversed) suffix matches the edge we want to traverse. Then, we use the $parent_t$ pointers to read upwards the (reverse) string associated to the block in the reverse trie.

For the $Node$ mapping we simply have a full array of $n \log_2 n$ bits.

Finally, we need to represent the data structure for range searching, $Range$, where we store n block identifiers k (representing the pair $(k, k + 1)$). Among the plethora of data structures offering different space-time tradeoffs for range searching [1, 11], we prefer one of minimal space requirement by Chazelle [4]. This structure is a perfect binary tree dividing the points along one coordinate plus a bucketed bitmap for every tree node indicating which points (ranked by the other coordinate) belong to the left child. There are in total $n \log_2 n$ bits in the bucketed bitmaps plus an array of the point identifiers ranked by the first coordinate which represents the leaves of the tree.

This structure permits two dimensional range searching in a grid of n pairs of integers in the range $[0 \ldots n] \times [0 \ldots n]$, answering queries in $O((R+1) \log n)$ time, where R is the number of occurrences reported. A newer technique for bucketed bitmaps [9, 18] needs $N + o(N)$ bits to represent a bitmap of length N, and permits the *rank* operation and its inverse in constant time. Using this technique, the structure of Chazelle requires just $n \log_2 n(1 + o(1))$ bits to store all the bitmaps. Moreover, we do not need the information at the leaves, which maps rank (in a coordinate) to block identifiers: as long as we know that the r-th block qualifies in normal (or reverse) lexicographical order, we can use rth_t (or rth_r) to obtain the identifier $k + 1$ (or k).

5   Space and Time Complexity

From the previous section it becomes clear that the total space requirement of our index is $n\lceil \log_2 n \rceil (4 + o(1))$. The $o(1)$ term does not hide large constants, just $\frac{5 + 2 \log_2 \sigma + 2 \log_2 \log_2 n}{\log_2 n} + o(1/\log n)$. The tries and $Node$ can be built in $O(u \log \sigma)$ time, while $Range$ needs $O(n \log n)$ construction time. Since $n \log n = O(u \log \sigma)$ [3], the overall construction time is $O(u \log \sigma)$.

Let us now consider the search time of the algorithm.

Finding the blocks that totally contain P requires a search in $RevTrie$ of cost $O(m \log \sigma)$. Later, we may do an indeterminate amount of work, but for each unit of work we report a distinct occurrence, so we cannot work more than R, the size of the result.

Finding the occurrences that span two blocks requires m searches in $LZTrie$ and m searches in $RevTrie$, for a total cost of $O(m^2 \log \sigma)$, as well as m range searches requiring $O(m \log n + R \log n)$ (since every distinct occurrence is reported only once).

Finally, searching for occurrences that span three blocks or more requires m searches in $LZTrie$ (all the $C_{i,j}$ for the same i are obtained with a single search), at a cost of $O(m^2 \log \sigma)$. Extending the occurrences costs $O(m^2 \log m)$. To see this, consider that, for each unit of work done in the loop of lines 27–29, we mark one C cell as *used* and never work again on that cell. There are $O(m^2)$ such cells. This means that we make $O(m^2)$ binary searches in the A_i arrays. The cost to sort the m arrays of size m is also $O(m^2 \log m)$. The final verifications to the right and to the left cost $O(1)$ and $O(m \log \sigma)$, respectively.

Hence the total search cost to report the R occurrences of pattern $P_{1 \ldots m}$ is $O(m^2 \log(m\sigma) + (m + R) \log n)$. If we consider the alphabet size as constant then the algorithm is $O(m^2 \log m + (m + R) \log n)$. The existence problem can be solved in $O(m^2 \log(m\sigma) + m \log n)$ time (note that we can disregard in this case blocks totally containing P, since these occurrences extend others of the other two types). Finally, we can uncompress and show the text of length L surrounding any occurrence reported in $O(L \log \sigma)$ time, and uncompress the whole text $T_{1...u}$ in $O(u \log \sigma)$ time.

Chazelle [4] permits several space-time tradeoffs in his data structure. In particular, by paying $O\left(\frac{1}{\varepsilon} n \log n\right)$ space, reporting time can be reduced to $O(\log^\varepsilon n)$. If we pay for this space complexity, then our search time becomes $O(m^2 \log(m\sigma) + m \log n + R \log^\varepsilon n)$.

6   Conclusions

We have presented an index for text searching based on the LZ78/LZW compression. At the price of $4n \log_2 n(1+o(1))$ bits, we are able to find the R occurrences of a pattern of length m in a text of n blocks in $O(m^2 \log(m\sigma) + (m + R) \log n)$ time.

Future work involves obtaining a real implementation of this index. Some numerical exercises show that the index should be practical. For example, assume a typical English text of 1 Mb, which is compressed by *Unix's Compress* to about $1/3$ of its size. Given the space used by this program to code each block, we have that there are about $n \approx u/10$ blocks. Our index needs $4n \log_2 n(1+o(1)) \approx 9.7u$ bits, little more than the size of the uncompressed text ($8u$ bits in ASCII). This should stabilize for longer texts: the 11-th order entropy of English text has been found to be 2.4 bits per symbol [3], and our index takes under this model $4uH_{11} = 9.6u$ bits of space. It is estimated [3] that the true entropy H of English text is around 1.3 bits per symbol (considering orders of 100 or more). Under this model our index takes $4uH_{100} = 5.2u$ bits, smaller than the uncompressed text. Note that in this space we also store the compressed representation of the text.

References

[1] P. Agarwal and J. Erickson. Geometric range searching and its relatives. *Contemporary Mathematics*, 23: Advances in Discrete and Computational Geometry:1–56, 1999. 334

[2] A. Apostolico. The myriad virtues of subword trees. In *Combinatorial Algorithms on Words*, NATO ISI Series, pages 85–96. Springer-Verlag, 1985. 325

[3] T. Bell, J. Cleary, and I. Witten. *Text compression*. Prentice Hall, 1990. 327, 334, 335

[4] B. Chazelle. A functional approach to data structures and its use in multidimensional searching. *SIAM Journal on Computing*, 17(3):427–462, 1988. 334, 335

[5] P. Ferragina and G. Manzini. Opportunistic data structures with applications. In *Proc. 41st IEEE Symp. Foundations of Computer Science (FOCS'00)*, pages 390–398, 2000. 326, 327

[6] P. Ferragina and G. Manzini. An experimental study of an opportunistic index. In *Proc. 12th ACM Symp. on Discrete Algorithms (SODA'01)*, pages 269–278, 2001. 326

[7] P. Ferragina and G. Manzini. On compressing and indexing data. Technical Report TR-02-01, Dipartamento di Informatica, Univ. of Pisa, 2002. 326, 327

[8] R. Grossi and J. S. Vitter. Compressed suffix arrays and suffix trees with applications to text indexing and string matching. In *Proc. 32nd ACM Symp. Theory of Computing (STOC'00)*, pages 397–406, 2000. 325

[9] G. Jacobson. Space-efficient static trees and graphs. In *Proc. 30th IEEE Symp. Foundations of Computer Science (FOCS'89)*, pages 549–554, 1989. 334

[10] J. Kärkkäinen. Suffix cactus: a cross between suffix tree and suffix array. In *Proc. 6th Ann. Symp. Combinatorial Pattern Matching (CPM'95)*, LNCS 937, pages 191–204, 1995. 325

[11] J. Kärkkäinen. *Repetition-based text indexes*. PhD thesis, Dept. of Computer Science, University of Helsinki, Finland, 1999. 326, 327, 334

[12] J. Kärkkäinen and E. Ukkonen. Lempel-Ziv parsing and sublinear-size index structures for string matching. In *Proc. 3rd South American Workshop on String Processing (WSP'96)*, pages 141–155. Carleton University Press, 1996. 326, 327

[13] J. Kärkkäinen and E. Ukkonen. Sparse suffix trees. In *Proc. 2nd Ann. Intl. Conference on Computing and Combinatorics (COCOON'96)*, LNCS 1090, 1996. 325

[14] R. Kosaraju and G. Manzini. Compression of low entropy strings with Lempel-Ziv algorithms. *SIAM Journal on Computing*, 29(3):893–911, 1999. 326

[15] S. Kurtz. Reducing the space requirements of suffix trees. Report 98-03, Technische Kakultät, Universität Bielefeld, 1998. 325

[16] V. Mäkinen. Compact suffix array. In *Proc. 11th Ann. Symp. Combinatorial Pattern Matching (CPM'00)*, LNCS 1848, pages 305–319, 2000. 325

[17] U. Manber and G. Myers. Suffix arrays: a new method for on-line string searches. *SIAM Journal on Computing*, pages 935–948, 1993. . 325

[18] I. Munro. Tables. In *Proc. 16th Foundations of Software Technology and Theoretical Computer Science (FSTTCS'96)*, LNCS 1180, pages 37–42, 1996. 334

[19] I. Munro and V. Raman. Succint representation of balanced parentheses, static trees and planar graphs. In *Proc. 38th IEEE Symp. Foundations of Computer Science (FOCS'97)*, pages 118–126, 1997. 331

[20] I. Munro, V. Raman, and S. Rao. Space efficient suffix trees. *Journal of Algorithms*, pages 205–222, 2001. 331, 333

[21] G. Navarro, E. Moura, M. Neubert, N. Ziviani, and R. Baeza-Yates. Adding compression to block addressing inverted indexes. *Information Retrieval*, 3(1):49–77, 2000. 325

[22] K. Sadakane. Compressed text databases with efficient query algorithms based on the compressed suffix array. In *Proc. 11th Intl. Symp. Algorithms and Computation (ISAAC'00)*, LNCS 1969, pages 410–421, 2000. 325

[23] T. Welch. A technique for high performance data compression. *IEEE Computer Magazine*, 17(6):8–19, June 1984. 327

[24] I. Witten, A. Moffat, and T. Bell. *Managing Gigabytes*. Morgan Kaufmann Publishers, New York, second edition, 1999. 325

[25] J. Ziv and A. Lempel. Compression of individual sequences via variable length coding. *IEEE Trans. on Information Theory*, 24:530–536, 1978. 327

Author Index

Lecture Notes in Computer Science

For information about Vols. 1–2387
please contact your bookseller or Springer-Verlag